Communications, Media and the Imperial Experience

Also by Chandrika Kaul

REPORTING THE RAJ: the British Press and India c1880–1922 (2004)

MEDIA AND THE BRITISH EMPIRE (2006 & 2013)

EXPLORATIONS IN MODERN INDIAN HISTORY AND THE MEDIA (2009)

INTERNATIONAL COMMUNICATIONS AND GLOBAL NEWS NETWORKS: Historical Perspectives (*with P. Putnis and J. Wilke*; 2011)

Communications, Media and the Imperial Experience

Britain and India in the Twentieth Century

Chandrika Kaul
University of St Andrews, Scotland

Softcover reprint of the hardcover 1st edition 2014 978–0–230–57258–4

First published 2014 by
PALGRAVE MACMILLAN

Palgrave Macmillan in the UK is an imprint of Macmillan Publishers Limited,
registered in England, company number 785998, of Houndmills, Basingstoke,
Hampshire RG21 6XS.

Palgrave Macmillan in the US is a division of St Martin's Press LLC,
175 Fifth Avenue, New York, NY 10010.

Palgrave Macmillan is the global academic imprint of the above companies
and has companies and representatives throughout the world.

Palgrave® and Macmillan® are registered trademarks in the United States,
the United Kingdom, Europe and other countries.

ISBN 978-1-349-36434-3   ISBN 978-1-137-44596-4 (eBook)
DOI 10.1007/978-1-137-44596-4

A catalogue record for this book is available from the British Library.

Library of Congress Cataloging-in-Publication Data
Kaul, Chandrika.
   Communications, media and the imperial experience : Britain and India in
the twentieth century / Chandrika Kaul, University of St Andrews,
Scotland.
      pages   cm
Includes bibliographical references and index.

   1. India—Politics and government—1919–1947.   2. Great Britain—
Foreign relations—India.   3. India—Foreign relations—Great Britain.
4. India—In mass media—History—20th century.   5. India—History—
20th century.   I. Title.
DS480.45.K349 2014
303.48′25404109041—dc23   2014023267

Transferred to Digital Printing in 2015

To Ishypooh and Mum

Contents

Tables and Figures

Tables

Figures

Acknowledgements

This book reflects several years of engagement with issues relating to communication, media and the British imperial experience in and of India. My debt of gratitude to individuals and institutions is a correspondingly large one. The final draft of the book was completed whilst I was a visiting research fellow in the invigorating environs of the Cluster of Excellence: Asia and Europe in a Global Context at Heidelberg University. I must record my deep gratitude, especially to Prof. Ronald Wenzlhuemer and also to other colleagues, for making this such a profitable and enjoyable experience. Much needed funds for a research trip to India came from the Carnegie Trust for the Universities of Scotland, to whose trustees I acknowledge my thanks. For giving me permission to reproduce cartoons and images from their collections, I am indebted to the literary trustees of William L. Shirer, Andre Gailani and the trustees of Punch Ltd, the *Radio Times*, Associated Press Corporate Archives in London and New York, James Houssemayne Du Boulay in London and Max Desfor in Silver Springs, Maryland. For technical help with computing, my appreciation is reserved for Andy C. Eccles and Stephan P. Welz. A small grant from the School of History at St Andrews helped towards meeting some of the reproduction costs of images.

I owe heartfelt thanks to Jill Jack, director of Library Services and college archivist at Coe College, who has been the epitome of professional courtesy and generosity, as well as to her assistant, Sara Pitcher. I am immensely grateful to William Shirer's daughter, Linda S. Rae, for her kind support and gracious permission to quote from her father's correspondence. I am deeply indebted to Valerie Komor and Francesca Pitaro at Associated Press Corporate Archives, New York, for their prompt and unfailing assistance with my numerous queries, and to Max Desfor for sharing his recollections of a pivotal time in Indian history. I would like to express my gratitude to Her Majesty Queen Elizabeth II for her gracious permission to quote from the Royal Archives, Windsor. My thanks are also reserved for Nick Mays, archivist, Times Newspapers Ltd Archive, News UK and Ireland Ltd, Jessica Hogg at the BBC Written Archives Centre, Caversham, and Pam Clark at the Royal Archives, for allowing me access to their records and, where appropriate, permission to quote from their collections. Finally, my thanks go to all other archivists and librarians at the following institutions: Bodleian Library,

Oxford; British Library, London; British Library Newspaper Library, Colindale; Cambridge University Library; National Archives of Scotland, Edinburgh; Royal Archives, Windsor; University Library, St Andrews; New York Public Library; Harry Ransom Center, University of Texas at Austin; Earl Greg Swem Library, College of William and Mary, Williamsburg; University Library and the South Asia Institute Library both at Heidelberg; and Nehru Memorial Museum and Library, Gandhi Peace Foundation and the National Archives of India, all in Delhi.

Early incarnations of these case studies have been presented at seminars in Britain and overseas, with three particularly memorable occasions being a lively discussion of Lord Mountbatten at the India International Centre in Delhi; debating the Coronation Durbar at a symposium marking its centenary held at the Manchester Metropolitan University; and analysing the wider implications of media and empires in world history at an international symposium held at the Centro de Belem in Lisbon. I am grateful for the constructive feedback from attendees at these events and at all other conferences and keynotes over the past few years. My thanks are also due to Richard Delahunty at Routledge and to the *Round Table* for permission to publish from an early version of what has become Chapter 5: 'At the stroke of the midnight hour': Lord Mountbatten and the British media at Indian independence', *Round Table*, Vol. 97, No. 398, October 2008, pp. 677–693. I have had the pleasure of working for several years with Michael Strang, publisher of history at Palgrave Macmillan, and I owe him a debt of gratitude for his unflagging enthusiasm. He left Palgrave before the completion of the book but his successors, Jenny McCall and Clare Mence, have ensured a smooth transition and I am most grateful for their expertise and consistent support.

Finally, my research was greatly facilitated by Paddy and Angela Coulter, who graciously allowed me the use of their charming home near Oxford as a writing base, and I have cherished their friendship for many years. I am also most grateful for the continuing encouragement of Joel Wiener, Bridget Griffen-Foley and John Darwin. I am deeply indebted to Joel Wiener, Edwin Hirschmann and Sian Nicholas for reading several sections of the manuscript and improving these immeasurably by their thoughtful suggestions. My largest debts are due to my mother, Minoti, and to my young son, Lawrence Ishan Anand, who has lived with this book as long as he can remember. His love and encouragement ('Hurry up, Mum!') has kept the project going. I dedicate it to both of them with the deepest affection.

Heidelberg, 2014

Abbreviations

AINEC	All India Newspaper Editors Conference
AIR	All India Radio
AP	Associated Press of America
API	Associated Press of India
BBC	British Broadcasting Corporation
BLI	British Library of Information, New York
CMG	*Civil and Military Gazette*
DIL	Department of Industries and Labour, GoI
DPI	Department of Public Information, GoI
EPU	Empire Press Union
ES	Empire Service, BBC
Express	*Daily Express*
FO	Foreign Office, London
FPI	Free Press of India
GoI	Government of India
Guardian	*Manchester Guardian*
Herald	*Daily Herald*
HPoll	Home Political files, NAI
IBC	Indian Broadcasting Company
ICS	Indian Civil Service
IJA	Indian Journalists Association
ILN	*Illustrated London News*
INC	Indian National Congress
IO	India Office, London
IOLR	India Office Library and Records, British Library, London
IRTC	Indian Radio Telegraph Company
ISBS	Indian State Broadcasting Service
L/I	Information Department, IOLR
L/PJ	Public and Judicial Department, IOLR
L/PO	Private Office, IOLR
Mail	*Daily Mail*
NAI	National Archives of India, New Delhi
New Statesman	*New Statesman and Nation*
PAFS	Press Association Foreign Special

RA	Royal Archives, Windsor
Rs	Indian rupee
RTC	Indian Round Table Conferences, London
Telegraph	*Daily Telegraph*
ToI	*Times of India*
Tribune	*Chicago Herald Tribune*
UP	United Press of America

Currency and Exchange Rates

In the 1930s:

1 Rs (rupee) = 1s 6d
1 lakh = Rs 1,00,000 = £7,500

NB: For the sake of consistency and historical accuracy, I have retained the original spelling of South Asian placenames throughout, so Bombay and not Mumbai, Ceylon and not Sri Lanka. The terms New Delhi and Delhi are used interchangeably throughout the book. The place of publication of books is London unless specified otherwise.

1
Communications, Media and the Imperial Experience: Perspectives and Perceptions

Introduction

As part of its Empire Day number in 1911, *The Times* argued that India was 'the centre of the east' and of an Asia that was 'neither changeless nor asleep...we are the guardians of a great tradition, but the conditions are changing and with them the forms of guardianship must also change. As we associate the Indian peoples more closely with the mechanism of rule, so must we give more and more consideration to their sentiments and views in the policy of rule.'[1] Arguments for a realignment of imperial ideology to account for the 'sentiments and views' of the governed must be contextualised within wider perceptions prevalent in the early twentieth century that emphasised a revitalised Asia, in sharp contrast to Matthew Arnold's well-known verse about the unchanging East, alluded to above by *The Times*. The unexpected and resounding nature of the defeat inflicted on imperial Russia by the tiny island state of Japan in the Russo-Japanese War during 1904–5, was a critical turning point. This war was covered by nearly two hundred western journalists (despite strict censorship by the Japanese), civilian observers and many military attachés, including Sir Ian Hamilton of the Indian Army. Major British, US and European newspapers and news agencies utilised advanced communication technologies, including the wireless, which was used for the first time in war reportage.[2] Historians have argued that after 1905, India too had 'new interests and objectives and compelled new lines of British policy'.[3] In less than four decades after George V's reaffirmation of imperial grandeur at the 1911 Coronation Durbar, Britain was not simply associating Indians 'more closely with the mechanism of rule', as *The Times* had noted. Instead, a great grandson of Queen Victoria was compelled to hand over the Raj entirely into Indian (and Pakistani) hands and the *Times of India* was proclaiming the 'Birth of India's Freedom'.[4]

These two events, in 1911 and 1947, respectively, help frame the parameters of this book, the aim of which is not to rework the standard theses of the rise of mass nationalism and the onset of imperial decline, punctuated by two world wars. Instead, the essays in this volume seek to offer an alternative window into the rich Raj experience through the prism afforded by communications and the media. All empires, as large conurbations, are predicated on means of control – control of both mind and movement. Jürgen Osterhammel has observed how power was exercised through 'communication imperialism'.[5] The British worldwide empire was no exception. Further, the twentieth century itself was a media and communications century *par excellence*. Whilst many historical periods can lay claim to remarkable advances in technology, there are, nevertheless, defining developments that make the twentieth century epochal. More people communicated with others, with greater speed and more cheaply than ever before, utilising more diverse and developed media over a wider geographical and temporal range. Ironically, this also enabled the twentieth century to become the most officially controlled and regulated era to date. The intense government propaganda of Britain and other combatant nations during the First World War, Bolshevik control of communist Russia after 1917, Nazism's iron grip on Germany during the period after 1933 and in the Second World War, and the Cold War propaganda of the superpowers beginning soon after – all serve as emphatic illustrations from the period under review.

Communications, Media and the Imperial Experience aims to explore the minds of those who utilised the media and those who controlled it, as well as to examine its output and impact, within the context of Britain and its Indian Raj. Of necessity, it is a limited exercise in the study of a vast and complex field. The role of 'communication' is interpreted broadly to include both specific communication and media channels as well as the ways in which the political and sociocultural roles of such channels are envisaged. The book focuses on the media environment of empire as a conceptual tool to investigate its political culture and role in shaping the imperial experience during the twentieth century. The principal area of investigation is the British media, including the national press, Reuters and the BBC, but Indian newspapers and nascent broadcasting as well as US news agencies and select newspapers are also analysed.

Perceptions of the communication process impacted reciprocally, and attention will be focused on the perspectives of the media industries and personnel as well as imperial proconsuls and leading Indian politicians, paying regard to the volatile context of mass nationalism during these years. How did the primary stakeholders frame arguments about the changing communication process and the media as a positive or negative force? Was the media viewed as agents of change by contemporaries? Commentators have ascribed a pre-eminent role to journalism in the creation of modernity: 'it is easy to describe each in terms of the other', claims John Hartley, with both being products of European societies over the past few centuries. Both are linked to advances in science, exploration and industrialisation, and both 'promote notions of freedom, progress and universal enlightenment, and are associated with the breaking down of traditional knowledge and hierarchies, and their replacement with abstract bonds of virtual communities, which are linked by the media'.[6] In the context of the Raj, is there also a counterhistory of media promoting deference and establishing order? In sum, what have been the role and impact of media in shaping the Raj experience in the first half of the twentieth century?

In terms of its approach and archival focus, the book aims to integrate imperial and media history in the manner popularised by the 'new imperial' history, which has sought to demonstrate the significance of the empire in British culture along with the values and ideologies that created and sustained this experience. This is reflected in the variety of primary sources that I have utilised which encompass the archival territories of both imperial and media history. I have relied on official reports, departmental memoranda, proconsular correspondence and memoirs, as well as newspapers, periodicals, news agency output, broadcasting transcripts, newsreels, institutional records of media organisations, recollections of journalists and proprietorial correspondence. Explored in conjunction with each other, these present an assessment of the relationship between media and imperial culture as manifested within different locales – metropolitan, peripheral and transnational – as well as the networks that bound them within a comprehensive frame of reference.

During the twentieth century the Indian empire was increasingly not just 'read' about but 'seen' and 'heard' as well. Varieties of print, photography, theatre, newsreels, cinema and radio all served to transform the imperial experience and transport the consumer over long distances and across time. Such transformations were not limited to media representations. Swift ocean liners now faced competition from civil aviation, which took off, quite literally, in the interwar years, with the subcontinent soon to be within a week's journey time of European imperial metropolises. 'Was it not significant of the change that a new invention had brought with it, that our machine had jumped the Channel in ten minutes and had surmounted the Frontier peaks [Northwest Frontier] as a Rolls would take the Newmarket road?'[7] Thus rhapsodised Sir Samuel Hoare, Secretary of State for Air, upon completing the inaugural passenger flight to India in 1927. What was key, he claimed, was not simply the speed of the travel but its regularity: 'An ordinary commercial machine with a full load of passengers and luggage had, day after day, carried out its time-table with the precision of a pre-war express train.'[8]

Correspondingly, as will be argued in the book, more intensive exploitation of the media was attempted by various stakeholders, with 'image' and 'perception' coming to play a critical part in the processes of imperial rule. We witness attempts by the Raj to combine 'hard' and 'soft' power, utilising Joseph Nye's categorisation of the changing nature of contemporary US foreign policy. Nye claims that these forms of power are related, can occasionally reinforce or interfere with each other, and that overall the distinction between them is perhaps merely a matter of degree. He defines 'soft' power as the ability to get 'others to want the outcomes you want' through co-option rather than coercion, which 'rests on the ability to shape the preferences of others'.[9] It is not, Nye argues, 'merely the same as influence' but the 'ability to attract, and attraction often leads to acquiescence'.[10] 'Soft' power can also be seen as the exercise of 'co-optive power' and can depend on factors such as 'the attractiveness of one's culture and values or the ability to manipulate the agenda of political choices in a manner that makes others fail to express some preferences because they seem to be too unrealistic'. On the other hand, 'hard' power tends to be associated with 'Command power', which he suggests is 'the ability to change what others do' utilising 'coercion or inducement'.[11]

The case studies in this book focus on the deployment of 'soft' power by the Raj through the channels afforded by communications and media as well as applied news management, including censorship. This strategy was combined with the exercise of 'hard' power, which in this context included punitive legislation and imprisonment, as well as physical force, as witnessed, for instance, in its response to demonstrations during the Civil Disobedience movement. 'Soft' power ought not to be discounted merely as an ephemeral bid to seek popularity by the imperium, but rather seen as a significant strategy in its approach to the increasingly problematic governance of India in the twentieth century.

Nye contends that 'Winning hearts and minds has always been important, but it is even more so in a global information age. Information
is power, and modern information technology is spreading information
more widely than ever before in history.'[12] However, this is not a new
phenomenon and such an approach can equally be applied to considering the impact of the information revolution during the first half of
the twentieth century and in the context of imperial Britain as a global
power.

As the twentieth century unfolded, the British were confronted with
the problem of the exercise of hegemony in a changing national and
transnational context, and attempted to combine the 'hard' power of
the sword with the 'soft' power of publicity, propaganda and news
management through newspapers and news agencies, as well as broadcasting, especially under the impetus of the Second World War. During
the interwar years, it became politically imperative to have the support of Indian moderates, liberals and constitutionalists, both to counter
aggressive forms of mass nationalism and to help manage their Constitution, as embodied in the 1919 Government of India (GoI) Act and,
most importantly, in its successor, the monumental GoI Act of 1935. The
war also weakened the military might of the Raj, and the Amritsar massacre in 1919 helped transform Indian nationalism from its relatively
exclusive and elitist nature into a popular movement. As I have argued
in *Reporting the Raj*, formal strategies of information management and
imperial publicity came into their own during 1914–22, due to external
pressures combined with a new angle of vision brought to bear upon
imperial governance by the Liberal Secretary of State for India, Edwin
Montagu (1917–22).[13] Montagu was convinced that 'the feeding of the
newspapers, the answering of enquiries, the touch between the Government and those who would support it – all this wants doing . . . It would
be so splendid if political methods rather than coercive ones were successful in downing the opponents of the British government.'[14] Building
on such initiatives, the 1930s witnessed the next significant watershed with respect to the official implementation of propaganda and
publicity strategies largely undertaken through the media. By the end
of the decade, these had become an accepted facet of imperial governance enshrined in institutional structures as well as administrative
procedures. Equally striking was the terminology routinely utilised by
proconsuls and civil servants with respect to the integration of such
activities as being not just necessary but also routine actions of imperialists. Thus A. H. Joyce, the veteran India Office (IO) publicist throughout
the 1930s and 1940s, who was appointed to the new post of Adviser on

Publicity Questions in 1941, remarked to Leonard Matters, the London representative of the *Hindu* (Madras), who had written to congratulate him: 'I like to think of my job, and that of the representatives in London of the Indian Press as a sort of partnership, not merely in a profession of publicity and journalism, but in a crusade in which we strive to replace doubts and fears by understanding and goodwill.'[15]

However, as Nye has posited, 'the effectiveness of any power resource depends on the context'.[16] The case studies featured in this book focus on a number of such contexts and engage, on the one hand, with the evolving approaches to communicating power via the media and, on the other, with the media's purported influence as a political tool. The book seeks principally to demonstrate how and why British politicians, civil servants, journalists, broadcasters and even George V sought to mediate imperial politics through the popular culture of communication. In addition, one case study directs the spotlight on the increasingly influential US press and news agencies (which had begun to challenge the monopoly of Reuters), examines their response to Indian nationalism during the interwar years, and considers the impact of such developments upon a Raj anxious about American public opinion, an area that has been relatively under-researched. The reactions of nationalists and the Indian press are also discussed at apposite junctures, with M. K. Gandhi's interaction with the media coming under detailed scrutiny.

Percival Spear wrote more than fifty years ago that 'The very weapons and arguments used by the Congress against the British were largely of western provenance. India broke her British fetters with western hammers. And it was significant of the community of ideas between the two sides that the fetters were never in fact broken by force, but began to be removed by one side as soon as they began to be rattled by the other.'[17] For the nationalists – many of whom were journalists themselves – the media became an increasingly prominent tool of opposition. The link between print and nationalism has been subjected to differing analyses. For example, Benedict Anderson's thesis of the growth of nationalism through the creation of imagined communities knit together by common cultural and political ties envisages the evolution of a Habermasian public sphere.[18] And while both Anderson and Jürgen Habermas have had their share of critics, there is no denying the impact of more extensive communication links as well as newspapers, pamphlets, periodicals, books and the emergence of a viable reading and debating public on the growth of anti-colonialism in India from the mid-nineteenth century onwards.

The intimate interconnections between media forms and political praxis in the protest movements of the nineteenth and twentieth centuries has been variously explored by contemporaries and historians.[19] Ironically, despite rampant illiteracy, print and the written word were utilised in unprecedented fashion to play a seminal role in the life of the nation under the Raj. The complex explanatory factors for this, and indeed for the development of the Indian press, cannot be examined here except insofar as to acknowledge that by the twentieth century, concepts such as public opinion, mass mobilisation, publicity and propaganda were established watchwords for nationalists and imperialists alike. The interest in public affairs went beyond the saloons and debating clubs of elite, English-educated Indians, with the press, pamphlets and periodical literature helping to inculcate, develop and sustain such interactions. Nationalists who exploited the media were aware of the need to reach the largest audience possible. Thus B. G. Tilak, whose *Kesari* was a longstanding critic of the Raj, exhorted his journalists: 'No Sanskrit quotations and no frightening statistics.'[20]

Though ambitious in scope, the *raison d'etre* of this book is not to exhaust an area of research but rather to explore select panoramas of the landscape – to wit, monarchy and empire; nationalists and the media; new communication technologies and the Raj; and Independence as the endgame of empire. Case studies analyse the Coronation Durbar in 1911 as a 'media event' and imperial 'spectacle'; Gandhi, the US media and responses to the Civil Disobedience movement during 1930–1; broadcasting and the Raj in the interwar years; and, lastly, media and the decolonisation project under the Viceroy, Lord Louis Mountbatten, during 1947. In sum, these case studies serve to demonstrate the extent of the media's impact upon Indian affairs, assess its influence and limitations, and evaluate the success of imperialists and nationalists alike at winning hearts and minds in these seminal decades leading to Indian independence.

I

Over the course of the twentieth century, Britain and India, each in their turn, became arenas of competitive publicity wherein official propaganda vied with that of Indian political parties, commercial organisations, non-official Europeans, popular pressure groups and their respective media. The two world wars intensified the need for imperial control and news management, albeit in ways that were specific to large-scale international conflict. It is not intended to examine official war propaganda in this book – a field that has received its fair share of academic attention – except to emphasise the advances made between the conduct of first and the second world wars by the GoI and Whitehall, both in their approach to the imperative for such actions, civilian and military, as well as the resources deployed towards this end.[21] London continued to serve as the pre-eminent geographic epicentre for political news, as it had in the nineteenth century, yet it is necessary to underline the global dimension of the information networks that had matured by the twentieth, encapsulated by, but not limited to, institutional developments such as the Empire Press Union (EPU), as well as advances in transport technology (e.g. aviation) and the birth of new media (e.g. radio). Founded in London during 1909, the EPU brought together under the aegis of the British press, journalists and news agencies of her dependent empire, including India, the Dominions, Crown colonies and protectorates. The initiative was designed to harness the influence of communication and media technologies to the cause of imperial unity and to encourage intra-imperial cooperation and cultural interchange in the sphere of journalism, with the overall aim being to create a transnational information community.[22]

The prominent role of the British national press (Fleet Street) and Reuters international news agency as conveyors of information and conduits of influence continued apace, and is discussed in the case studies, as did the reach of Reuters subsidiary catering to domestic news, the Associated Press of India (API), established in 1908.[23] Yet there were challenges to this supremacy: the substantive threat to Reuters' foreign monopoly, as analysed further in Chapter 3, was led by the Associated Press of America (AP) and the United Press of America (UP). Indians, too, had long resented Reuters' symbiotic relationship with the Raj, accusing the agency of subversion and subterfuge. The *National Herald* appeared to sum up such sentiments on the eve of Independence:

> it has been the lot of India, [and] almost all the countries of Asia, since daily journalism became a permanent feature to have been fed on the mass communication of a British concern … In elegant phrases of choice English, Reuters has told us for decades, with unrelieved monotony, the beneficial influence of European racialism and colonialism. It has faithfully, and with meticulous care, transmitted the denunciatory epithets of Mr Churchill in the days when … India had not ceased to be his pet aversion … As the monopoly purveyors of news its supremacy has yet to be challenged. It had the support

of the British Government and it remains to be seen whether it will continue to receive the support of the national government.[24]

The combined assets of Reuters and API in 1947 were worth about £100,000. However, despite the former's aim to keep India 'permanently as a Reuter territory', the monopoly survived only a few months after the transition to Independence.[25] There was also a spirited attempt by the mercurial Swaminath Sadanand to establish an Indian agency to challenge the Reuters-API monopoly in the shape of the Free Press of India (FPI). The FPI began in 1925, enlarged its operations to include foreign news in 1927, and by the early 1930s was offering a world news service under the direction of Margarita and Charles Barns, in alliance with the Exchange Telegraph Company, Central News and the British United Press. Funded intermittently by a coalition of nationalists, businessmen and journalists based in Bombay, and by subscription, its operations were stymied by a lack of finances, high operating costs and occasional political obstruction. Thus Margarita Barns describes how the security deposit of the principal Bombay newspaper sponsoring the news service was forfeited under the 1930 Press Ordinance and they had to 'run a 24-hour cable service of news for three nights by candle light!'[26] By the time the third Round Table Conference (RTC) met in London, she claimed that 'the organization was in full swing'.[27] However, despite some success, the FPI folded in 1935.[28]

Within Britain, the Great War helped precipitate key structural and ideological changes in the national press landscape, given the astronomically high costs of production, increasing concentration of media ownership, rising commercialism and an advertising boom, and an overtly populist thrust, symbolised by the so-called 'war of the populars'. These years witnessed both an aggressive assertion of proprietorial interest in domestic political and imperial crusades and a marked degree of deference, as observed in the response (or lack of) to the successive crises of Abdication and Appeasement.[29] With coverage of India, Fleet Street continued its engagement along lines based on the political predilections of individual titles, broadly similar to the 1880s–1922 years, as analysed in *Reporting the Raj*. A generalised pride in imperial achievement, often assumed rather than articulated, coloured their outlook, as it did at the BBC under Director General Sir John Reith, whose personal role in the nascent development of broadcasting in the subcontinent is analysed in Chapter 4. Yet there existed, as before, a range of opinions and ideological differences regarding events and policies across the spectrum of the industry. The domestic pulls on a newspaper's loyalty also continued to conflict with its imperial rhetoric. In the campaigns against the 1905 Partition of Bengal, Surendranath Banerjea, a prominent moderate nationalist (and proprietor-editor of the *Bengalee*), who advocated the case for revision, met with C. P. Scott, editor of the *Manchester Guardian* (hereafter *Guardian*) and doyen of Liberal pro-nationalist journalists: 'His sympathies were all with us. I pressed him to write in the columns of the *Manchester Guardian*, but his difficulty was that Lord Morley [Secretary of State for India] was a Liberal leader, and above all a Lancashire man.'[30] Further, one must not assume automatic hostility by the conservative press towards nationalism, nor left-wing newspaper sympathy for anti-imperialism, as shown, for instance, in Fleet Street's response to decolonisation studied in Chapter 5. This mirrors the complex picture that Nicholas Owen has painted of the relationship between the British Left and 'metropolitan anti-imperialism'. He argues that during the 1920s and 1930s, much of the Left was too fragmented to achieve any degree of coherence with respect to Indian policies, that several socialists saw eye to eye with their imperialist counterparts regarding the progressive benefits of imperial rule, and that decolonisation was due largely to electoral and economic realism, rather than a widely held ideological commitment.[31]

II

The British, whether acquiring military support or enforcing a reform agenda, were consistently faced with the problem of securing, at the very least, a workable measure of consent to their rule. Recourse to the law served as the first line of defence and offence in official attempts to control and censor dissent. However, as I have analysed elsewhere, the complex and multifaceted response to the freedom of the press ebbed and flowed largely as a reactive process, appealing to the cloak of ideology when convenient.[32] Some administrators encouraged the development of the press, arguing that it might prove to be an auxiliary to good government. Others imposed stringent measures to control all printed matter. The contradictions between liberalism and authoritarianism, which the working of this imperial experiment exposed, tended to eventuate in acts of legislative and executive fiat on the grounds that press freedoms inevitably impacted on other institutions, and that, because the Raj was by its nature despotic, unrestricted freedom of the press was inherently incompatible with imperial governance. Thus a complex set of laws intended to censor and curtail a plethora of civil freedoms made its way into the statute books, including Indian Official

Secrets Act (amendment) 1903, Newspapers (Incitement to Offences) Act 1908, Indian Press Act 1910, Criminal Law Amendment Act 1913, Defence of India Act 1914, Rowlatt Acts 1919, Princes Protection Act 1922, Indian Press Ordinance 1930, Indian Press (Emergency Powers) Act 1931, Emergency Special Powers Ordinance 1932, Criminal Law Amendment Act 1932, Foreign Relations Act 1932, Indian States Protection Act 1934 and Defence of India Rules 1940. Gandhi was tried in 1922 under the Press Act of 1910 (shortly before the Act was rescinded) and sentenced to six years in jail. In 1930 the Press Ordinance netted securities worth Rs 2,40,000, and 450 papers had ceased to exist by 1935 on account of the high levels of security demanded of them.[33]

However, we also witness concerted attempts to incorporate 'soft' power and public relations into imperial culture, driven, on the one hand, by constructive realism: the necessity to respond to the evolving nature of opposition and the sophisticated use of the media – both Indian and international – by politically savvy colonialists. Thus the funding of official propaganda in the US during the 1930s through Secret Service funds, as discussed in Chapter 3, was now considered politically unviable, given the need to defend such expenditure before rising numbers of Indian members of the Legislative Assembly, a position further consolidated after Indian political parties assumed control of provincial governments following elections under the GoI Act of 1935. A more coordinated and organised institutional response also became essential due to the perceived unreliability of allies amongst the Anglo-Indian press, the emergence of potentially disruptive new media, such as radio, and the general impact of greater networks of information linking the subcontinent into a wider web of news flows. The development of broadcasting for imperial purposes instituted a form of media divergence, which challenged the existing arrangement between press, cable and news agencies. However, as my research into broadcasting under the Raj demonstrates (Chapter 4), a complex set of factors combined to pose almost insuperable problems for its adoption as a means of all-India communications before the Second World War.

On the other hand, the Raj was also motivated by the belief that successful policy outcomes were predicated, in an increasingly mediated world, upon the official ability to deploy 'soft' power: to sell its product/point of view to a discerning, potentially hostile, audience in as attractive a package as possible. Therefore it was considered imperative to create a positive and supportive environment for the reception of government initiatives, to convert the disaffected by means of persuasion through formal and informal methods, as well as pre-empt hostile criticism, where possible. These involved a more intensive personal cultivation of journalists, foreign and Indian; increasing advertisements in pro-government papers within India; continued subsidies to Reuters and API; institutional developments within India, such as the enlargement of central and provincial departments of information; and subsequently, during the Second World War, a separate Ministry of Information and Broadcasting in Delhi.

The expansion of the central news services in Delhi, under the Department of Public Information (DPI), and replicated in the provinces, formed an important aspect of the Raj's endeavours to streamline its approach to media and communications, and the exercise of 'soft' power, after the Great War. To an overwhelming extent this revolved around the press, since it was widely accepted that Indian public opinion was a press-made opinion. The DPI was also concerned with foreign media, including Fleet Street, Reuters, the BBC, newsreel companies, and US news agencies and journalists. The 1930s witnessed the most concerted attempts yet to overhaul the machinery of the DPI, simultaneously transforming what was essentially a press office into a public relations office, with the professionalisation of services aimed at improving the public face of imperial rule – a process both reactive and proactive, as the case studies in this book seek to demonstrate.

Such activities were replicated in London at the Information Department of the IO, which was established in 1921.[34] The department continued to expand in size and scope and was headed by experienced British journalists, A. H. Joyce being the first civil servant to be appointed as Publicity Officer (the title was used interchangeably with Information Officer) in 1937, having earned his spurs as deputy to his predecessor, Hugh MacGregor, a veteran of *The Times*. It functioned in coordination with the Foreign Office (FO) news department, official organisations in America and the US embassy in London, as well as the Ministry of Information during the Second World War. The remit of the Publicity Officer encompassed a staggering range of activities, including the more routine work involved in the daily collection and distribution of newspaper cuttings about India within the IO and in Whitehall; recording India-related activities in London, including public events, visits of personalities and replies to parliamentary questions; maintenance and loan of collections of official photographs; preparation of a weekly summary of the Indian and Burmese press; responding to telephone enquiries and issuing official communiqués; and issuing announcements to news agencies and the press. However, of greater portent, and what was regarded as the 'chief work' of the Information

Officer, lay in 'ascertaining the policy which he is required to follow, settling the terms in which views may be expressed and in interviewing journalists and others, placing before them an exposition of policies or views, in discussion with them, and answering questions'.[35] He was also responsible for organising press conferences and arranging interviews by journalists of high officials, encompassing not just the British press but also the London correspondents of Indian and Burmese newspapers, as well as representatives of the Dominion and foreign press, especially the US media since 'American interest in India, in particular, has been very keen for a very long period.'[36] The requirements of other media, including broadcasting and film, were also addressed. By the 1930s the Officer had established 'close contact' with the BBC 'by whom he is frequently consulted before an item of news, relating to India, is broadcast in the Home or Empire News programmes'.[37] When dealing with confidential matters or a delicate negotiation, the Officer had to employ his discretion to contact only the select few 'responsible editors': 'The influence of the Information Officer on occasions of this kind obviously depends to a large extent on his own personal standing with the Press.'[38] It becomes apparent even from a cursory glance at the complexities of the Indian situation and the wide platform upon which the Information Officer functioned that the incumbent had to command a wide knowledge and experience, and the 'qualities of judgement and tact'.[39]

Negotiations between Delhi and London regarding both the *raison d'etre* and the praxis of official publicity and propaganda were undertaken throughout these years. The three RTCs convened in London (1930–2), and the protracted negotiations leading to the GoI Act of 1935 were the key constituents of the reform agenda being pursued by the Raj. Joyce was seconded from the IO to help with the official restructuring of government propaganda and played a key role in influencing the imperial mindset. He was convinced that the 'first duty' of a government publicity organization was to 'safeguard' official interests.[40] Moreover, it was 'vital' that the 'general public should be acquainted with its policy, and should be kept informed of the steps taken by the Administration to implement that policy. Upon a recognition of this fact depends both the strength and the life of a Government.' Such a publicity machine was 'the connecting link between the Administration and the public which it serves. It is in itself part of the Administrative machine.'[41]

The Hoare-Willingdon correspondence in the first half of the 1930s indicates the concerted regard at the highest levels about the necessity of publicity and news management as integral dimensions of the imperial experience, and this is discussed further in Chapter 4. Thus the Viceroy,

Lord Willingdon, responding on one occasion to a directive emanating from the Secretary of State, argued:

> I am sure you will recognise that it is a very different job to create efficient publicity in a huge continent like India than it is in our country at home. If *you* want anything put out in the Press you simply telephone round to the various Press correspondents who are in London and the thing is done. Here at the moment I have one Press correspondent who represents the *Statesman* and, in Peterson's absence, also represents the *Times*, and if I want to get anything out to the Press, it has to be done through agencies, for I can't summon individuals from all parts of the country to make a statement to them at any particular time. But I do appreciate ... all that you say with regard to its importance, and we are seriously trying to place this matter on a much more efficient scale.[42]

In London, Hoare was enthusiastic and proactive. Writing in December 1931, he affirmed how the potentially adverse RTC propaganda by Indians following Gandhi's disappointment with the Second RTC (as described in Chapter 3) had to be countered by GoI propaganda undertaken by 'Indian friends' and 'inspired article-writers' in the Indian press. Whilst this was not a novel idea, Hoare was worried about the unreliability of moderates such as Tej Bahadur Sapru: 'They are full of forensic zeal when over here, but it seems somehow to evaporate between London and Bombay.'[43] A month later he claimed to be 'trying to arrange for a close contact with the Press, British, American and foreign, whilst these critical affairs are going on in India. I am also going to broadcast one night to England and I believe another day to America. So far the Press have behaved well.'[44]

During the summer of 1932, Hoare again spelt out the importance of creating a positive environment for government policies, urging action upon his Viceroy: 'Is it not pretty certain, first of all, the communal decision [Communal Award] and, secondly, the Government Bill [leading to 1935 Act] will both fall short of the wishes of several sections of Indian opinion. If this is so, it seems to me quite essential that we should be in a position to get our own case across India.'[45] Hoare was particularly anxious because of what he felt was the 'apparent absence in India of all the most modern methods of propaganda, upon which we depend at home – the Prime Minister from Downing Street or Willert at the Foreign Office'.[46] He was convinced that imperial success was predicated on the 'kind of atmosphere that we can create and that it is almost entirely by this sort of propaganda that we shall create it'.[47] Whilst appreciating the difficulties in India, he nevertheless reiterated: 'you should know how strong is the feeling here and how certain the experts are that very much could be done with new methods'.[48] Hoare included films and wireless in his assessment, stressing how Reith and the BBC were eager to help. 'The question of publicity is, however, so vital if we are ever to get the new constitution accepted in India, that I am sure we must be prepared to... be somewhat ruthless in our publicity methods... We all think here that the matter is not only vitally important but that it is also very urgent.'[49]

III

Lord Sykes, Governor of Bombay, writing to the Viceroy, Lord Irwin, in 1929, remarked: 'There is no Government in the world which has to carry on, as do Governments in India, without the active support of a single national newspaper.'[50] This is revealing in the context of a long-established and largely conservative Anglo-Indian press that might reasonably be expected to act as their natural allies. The comment by Sykes also points to the fact that the British adherence to a loosely defined, but widely accepted, concept of 'freedom of the press' meant that they could not contemplate overt support of any newspaper. John Coatman, Director of Public Information in the late 1920s, argued that 'we are dependent, for the effective presentation of our point of view', on the *Statesman* and the *Times of India*, 'and, of course, their point of view is not always exactly the same as ours. [We cannot, in fact, rely on them to quite the same extent as we could on the "Pioneer" in the old days.]'[51] The changing press landscape within India also revealed the competitive nature of the market wherein strategies for commercial survival combined with committed, non-racist British journalists meant that press support needed to be actively cultivated on a regular basis and could no longer be taken for granted. Thus despite the exigencies of war, Ian Stephens, editor of the *Statesman*, when asked in 1943 to produce a pro-government propaganda paper using its facilities, declined to do so, arguing that 'The Statesman is an independent paper, jealous of its position as such since, being British-owned, it is open to taunts from nationalist rivals that it constitutes a limb of Government. Establishment in its offices of a Governmental journal would carry awkward implications.'[52] These developments further accentuated the importance of Fleet Street, Reuters and the BBC in official policies of news presentation and media strategies, as analysed in the case studies.

There were several other factors that influenced a degree of mutual cooperation between the hitherto divided press communities in spite of the Raj, to create, at one level, a measure of shared journalistic discourse. The globalisation of communications meant that India was increasingly drawn into a transnational news network. Empire-wide collaboration, facilitated by the EPU, provided an international stage for the articulation of dissent by Indian editors alongside their British colleagues and meant that foreign focus began, slowly but surely, to be directed towards the conditions under which journalists were allowed to function in the Raj.[53] There was continued growth from the late nineteenth century of the transnational linkages between the British national and provincial papers, and the press in India. Men and machinery moved across continents, and expertise was shared and transferred. In addition, the Second World War acted as a catalyst to initiate a greater degree of formal cooperation between the larger Anglo-Indian and Indian newspapers, as evidenced by the creation of organisations to further common goals, such as the All India Newspaper Editors Conference (AINEC) and the Indian and Eastern Newspaper Editors Society.[54] The AINEC met in Delhi during November 1940 under the presidency of Kasturi Srinivasan, editor of the *Hindu*, whereby the combined efforts of the British and Indian papers helped defeat a GoI motion to impose prepublication censorship of any matter relating to the prosecution of the war. The edict was withdrawn after the AINEC's 'assurance' that the press, 'however strongly it might support the nationalist cause, had no intention of impeding the country's war effort'.[55] Sir Francis Low, editor of the *Times of India*, who played a key role in the proceedings, could note with satisfaction how 'For the first time in Indian history the entire responsible Press of the country, British as well as Indian owned, took united action in defence of their rights against administrative encroachment.'[56]

Further, as discussed in several case studies, the presence of larger contingents of overseas journalists and international news agency correspondents in India curtailed the scope of official censorship. Instead, more nuanced and covert operations were deployed with greater intensity, including coercive strategies to oust, even their compatriots, if sufficient provocation existed. I have analysed elsewhere the deportation in 1919 of B. G. Horniman, editor of the *Bombay Chronicle*, due to his hard-hitting attacks against the Amritsar massacre.[57] Whilst not resorting to such overt sanctions again, the GoI manoeuvred behind the scenes against, for example, Arthur Moore, editor of the *Statesman* (1933–42), who was a longstanding and strident critic of the Raj, as well as of Neville Chamberlain's Appeasement policies. Moore was finally forced to resign due to political pressure exerted on the paper's proprietor, Lord Catto, by the Secretary of State in collusion with the Viceroy.[58]

Within India the seminal links between nationalists, political parties and the press (in English and most major Indian languages) is well established, with the roll call of ideologically inspired journalists and newspapers being a distinguished one. Unsurprisingly, it included the two premier Indian National Congress (INC) families: the Nehrus and the Gandhis. Jawaharlal Nehru's father, Motilal, a successful lawyer and politician, was the first Chairman of the Board of Directors of the *Leader* in Allahabad, before launching his own daily, the *Independent*, in 1919. Jawaharlal went on to found the *National Herald* in Lucknow in 1938 (where later his son-in-law, Feroze Gandhi, was Managing Editor). Nehru took a keen interest in the *Herald*, writing frequently in its pages, and was also invited to contribute to a range of overseas journals and newspapers. Gandhi's long association with journalism is discussed in Chapter 3, and was to remain central to him to his dying day. One of his sons, Devadas, followed in his footsteps and became Managing Editor of the *Hindustan Times*, based in New Delhi. (The paper was established in response to the need felt by the INC for the capital to have an Indian-run daily in English.) Broadcasting a tribute to his father, Devadas recounted how when he called on him on 29 January 1948, as it transpired the day before Gandhi was assassinated: 'I stepped in and was greeted by "what news?" That was his way always of reminding me that I was a newspaperman.'[59] The most prominent of the Indian papers also began to achieve a small measure of financial stability and marginal profits, driven by a combination of factors, including the maturity of the press as an industry, modest rises in literacy and readership – fuelled by interest generated by the Second World War – and advertising revenue, as well as an upsurge in financial investment from patriotic business conglomerates – for example, G. D. Birla, who backed the *Hindustan Times*. However, these years were very challenging for the majority of the press, with the consequence that there was a high turnover of titles and short print runs across the spectrum of publications in English and in Indian languages.

Simultaneously, the twentieth century witnessed several Anglo-Indian and British printing houses suffer financial decline and rising competition for advertising revenue from Indian rivals. The prominent few that continued to prosper included the *Times of India* and the *Statesman*, with the latter claiming truly national status on account of simultaneous publication from Calcutta and Delhi, beginning in 1929. At a distance of

900 miles and without a direct teleprinter link until after the Second World War, this was indeed an astonishing technological and logistical feat. By the 1940s, both practical necessity and political imperatives had made the British-run press a more nuanced and sensitive barometer of Indian opinion. The *Statesman*, established by Robert Knight in 1875, was 'by long-standing tradition Liberal' and thus a discredit in the eyes of the conservative British expatriate communities, with its editorials 'thrust moreover over a readership largely Indian, seemed to many almost treasonable'.[60] However, it was precisely the commercial success 'based on wide Indian readership' that enabled the *Statesman* to flourish, and indeed in 1924 to buy up the *Englishman*, 'favourite of the local reactionaries and India's counterpart of the *Morning Post*'.[61] In addition, increasing scrutiny from Indian elected members of the legislature, especially after the introduction of provincial autonomy in 1937, made information and the media 'transferred' subjects, forcing many Anglo-Indian journalists to respond proactively to the changing dynamics of nationalism to survive. As a survey by J. Natarajan, undertaken for the DPI in 1938, contended, 'One noticeable feature is that the Anglo-Indian Press ... is more reluctant to criticise the Congress than it used to be. The three principal papers – The Statesman, the Times of India and the Madras Mail – represent in that order varying degrees of friendliness towards the Congress.'[62] The *Statesman* became the last newspaper to be retained in British ownership after Independence; the *Times of India*, whilst displaying Bennett Coleman as the publisher on its masthead, completed its transfer to the industrialist Ramkrishna Dalmia by early 1948, though Low continued to hold the editorial reins.

2
Coronation, Colonialism and Cultures of Control: The Delhi Durbar, 1911

Introduction; The Journalism Paradigm; The Imperial Paradigm; Imperial Media Event; Conceptualising the Coronation Durbar; Communications & the Coronation Experience; Press Coverage Prior to the Durbar; Gateway of India; Delhi & the Sovereign; *The Times* Coverage; Resonances & Impact; Concluding Remarks

> The journalist, the news-writer, and the stately historian have had, and will have, much to say of the Imperial Durbar at Delhi, when for the first time since the days of Aurangzeb a real *Badshah* has been seen to ride *coram publico*, for all who willed to gaze on.
>
> *Blackwoods Magazine*[1]

Introduction

The Coronation Durbar was a momentous interlude in the British imperial experience, not just contributing towards the creation of 'a uniquely royal and ritualised realm',[2] but also inaugurating a new political roadmap for the Raj. Held on the twelfth day of the twelfth month of 1911, the Durbar had preoccupied India for more than a year, involved the most elaborate preparations and much expense – just the new crown crafted by Garrads for the occasion cost £60,000 drawn on the Indian exchequer – and brought a quarter of a million people together from every part of India and overseas to the vast plains just beyond the ridge at Delhi. In spectacle alone it dwarfed previous durbars – 'none who witnessed the Durbar of 1903 deny', wrote Valentine Chirol, the veteran *Times* foreign editor and India expert, that 1911 was 'an incomparably bigger and more majestic spectacle'.[3] It was significant in being the first time that a reigning monarch had left Britain's shores for an extended visit to the East, reinforcing also a personal association, with George V and Queen Mary having earlier toured the subcontinent as Prince and Princess of Wales during 1905–6. Further, as Chirol hoped, the fact that the King's first visit to any overseas dominions should be to their country 'cannot but be regarded by all his Indian subjects as a special recognition of the great part which India plays, and must continue to play, in the Empire'.[4] Indeed, Dominions like Canada and South Africa had to wait considerably longer – 1939 and 1947, respectively – for the first visit by a reigning sovereign.

Fresh insights into this imperial experience can be provided by examining the Coronation Durbar as a 'media event', undertaken through a focus on the British press with special attention being paid to *The Times*, which was arguably the most influential newspaper to cover India. The aim will be to situate these metropolitan perceptions within official attempts at the creation of a distinctly British imperial project of cultural control, in part through and by the media spectacle, as well as to analyse its success. Due regard will also be paid to transnational linkages of communication, since newspapers were critical in creating networks of information as well as a shared virtual space for imperial debates transcending political boundaries. There will thus be two main paradigms informing the parameters of this enquiry – a journalism paradigm and a political one – and in the process concerning itself with both the 'official mind' and 'popular psychology'.[5]

The Journalism Paradigm

The Durbar was covered by every form of extant popular media, including newspapers, newsreels and the cinematograph, lantern slide shows, musical theatre and operatic compositions, paintings, photography, pamphlets and books. It effectively became a one-event money spinner for the media as most graphically displayed by the popularity of the newsreels and film footage produced by companies like Kinemacolor, Pathé and Gaumont. To a more limited extent, this was also true of the Dominion and global exposure including within Europe, the US and Japan. Accounting for the entirety of this coverage would require more space than is available here and would also amount to a different exercise.

An examination of the detailed and nuanced reportage offered in the pages of *The Times*, supplemented by coverage in other national newspapers and reviews, allows us to probe into the process whereby the Coronation Durbar became the supreme media event of the Raj, as well as to evaluate its impact. Chirol had covered the 1903 Durbar and had also accompanied the royals during 1905–6. However, in 1911, he travelled to India during the spring and late summer but elected to return to London before the Durbar, and virtually singlehanded produced the editorial comment upon the proceedings in conjunction with the specialists on the ground, who were two of the paper's most adept imperial commentators: Lovat Fraser and E. W. M. Grigg. Fraser had longstanding experience in India, having previously edited the pre-eminent Anglo-Indian newspaper, the *Times of India*, during Curzon's Viceroyalty. Coincidentally, his account of these years, *India under Curzon and After*, was published just prior to the Durbar to considerable critical acclaim, including from the pen of Sir Alfred Milner.[6] As Grigg informed Lord Northcliffe (formerly Alfred Harmsworth), proprietor of *The Times*, Curzon was 'a great friend' of Fraser and whilst the book was 'in no way subsidised or influenced' by him, Fraser had secured 'full access to private and confidential records'.[7] Other journalists of the Anglo-Indian press, such as Alfred Watson of the *Statesman*, had little doubt that Fraser's access to the Viceroy 'enabled him to write with almost unique authority and force'.[8] Edward William Macleay Grigg was head of the paper's Colonial Department and later entered politics, becoming an MP and then Governor of Kenya, and he received the peerage as the first Baron Altrincham. The Durbar trip involved a substantial financial outlay and, in the event, the £200 allocated to each for expenses (along with the gift of their court suits) proved inadequate, much to the consternation of Northcliffe.[9] These specialists complemented the newspaper's impressive network of local reporters headed by the editor of the *Times of India*, Stanley Reed, supplemented by Reuters despatches. Reed succeeded Fraser to the editorship and with a reputation for fair play was considered amongst the shrewdest minds in Indian journalism.

The Times and Fleet Street in general, along with the major Anglo-Indian newspapers, had developed official and personal links with the IO and the GoI from the mid-nineteenth century.[10] At this juncture, one striking instance of such cooperation was provided by Chirol and the Secretary of State, John Morley. Chirol had worked closely with Morley in promoting the GoI Constitutional Act of 1909 and was rewarded, in part for these services, with a knighthood in January 1912. He was also appointed to serve on the Indian Public Service Commission, which convened later that year. With Minto's successor, Lord Hardinge, Chirol enjoyed a friendship going back several years, which was to stand him in good stead during the Durbar. Thus, overall, we can pose the question, *apropos* Marshall McLuhan's celebrated dictum 'the medium is the message': to what extent was *The Times* implicated in this game of imperial shadow-boxing and how useful was its coverage in furthering the empire's political line? Alternatively, how far did media coverage overall create its own realities? Within this specific context, can the Durbar be considered a success, and what criterion do we utilise for judging its metropolitan impact and on the fate of the Raj?

It is worth reminding ourselves of the dominance exercised by the national press during the Edwardian era, and, most especially in terms of political influence, by *The Times*, which also had an enviable standing within the empire. Though undoubtedly damaged commercially by the growth of the so-called 'feather-brained' journalism of the popular press from the late nineteenth century, its reputation remained virtually unrivalled. It spoke for the political and intellectual elites but also for a range of middle-class and commercial interests, imperial pressure groups and institutions, as well as upholding its status as a paper of record covering parliamentary proceedings in detail. The daily sermonising from its Fleet Street pulpit continued to be required reading for the political classes and for all those with aspirations to public careers. The obsession of Northcliffe with acquiring control of *The Times* stemmed from this conviction, and it was said that Lloyd George never delivered an important speech without dictating it to the paper's correspondent beforehand. Amongst Liberal dailies, the *Guardian* under the editorship of C. P. Scott had, despite its provincial provenance, established a national reputation which rivalled that of the conservative *Times*. In terms of circulation, both newspapers were level pegging at this juncture, with *The Times* averaging 45,000 and the *Guardian* 35,000–42,000 copies daily.[11] In the burgeoning field of the popular press, the Harmsworth brothers owned a raft of national and provincial titles, and, along with Pearson and Cadbury, they controlled a staggering two-thirds of national morning and four-fifths of evening papers in Britain by 1910 – an unprecedented concentration of ownership. Northcliffe's flagship *Daily Mail (Mail)* was the largest-selling popular daily, averaging 800,000–900,000 copies. An often bellicose nationalism and a passion for empire marked the *Mail's* approach, yet, whilst Northcliffe would have considered himself an imperialist, his was not a blind fanaticism as evidenced by his critique of British economic policy and support of famine relief in India during the 1890s. He was unique amongst proprietors, as his insights were derived from having personally visited India twice.[12] The most highly regarded political weeklies were St Loe Strachey's *Spectator* (which he owned and edited) and the *Observer*, edited by J. L. Garvin from 1908, the latter with the added distinction of being the oldest Sunday paper in Britain. Both journals were infused with a sense of imperial mission reflective of the proclivities of their proprietor/editors and their commitment to the Unionist/Conservative cause; yet their editorial opinion was not tied to any political straitjacket and preserved a strong independent streak. The *Spectator* averaged sales of around 20,000, but the *Observer* had received a significant boost under the combination of Northcliffe's financial acumen and Garvin's spirited editorship. In less than two years, circulation went up from 20,000 to reach 57,000 in 1910. Though continuing at the helm after J. J. Astor became proprietor in 1911, Garvin was forced to relinquish his one-fifth share in its ownership. He also came to edit Astor's venerable *Pall Mall Gazette* from 1912.

The Edwardian years witnessed the maturation of the national press as an imperial institution. The British press not only provided the ideal platform and a conduit for a reaffirmation of the country's worldwide imperial status but also proved to be a significant participant in the process. The idea of simultaneity – the temporal and geographical compression of experience – now made possible by the rapid advances in communication meant that the daily press could indeed successfully present a depiction of the passage of imperial pageantry and spectacle. As has been argued for the era of television broadcasts, so can it be contended for press coverage of the empire: the 'reproduction' of the event and the image thus created could often be as important as the original, especially when the original was largely inaccessible to remote audiences. Through the technologically sophisticated media coverage now available, the transnational shared experience of ruler and subject became a reality as never possible before.

The Imperial Paradigm: 'demonstrating to ourselves our strength'

The precedents established by the previous durbars, especially Curzon's 1903 extravaganza to celebrate the accession of Edward VII, are significant, not just in terms of organisation and protocol but much more so for revealing the imperial mind and the rationale behind the staging of these spectacular events. This rationale, best articulated by Curzon, can also be taken as the guiding principles underlying *The Times* coverage in 1911. Curzon, more than any other proconsul, appreciated the impact of the imperial experience associated with a grand durbar as well as the seminal importance of ritual and performance in the Indian context. In defending his case for contemplating an acclamation durbar, Curzon raised several critical issues that remained pertinent a decade later and are worth revisiting. He considered the 'sacred' nature of the practice in the East that brought 'Sovereigns into communion with their people'. The so-called 'Installation Durbar' was, he noted, an accepted feature of ceremonial life throughout India and in all social hierarchies: the 'community of interest between a Sovereign and his people to which such a function testifies, and which it serves to keep alive, is most vital and most important.'[13] It was precisely this 'community of interest' that the organisers in 1911 sought to rekindle. Such a ceremony was also immensely helpful in projecting a virile image to the wider world. The 'life and vigour of a nation are summed up before the world in the person of its Sovereign' and in India it was the British Crown that had unified the country. Thus the 'political force' and the 'moral grandeur' of the British nation was 'indisputably increased by this form of cohesion, and both are raised in the estimation of the world by a demonstration of its reality'.[14] Eight years later it was precisely this demonstration of 'the community of interest' through the staging of the Durbar that was considered critical to cohere the nation together, as well as to project its force and grandeur to a wider world, for which the physical presence of the monarch was considered essential.

Far from being 'a mere pageant intended to dazzle the senses for a few hours or days', its significance for Curzon lay rather in it being 'an act of supreme public solemnity, demonstrating to ourselves our strength'.[15] And, as I shall argue, these reasons also lay at the crux of the Coronation Durbar in 1911. Curzon's total commitment to the cause is revealed in his meticulous attention to detail. For example, he refused to include a hymn, 'Onward Christian Soldiers', in the Delhi service because, as he put it, 'there is a verse in it that runs: *Crowns and thrones may perish, Kingdoms rise and wane*, which would not be particularly appropriate'.[16] Curzon also stressed that, unlike in 1877, what he wanted was to create 'a celebration not of officials alone but of the public'.[17] 'A good many eyes in a good many parts of the globe will be directed upon Delhi... and we shall have an opportunity not merely of testifying the enthusiastic loyalty of India... but also of demonstrating to the world that India is not sunk in torpor or stagnation.'[18] As will be elaborated later, in 1911 the main celebrations in Delhi were witnessed by about 100,000 spectators, with the number of visitors estimated at double that number. The occasion was orchestrated as never before through a ritualised pageant, which drew sustenance from the 'invented traditions' established by previous imperial assemblages, as well as reflecting the technological achievements of the intervening years.

Imperial Media Event

Garvin, as editor of the *Observer*, was at this juncture 'closer to the centre of political power than at any other time'.[19] Interestingly, he had spent three months in the subcontinent in connection with Curzon's Durbar, representing the *Daily Telegraph* (*Telegraph*) which instilled a continuing preoccupation with India.[20] Writing home one night after climbing a minaret at the Taj Mahal complex, he enthused: 'And this was ours and every city and plain and river steeped in the moon throughout India that night was ours. I never understood the greatness of England till that hour.'[21] Thus it was that eight years later, commenting on the impending tour of George V, Garvin argued: 'At our peril do we allow our minds to grow dull and cold as to the meaning of this tremendous heritage. We firmly believe that *an event raising conscience and imagination alike to a higher power* will be no hollow process of grandiose pomp and glittering ostentation, but will be for the permanent good of India and for the renewed strengthening of the Monarchy in the sight of all the peoples over whom the sceptre of Britain stretches its sway.' The Durbar, he contended, 'will be *an event opening vistas of political thought and carrying suggestions of sheer romance and practical idealism* to which only the genius of Disraeli or the stately eloquence of Lord Curzon could do justice.'[22] I would suggest that such perspectives continue to be reflected in the staging and coverage of more contemporary ceremonial events that were also royal, such as the coronation of Queen Elizabeth in 1952 or the marriage of Prince Charles and Lady Diana in 1981. This has been argued by Daniel Dayan and Elihu Katz in their seminal treatise, *Media Events*, which focuses on the late twentieth century and what they persuasively claim was 'the live broadcasting of history'.[23] Their insights, particularly into what they categorise as 'Coronation' events, draw upon the bases of legitimate authority as proposed by Max Weber – rational-legal, traditional and charismatic.[24] It also throws, as I will argue below, fresh light on the process and impact of media coverage within the imperial context and offers a new paradigm to evaluate its significance.

It was undoubtedly the case that in the past, as today, media coverage was made possible by the realisation of the full technological potential of the extant communication systems. By the Edwardian years the national press, aided by developments in printing, photography, telegraphy and speedy distribution, was the most pervasive, comprehensive and accessible media. The telegraph had enabled the British to establish an 'An All Red Route' linking their global empire by 1911. Such developments enabled the onsite special correspondent of the imperial press to conjoin with the organiser of the 'historic' ceremony, the Raj, to create a 'media event' centred on the Durbar and associated rituals. Dayan and Katz posit that the 'center' of the media event 'is the place where the organizer of a "historic" ceremony joins with a skilled broadcaster to produce an event'.[25] Were it not for the media coverage of the Durbar in all its multifarious dimensions then, arguably, the event, as it was understood at the time and evaluated later, would not have transpired, given that it was this reportage that provided a cynosure for all eyes – domestic and transnational – empowering the press, at least momentarily, to create its own constituencies.[26] Thus coverage of the Coronation Durbar as a 'media event' succeeded in creating differing and multiple identities.

Reminiscent of staged displays of twentieth-century revolutionary regimes, we also witness 'shades of political spectacle' in the Coronation ritual which was consequently reflected in journalistic accounts. But media events then, as now, were more than simply political manipulations. Contemporary western journalists are of course considered independent from government. And even in the early twentieth century, as I have argued in *Reporting the Raj*, the influence of Fleet Street derived in large measure from the fact that it was a free press operating nevertheless at the heart of an imperial system of coercion and control. However, Dayan and Katz contend that broadcasters of today often 'share the ceremonial occasion with the organisers and satisfy the public that they are patriots after all'.[27] They claim that 'journalists sometimes reluctantly – put critical distance aside in favour of the reverent tones of presenters. Broadcasters thus share the consensual occasion with the organizers.'[28] In 1911, Fleet Street exemplified the truth of this observation: these journalists for empire were at one in affirming the value of the sovereign's role within the empires of the East, where respect for the monarchical tradition was deep rooted and pervasive.[29]

Modern media events are preplanned and advertised in advance, giving 'time for anticipation and preparation' for both broadcasters and audiences, 'abetted by the promotional activity of the broadcasters.'[30] Likewise in 1911, the media built up anticipation for the Durbar in the weeks and months preceding the ceremonies. Media events also 'celebrate what, on the whole, are established initiatives that are therefore unquestionably hegemonic. They are proclaimed historic.'[31] The relevance of such an interpretation becomes apparent at every turn in *The Times'* coverage during 1911 with the 'meanings' divested in the ceremony by the organisers being shared and reinforced by the press.[32]

The rhetoric of journalism, and media events in particular, with their emphasis on 'great individuals and apocalyptic events', diverge from academic and historical rhetoric: 'Where social science sees long run deterministic processes, journalism prefers heroes and villains.'[33] As evident in the discussion to follow, for the British press in 1911, the heroes and villains were clearly identified as those that cooperated with the Raj and those that sought to undermine it, respectively, with the monarch reigning supreme above this melee and unsullied by it, and, in fact, going further by assisting in the process of conversion. Yet Dayan and Katz opine that for contemporary broadcast events to be successful, public approval is essential, at least in the democracies of the West.[34] In the empire it was, arguably, always possible for such events to be hoist on an unsympathetic public, but all evidence from media coverage and print opinion points to the Durbar's general acceptance.

Conceptualising the Coronation Durbar

George V and 'creating new precedents'

The Coronation Durbar was in significant ways a brainchild of George V and as such reflected a marked shift in impetus behind the conceptualisation of these pageants under the Raj. He had taken a continuing interest in the empire and it is undeniable that his long peregrination around India whilst Prince of Wales had proved a stimulating experience, and despite official protocol had allowed sufficient latitude for him to have developed an individual perspective. The tour had coincided with the beginnings of large-scale popular agitation against the Partition of Bengal, with the Prince being exposed to the dark underbelly of imperialism. Despite this, he had been moved by the genuineness of the welcome he felt he had received from the masses and the aristocracy, including, strikingly, in Calcutta, and had concluded upon his return to London: 'I cannot help thinking that the task of governing India will be mainly easier if we, on our part, infuse into it a wider element of sympathy.'[35] Interestingly, these sentiments were also widely recalled in the pages of the Indian press at this juncture – that is, at the time of George V's accession to the throne. Anglo-Indian newspapers like the *Statesman* and the *Times of India*, as well as Indian-run ones like the *Bombay Gazette* and *Amrita Bazaar Patrika*, also highlighted these sentiments, with many reproducing the speech verbatim as a good augury of things to come. The *Patrika* even reminded its readers that the King was 'specially dear to us personally' as he had granted an interview to the journal in 1905.[36]

A perusal of George V's diaries and correspondence makes apparent that the idea of returning to India as the monarch appeared to him a natural progression. His scheme was communicated to Prime Minister Asquith after his Coronation and the King also wrote to Morley, on the eve of the latter's departure from the IO, convinced that 'if this proposed visit was made known some time before, it would tend to allay the unrest'.[37] George V acknowledged that his proposal was 'an entirely new departure' but argued for 'the necessity of creating new precedents when circumstances justify them'.[38] Morley, having in a previous career edited the *Fortnightly Review* and the *Pall Mall Gazette*, was no stranger to the art of publicity, and in turn identified the two critical audiences that the project would best serve: it would 'strike the imagination' of Indians, and also give 'fresh life to English interest and feeling about Indian subjects'.[39] However, he shared with the Cabinet concerns at exposing the King to potential terrorist attacks, and, at the heavy expenditure entailed for staging the ceremonials, which would most likely have to be borne largely by the Indian exchequer.[40] Eventually, despite the 'surly reluctance' of the Cabinet, the tour was allowed to proceed.[41] In contrast, the press, spearheaded by *The Times*, greeted this announcement in November 1910 with fulsome approval and hoped that this imperial pilgrimage would be received positively in India, which was, as the paper put it, 'the only real Empire' that Britain possessed and one which should be regarded with 'a very special pride'.[42] Featuring in its pages the opinions of a range of Indian papers, including the *Times of India*, *Pioneer*, *Jam-e-Jamshed*, *Patriot*, *Bombay Gazette* and the *Madras Mail*, *The Times'* hopes appeared to be more widely shared.[43]

The sheer novelty of the situation created its own pressures – there were no blueprints to work with since no ruling British monarch had ever visited the subcontinent, let alone been crowned there. Could the King be crowned twice? Could the British crown journey across the oceans or would a new one need to be manufactured? Who would finance it and what would be its fate after the Durbar? Issues such as the grant of 'boons' now assumed heightened importance: gifts bestowed by a monarch must surely outshine those by a Prince of Wales or the Duke of Connaught. George V took a keen and continuing personal interest in all aspects of the preparations, communicating his ideas to the GoI on a frequent basis, moving Crewe to comment how 'HM is so desperately keen that he thinks out all manner of questions for himself'.[44] The King envisaged being crowned in person in India, but this proposal was turned down quickly for fear of setting a questionable political precedent, though his idea of granting 'boons' as part of his Coronation 'gift' to Indians, which he felt would help to heal the wounds inflicted by the Partition, as well as signify a suitable infusion of sympathy, was taken up with more enthusiasm. The artist, George Percy Jacomb-Hood, from the *Graphic*, was specially commissioned as Artist to the King, being paid £400 directly from the King's coffers.[45] Similarly, Ernest Brooks was the royal photographer, and Charles Urban and the Kinemacolor Company were appointed to film the proceedings. Several others, including Gaumont, Pathé, Barker Motion Photography and Warwick Trading Company, sent representatives, and, in fact, the Durbar was to provide a tremendous fillip to the popularity of newsreels within Britain. Many of these companies had been present at Curzon's Durbar and chose to rerelease this earlier footage 'to a trade that now had Durbar fever'.[46]

Apart from George V's direct input into specific facets of the programme, such as the honours to be awarded, the design of the sporting trophies, the redesign of the Star of India and other medals, and the role of Queen Mary, what needs emphasis is the extent to which he wanted to be associated directly with the people and not merely tied down in official routine. Thus he insisted to Crewe during a lengthy meeting at Windsor that it was 'imperative that the actual ceremony should not be at the Diwan-i-Am [the Hall of General Assembly in the Red Fort] but in a special arena, so that a great crowd may witness it'.[47] As it transpired, the Red Fort was utilised during a garden party following the Durbar when Their Majesties appeared in their Coronation robes and crowns, to give *darshan* (worshipful presence) from its ramparts to Indians – Hardinge estimated 100,000 – as they filed past in the grounds below. Dressed in Coronation attire and accompanied by their young princely pages, they sat like their Indian forbears, partaking of the customary ritual wherein a *Maharaja* (monarch) as God's representative on earth allowed himself to be gazed upon by a grateful *praja* (subjects]), simulating the secular equivalent of an age-old religious experience. As affirmed by the Maharaja of Bikaner, 'Kings have been held to be sacred and are not only revered but loved and . . . the *personal* element counts for so much.'[48]

Coincidentally, like George V himself, the two heads of Government in London and Calcutta – Crewe and Hardinge, respectively – were also newcomers to the job, both having taken over the reins during the autumn of 1910. Crewe had the advantage of having attended Curzon's ceremonial, and his biographer claims that the 1911 event was 'of deep and interesting importance' to him.[49] Indeed, he eventually accompanied the monarchs to India, which was a Raj milestone since it made him the first Secretary of State ever to do so. Yet Crewe had no direct experience of India, having previously served at the Colonial Office as well as in the Lords, where he was Leader of the Liberal Party, an onerous responsibility which he continued to fulfil even after taking over at the IO. Hardinge was a diplomat with extensive experience at the FO, though he did also have longstanding familial links to the subcontinent. His grandfather, Field Marshal Henry Hardinge, had served as the Governor General (1844–8), and later created the First Viscount Hardinge of Lahore largely on account of his successful conduct of the First Sikh War. The grandson now left for India, 'full of enthusiasm' and 'more than happy at the realization of my highest ambition'.[50] Crewe and Hardinge had known each other since their days at Harrow, which was fortuitous given that the burden of the gargantuan preparations involved in the Durbar took a heavy toll, especially on Hardinge, who felt driven to confess: 'This Durbar is a tremendous business and very overwhelming for one's first year of office.'[51]

A Liberal Masterstroke

Key facets of the multidimensional Coronation project were encapsulated by the imperial paradigm, as discussed earlier. However, an important aspect of the political rationale for the Durbar as it developed and which, in turn, further reinforced the necessity of staging a supreme media event, needs further elucidation. What has not been given due weight is the extent to which this initiative, far from reflecting only the Conservative paradigm of the monarchical association with empire, as enunciated so expertly by Disraeli at the time of the first Imperial Assemblage, was now also centre stage as part of a Liberal political strategy.[52] The King had raised the prospect of a revision of the Partition almost simultaneously as he had broached his Durbar plans, and Crewe was sympathetic to this suggestion. As he informed the Viceroy, the King had 'set his heart upon doing something which would, to some extent, satisfy that section of opinion in India which regarded partition as a mistake. He himself had always disliked the change.'[53] Initially, Hardinge had baulked at the enormity of such a move, hastening to inform London upon his arrival in Calcutta: 'we must regard that ... as a closed chapter'.[54] Though increasingly enthused about the idea of a Durbar and the granting of imaginative 'boons',[55] he continued to be reluctant to address this issue, reiterating in February 1911: 'Feeling about the partition has almost entirely disappeared, and in a year or two nobody will think of it. What we want is quiet, and any tinkering with what was done six or seven years ago would raise a terrible storm. I shudder to think of it.'[56]

Yet, as the year progressed and Hardinge was able to gauge the mood of the agitation outside his office windows and through meetings with moderate nationalists like Surendranath Banerjea and Gopal Krishna Gokhale, as well as in consultation with his Council, he became convinced that the key to re-establishing political harmony lay in a reversal of Curzon's Partition and the territorial readjustment of administrative boundaries with the creation of new provinces. However, critically, Hardinge also rekindled the idea of simultaneously deprovincialising the capital of British India. Sir Alfred Lyall had argued cogently in 1883: 'nothing can be worse for Viceroys than the present system of dividing time chiefly between Calcutta and Simla – at Calcutta the Viceroy is surrounded by eloquent baboos, at Simla by confident officials'.[57] The continuing Indian opposition played a significant role in motivating Hardinge to consider yoking a reversal of the Partition with a move towards autonomy for the GoI. Such a shift would allow the Raj to extricate itself from the turmoil in Bengal and allow it to function independently of well-entrenched provincial and commercial interests. Also significant from the perspective of liberal ideology, Hardinge argued that this would allow for a greater development of the institutions of provincial self-government in Bengal, initiatives which were part of the British constitutional strategy, and mentioned in official pronouncements since Lord Ripon's local self-government initiatives in the 1880s and made manifest more recently in the 1909 GoI Act. The Act increased Indian participation in the administration with the first Indian nominated to the Viceroy's Executive Council and two others to the Secretary of State's India Council, as well as extended both nominated and elected representatives at the provincial and local levels.

Thus Hardinge's political masterstroke was to marry the two imperatives by adroitly shifting the capital from Calcutta to Delhi, utilising the critical cover provided by the King's presence at the Durbar to formally announce the decision. The shift of the capital would hopefully signal the re-establishment of a strong centralising imperium unfettered by regionalism. As Harcourt Butler noted, 'The transfer of the capital marked the end of the old epoch and the beginning of the new. Henceforth the GoI had a habitation of its own, free from any preponderant provincial influences.'[58] Hardinge acknowledged the critical advice he received from Fleetwood Wilson and John Jenkins, the Finance and Home Members, respectively.[59] And whilst it is undoubtedly the case that the need for a new capital had been discussed for many years, no proconsul before him had taken the decisive step of bringing these suggestions to their logical conclusion, displaying a willingness to formulate and implement policy in a decisive and prompt fashion.

The aim now became to push through imperial policy with the maximum of speed and the minimum of political damage, which would inevitably follow a prolonged debate in Parliament, especially from a Conservative dominated Lords whose peers could be counted upon to lead the cavalry charge. Crewe had had to contend with their habitually obstructive behaviour since 1908, so a plan which would also bypass a pre-emptive attack in Parliament was especially attractive. Therefore, to ensure success, covert operations were considered essential, which explains the secrecy which shrouded the contents of the King's Proclamation. Hardinge sent the detailed memorandum to Crewe on 19 July, 'advocating strongly its acceptance as the best and only certain means of securing peace and reconciliation' in Bengal and simultaneously 'a statesmanlike change' in the situation of the GoI. Urging upon Crewe the necessity for 'extreme secrecy', Hardinge re-iterated how 'I felt this need so strongly that I myself made copies of all my letters on the subject, while the notes of the Members of my Council had been privately typewritten.'[60]

During August, George V (though not Queen Mary) became amongst the handful in London privy to this momentous decision when both Crewe and Hardinge wrote in secret, hoping the King could see how their proposals fulfilled the latter's own aspirations. The revocation of Curzon's Partition, Hardinge was convinced, would be 'welcomed as the rectification of what must...be conceded on all sides to have been an unintentional but grievous mistake'.[61] Further, a shift of the capital was urgent, owing to the 'undue influence' that Bengal was exercising over Indian politics. Delhi was the 'only possible site' given that it had been the ancient capital of both Hindu and Muslim dynasties, and was 'full of historic memories'.[62] Stressing yet again, the need for absolute discretion, Hardinge argued that

> secrecy is the first & very greatest requisite in order that your Majesty's words may have a really striking effect upon the imagination of the people. They will, I am sure, feel that something really big has been done when their Sovereign Emperor announces to them in open Durbar his decision that the capital is to be transferred to Delhi...Nothing so striking will have occurred since the establishment of British rule in India.[63]

It was barely three days prior to the actual ceremony that Hardinge arranged for the erection of a 'Mystery camp' in the Durbar city, with a strong police cordon, which housed the machines and the staff who would prepare and print copies of the announcement, gazettes and news-sheets to be distributed in sealed envelopes after the King's announcement.[64] Thus, prior to the Durbar, this decision was only known by about a dozen people each, in England and within India, and must surely rank amongst the best kept secrets in imperial history, a stratagem which undoubtedly enhanced its impact when made public at the subsequent media event (Figure 2.1).

Communications and the Coronation Experience

'wonders were attempted and wonders done'[65]

'One's instinct is to avoid the theatrical, but, it does not follow that the instinct is sound', observed Crewe.[66] In the event, his aversion to theatricality was ignored, for we witness in the planning and execution

Figure 2.1   Lord Hardinge, Viceroy of India
Source: James Houssemayne Du Boulay private collection, London.

of the Coronation Durbar the apogee of a propaganda Raj. This was an imperium determined to project a grandiloquent and spectacular image to capture the imagination of subcontinental as well as transnational publics.

What had to be organised to perfection was the staging of the main coronation event itself, which would be the cynosure of all eyes. Sir John Hewett, Lieutenant-Governor of the United Provinces, was in charge of the Coronation committee, but Hardinge displayed an indefatigable interest in the proceedings which, Irving claims, reflected his experience of the diplomatic service with its lavish receptions, liveries and protocol.[67] Finally, after months of Indian toil and at considerable Indian expense – the budget for the ceremonial was estimated at £1 million though the GoI claimed the final cost amounted to £660,000 – the Viceroy telegraphed Crewe, excited about the physical transformation of Delhi, which was 'enthralling to the prospective visitor'.[68] Sited at the same location as the previous durbars to emphasise continuity and tradition, it was, nevertheless, envisaged on a grander scale than anything before in the history of the Raj. As a ceremonial itself it is worthy of scholarly attention. Two amphitheatres were constructed – a smaller one to seat about 12,000 special dignitaries, both royal and official, and a much larger one for around 50,000, including a seating area to accommodate 6,000 schoolchildren and 8,000 other civilians, as well as 20,000 troops. The focus of the assemblage was the pavilion at the centre with a double platform and surmounted by a bulbous golden dome, where homage would be paid and proclamations read out. Bhai Ram Singh, who designed the amphitheatre, was Principal of the Mayo College of Art in Lahore.[69] Their Majesties would process from the smaller to the larger amphitheatre, accompanied by young princes as royal pages holding up their ermine trains. Amongst other spectacular events was to be a review of 50,000 troops on the specially prepared grounds. In the event, the line of troops stretched for four miles and included two seven-year-old princes leading their respective contingents: the Maharaja of Jodhpur and the Nawab of Bhawalpur.

The Media of Communication: Posts and telegraphs, press and telephones

> The tall slim masts of the radio telegraph station, with their connecting wires rise in silent testimony to the wonders which science has achieved ... So the Fort stands now with a new ally within its walls, who keeps it in touch with the wide outer

world...they are symbolic and we must accept them as part of the modern order of things.

This reflection in the *Pioneer*, on the day of the King's arrival in Delhi, is testimony to the novel presence of technological innovation as epitomised in the Marconi tower, situated at the symbolic heart of the traditional order, which also served to link India into a worldwide web of communications. It is also a fitting epitaph to the modernity of the Durbar, as envisaged by a Raj which saw facilities for communication as critical to the success of what was paradoxically also conceptualised within the ancient tradition of divine communion between a sovereign and his subjects.

George V's journey itself reflected impressive advances in technology: as the 'Medina' steamed through the Suez Canal, which had revolutionised sea voyage to the East four decades earlier, Petty Officer E. A. Philp looking to the shoreline enthused about 'the telegraph messenger on the back of his camel awaiting his orders, and as the train runs along it makes me realize what a wonderful piece of work the whole thing is'.[70] Another prominent feature of the trip was the results obtained by wireless telegraphy whereby the cruiser, *Defence*, providing royal escort, managed to maintain communication with England until 23 November and at a distance of 3,000 miles. Outward and inbound messages were received from Aden, and *Defence* was also in touch with the new Marconi station at Delhi, referred to above, from whence a message of welcome was sent to their Majesties.[71]

Within Delhi, facilities for the media were made available on an unprecedented scale. As detailed in *Reporting the Raj*, by the turn of the century, imperial administrators were increasingly aware of the rising influence of the press on political and popular opinion, as well as the strategic potential of exploiting new technologies of communication. Crewe's sensitivity to press opinion was reflected in his desire to assist journalists attending the Durbar, arguing that it was 'bad policy not to treat the Press generously'.[72] The Viceroy reassured him: 'I have made enquiry, and find that accommodation is luxurious and situation excellent. As regards conveyances, fifty seven *tongas* [horse-drawn traps], seventeen motor-cars, and one motor-omnibus will be at the disposal of the camp. There is absolutely no cause for dissatisfaction.'[73] It was also arranged for Fraser and Grigg, as well as Perceval Landon of the *Telegraph*, who were arriving in advance, to be 'shown over the camp, and attention will be paid to any suggestions they may offer'.[74] Journalists, photographers and newsreel cameramen were enabled to view the state entry from at least two, if not three, different vantage points to ensure fuller reports. About fifty newspapers and agencies, which included the *crème de la crème* of Fleet Street and other foreign correspondents, including from France, Holland and Italy, were resident in the Press camp, each being charged a one-off fee of £120 per person, with double this number having to make private arrangements in the city. However, racial segregation was imposed in the camp, with Indian and European journalists housed separately.[75] Newsreel companies competed to have the finished product available for screening as quickly as possible, using innovative onsite facilities. Thus, in Bombay, the firm of Barkers developed the film from the royal visit within a few hours, which was then screened at the Excelsior's Novelty Theatre from 6 December.[76] The royals were themselves entertained to a cinematograph of the Durbar on 6 January, whilst in Calcutta.[77]

More significantly, there were new and sophisticated communication infrastructures created. To supplement the ten permanent telegraph offices within Delhi, there was one main 'Coronation Durbar' office established which remained open 24 hours a day, as well as nine local telegraph offices with 'Coronation Durbar' status. In addition, there were eight railway telegraph offices which received paid telegrams. A Central Telephone Exchange was set up at the Durbar telegraph office and all post offices were equipped with facilities for public calls, where a three-minute conversation cost four annas. Each camp was allocated at least one telephone set in addition to a number of official lines which were available for Government use and had necessitated eighteen miles of underground cables being laid. A specially designated Coronation Durbar Post Office was located in the centre of the civilian and military camps, with 24 outlying suboffices within a five mile radius and 125 letterboxes. This postal system was serviced by 200 staff, 16 inspectors, 150 postmen and 80 coachmen to drive *tongas*, despatching on average 25,000 and receiving 50,000 articles daily.[78]

Transport and Communications: Roads, railways and motor cars

One of the most striking differences with Curzon's Durbar was the organisation of the Camp itself, which occupied 25 square miles with upwards of 40,000 tents and 300,000 occupants, the living quarters arranged in strict hierarchical order. Instead of the 'disorderly spread' in 1903, there was now 'a carefully planned city of canvas' grouped around an extensive royal camp and traversed by metalled roads, in contrast with the 'primitive dust-encumbered roads' of before. This, in turn, reflected what the *Guardian* claimed was the most marked development between 1903 and 1911: the modes of conveyance. The metalled roads were now essential because of the widespread use of motor vehicles, 'in excess of anything hitherto known in India'. For the royal dignitaries a fleet of luxurious cars was put into service, and the Indian rulers sought to outdo each other in displaying the latest in four-wheeled technology that money could import, forcing the press to remark that cars were arriving in Delhi 'not in single spies, but in battalions'.[79]

Railways, emblematic of Victorian progress, were also showcased at the Durbar, which provided the perfect opportunity to demonstrate technological efficiency and skill, and, by implication, public legitimacy for the Raj as representative of 'superior' western civilisation, an argument that had gained increasing currency in imperial and popular discourse from the late nineteenth century.[80] A striking innovation was the extensive use of the light railway within the Canvas city, unlike the dependence on 'ramshackle carriages and tongas' witnessed in 1903.[81] There was a new circular broad gauge railway that circled the Durbar amphitheatre, skirted the parade ground and ran to the Red Fort. There were also a series of narrow gauge lines that served the entire camp and which connected up with the seven major lines that converged in Delhi. Temporary new railway stations were constructed and the main Kingsway terminus fitted with an extended platform to receive visiting dignitaries and their elaborate retinues. Other stations included to the North East the army camp, to the North West the cavalry camp, to the West the Imperial Service troops, the provincial camps and the Punjab camp, the names being indicative of the primary constituencies which these were intended to serve. A regular service of 150 trains per day was organised to run between the Camp and Delhi. Cheaper fares were offered to those 'travelling by light railway in the early morning to provide facilities for the servants of visitors to proceed to the central market or the city for provisions'.[82] This dedicated railway network, as *The Times* noted cost almost £100,000. Most Indian papers agreed with the *Pioneer* that 'in the matters of organisation and direction', this Durbar was 'far ahead' of that in 1903 and showcased 'clockwork precision' in all its arrangements.[83] The *Times of India* concluded that it was nothing short of 'a miracle of improvisation, so bold, so complete, so meticulous'.[84]

Let There Be Light: Electricity and progress

The mammoth task of supplying fresh water, food and milk for the Durbar camp was organised with military precision. However, it was the universal use of electricity that evoked the most fulsome praise from the assembled media. The supply of electricity to 7,500 lamp posts, double that required for a town the size of Brighton, and which the *Guardian* claimed was the largest overhead installation in the world, testified to the energy and scale of the proceedings.[85] A special power plant was set up on Bawari Plain, which supplied the current carried through 300 tons of copper wire for 70,000 lights. Reed, living in the press camp, rhapsodised about how the main roads were 'as brightly lit as Piccadilly and each tent has a perfect arrangement of lights and switches.'[86] This vast-scale electrification of the Canvas city, expanded enormously from the precedent established by Curzon, offered a striking metaphor – along with the metalled roads, the ubiquitous motor cars, the dedicated railway network, postal services, the latest in telephony and telegraph technology – of the modernity that the organisers were keen to associate with the new monarchy and, by association, with the imperium that it would help inaugurate in twentieth-century India.

The King himself appeared eager to partake of the new, whether it be discarding the paraphernalia associated with the lugubrious but traditional elephant *howdah* in favour of the more agile horse for his state entry into Delhi, or preferring the sleek motor car to the stately carriage, and, in general, being much more willing to communicate directly with the masses. Despite being a traditionalist, his mission to India displayed a willingness to adapt and change, which was to remain a feature of his reign, culminating symbolically two decades later when he became the first monarch to broadcast to his people, delivering the BBC Christmas message in 1932. Nicolson, his biographer, argued that whilst George V 'preferred the usual to the unusual, the familiar to the unaccustomed, the old to the new', he was also convinced that the monarchy could not remain 'the sole static institution in a dynamic world' and accepted changes in the sovereign's functions 'as necessities of evolution'.[87]

Building Anticipation: Press Coverage Prior to the Durbar

The Times offered a range of coverage to whet the appetite of its readership, which was far larger than the total subscriptions would indicate, given that its reports circulated widely in national and transnational networks across and beyond the empire, including in North America. In keeping with its claim to be a paper of record, it published on 24 May a special Empire Day number, which was subsequently enlarged and reprinted as a book by Macmillan titled *India and the Durbar*, priced at five shillings.[88] Though written by experts, the paper hastened to assure the public that it was 'designed for general readers and examines, in not too technical a manner, many current Indian questions'. While 'primarily intended' for visitors to the Durbar, it was hoped that the volume would also be 'of value to the far larger public who will watch that unprecedented event from afar'. In addition to historical details of previous tours and the Princes of India, the collection also thoughtfully included chapters on 'Touring in India' and a 'compact Guide to Indian shooting'.[89] Likewise the Official Durbar Directory issued by the GoI featured reports on sightseeing, a map and recommended travel itineraries. Such efforts to publicise the visit (along with the continuing media preoccupation as detailed below) were so successful that it was estimated that 200,000 tourists would descend on Delhi and its environs during December–January and there was official concern about whether the city's already overburdened public services could meet this challenge.

Throughout the summer and autumn of 1911, Fleet Street helped create an air of anticipation for the forthcoming extravaganza.[90] Issues addressing the more social aspects of the celebrations – the lavish balls, garden parties and sporting events – were prominently covered. The illustrated papers added a visually dramatic dimension with the *Sphere*, the *Daily Graphic* and the *Illustrated London News* (*ILN*) all featuring extensive photographic and painted panoramas, beginning with naval scenes at the departure from Portsmouth, portraits – of the royal family, the Hardinges, the ladies in waiting to Queen Mary, the Maharajas attending the Durbar – and later the various ports of call *en route*, culminating with the highlights of their progress through India. The *Sphere*'s coverage was impressive given that its staffer Jacomb-Hood was the royal Artist, and his impressions of the Durbar itself were particularly striking and were given full-page spreads in the paper. However, quality dailies too invested in photography, featuring large montages supplied chiefly by the firms of Central News, Bourne & Shepherd and Johnstone & Hoffman, thus helping to bring home the totality of the experience across the spectrum of the reading public.[91] Whilst understandably focusing on the opulent East of the Maharajas and romantic images from the Durbar, such as the luxurious silk-lined and carpeted tents of the royal couple, complete with the obligatory electric fixtures, these images also included relatively mundane aspects. For instance, the *Guardian* had extensive displays devoted to themes such as 'Getting ready for the Durbar', 'Natives working on the amphitheatre', Indians arriving on richly decorated camels and bullock-carts for the festivities, and views of the official dairy lined with large vats and modern processing equipment.[92] Thus the major behind-the-scenes logistical operation was also conveyed to British readers.

Closer to the departure date, detailed accounts discussed the large royal suites (which included the military historian and librarian at Windsor, John W. Fortescue, who was elevated to the rank of official chronicler); the royal quarters on the new P&O ship, *Medina*; as well as the unprecedentedly large military entourage of battleships, including dreadnoughts.[93] The royal routines in the lead-up to sailing day and a detailed itinerary of their voyage with stops *en route* combined with the atmospheric eye-witness coverage of the actual departure from the massed numbers of correspondents lining Portsmouth docks on a grey and wet winter's day, all helped to build up reader anticipation as well as any adventure novel would. Journalists appeared fascinated by the large naval escort: 'such a powerful force cannot fail to add to the impressiveness of the departure'.[94] Seven battleships (*Neptune*, *St Vincent*, *Vanguard*, *Temeraire*, *Dreadnought*, Superb and *Collingwood*) and three cruisers (*Indomitable*, *Indefatigable* and *Invincible*), all recently built dreadnoughts, would escort *Medina* out to sea and part way up the Channel. Four additional cruisers would then provide the entourage all the way to India's shores.[95]

One of *The Times'* leader writers, the historian Walter A. Phillips (later Lecky Professor of Modern History at Trinity College, Dublin) argued that despite the rising tensions in Europe, North Africa and the Red Sea littoral, the nation was united in supporting this monarchic sojourn.[96] Applauding rather than criticising the monarch for setting aside his national obligations for imperial ones, *The Times* expressed confidence that the tour should assure all 'of our goodwill... since, in spite of these risks, we are prepared to suffer his absence from among us, and to entrust him to the loyalty and affection of our Indian fellow subjects'.[97] This link between domestic, European and imperial agendas ensured that the visit was elevated to a transnational status, with the unprecedentedly large military escort a response to the escalation in European tensions, but also a hint of imperial posturing at a time when Britain's naval supremacy had been successfully challenged. Similarly, Garvin argued how 'the whole heart, sympathy and allegiance of their people go with them'.[98] The *Mail* elected to send William Maxwell, who had earlier accompanied the royals in 1905–6, and he concluded that the royal couple would 'inaugurate a new era' in the history of the empire.[99]

The unfolding of this sea passage to India was covered in the press in a manner akin to a dramatic performance in many acts. Thus interesting excursions at ports of call *en route*, as well as detailed itineraries featuring not just the daily but even the hourly schedule of the royals, enabled readers to become virtual participants in their progress. Simultaneously, *The Times* also began to cover the preparations being made within Delhi, which Chirol described as 'one of the busiest scenes of human activity in the whole world'.[100] Extolling the Durbar city which had risen like the proverbial phoenix from the dusty plains, *The Times* compared the synergies resulting from this conjoining of East and West:

> The West contributes its wonderful powers of scientific organization, the East its inexhaustible resources of patient toil, and by the magic of their combined energy a vast canvas city, equipped with all the requirements and many of the luxuries of modern civilization, is being rapidly evolved out of a waste of ploughed fields and meagre pasture lands.[101]

Overall, Liberal planners had reason to be satisfied by the overwhelming endorsement and popular support received via a reverential Fleet Street basking in the afterglow of a newly crowned sovereign.

The Gateway of India: 'I feel myself no stranger in your beautiful city'

2 December witnessed the royal arrival at Bombay, the occasion being commemorated later by the construction of the elaborate Gateway of India. The details of the reception, including a bird's-eye view of their route and the various meet and greet ceremonies, was accompanied by sketches of the reception at Apollo Bunder and architectural embellishments, like elaborate ceremonial arches, with multiple pages in *The Times* being devoted to the story. This was the first time that a full imperial salute would be fired in Indian waters and the 'expectations of the multitude' were at 'fever point'.[102] Chirol reminded readers how Bombay was 'royal and dower-royal' being part of the wedding dowry of a Portuguese princess to an English king 250 years ago. Bombay's transformation since then into a premier province paralleled the expansion of the empire and the growth of British power in the East. *The Times* was confident that 'In its glorious setting, the blue waters of the harbour in front, the clustered towers and roofs of the city behind, this shimmering palace will make a landing-place worthy of the first Western Emperor to set foot upon an Eastern realm.'[103] Its coverage of the royal arrival was euphoric, 'a splendid dream which history might belie. But today the dream has come true.'[104] This juxtaposition of East and West was also picked up by other newspapers, thus the *Morning Post* argued that the

port city's 'right royal welcome ... seems to unite the colour and glamour of the East with the discipline, power, and energy of the West'.[105]

The Press Association Foreign Special (PAFS) service provided fulsome coverage of all major events fulfilling the demands of the provincial papers, including the *Guardian*, which despite an abiding interest in India had been precluded by expense from sending its own correspondents. The PAFS reports conveyed eyewitness accounts of the 'stir and colour in the streets', the 'cheering and enthusiasm' of the crowds and a copy of the King's speech, which was reproduced by most dailies.[106] The *Guardian*'s leader writer enthusiastically proclaimed:

> When an Emperor comes to visit his people how much his coming gains in spectacular dignity if his road is the sea and his landing place a beautiful natural harbour like that of Bombay, affording a great amphitheatre from which hundreds of thousands can watch his approach and arrival. At Bombay there was no slinking of the royal train past the backs of slum houses into a cavernous railway station; no tedious navigation of a soiled and tortuous stream flanked with ugliness, as there would be if a Royal ship came to London or Glasgow or Newcastle; no undignified business with locks or dock gates.[107]

Maxwell wrote in the *Mail* of the royals driving through miles of 'crowded magnificence, receiving vociferous homage',[108] and the *Daily News* affirmed the 'greatest excitement' amongst Indians.[109] Reuters telegraphed accounts of the Anglo-Indian and the Indian press's gratification at the 'sympathetic tone' of the King's speech, extracts from which were quoted 'with the greatest approval'.[110] News agency coverage helped convey a wide array of Indian opinions to Fleet Street, thus helping to sustain multiple networks of support for the imperial project.

Delhi and the Sovereign: 'An incomparable spectacle'[111]

'I rode a nice looking & quiet horse called "Smoke" & May drove. The whole route was lined with 50,000 troops. There were large crowds all the way, but they were not particularly demonstrative.'[112] Thus reflected George V upon his journey from Selimgarh station – purpose built near the Red Fort to welcome the royal train on 7 December – to the Durbar city five miles away. Freda Du Boulay, wife of Hardinge's private secretary, James Du Boulay, and lady-in-waiting to the Queen, privately claimed that the 'crying trouble' was that the King would not agree to ride the traditional elephant and 'at the last moment the procession was made to close in on the King, so that he was lost in the Viceroy and his escort. Consequently he was not recognized and was scarcely cheered at all.'[113] Some others have similarly questioned the extent of popular enthusiasm evoked by the visit, based largely on this one episode. In his official history, Fortescue remarked that despite the presence of thousands of spectators, they were 'silent after the Oriental fashion' and the King went unnoticed.[114] Reed referred to the 'depressing chilliness' of the State Entry,[115] and Rose, George V's biographer, argued that it 'lacked grandeur'.[116] However, this version of events is disputed by contemporary press accounts. For instance, the *Mail* confidently claimed that 'the fervour of the native welcome was beyond question' after the royal procession left the Delhi gate.[117] Percival Phillips, the *Daily Express* (hereafter *Express*), special correspondent, wrote about the 'tumultuous welcome' accorded by the 'natives of every caste and condition filling the bazaar from end to end'.[118]

Certainly in the days that followed, events were to disprove sceptics. At the final of the football tournament, George V noted how 'there was an enormous crowd of soldiers both British and Native who gave me a tremendous reception'.[119] Similarly at the polo finals on 11 December, 'We got a tremendous ovation from the thousands of people there'.[120] In order to further engage the populace, Sir Louis Dane, Lt. Governor of Punjab, organised a 'Badshahi Mela' (Emperor's Fete) on 13 December, which involved all the main religious communities, including the Sikhs, and strove to emphasise fraternity amongst the sovereign's diverse subjects.[121] Indeed, such instances of popular participation were frequently alluded to by the King and Queen, including at Calcutta, which acquires added significance in view of official unease at the possibility of a popular backlash there. Instead, there was much evidence of general enthusiasm. Thus with reference to the Indian pageant on 5 January 1912, George V confided to his diary: 'We then drove around the arena at a walk for the enormous crowds to see us & they gave us a most splendid reception, there must have been a million people on the Maidan.'[122] Queen Mary's entry reads: 'a most interesting Indian Pageant...The crowds were wonderfully enthusiastic when we left.'[123] Likewise, at their departure from Bombay some days later, the King noted the 'very large crowds who were most enthusiastic'.[124]

So the moot question remains: How do we explain this apparently singular lapse in popular welcome at the entry into Delhi? Amongst the most plausible explanations was provided by T. Y. Chandavarkar, Vice Chancellor of Bombay University and a judge of the Bombay High Court, who was in attendance. He contended that the arrival of the royal procession was 'a great disappointment because the Police regulations were so strict that people were almost kept out'. The King was on a horse and few could recognise him. Further, Indians 'took it all to be an official function, and Indians feel bound to observe silence at such functions'. More pertinently, the public had been issued with orders such as 'Don't raise your hands – don't shout – go away.'[125] These police restrictions and controlling orders were especially enforced in the crowded parts of the route and were remarked upon by several contemporaries. However, there was an abrupt reversal of policy once the organisers realised that such measures were counterproductive: 'from the next day all Police regulations were considerably relaxed and Delhi became "a City of Joy" '.[126] A change in atmosphere was also perceptible to journalists: Phillips described how, amongst the polo players and in the football fields, the 'natives made the air resound'. 'I understand', he concluded, 'that the King was delighted and touched with the spontaneous demonstrations.'[127]

Thus the scale of evidence points to the state entry episode being a relatively minor blip in an otherwise faultless imperial spectacular. *The Times* coverage was magisterial and emphasised how the 'heartfelt emotions' on display 'so visible and so sincere, counted for immeasurably more than transient and limited outbursts of opposition'.[128] The passage of the King 'through vast throngs of his revering peoples' exemplified the 'increasing validity' of an imperium which was 'freely accepted by India in recognition of a long era of just and beneficent government. Though China totters and Persia is in chaos,' the British Raj 'stands four-square upon firm foundations. No one who witnessed the august ceremonial at Delhi this morning can doubt it.'[129] Imperial paternalism, which constituted an active ingredient in Raj ideology, was reinforced by *The Times*, whose lead was followed by most publications.

The Times cartographic department did itself proud by creating extensive maps conveying a bird's-eye view of the processional route through the Red Fort, across the Maidan, round the Jama Masjid, along the Chandni Chowk, through the Mori Gate and over the historic Ridge to the King's camp in the Durbar city. In picturesque description and evocative language, the reports from Grigg and Fraser, accompanied by stellar leaders from the pen of Chirol, succeeded in transporting readers from their sitting rooms in a cold and wet Britain to the crisp air of Delhi where the bright sunshine soon dispelled the chill of the early morn: 'We have cloudless blue skies from dawn to dusk and neither heat enough by day nor cold enough by night to detract in any way from the pleasures of camp life.'[130] 'No conqueror in war, no Imperial guardian of peace and good government, ever gazed upon a scene more spaciously magnificent than that which lay outspread before the Emperor', enthused the duo.[131]

Foreign correspondents were immeasurably aided in achieving a grandiose coverage by the ornamentation and ostentatious display of the Indian princes, who sought to outdo each other through the lavishness of their procession, entourage and livery of their retainers, as well as in the magnificence of their camps. By common consent, one of the most ornate of these housed the Maharaja of Kashmir. It was 460 feet in length and enclosed in a 'beautiful carved and polished walnut open-work screen with carved walnut temples as guard rooms on each flank', fronted by two 'superbly carved' entrance towers, 33 feet high.[132] The roofs and projections all round were covered with polished copper, while the finials appeared to be in gold (Figure 2.2):

> The portions of the screen filling the spaces between the two guard rooms...are arranged in panels each representing some Kashmir fruit, flower, or plant...Each gate tower is composed of four smaller towers, connected by solid panels of carved walnut 3 feet broad and 15 feet in height, roofed over with polished copper. These four towers support a copy of a Hindu temple of the same design as the guard rooms, and this temple is also roofed with polished copper and carries golden finials with the Maharaja's coat of arms embellished everywhere.[133]

Such detailed descriptions were supplemented by a deeper knowledge and sensitivity which *The Times* had long sought to cultivate *vis-à-vis* India, and which was now allowed full creative rein in the hands of Chirol. Thus, for instance, the hyperbolic description of the King's entry into Delhi was accompanied by a thoughtful essay that displayed Chirol's considerable historical expertise, presenting a graphic image of a city where multiple religious faiths and regimes had left their distinctive marks. Acknowledging that, for most Europeans, Delhi was chiefly associated with the Mughals, Chirol argued it contained 'so many memories of Indian history at least as precious to the Hindu as to the Mahomedan'. Beginning with the prehistoric era when the plains of Delhi lay besieged by ancient Aryan races 'round which the poetic

Figure 2.2   Sir Valentine Chirol
Source: James Houssemayne Du Boulay private collection, London.

genius of Hinduism has woven the wonderful epic of the Mahabharata',
to the story of Hastinapura where King Pandu held court, or to that
of Indraprastha, the city founded by the Pandavas, and overlain by
Emperor Humayun many centuries later. Readers were enlightened
about the Asvamedha or great horse sacrifice performed on the banks
of the Yamuna by Yudhisthira, and how 'the whole plain of Delhi is
sacred soil to the devout Hindu'. For the Buddhists, too, there was
the famous Pillar of King Ashoka, who had renounced warfare and
become a devout follower of Buddha. Other Iron Pillars – now part
of the Kutub Minar complex constructed by the Muslim rulers of the
Delhi Sultanate – were further testimony to the grandeur of Hindu war-
rior princes, like Chandragupta Vikramaditya, or the valiant heroes of
the Rajput dynasties who founded the first city known as Delhi in the
eleventh century, such as Rai Pithora, whose name 'still lives in song
as the embodiment of Indian chivalry, equally gallant and daring in
love and in war'. Delhi was raised to the stature of an imperial city *par
excellence*:

Historically as well as geographically it represents the very heart of India; and whenever occasion requires some great and solemn gathering at which expression is to be given of the majesty and power of the Indian Empires, Delhi, at once and without question, resumes its inherited position of primacy as 'the King's house'.[134]

Laying claim to a long heritage of rule in Delhi proved, in retrospect, fortuitous in establishing the groundwork for the King's proclamation, and one must speculate as to whether Chirol was told of its contents and thus took a calculated decision to utilise the pages of *The Times* for an astute piece of agenda-setting.

The Times Coverage of the Coronation Durbar

The Durbar took place, Chirol wrote, 'amid scenes of unparalleled splendour and universal rejoicing'.[135] The descriptions of the coronation ceremonies before, during and after the actual Durbar have been detailed elsewhere by contemporaries and later historians, and it would serve little purpose in recounting these again. Suffice it to say that through word and image the scenes of princely homage, military parades, rousing military music, the panoramic vistas and the sheer numbers massed together were described in the popular press with great verve and palpable excitement.[136] In terms of column inches *The Times* had the most extensive layout amongst the English-language press of the empire. The extract below serves to convey some flavour of this coverage in the words of Fraser and Grigg (Figure 2.3):

> The ceremony at its culminating point exactly typified the Oriental conception of the ultimate repositories of Imperial power. The Monarchs sat alone, remote but beneficent, raised far above the multitude, but visible to all, clad in rich vestments, flanked by radiant emblems of authority, guarded by a glittering array of troops, the cynosure of the proudest Princes of India, the central figures in what was surely the most majestic assemblage ever seen in the East...Not a soul who witnessed it, not even the poorest coolie who stood fascinated and awed upon the outskirts of the throng, can have been unresponsive to its profound significance.[137]

Commenting later on the significance of the occasion, they reflected how

From first to last the Durbar partook of the character of a solemn rite performed with stately and almost sacramental fervour, tinged with high emotions...no one who stood on the plains of Delhi to-day can have failed to feel that it recalled and symbolized the long and majestic story of two races whose fate had become interwoven...It epitomized the centuries; it made visions of the years to come seem real and immediate. Ships sailing into unknown seas, handfuls of men battling amid myriads, had set in motion a train of events culminating in this mighty gathering; all the past strife and turmoil of India, the splendour and the misery,...had been a preparation for this day of days...One felt...that the Durbar was not the apotheosis of a tinsel Imperialism; it was the ritual of that unreasoned but increasing faith which has linked the people of a distant island with the ancient nations of the East in a common striving towards an exalted end.[138]

For George V, acknowledging publicly the presence of his Indian potentates was a critical element of his performative role, and he had

Figure 2.3   Crowds at the Delhi Durbar, 12 December 1911
Source: James Houssemayne Du Boulay private collection, London.

insisted on personally receiving all of them (many of whom, like Sir Pratap Singh of Jodhpur, he had befriended on his earlier tour), noting with disfavour that this aspect of the ceremonials had not been observed diligently by Curzon.[139] He greeted dozens of them upon arrival at Selimgarh station, including the Nizam of Hyderabad, the Gaekwar of Baroda and the maharajas of Mysore and Kashmir, who then joined his entourage as they traversed through Delhi to the Durbar city. Once ensconced in the royal camp, he met a further 20 rulers individually the same afternoon, followed by another 17 the next day, and 59 the day after.[140] The prominent role of the Indian princes in the ceremonial, with the public and ritualised obeisance to the monarch, who, in turn, bestowed imperial honours upon them, was intended to cement still further their significant role as political allies, one which Barbara Ramusack argues was made overtly manifest during the 1910s.[141] The mantra which considered the princes as the pillars of the throne and the embodiment of the spirit of loyalty formed an integral aspect of the British theory of indirect rule over princely India, which accounted for a population of over 70 million and two-fifths of the land surface of the subcontinent, and was established in the aftermath of the Great Rebellion to reinforce control without further annexation or expenditure.[142] These ceremonies were intended to assimilate Indian rulers into British royal rituals, with the rituals helping to bring into being the relationships expressed in them. Honours from the British Emperor were considered as important as land and wealth to securing their position in an imperially constructed social system where prestige was the most valued commodity, surpassing in importance even the hierarchy of wealth. Further, in conjunction with the enormous efforts to transform the city, the Durbar provided an ideal platform for these aristocratic bastions of traditional power to assist, in their turn, in the creation of the proverbial magical East, where the disturbing realities of urban squalor, overcrowded native quarters and widespread poverty were airbrushed from the pages of the press and hence from the first draft of history.

'It came like a bombshell'[143]: The Durbar announcements

Inevitably, however, the two 'boons' announced via the royal proclamation claimed the focus of *The Times'* attention, as indeed it did for the entire press corps, British and Indian. Both were momentous decisions and unprecedented in the annals of the Raj, so intense media engagement was anticipated and inevitable. What, however, were the key preoccupations as evidenced in popular coverage?

'New partition of Bengal'[144]

The annulment of the Partition put Fraser in a particularly awkward position, having now to rationalise the reversal of an initiative which he had praised as the crowning achievement of Curzon's tenure only a couple of months before. This might go some way towards explaining the more nuanced tone of *The Times* as well as the reaction amongst Curzon's other press supporters, including St Loe Strachey and Northcliffe, all of whom claimed that the King's announcement was not a *volte face* due to 'the intrigues of insurgent Bengalis'.[145] Instead, they sought to echo the lead of *The Times* and emphasise that the 'essential principle' of the Partition – that Bengal as a single province was too large to be governed efficiently – had in fact been upheld 'rather than denied by a division of the old province into three instead of into two'.[146] Chirol, who had been Curzon's ally, but was also Hardinge's friend, was markedly confident that the new proposals 'conflict in no way with the avowed purposes of Partition'.[147] The *Mail* referred to it as the 'New Partition of Bengal', explaining, with the help of a map, how the view that Curzon's policy was being reversed was erroneous: 'The ends which he sought are attained, but by a slightly different means, and at the same time popular feeling is conciliated.'[148] Thus the overall emphasis, from this section of the British press, was on an administrative readjustment as opposed to a reversal of Conservative policy. On the other hand, the *Guardian*, like most Liberal papers, welcomed the decision as a progressive measure, though accepting that the devil would lie in the detail. However, it was all praise for the initiative itself which 'for boldness and originality of imagination has thrown into the shade every declaration of policy made in India'.[149] Whilst Indians had been expecting some concessions, not even the 'most sanguine', it claimed, could have been prepared for these 'gifts' which were 'so brilliantly conceived and generously stated'.[150] Most Indian-run papers rejoiced at the revocation of this running sore in the Bengal body politic.[151]

'Delhi reborn'[152]

The other boon announced to 'an astonished world'[153] was the transfer of the capital – 'Delhi reborn' as the *Guardian* put it. This measure received widespread support from journalists across the political spectrum in Fleet Street, though here again we need to strike a note of caution and acknowledge that there was some criticism, but most of it was directed more at the form of the announcement than at the decision itself. The *Edinburgh Review* complained about 'the manner in which so tremendous a move was announced', though admitting in its defence that 'if the matter had been submitted to public discussion it would have been hung up indefinitely'.[154] For the *Edinburgh Review*, a critical explanation behind the move was decentralisation, which was 'a necessity' and impossible as long as the capital of British India served also the needs of a province.[155] The overwhelming British perspective was embodied in Chirol's contention that the transfer was 'a demonstration of the Royal power no less impressive than the splendours of the great Durbar' and would 'commend itself to the dispassionate judgement of both Englishmen and Indians'.[156] Over the following week, Fraser and Grigg's reports on the public mood in Delhi conveyed a largely positive picture, with the laying of the foundation stone for the new capital (after the Durbar) signifying that the decision was 'fixed and irrevocable'.[157] The *Spectator* concluded that the change would advertise 'the hollowness and absurdity of the talk of our abandoning our sovereignty over India...we are not relaxing our hold upon India, but making it firmer'.[158]

However, not all Indians and Anglo-Indians were as sanguine about the move, especially in Bengal, where it occasioned controversy. As Harcourt Butler wrote, the Muslims felt it 'as the wound of an enemy...the Bengalees felt that they were paying a heavy price for their victory'.[159] The *Guardian* noted how 'European Calcutta...is up in arms, and the leading English journal...has raised the cry of "Hardinge must go". The secret decision without reference to local opinion was "insulting to a great city".'[160] The newspaper that raised the Hardinge Must Go cry was the *Statesman*, and in a subsequent meeting Hardinge claimed to have replied to the editor that he 'quite agreed, but from Calcutta only'.[161] The proposed change inevitably also awakened wider debate about the nature of British rule and its future. The *Spectator*, like *The Times*, claimed that 'trusteeship' was the only 'moral base' for domination: 'It is a condition of that trust...that we should govern in the best interests of the governed.'[162] The journal was convinced that British rule was a 'necessary condition to the enjoyment of law, order, and just government'. In juxtaposing the arguments of Pax Britannica and the 'white man's burden' against Indian disunity and difference, the weekly was repeating well-worn imperial sentiments. After all, not even Gladstone in his Midlothian rhetoric had ever contemplated the giving up of empire. As Bernard Porter has argued, 'Liberals had different ideas about the empire from those of the Unionists. But they were not against it...Ideologically imperialism could be squared as easily with Liberalism as with Conservatism.'[163] The *Spectator* issued a prophetic warning: 'To exploit India in British interests would be a crime of the first magnitude, and would be justly rewarded by the downfall of our Empire.'[164]

'a triumphant and resplendent progress': Resonances and Impact

Multiple approaches to understanding the impact of media events are offered by Dayan and Katz, and many of these resonate with the evidence from this case study – despite the differing contexts and technologies separating the early from the late twentieth century. What follows is a distillation of some of their complex contentions, before offering a more directed summary of the press and political response to the Durbar which will serve to flesh out these arguments. Dayan and Katz distinguish broadly between effects that take place 'inside' the event and those which transpire 'outside', which could occur not just after the event but before and even during it. They distinguish between 'effects on the participants', such as the organisers, journalists and spectators, and 'effects on institutions', including politics, leisure and collective memory.[165] Thus, in the case of the latter, one could conclude that the genres of public ceremonial associated with the Raj, with the Coronation Durbar at its apex, engendered the expectation of the greatest cooperation between Indian elites and the British, whilst the specific boons announced by the King assuaged the Indian political classes and popular opinion, as well as contributed to reinforcing imperial control.

However, to begin with 'inside effects', they claim that the 'public commitment to mount an event makes the organizers politically vulnerable even before the event takes place'.[166] In 1911 there was political pressure on the Liberal Government as evidenced by the initial reluctance to allow the tour to proceed, and later in organising the elaborate ceremonials on an unprecedented scale. Next, they argue 'during the event, principals are cast in mythic roles, often by the media...The principals may also use the spotlight to recast themselves.'[167] As I have argued earlier, from the turn of the century, royal visitors sojourning around Britain's empire were well served by a largely reverential and enthusiastic Fleet Street and colonial press. The press exalted the station of monarchy and the person of the sovereign, and succeeded in 'casting' them in 'mythic roles'. In India, however, they worked within the ceremonial cultures of control incorporated by the Raj as part of their governing strategies, as well as the pre-existing traditions of reverence, as testified repeatedly by journalists and political commentators alike. As far as recasting by the principal is concerned, we noted how the Durbar was an innovation where the monarch himself had taken the initiative in calling for the event as well as in pressing for the type of 'boon' he would announce, which would best serve to undo the grievous mistake of partitioning Bengal. We have evidence to suggest that George V saw himself as a force for change in the Raj.

Further, Dayan and Katz suggest that 'live' broadcasting creates 'not only moral but aesthetic' pressure on the event to succeed 'in full sight of the cameras. The emotion generated by the event can only be sustained if the ceremonial progress culminates in a cathartic conclusion.'[168] Clearly the nature of the medium – that is, broadcasting, and live broadcasting at that – is seminal to such a contention. However, even discounting for this, it can be argued that there was considerable ink devoted in the press and by contemporary commentators to gauging the level and nature of public response during the tour, and specifically in relation to the Durbar, where the additional presence of cameras and newsreel companies, who were able to produce footage within hours, ensured that through image and word, the technological capacities of the extant media were exploited to their utmost. For the Raj it was imperative for the Durbar to be an outstanding success and, as evident from the discussion in this chapter, this goal was considered to have been substantially achieved, with the additional benefit of having this euphoria conveyed to audiences across the British world. And, finally, the 'cathartic conclusion' was evidenced in the response to the contents of the King's proclamation at the end of the Durbar – a matter of hours from start to finish. In general, just as 'Live broadcasting enhances the status of the principals, conferring both legitimacy and charisma during the event and after',[169] so it would appear to have been the case with the coverage of the royal couple in 1911, as well as the proconsuls and civil servants involved with the staging of the Durbar media event.

Moving next to consider the effect on organisations, Dayan and Katz posit that media events 'redefine the rules of journalism. Journalists become priests.'[170] They claim that journalists and broadcasters 'tend to be neutralized by their ceremonial role, trapped in the rhetoric of reverential lubrication', whilst some who 'overspecialize in the reporting of such events sometimes turn into establishment panegyrists'.[171] The British media establishment was unashamedly royalist, and to that extent it might well be considered panegyrist. However, whether or not the press was 'trapped' in this reverential mode is difficult to ascertain in the imperial context. Certainly, as argued in *Reporting the Raj*, the symbiotic relationship that the Government sought to create with the press and Reuters was successful to a considerable degree, and in their turn the writings of prominent journalists and proprietors at least contain more than a hint of their self-perceived didactic role: one need only think of Northcliffe, Garvin, Strachey and Chirol. Overall, there is little doubt that, at a critical juncture in the history of the Raj, journalism as an institution played a key role in mediating the monarchy to the empire as well as to the British at home. In return, Dayan and Katz claim that 'broadcasters are rewarded with status and legitimacy for abandoning their "adversarial" stance in favour of an integrative role [and] the opportunity of repledging their allegiance to the central values of the commonwealth'.[172] Yet with respect to the monarchy, it is difficult to see the media in 1911 in such binary terms. Instead, it can be argued that the Durbar as a media event provided the press with an opportunity to display its value as an imperial asset – a role it appeared to crave. There is a persuasive case to be made that it was, instead, the adversarial party political context within Britain that allowed journalists an opportunity to display media support to best advantage by rising above partisanship.

In terms of effects on viewers, their contention that media events invite 'more active participation' is certainly borne out by press coverage during the tour. But whether this transform(ed) the ordinary role of viewers is difficult to gauge at this distance in time and in the absence of opinion polls. Within the empire, we do have some evidence of adulatory treatises and valedictory musical scores composed by ordinary Indians, but these are fragmentary. There is also considerable anecdotal oral evidence from journalists covering the event on the ground, all of which testifies to the widespread acclamation which greeted George V – in both his personal and institutional capacities – and how it was a transformative moment for many Indians. Similarly, there are several accounts by foreign visitors which attest to its popular impact. For example, a young American, Shelland Bradley, remarked how 'the whole atmosphere of Delhi was so alive with expectation that even the most rigidly official of officials showed something of it'. She described the 'extraordinary tension in the air' and the 'startling announcement that literally took away the breath of all India ... Astonishment and incredulity were on every face.'[173] But how we attribute wider significance to such anecdotal and oral evidence remains a thorny issue, so we can but note its presence at this juncture.

However, what is repeatedly reinforced by coverage of the Durbar media event is what Dayan and Katz refer to as 'an upsurge of fellow feeling, an epidemic of communitas'. The event connects centre and periphery 'through direct communion with central symbols and values...The event offers, and affirms, shared membership in a national or international community.'[174] In 1911 the rituals of the Raj accompanying the King and Queen, the panoply of ceremony, as detailed in the media, allowed subjects in Britain and within India to have shared communion as part of the larger imperial family. The enthusiastic letters to the editors of Fleet Street and the popularity of Durbar newsreels attest further to this shared experience.

With respect to 'outside effects' on institutions, the Durbar media event offers scope for reflection on several genres identified by Dayan and Katz. They claim that media events 'confer status' on the institutions involved and help to 'focus public opinion and activate debate' on a specific set of issues, thereby exercising 'an agenda-setting power'.[175] In both Britain and India, the Durbar dominated popular discussion in the preceding few months and, thanks largely to newsreels and the cinema, it carried over into the months immediately following as well. The Disraelian experiment from the 1870s had been largely successful and the prestige of the monarchy reached unprecedented heights in the early decades of the twentieth century. David Cannadine demonstrates how this process was systematically cultivated by politicians when arranging for the royal family to become more accessible to the publics of Britain's far-flung empire and Dominions.[176] The critical role exercised by the media in elevating the institution of monarchy and enabling it to reach vast audiences, as well as recording such events for posterity, cannot be overstated.

The Durbar as a media event was largely seen by Raj commentators to have reaffirmed the governing ethos, or, in the words of Dayan and Katz, 'reinforce[d] the status of leaders'.[177] They also argue that some media events 'lead directly to social and political change'.[178] With respect to the Durbar, one can plausibly point to the King's pronouncements as leading to major administrative and policy shifts. Linked to this are the effects on diplomacy which could become 'infected by the personalization of power'.[179] In 1911 we witness how the power of the Raj was embodied in the person of the sovereign, which at one remove made it both sacrosanct and indivisible. Indeed, in the act of conferring 'boons', laying the foundation stone of New Delhi and so forth, it can also be contended that the 'diplomacy of gesture' was to the fore. This facet of negotiation is but one of many; yet, like today, media events can 'manage to deliver different messages simultaneously'. This is apparent in our analysis of the Durbar media event, which in both its conception and its realization was intended to address many constituencies within the subcontinent as well as transnationally. In creating the Durbar as a dramatic spectacle and choreographing it to come together as a unified whole, its organisers saw its potential to impact on the imagination of both Indians and the British via the reports of the amassed foreign media. For critically 'the event as represented is the one that is experienced and remembered ... The reproduction is now more important than the original.'[180] This, in turn, frames collective memory. With the Durbar there is an overwhelming sense that it represented the beginnings of a new era in the history of the Raj.

Press and Politics

Whilst members of the British media competed to outdo each other in conveying this imperial spectacle, the *Observer* spoke for many when it claimed that 'the ablest correspondents have failed to do more than suggest the splendours and significance of an unparalleled scene. As a spectacle it beggared all the opulence and glories of the past.'[181] Maxwell went a step further to argue in the *Mail* that attempting to describe the magnificence would 'exhaust the resources of language'.[182] Yet, what made this a media event *par excellence* was that it was the gentlemen of the press who served as the main interlocutors between the images and the reality, and, indeed, defined to an extent what constituted 'reality' based on journalistic perspectives and notions of objectivity. The special correspondents, photographers, artists and cinematographers all became first-person narrators, helping to create an imperial collective memory. The mental imaginaries they constructed helped define the public and popular impact of the Durbar, as well as its political significance for the Raj, and indeed for the monarchy at home.

Upon the conclusion of the tour in January 1912, Grigg and Fraser wrote at length about what they considered to have been 'from first to last ... one unbroken record of success'. The visit had 'deepened the sense of loyalty', 'gratified the Princes' and 'tended to pacify many conflicting interests'.[183] Beyond these lay the issues raised by the momentous pronouncements which *The Times* claimed were now universally accepted with the 'profound influence' of George V behind them. Nevertheless, they were realistic enough to conclude the impossibility of predicting whether 'this peaceful atmosphere, with its undercurrent of somewhat strained feelings', was likely to be preserved.[184] From this perspective of underlying tensions within the Raj, the fact that the Durbar

took place at all, and with the King in attendance, was a calculated political gamble. Individual acts of terrorism, though peaking during 1905–8,
were still likely and the 1909 constitutional reforms, intended as a pallia-
tive to the rising political aspirations of Indians, had done little to quell
such violence. Minto's Viceroyalty had been marked by stringent press
laws, regulations against public associations and deportations. Chirol's
book *Indian Unrest*, published in 1910, had received wide coverage and
drawn attention to the role of secret revolutionary organisations, Indian
newspapers like *Yugantar* and *Kesari*, and charismatic leaders, such as
Tilak and Aurobindo Ghosh, the latter's pervasive influence was especially noticeable amongst the educated youth. As late as October 1911,
Mr Cleveland, Director of the CID in India, contended that most of
the itinerary, including the trip to Nepal, could be 'carried out without real danger'. But he was far less sanguine when it came to Calcutta:
'I am certainly apprehensive of some kind of demonstration there from
the extreme party of violence', and was 'averse to His Majesty trusting
himself within small distance of any Calcutta crowd'.[185] Several British
papers echoed such sentiments and highlighted the potential threat
when the royals went amongst the masses. Prior to their arrival, *The
Times* had been critical about what it considered inadequate police protection along the ceremonial route in Bombay, and in Delhi. Hardinge
affirmed that the royals were 'elaborately guarded', with the crowded
streets of Chandni Chowk thoroughly searched. Under these conditions
the *Spectator* commended the actions of the royals in Calcutta: 'To walk
unconcernedly among a crowd every man in which might conceivably
be an assassin is a greater proof of courage than to head a charge in the
field.'[186]

The Raj, in allowing the tour in relatively unsettled times, was
undertaking a challenging 'experiment', testing the waters of the subcontinent by situating the presence of the monarch within it. Yet they
were reassured by the experience of 1905–6 when, despite the Partition
of Bengal having only just been announced, Calcutta had been retained
as a key part of the tour, a faith that had been justified by its enthusiastic public response. The British had reason to be optimistic about the
Indians' seemingly instinctive allegiance to a personal sovereign. The
Edinburgh Review remarked about how the Bengalis, 'these Irishmen of
the East were as exuberant in their loyalty to him as they had been
conspicuous in their antagonism to his Government'.[187] Fleet Street
affirmed that the 'black cloud of unrest that had been hanging over
India for five years...disappeared in an instant before the sunshine of
Delhi'.[188] The Indians were distinct in most respects from the British,

claimed the *Spectator*, 'but in enthusiasm, in devotion, in all that makes the romance of the relation of people to Sovereign, they are one with ourselves.'[189]

Monarchy and the Raj

It was the conjuncture of two processes – political and monarchical – that made this visit so strikingly different. Bagehot had warned against letting daylight in upon the magic of the monarchy, yet in 1911 the Raj came to utilise the Crown more efficiently than ever before. The association was fraught with pitfalls, which explains the imperative need for secrecy. When Morley rose to inform the House of Lords soon after George V's pronouncement, there was an immediate backlash from Unionist MPs. The Marquess of Lansdowne, who had been Viceroy, claimed that both the content of the proclamation and the manner of its disclosure 'cannot fail to mark an epoch' in the history of the Raj.

> But what makes these proposals really of quite exceptional importance is the fact that they are to be connected with the personal intervention of the Sovereign. That is a very serious matter indeed. These are new departures which I can only characterize as of the utmost gravity, and, unless I am mistaken, they will provoke in India every variety of feeling, ranging from great elation to great disappointment, and from the highest hopes to serious mortification. These changes will certainly provoke criticism.[190]

However, Lansdowne was unwilling to enter upon a 'critical discussion' which might introduce 'a jarring note', especially since the House of Lords was powerless to alter what had been announced: 'The word of the King-Emperor has been passed, and that word is irrevocable.'[191] Predictably, Curzon expressed his views rather more forcefully, contending that the changes announced 'involve so abrupt a departure from what has been the traditional and accepted policy' of the GoI, bore 'so strong a political flavour' and were 'invested with so novel and unprecedented a character in being placed at a moment of great solemnity in the lips of the Sovereign' that Parliament would need to subject these to detailed scrutiny.[192] These issues continued to fester into 1912, and upon the King's return he was faced with a Conservative delegation headed by Lansdowne, who had been instructed by his conservative peers:

> Do tell him in plain language that no Tory Minister, not even Dizzy, at the height of his power, would have dared to make such a use of the

Crown. Just imagine what would have happened if Dizzy had caused Queen Victoria to proclaim herself Empress of India at Delhi without a word of prior communication to Parliament, and had come three months later to the House of Commons for the necessary legislative sanction.[193]

A similar theme had earlier been raised by *The Times*' special correspondents based on anecdotal evidence from the Durbar camp: 'It is noticeable that even among Indians who are jubilant about the change of capital there is a marked tendency to criticise the Government for advising the Emperor to intervene in the bitter controversy about the Partition.'[194] However, the Liberal Party was prepared for the potential backlash, eventually managing to steer a bill through Parliament in spring 1912 which sanctioned the measures *ipso facto*. Hardinge, who had known Curzon since college days, was to reminisce how the reversal of the Partition was 'a blow which Curzon never forgave'. Another was the shift of the capital from 'his beloved Calcutta' and for the remainder of his Viceroyalty, 'I found him ... my implacable enemy.'[195]

Nevertheless, for the British this was arguably the most successful Durbar, serving simultaneously an imperial, domestic as well as a transnational agenda. The King had 'revealed himself not only to his Indian but also to his English subjects. He has shown to a wider world ... that he is a strong man as well as an hereditary sovereign. He has shown he has a clear grasp of the problems of his Empire.'[196] The domestic party political context and Liberal policy *vis-à-vis* India in the aftermath of the 1909 GoI Act adds a critical dimension to understanding the function of the Durbar. The purpose of the reforms was 'benevolent but still autocratic',[197] and Morley's radicalism appeared in practice to be lukewarm at best. Rather, the presence of prominent liberal-imperialists in the new Cabinet, including Prime Minister Asquith, signalled that the advent of the Liberal Party to power did not herald a radical shift in imperial policy over India as hoped for by the INC. The emphasis was on conserving the *status quo* whilst making nods towards wider representation and increased responsibility for a small section of educated and moderate Indians. The Liberals differed from the Conservatives much more with respect to the means, rather than the ends, of imperial rule – hence the widespread dissatisfaction with the manner of Curzon's Partition of Bengal. With the departure of Morley, Crewe had large shoes to fill, and the fact that he became, in the end, the first Secretary of State ever to set foot on Indian soil demonstrates the political significance in Liberal eyes of the royal visit.

This was an occasion of state that was skilfully utilised to pilot through a series of reforms that had long been discussed but entailed a degree of party-political controversy that the new Liberal incumbents, facing a vociferous Conservative clique, especially in the Lords, were keen to avoid. To utilise the monarchy to side-step political opposition was a creative act of statesmanship. By claiming that the shift of the capital to Delhi would inextricably involve an administrative reorganisation of provincial government in Bengal, the GoI was able to justify the dismantling of the Partition. Even the latter policy was, as *The Times* stressed, not a reversal of the principles underlying the Partition, since a division of geographic areas and the creation of new administrative boundaries was intrinsic in the new schema, just as it had been in the Curzonian one.

Hardinge, basking in the afterglow of the Durbar, was convinced that the visit had assuaged Indian demands and had acted as a salve to the wounded sensibilities of nationalists. 'The agitation amongst the British community of Calcutta against the transfer of the capital is now dead', he noted in March 1912, and 'the Indian community everywhere is delighted.'[198] Reed, writing to Northcliffe soon after George V's departure, also attributed the decline of anarchical crime to the 'amazing success' of the visit. 'The King had been wiser than all of us. We were all filled with doubts.... [but] there was no interruption in the crescendo wave of popular enthusiasm. It reached an unparalleled pitch in Calcutta, and has left a deep and ineffaceable impression behind it.'[199] The personality of the monarch was frequently lauded by Indian papers, and a writer in the *East and West* emphasised how 'His desire to make himself accessible to the people has greatly tended to endear him to them. The Durbar was a success not only in point of grandeur but in the spirit that pervaded it.'[200] Indeed, as in 1905, the King's demeanour and the popularity of the extravagant *tamasha* afforded by the ceremonies surrounding the visit no doubt also served to provide the common man with a welcome diversion. Thus an anonymous writer in *Blackwood's Magazine*, being an eyewitness on the streets of Delhi, wrote of the 'peasant from the fields of Hindustan and the villages of the five rivers, of the trader from the stalls in the packed bazaar, of the American cousin with his camera and lust for souvenirs', 'the soldier off duty, the long suffering constable, European tourists of every nationality, Burmans, and Shans'.[201] 'Enthusiasm, real genuine enthusiasm, was moving the crowd as no man had ever seen them moved before.'[202] Chirol argued that in Calcutta, where George V 'moved cheerfully amongst the delirious crowds', the 'wound' inflicted on the Bengali psyche by the 'detested'

Partition had been 'healed' by the King's hand.[203] Even after the lapse of several months, similar prognoses were being offered. Field Marshall Lord Nicolson wrote in June 1912 that India 'seems to be enjoying a peaceful time at present, and there can be no doubt that their Majesties visit has produced an excellent effect'.[204] In November, Chirol, accompanying Hardinge on a tour through central India on behalf of the Indian Public Service Commission, claimed that 'Unrest is at least temporarily at a discount.' The move to Delhi was widely popular, he reported, adding that every Indian ruler he had met had alluded positively to it, including Scindhia, which coming from 'one of the greatest Mahratta chiefs is significant'.[205]

What about the chief protagonist's views? For George V, the Durbar was the 'most beautiful and wonderful sight I ever saw & one which I shall never forget. All the arrangements were perfect & everything went without a hitch.'[206] Indeed, the King noted in his diary how the warmth of his welcome had increased and 'the people became more and more enthusiastic each day'.[207] He was so genuinely moved at the farewell in Bombay that he confessed: 'I quite broke down in reading my answer which rather upset me.'[208] Confident that the tour had been 'an unqualified success from first to last', he reiterated how 'It was entirely my own idea to hold the Coronation Durbar at Delhi in person & at first I met with much opposition, but the result has I hope been more than satisfactory & has surpassed all expectations. I am vain enough to think our visit will have done good in India.'[209] George V argued that if the momentum from the fact that 'all the classes and creeds have joined together in true-hearted welcome' could be translated into the wider public sphere, the 'same unity and concord may for the future govern the daily relations of their public and private lives'.[210]

In general, historians have paid relatively little attention to the Coronation Durbar, and those who have alluded to it are divided as to its practical consequences. Denis Judd appears to side with the sceptics when he claims that the impact was 'hardly profound'. The Durbar was 'both the ceremonial apotheosis of the Indian Empire and a rare, isolated moment stolen from the pressures of nationalist agitation'.[211] Robert Frykenberg, whilst not critiquing the Durbar *per se*, claims that a deleterious consequence of the move to Delhi was the alienation of Bengali Muslims, which served to 'aggravate local opinion' and thus the growing communal antagonism within the Indian body politic.[212] On the other hand, R. J. Moore considers it to have been a fine moment in the Liberal experiment, reserving his praise, in particular, for Hardinge, whose scheme was 'a stroke of intelligent and enlightened liberal statecraft', reflecting the 'most astute Viceregal appreciation' of Indian politics since Dufferin.[213] B. R. Nanda contends that the Durbar and its associated 'boons' were 'a magnificent spectacle and a political masterstroke', creating an 'excellent effect on public opinion' within India and vindicating the faith of Moderates like Gokhale in the 'sincerity' of the Raj.[214] Rose highlights a different perspective, noting that in 1912 India had already begun 'her chequered progress' towards self-government, yet 'paternalism and pageantry, it seemed, still retained their place in her national life: at best ties of affinity between one civilization and another, at worst the bread and circuses with which an earlier empire stilled disaffection'.[215] This approach has received robust support from Bernard Cohn and Cannadine. Cohn in a landmark essay focusing on the 1877 Assemblage posits that the ritual idiom constructed by the British chiefly as a means to create authoritarian legitimacy survived and flourished till the Great War. Overall, the success of this strategy can be judged by the fact that this 'set the terms of discourse of the nationalist movement in its beginning phases'.[216] The single unquestionably concrete result of such an approach was the construction of that monument to imperialism: the New Delhi of Lutyens and Baker. Crewe's biographer gives him prime credit, claiming that he was 'very really and very directly responsible', having pressed the case of Lutyens who seemed to possess 'singular purity of taste'.[217] Lutyens was, in turn, an enthusiastic supporter of the Raj, finding in it 'the ideal of an enlightened imperial despotism, dedicated to public service'. He was determined to supply it with an 'architecture fitting its lofty ideals'[218] and envisaged creating 'an Anglo-Indian Rome'.[219]

Finally, with respect to the British theory of indirect rule and in terms of shoring up support for their aristocratic allies, the Durbar was undoubtedly an important milestone. With the escalation of nationalist opposition as the twentieth century unfolded, it was even more contingent for the Raj to be able to display publicly the strength of its princely collaborators. The Durbar provided an ideal pan-India forum where administrators were able to accomplish this goal without getting entangled in the domestic politics of hierarchy, religion or size that dogged the internecine relationship among these potentates. Whilst their order of precedence was respected, they were all, nevertheless, equally subservient in the presence of the imperial sovereign. George V was particularly keen to strengthen this aristocratic alliance, and he specified the protocol to be followed at the Durbar and at various stages of the tour. This personal touch was much appreciated, in their turn,

by the Indian rulers, some of whom also served on the official Coronation committee, including the maharajas of Gwalior, Bikaner and Idar,
as well as the Nawab of Ranpur.

This perspective goes some way towards explaining the furore occasioned by the 'one uncouth incident'[220] that was caused by the 'seemingly indifferent manner' of the Gaekwar of Baroda's homage at the
Durbar in turning his back to their Majesties whilst descending from
the steps of the amphitheatre afterwards.[221] Whilst this event did indeed
occur, a creditable eyewitness testimony provided by a young equerry
to Queen Mary is worth noting. Harry Watson, who later became a
Major General and was knighted, recalled how he had been 'in full
view' of the throne at a distance of only six yards and had witnessed
the Gaekwar unaware that he had to climb up one flight of stairs but
return via a second set, was 'rudely handled' by the Political Officer
and 'pushed past' His Majesty. 'I happened to know the Gaekwar very
well', Watson added, claiming that he was 'a nervous little man, very
kindly and very simple. I was sad to see him so rudely handled at the
Durbar and quite realised his nervousness had upset him.' According
to Watson, Hardinge 'most stupidly made an awful fuss of what he
called the Gaekwar's disloyalty and allowed the Press to make a fuss
about it too, and the story got to England and the Gaekwar was not
forgiven for a very long time'.[222] *The Times*, for instance, suggested
the Gaekwar's disloyalty in a provocatively titled piece, 'The Gaekwar
and Indian sedition'.[223] These sentiments were juxtaposed, ironically
in the same edition of the paper, with a public apology on behalf of
the Gaekwar in which arguments similar to those espoused by Watson
were explicitly made. Such was the press furore that Phillips, who had
been amongst the minority in not considering the incident worthy
of coverage for the *Express*, found himself at the receiving end of a
cablegram from his irate proprietor, Lord Blumenfeld, questioning his
judgement.[224]

This episode created further consternation later when newsreels of the
Durbar began to be screened in London and elsewhere. Bottomore offers
an intriguing counterperspective from a perusal of the film footage,
arguing that there were two very similarly dressed princes – the Gaekwar
and the Maharaja of Mysore – who both turned their backs to the
monarch, as indeed did the Begum of Bhopal. Thus he concludes
that the evidence points not to the exceptionalism of the Gaekwar's
behaviour 'but that others behaved in a very similar manner'.[225] However, Hardinge was intent on making an example of the Gaekwar and
succeeded in extracting 'a full apology' for his 'attitude of disrespect' to

the King.[226] Yet, as his memoirs reveal, his 'firmness' was motivated far more by *realpolitik*, given the Gaekwar's record both overseas, where 'he associated with Indian extremists', and within his state, which was considered to be 'a hot-bed of sedition and contained printing presses where seditious literature was printed for dissemination throughout India'.[227] The fact that Baroda was a progressive ruler who prioritised issues such as public education, health and sanitation was conveniently ignored.

Concluding Remarks: 'the golden link of Empire'[228]

The year 1911 was a transformative moment in the imperial experience. It was conceived primarily as a demonstration to the British at home and to the wider world that the Raj continued, in the twentieth century, to ride high on a wave of pomp and circumstance and, by implication, also of power. As the shrewd manipulator Benjamin Disraeli, vigorous proponent of the first Imperial Assemblage, had argued, the key to India lay in London. And, as his moral heir, George Nathaniel Curzon, had declared of the subsequent event in 1903, it was 'an act of supreme public solemnity, demonstrating to ourselves our strength'.[229] This was truer of the Coronation Durbar – 'the greatest pageant of all time'[230] – where, arguably, the domestic Indian agenda served to reinforce the metropolitan and transnational one. The immaculate staging of the Durbar and the highly coordinated and carefully produced coverage resulting in the media event, masked, in the process, the harsher realities of the Raj – its inequalities and deprivation, brute force and racism. And herein lies its inherent paradox and the key to appreciating a critical *raison d'etre* for the coronation media event: it was not intended to illuminate the Raj but rather to obscure it, by reducing it to a template and backdrop against which was played out an elaborate ritual for the display of imperial grandeur and self-confidence. The masses, whose loyalty to the British throne was repeatedly proclaimed by politicians and the press alike, were almost always this distant and murmuring sea of people who appeared to gaze in wonder at the imperial spectacle. The chosen few who were allowed to assume a distinct personality were the traditional royal elites (the Indian princes) and the faithful retainers – that is, the Indian veterans of the 'Mutiny', both constituencies beyond reproach and who offered no threat to the imperial *status quo*, rather serving to reinforce the official narrative of stability and loyalty. Thus *The Times* was convinced that the Delhi ceremonies would 'link up as never before the history of the British rule in India with all the greatest traditions of India's past, and will establish as nothing else

Figure 2.4a and 2.4b Contemporary views of the site of the 1911 Coronation Durbar, Delhi

Source: Author, 2011.

could the continuity of Indian history under the beneficent supremacy of the British Power'.[231] And the *Spectator* argued that, from the new capital, the British would in future 'stand with their backs against the wall of the Himalayas, ready to make good their right of rule against all comers'.[232]

The Coronation Durbar was not conceptualised in isolation but within the wider ceremonial strategies of British rule. For the Raj, the event represented the apogee of performance as a mode of imperial politics. A host of commentators have reflected upon the complex late nineteenth-century processes involved in the creation of an imperial culture associating monarchical symbolism with imperial force. By the early twentieth century these were well established and had developed to become sacrosanct touchstones by which the success of British overseas endeavours and, by implication, of the British themselves were judged. In 1911 India, this was revealed most distinctly by the centre-staging of George V at the Durbar; additionally, he was also prominently associated with, and acted as the conduit for, the articulation of imperial policy. Unionist critics cried foul play, claiming an attack on the institution of constitutional monarchy and parliamentary privilege. Yet the Liberal strategy of promulgating major administrative and policy shifts, under the radar of political controversy and cloaked with monarchical privilege, proved successful. Garvin at the *Observer* was able to appreciate the skills involved in this process, remarking that it demonstrated the 'vitality, daring and elasticity' that the British were able to bring to imperial problems. The *Mail* considered the changes 'in their boldness and breadth of imagination [to be] worthy of idealism of the first British Sovereign who has been crowned in Delhi. They add alike to the glory of the King-Emperor and to the strength of that modern miracle, the British Raj.'[233] And the *Guardian* concluded: 'in political significance the Imperial Assemblage would enormously outweigh its spectacular effect'.[234]

Perceptions of empire created their own reality, and the Raj had slowly but surely begun to accept the political imperative of propaganda and publicity as integral to official strategy. As the *Edinburgh Review* emphasised, 'England in her relations with India must not only be just but must also appear so.'[235] In the context of the wider British world, the ceremony as reported across the globe also served to shore up national confidence in a post-Boer War era with the threat to her naval supremacy and the impact of European colonial posturing. As *The Times* had proclaimed on the occasion of the royal departure for India: 'For nothing could more grandly illustrate the fact that Great Britain is still Mistress of the Seas than the spectacle of her King calmly sailing, on a mission of peace, through waters where war is supposed to be raging.'[236]

It has been widely acknowledged by newspaper historians that this was a seminal period – often referred to as a golden age – in the political maturity and influence of the British national press, and it was in the conjuncture of these processes that the impact of the Durbar was made manifest as a media event. *The Times'* coverage revealed a sophisticated grasp of the ceremonial, its implications and an evaluation of the wider policies inaugurated by the Raj. The close and symbiotic relationship between the press and imperial elites was displayed most dramatically by the fact that amongst only a handful in Britain entrusted with the details of the King's announcement were two journalists, Chirol and J. A. Spender, editor of the *Westminster Gazette* which was 'run as a mouthpiece of the Asquith/Grey wing of the Liberal party relying heavily on party donations'.[237] Thus Spender reminisced about how he travelled out for the Durbar 'burdened with the secrets' of the proclamation on which 'I had written articles and left them behind me in sealed envelopes for publication on the appropriate dates'.[238] The complex network of British media and its Anglo-Indian counterparts represented also a professionalism borne of experience, and it is noteworthy that many of the senior British journalists covering the Durbar had also reported on earlier royal events, most notably Curzon's Durbar and the 1905–6 tour, and had established reputations as India experts. These included *The Times* men and Reed of the *Times of India*, Phillips representing the *Express*, Maxwell writing in the *Mail*, Landon of the *Telegraph* and the ubiquitous Reuters correspondents.

Dayan and Katz argue that the broadcasting of media events may help shift perceptions and shape political responses. One needs to be wary of attributing causality too literally to press coverage, and questions such as how successful the British press was as a vehicle of popular cultural imperialism and to what extent it managed to impart its worldview to the public, continue to remain pertinent. Yet then, as now, tendencies can be highlighted and inferences made. Whilst it was undoubtedly the case that the British public, as John MacKenzie posits, 'never came to grips with the principles or practice of imperial rule', it was equally true that empire, in its multifarious dimensions, was a fundamental preoccupation of all shades of press opinion, and newspaper circulation was at an all-time high with both quality and popular papers reaching more numbers and across a wider social spectrum than ever before.[239] Though, at home, Fleet Street had displayed a largely reverential – if occasionally distant and even critical – attitude towards the reclusive Queen Victoria, with the advent of Edward VII, and more especially George V to the throne, royal coverage appeared to be revitalised. It is in this context that the press preoccupation with a magnificent and grandiloquent Assemblage on the faraway sunlit plain from which rose 'the glorious city of Delhi – a plain heavy with the dust of empires dead and gone but now stirring with the promise of a new and more hopeful age' – appeared to herald a new imperial dawn as well.[240] A new emotional power appeared to be vested in the office of monarchy. Such an interpretation of the imperial-media event would appear to be vindicated by the in-depth study undertaken in this chapter, and, to the extent that this played into the machinations of the Raj, the press was complicit in imperial manipulation. Curzon's was 'an elephant Durbar... This will be a motor Durbar', the *Times of India* had noted. Indeed, the efforts of imperial propagandists in creating a modern communication and information environment that would be conducive to this outcome appeared to have paid handsome dividends.[241] However, the degree to which this manipulation was the act of a coconspiratorial press is impossible to prove conclusively.

The Times had demonstrated an extensive range and degree of involvement with Indian issues since the early nineteenth century, and its coverage a hundred years later circulated widely in numerous national and transnational networks, including in diasporic circuits, and within the Anglo-Indian and indigenous press. In the constant reiteration of Indian themes and in the quality and nature of debates that found a platform amongst the pages of *The Times*, and of Fleet Street more generally, it succeeded in creating communities of interest and collaboration transnationally. Thus as *The Times* concluded at the departure of the royals from Delhi, 'From the graphic descriptions sent to us day to day by our Special Correspondents, even those of our readers who have never seen the gorgeous East have been able to gather something of the splendour of these great solemnities, amidst impressive surroundings hallowed by the most ancient traditions of Indian history, under the glorious canopy of the Indian sky.'[242] What was of seminal importance to the process was to convey this choreographed image of India to a vast audience: in that instance via the Durbar media event, a world was epitomised in the writings of the press, agency reports and foreign despatches, as well as evoked through photographs and the cinema. India became 'a visualised unit and reality, the Orient and our Empire in it were caught and held to a single point'.[243]

At this historic juncture, the press provided a reliably consistent source of reference to gauge wider opinion, and in the face of over-whelming newspaper praise and support – including from Indian, especially Bengali publications – it would be a strong Opposition that would seek to overthrow the political changes announced at the Durbar, without also seemingly denouncing George V who articulated them, as Lansdowne's discomfiture made apparent. The Conservatives were hoist on their own petard, impotent to seek to alter or mod-ify the decision without damaging monarchical prestige within the empire, a cornerstone of their ethos. Thus the press and the Liberal Government appeared to sing from the same imperial hymn sheet proclaiming the successes of the Durbar. The honeymoon period imme-diately following the Durbar was pregnant with anticipation under-pinned by the expectation of real change that the King appeared to promise.

Yet, unsettling portents could also be detected on the horizon and, akin to a Shakespearean drama, natural forces appeared to forewarn of the dangers ahead. Keeping with a nautical theme, the King's con-voy was faced with a severe gale and exceptionally heavy seas soon after departure for this imperial mission, mirroring the turbulence in Britain's foreign relations. And, subsequently, even before the dust had settled on the Durbar, readers were informed of the sinking of the aptly named *The Delhi* on 14 December. This P&O liner was on its way to India when it sank near Cape Spartel, a few miles off the Moroccan coast. On board were George V's sister, Princess Louise, and her family, who were saved amidst high drama, with their rescue boat itself cap-sizing, throwing the royals into the churning waters.[244] In India, too, the fragility of the truce bought by the Raj through the stratagem of the Durbar was brutally demonstrated by the audacious attempt to mur-der the Viceroy – almost a year to the day of the Durbar. The incident in Chandni Chowk involved a bomb thrown onto the elephant howdah in which the Hardinges were making their state entry into the new capital. This came, argued Chirol, 'as a painful reminder that the fangs of Indian anarchism had not yet been drawn'.[245] As Reed was to note presciently, the enthusiasm for the royal house witnessed at the Durbar was

> generated by a revived consciousness of Indian nationality, a quick-ened confidence in the realisation of Indian ambitions ... So far from allaying the national spirit the visit has strengthened it, so far from calming Indian aspirations it has made them stronger. True, Indians

now work for the realisation of those aspirations within the Empire, but they will press for this realisation strongly nevertheless. The situation we have to face in India is India for the Indians, politically and economically. We are surrounded by evidences of this spirit every day. If these hopes are frustrated, there will be a revival of stormy agitation.[246]

We turn, in the next chapter, to examine Gandhi, arguably the greatest exponent of the agitational genre in twentieth-century India. The imperial game of cultural control utilising the weapon of monarchy was fraught with peril and needed to be played with caution and within a wider political strategy, as became apparent with the subsequent visit of George V's son, the future Edward VIII, albeit in a fundamentally altered context following the First World War.[247]

3

India as Viewed by the American Media: *Chicago Daily Tribune*, William Shirer and Gandhian Nationalism, 1930–1

Introduction; Indian Publicity & the US; American News Agencies & India; *Chicago Daily Tribune*, McCormick & Overseas Coverage; McCormick & India; Shirer & India; Shirer & Gandhi; With Gandhi in England; Gandhi & the Western Media; British Propaganda & the American Press; Concluding Remarks

> The little old man may look weak and sickly and have only two teeth and almost no clothes – but he's strong, powerful and able, very able. I was amazed at the efficiency of his party organization, the Indian National Congress.
>
> Shirer to McCormick, 21 August 1931

Introduction

William Lawrence Shirer first encountered India, in his own words, as 'an ignorant young American foreign correspondent' of the *Chicago Daily Tribune* during 1930.[1] He was only twenty six, and with a journalistic experience hitherto limited to western Europe, when he was sent to cover what he referred to as 'Gandhi's peculiar revolution'[2] – that is, the mass Civil Disobedience movement inaugurated in March 1930 by one of the great ideologues, politicians and moralists of the twentieth century, M. K. Gandhi. 'It was a difficult revolution to understand even for Indians,' he was to confess in his *Memoir* fifty years later, 'and especially for one like me who came to India loaded down with all the foolish prejudices and myths of the West, which had been dominated so long by force and violence.'[3] However, ever since he had read about Gandhi's imprisonment in 1922 at the end of the Non Co-operation

71

movement, Shirer had harboured a wish to meet him. Now he was to realise this ambition in full measure, becoming part of a select coterie of foreign correspondents who enjoyed the trust and cooperation of the nationalist leader.[4] Concluding his *Memoir* of this seminal encounter, he wrote:

> I count the days with Gandhi the most fruitful of my life. No other experience was as inspiring and as meaningful and as lasting. No other shook me out of the rut of banal existence and opened my ordinary mind and spirit, rooted in the materialist, capitalist West as they were, to some conception of the meaning of life on this perplexing Earth. No other so sustained me through the upheavals and vicissitudes that I lived through in the years after I left India...What I had got from Gandhi helped me to survive.[5]

In the intervening decades, Shirer had become immensely successful in making the transition from reporting news to writing history, and one needs to bear this in mind when interpreting his subsequent observations about Gandhi and decolonisation. The aim in this microstudy is to juxtapose Shirer's contemporary despatches, the coverage accorded in the *Tribune* and his private reflections, against the broader context of American media interest, official British propaganda strategies directed at the US, and an appreciation of the Gandhian oeuvre of political publicity. Such developments and their impact deserve much more credit than they have been accorded in the annals of Anglo-American journalism history as well as in shaping the Raj experience during the twentieth century (Figure 3.1).

Indian Publicity and the US

Official US connections with India are conventionally attributed to having begun with President Washington's appointment of Benjamin Joy as consul in Calcutta in 1792. Such initiatives were intermittent over the following century and it wasn't until the 1940s that regular diplomatic contact was established. However, trade and commerce had thrived in the interim, whilst India had always been a subject of public interest, though limited largely to specialist interest groups, such as transcendental meditation associations, Christian missionaries, as well as writers and philosophers. Amongst the best-known Indologists were William D. Whitney and E. Washburn Hopkins, both of Yale, Charles R. Lanman (Harvard), Maurice Bloomfield (Johns Hopkins)

73

Figure 3.1 William L. Shirer on board ship *en route* to India, 1931 [photograph, copy], reprinted by permission of the Literary Trust of William L. Shirer, George T. Henry College Archives, Coe College, Iowa

and A. V. Williams Jackson (Columbia). Other prominent personalities, such as Bronson Alcott, John Greenleaf Whittier, Herman Melville, Walt Whitman, Henry David Thoreau, Ralph Waldo Emerson and Mark Twain, also did much to enlighten the reading public and impact popular sensibilities. Twain's three months in the subcontinent during 1896, which occupied a central part of his book *Following the Equator*, is an oft overlooked episode in the cultural awakening of Americans, but one which also had a profound impact on 'the father of American literature'. Upon his return, Twain spoke on numerous platforms, wrote copiously for the press and concluded that India was the 'mother of history, grandmother of legend, great-grandmother of tradition ... the one land that *all* men desire to see, and having seen once, by even a glimpse, would not give that glimpse for the shows of all the rest of the globe combined'.[6]

However, it was largely under the impetus of the First World War and in the early 1920s with Gandhi's Non Co-operation movement that the US press awoke to the potentialities of regular reporting from the subcontinent. Much was made in India of President Woodrow Wilson's Fourteen Points and proclaimed right of self-determination for all peoples, and 'veils of distance and culture were penetrated to introduce the Mahatma to the American readers'.[7] Press coverage juxtaposed attempts at explaining Gandhi's political strategies with descriptions of his physical appearance: the toothless grin, seeming frailty, asceticism and scanty attire.[8] None other than William Randolph Hearst writing in the *Washington Times* questioned how the US could 'consistently and conscientiously support England in her domination of India against the will of her three hundred million people'.[9] Nevertheless, it is instructive to note that British censorship delayed full details of defining events, such as the Jallianwallah Bagh Massacre, from reaching American shores.[10] This is unsurprising given that news obfuscation methods had ensured that it was eight months before the full details of the killings and their cover-up emerged, even within Fleet Street.[11] US newspapers did not have permanent staff stationed in India at this juncture and were heavily reliant on their London correspondents, the British press as well as Reuters. Thus misconceptions persisted and were perpetuated, as Lala Lajpat Rai observed in 1919: 'more the result of ignorance than of prejudice, or say, prejudice born of ignorance'.[12]

The radical traditions of North America-based Indian support for nationalism can be meaningfully dated to the turn of the twentieth century and are symbolised by the iconic San Francisco-based Hindustan Ghadr Party, established by Har Dayal, and its eponymous journal.[13] They were joined by a steady stream of students from India like Taraknath Das (who began publishing *Free Hindustan* from 1908), activists such as Rai, Vithalbhai Patel and Sarojini Naidu, as well as writers and philosophers such as Rabindranath Tagore and Dr S. Radhakrishnan, following in the footsteps of Swami Vivekanand, who electrified audiences during two tours, the first undertaken in 1893 and lasting two years, followed by another in 1900. Tagore made several visits and was a most prolific communicator through private and public engagements and via his writings. Rai came to reside for several years in the US, being much impressed by American democratic institutions, and upon his return penned *The United States of America: A Hindu's Impression*. (Jefferson's American Declaration of Independence is widely considered to have influenced, in word and spirit, the framers of the INC declaration of Purna Swaraj on 26 January 1930.)[14] These sojourners engaged in propaganda campaigns through the press and platform, but also via political organisations such as the India Home Rule League of America established by Rai in New York in 1914, with its monthly organ *Young India*. Funded by their American sympathisers and donations from Indians – for example Rai was funded by B. G. Tilak to the tune of £5,000[15] – such initiatives successfully targeted opinion-makers and political elites, such as Roger Baldwin, founder of the American Civil Liberties Union, and several Congressional members. Another base of support were missionaries and Church groups with their attendant publications, as will be discussed later. Such endeavours were slowly but steadily subjected to scrutiny by American intellectuals and journalists, many of whom became involved in the setting up of organisations to further the Indian cause, such as the American League for India's Freedom (1932) and the India League of America (1937). (The latter also published the monthly *India Today* and was led by the indefatigable J. J. Singh.) Overall, such initiatives lacked large investment of funds and were not institutionally directed from India or part of the sustained political strategy of nationalist parties, though some prominent leaders, such as Jawaharlal Nehru, maintained a consistent interest in cultivating western support and pushed the INC to be more proactive. Nevertheless, over the interwar years, Indian publicists could justly claim a measure of success in their collaboration with myriad networks of support in the US.

Parallel to this largely positive US reception, it is possible to discern a more negative response, especially amongst some missionary groups from the early nineteenth century. These were largely directed at what they considered deleterious religious and social practises, attitudes that persisted into the twentieth century and can also be discerned in the book which caused the greatest furore ever unleashed in US publishing circles *vis-à-vis* India: Katherine Mayo's 'crudely propagandist' *Mother India*. Published in 1927 it sold 250,000 copies within only a few months.[16] Gandhi was disturbed as much by its contents, which he referred to as a 'drain inspector's report', as by the adverse impact on India's public image due to the international controversy unleashed in its wake. Edward Thompson wrote how, whilst visiting Vassar College in 1929–30, he was 'drawn in the Indian controversy'.[17] Indians felt that 'their civilization was held up to contempt' and in subsequent campaigns they 'found a ready audience for their sorrowful stories'. It was 'generally believed', argued Thompson, that the 'diabolically ingenious' Raj had 'suborned' Miss Mayo to write the book which 'poisoned the political atmosphere to a terrible extent'.[18] Naidu's visit to the US in 1928–9 was an attempt, in part, to offset the impact of Mayo. There were also several pro-nationalist books by Americans at this juncture, including Rev. J. T. Sunderland's *India in Bondage*. Sunderland's association with India began in the late 1890s on behalf of the Unitarian Missions. He came to author multiple volumes, edit *Young India* and serve as President of the India Society of America. The transnational impact of such publications is well illustrated by the subsequent history of Sunderland's book, which was widely extracted in *The Modern Review* (Calcutta), whose editor, Ramananda Chatterjee, had become a close confidante. This action, along with Chatterjee's republication of an Indian edition of the book entitled *Her Right to Freedom*, incurred the wrath of the GoI, which banned the book, charging Chatterjee with sedition. Such bans were hardly new but their frequency intensified in the wake of the upsurge of mass nationalism during the interwar years.[19]

However, the Raj could not censor with such impunity the massed numbers of American journalists, and herein lay their strength. In terms of US media coverage of nationalism, it was the 1930s that marked a watershed. Undeniably, the Civil Disobedience movement, beginning with Gandhi's iconic Salt March to the sea, served as the critical launchpad for a much more popular and sustained US media focus reaching larger audiences than ever before. Gandhi's protest, conceptualised and staged as a pilgrimage, was advertised through his newspapers and duly transmitted worldwide by Reuters, as well as via numerous interviews with foreign journalists, all of which served to create public anticipation and widespread publicity, much to the chagrin of the Raj.[20] 'We have recognised from the beginning that Gandhi's campaign depends to a very large extent for its effectiveness on publicity', ran a Home Office secret memo dated 2 April 1930. 'Consequently our policy has quite definitely been to curtail the Gandhi publicity and to do as much counter-publicity of our own as is feasible.'[21] Another secret despatch expressed grave concern about the impact of special telegraph and postal facilities arranged along the line of Gandhi's march, considering it 'a mistake thus to facilitate the advertisement that Mr. Gandhi and his followers no doubt desire'. Reiterating how government policy had curtailed all Gandhi-related publicity, including films, which were 'banned all over India',[22] it appeared 'quite contrary' to have special facilities enabling journalists to broadcast 'highly coloured and frequently inaccurate accounts of the success of the march'.[23] The Postmaster-General of Bombay, G. V. Bewoor, responding to such admonitions, was at pains to stress that while they had 'not facilitated the advertisement of the march', the telegraph branch in the proximity of the march had been 'strengthened in order to cope with the anticipated telegraph traffic'. The additional facilities would avoid severe congestion of Government traffic and deter complaints from journalists. 'We could not refuse press traffic', claimed Bewoor, 'when offered by duly authorised correspondents. We obtain payment for this and it is our duty to dispatch the messages.'[24] He emphasised nevertheless that 'a very large number' of contentious telegrams had been 'detained under proper advice'.[25] Bewoor's justification exemplifies the ambiguity inherent in the British response to press freedom in an imperial context.

Lord Sykes, Governor of Bombay, though 'uneasy about the propaganda effect' of the march, was powerless to countermand Irwin's disinclination to take pre-emptive action since the law 'did not permit any interference with the march, provided that it was undertaken in a peaceful and orderly manner'.[26] Irwin was also hoping that Gandhi's call to the nation would receive a muted response, a position his biographer Gopal claims 'suggested a lack of imaginative understanding'.[27] US newspapers, magazines and film companies did not share Irwin's hopes and 'recognized the drama of the event and participated actively'.[28] At Sabarmati ashram, 'Scores of foreign and domestic correspondents dogged Gandhi's footsteps...what exactly would he do?...The excitement spread abroad. Cables kept the Ahmedabad post office humming.'[29] Gandhi continued to write for *Navajivan, Young India* and the *Bombay Chronicle*, grant interviews to papers such as the *New York Times* and the *Guardian*, and make direct public exhortations to journalists. For example, at Navagam on 14 March, he apologised to them for having to suffer the same privations as the marchers but issued a reminder: 'we do need the help of newspapers....this struggle is a unique one....In the last analysis, even the Press representatives have come for public service, have they not?'[30] Thus Gandhi managed in the conceptualisation and execution of the march to incorporate the media into the heart of his struggle and turned journalists from passive bystanders into unwitting participants.

In 1930 it was the dramatisation of Indian nationalism that prompted *Time*, the American news magazine, to feature Gandhi on its cover with the title 'Saint Gandhi'. Under the heading 'A Pinch of Salt', the magazine argued that if a western politician in a loin cloth had walked barefoot the 80 miles to London, 'Englishmen would have thought him mad.' However, as Gandhi 'trudged along last week...Englishmen were not amused but desperately anxious'.[31] *Time* was also to name Gandhi 'Man of the Year' in January 1931 (Gandhi making the cover again), contending that more than Sinclair Lewis, Stalin or Hitler, the Mahatma – 'the little half-naked brown man whose 1930 mark on world history will undoubtedly loom largest of all' – deserved the award.[32] *Time*'s ironic and occasionally pointed critique of Gandhi succeeded in keeping the news story on the front pages with the US press comparing his breaking of the salt tax to the Boston Tea Party. The year 1930 also witnessed an apogee in book output with more than twenty volumes by Americans published in that year alone, including Gertrude Emerson's *Voiceless India*, Will Durant's *The Case for India*, A. Henderson's *Contemporary Immortals* and *Eminent Asians* by Upton Close (a.k.a J. W. Hall). Durant made a spirited case for enlisting American help and referred to Gandhi as 'in all probability the most important, and beyond all doubt the most interesting figure in the world today'.[33]

Gandhi deliberately courted US opinion. Before embarking on the march, and again upon breaking the salt laws, he was in touch with T. H. K. Rezmie, Director of the Indian Independence League in New York, directing him to publicise the protest. Thus the *New York Times* came to publish Gandhi's appeal under the caption: 'Gandhi Asks Backing here: Urges Expression of Public Opinion for India's Right to Freedom.'

I know I have countless friends in America who deeply sympathize with this struggle to secure liberty. But mere sympathy will avail me nothing. What is wanted is the concrete expression of public opinion in favour of India's inherent right to independence and complete approval of the absolutely non-violent means adopted by the Indian National Congress.[34]

The Rev. C. F. Andrews, Gandhi's close associate, was also in the US during 1930 and writing in the *New York Times* on Gandhi's motivations in launching civil disobedience, providing a short history of his experiments with non-violent resistance and offering a critique of imperial economic policies. His article appeared to have hit home, since a month later the same paper published a rejoinder from government officials refuting the Mahatma's version of developments.[35] Thereafter, other newspapers and specialist reviews, such as the *Wall Street Journal*, *Chicago Daily Tribune*, *Chicago Daily News*, *Washington Post*, *Los Angeles Times*, *San Francisco Chronicle*, *Christian Science Monitor*, *Nation*, *New Republic*, *Atlantic Monthly*, *Yale Review* and *Time*, as well as the Associated Press (AP) and United Press (UP) news agencies, intensified their reporting from India, pooling resources and utilising roving correspondents. However, increasing output devoted to India should not necessarily be equated with rising press support for Indian nationalism. British imperialism had its champions too, for instance, in the *New York Herald*, *Los Angeles Times*, *Los Angeles Examiner*, *Baltimore Sun*, *Washington Star*, *Philadelphia Inquirer* and *Christian Science Monitor*.

Finally, much has been made of the impact of Gandhian ideology and praxis on the black civil rights movement and on Martin Luther King Jr. Actually, this process of transnational influence began decades earlier during the 1920s and 1930s when numerous individuals and delegations, including leaders such as Marcus Garvey and W. E. B. DuBois, undertook long sea voyages to the subcontinent, and the African-American print media extolled Gandhi. There was rising awareness amongst African-American communities of the links between Gandhian experiments with freedom and their own struggles for equality. Sudarshan Kapur has enumerated how such publications as *The Crisis* provided information as well as a platform for debate about comparative struggles.[36] Gandhi warmly welcomed such delegations, many of which had missionary and Christian connections, and communed with his American audience via messages of encouragement and exhortation which were published to wide acclaim in the African-American press as well as in his own newspapers.[37] Other African-American visitors to India in 1935–6 included such prominent educators as Dean Howard Thurman of Howard University and Benjamin Mays, President of Morehouse College, and, after Gandhi's assassination, Mordecai Wyatt Johnson, President of Howard University, whose sermons were credited by King with introducing him to the powerful potential of a black *satyagraha*.

American News Agencies and India

Both the AP and UP, as the leading international news agencies, covered India during these years. However, India was at the heart of Reuters' sphere of influence and yielded high commercial dividends. As analysed in *Reporting the Raj*, whilst claiming independence, Reuters had established a mutually beneficial relationship with the GoI from the nineteenth century and was in regular receipt of preferential access and substantial subsidies. Thus the Viceroy confirmed to the Secretary of State in September 1930: 'for some years we have paid Reuters Rs 9,000 per year for transmission to England of news of Government importance, outside the scope of the ordinary service.'[38] During special occasions like the first RTC, additional sums were also paid out to individuals. For instance, Rs 5,000 was given to U.N. Sen of API to enable his passage to London and facilitate enhanced coverage of the official proceedings. Defending such actions the Home Secretary, W. H. Emerson, argued that the '*very important object of creating in India the right atmosphere* regarding the RTC and of counteracting the malicious propaganda that is likely to be disseminated cannot be satisfactorily carried out, unless Reuters gives an amplified service'.[39] The Raj was further prepared to sanction, if need be, 'a direct subsidy to Reuter for an amplified service' not exceeding Rs 10,000, 'on the understanding that the matter will be kept strictly confidential, at any rate until the Conference is over'.[40] Despite its official allegiance, from the interwar years and due largely to commercial pressures rather than any ideological conversion, Reuters had simultaneously become increasingly sensitive to Indian market conditions as well as nationalist opinion.[41] Its subsidiary, API, provided, according to Milton Israel, 'special opportunities for an extraordinary kind of professional collaboration' between Indian journalists and the Raj.[42]

Reuters had also carved up the wider world, aided by Britain's imperial hegemony, into sectors of monopoly utilising a news share scheme with its rival European, American and Far Eastern counterparts, a system which worked much to its advantage. Thus, by 1900, the AP had secured through membership of this 'ring combination' exclusive rights to distribute news from Reuters, Havas and Wolff throughout North America and undertook *vice versa* to supply US news to their agents in New York. AP was to remain the junior partner in this relationship, having to pay several thousand pounds annually in differential, though by the outbreak of the First World War it had managed to enlarge its exclusive influence to encompass Central America, Cuba and the Philippines.[43] Following the war and in large part due to the skilful machinations of its General Manager, Kent Cooper, this situation was reversed to the detriment of Reuters' influence.[44] Cooper was keen to break free of the 'overlordship of Reuters' and its financial burden, an inequality which he contended was 'not only antiquated but is wholly inconsistent with the progressive thought of today'.[45] He railed against the 'restraining and forbidding hand of an ally who maintains position of arbiter, controller and fee collector of the activities, hopes and aspirations of news agencies in countries other than his own'.[46]

Beginning with Japan and the Far East in the 1920s, Cooper successfully managed to renegotiate news share deals and ultimately to become independent of Reuters, dealing directly with Britain's Press Association to supply provincial papers with US news. By the early 1930s, AP was also commercially profitable enough to dictate terms and 'feeling less and less obliged to humour Reuters. It was now strong enough to stand alone anywhere in the world.'[47] The Reuters–AP agreement finally ceased in 1933. The other major US agency, UP, had been excluded from formal partnership within these multinational arrangements, though Roderick Jones, Chairman of Reuters, did attempt, albeit unsuccessfully, to pressurise AP by dangling its rivals as a counterpoise. It would therefore appear that Cooper's assertion that, prior to the Great War, 'news went to the world east, west, south and north from London', but in the interwar years New York became 'a distributor of news to the world', had considerable merit.[48] By 1945 the services of AP reached 2,604 newspapers and radio stations worldwide, more than doubling the figure for 1920.[49] And thus it came to pass that in 1930 from amongst these rival news agencies there emerged two outstanding foreign correspondents who were to exert a profound impact in the annals of Indo-American media interactions – James Aloysius Mills of AP and Webb Miller representing UP.

J. A. Mills and the Associated Press

Kent Cooper had global ambitions for AP which included further exploration of the Asian market, and Mills, its veteran correspondent, was sent to report from India, reaching Bombay in November 1930. Of Irish descent, Mills joined AP in 1905, was widely travelled in Europe and Russia, had made a *forte* of covering Romania and royalty, and is considered to have inspired Evelyn Waugh's *Scoop*, being loosely based on his reporting from Ethiopia in the 1930s.[50] Mills had the foresight to contact Sir Arthur Willert at the FO with whom he had prior acquaintance, to secure the diplomatic foundations for his imperial travels, explaining how he was 'on my way round the world ... on a sort of roving assignment'. He reassured Willert, 'As you know, my personal views towards the British Empire and British interests have always been very friendly and sympathetic', and requested in turn 'a quiet word along to the proper British officials in Palestine, Egypt and India...that I will be eager to present the situation...in the fairest and most impartial manner...and that any help on their part in furnishing me with information or guidance will be appreciated.' Further emphasising his loyalist credentials, Mills proclaimed:

> No newspaperman could have spent a dozen years in Europe and Asia, as I have, and not realize the tremendous civilizing, pacifying and stabilizing force exerted by the British Empire. That thought will guide me in all my despatches. It will be of great service to me if your own people in the countries I have mentioned will help me put before the American public the true situation in those places from a British standpoint.[51]

Mills' letter appeared to have had the desired effect, with the FO urging the Home Department to respond proactively:

> It seems to us here, in view of recent experiences of American press correspondents, and of the general attitude in the States towards the Indian problem as indicated in the Press, that it might be well worth while to take some trouble to see that Mr. Mills is well handled, and we thought the GoI might be inclined to take some steps towards this end which a mere letter of introduction to your Publicity Officer would not be likely to produce.[52]

In a revealing admission, the FO News Department acknowledged that whilst it did not routinely supply personal letters of introduction, it was going to make an exception in this case and was requesting HMG representatives in Constantinople, Cairo and Addis Ababa 'to give Mr. Mills all the assistance they properly can'.[53] Emerson reacted to the urgency of the situation, affirming how he was 'only too glad to meet American press correspondents and to do what I can to put them on the right lines'.[54] (American journalists and prominent professionals, especially those with pro-Raj sympathies, were routinely in receipt of official assistance – for instance, Alexander Inglis representing the *Christian Science Monitor* during November 1930.)[55] In Bombay administrators were instructed to help Mills upon arrival, and Emerson wrote warmly, emphasising how he was 'particularly anxious to have a talk with you'.[56] In early 1931, meetings were arranged with the Viceroy and his Private Secretary, G. Cunningham who also requested the DPI to prepare special memos for Mills' personal use on topics such as education and fiscal policy.

However, in the event, the Raj might well have had reason to feel aggrieved since Mills, though scrupulous about factual evidence and following leads conscientiously, came, nevertheless, to strike up a special rapport with Gandhi. Sailing with him to London for the second RTC, Mills persuaded Gandhi to sit for the famous American sculptor Jo Davidson, who acknowledged how AP was 'responsible for my making this bust of Gandhi', with its photographer duly capturing the event for posterity. Davidson found the process especially trying as Gandhi 'continued to ignore' him during the entire process: 'I received absolutely no help from my sitter.'[57] Covering Gandhi's travels in England and being in close and constant contact with Indians on board ship facilitated the development of mutual regard and a close working relationship between Mills and the nationalists. Returning to India with the RTC contingent in December 1931, Mills was to remain till the following summer, reporting on the relaunch of the Civil Disobedience campaign and being present at the times of Gandhi's arrest and release from jail. Such devotion formed the basis for the story, possibly apocryphal, that on one such occasion Gandhi, sighting Mills in the misty dawn on a deserted railway platform, remarked that the first person to greet him at the Pearly Gates would most certainly be an intrepid AP reporter.[58]

One of the unique results of the shared long sea passage from Bombay to Marseilles was that Mills was able to shoot 'thousands of feet of film' of Gandhi, as well as many stills for reproduction in US newspapers and magazines. Writing about this astonishing feat, Mills acknowledged that he filmed Gandhi 'without his permission' and was fully aware of the latter's hatred of everything mechanical. Gandhi was 'pained and displeased', and frequently complained of his 'torturer'. 'Never did he willingly lend himself to pictures. Yet never did he forbid me to photograph him. Always he maintained a curiously detached, impersonal, negative attitude towards my efforts to capture his features for the screen and for history.' Invariably Gandhi kept his eyes downcast but whilst on the steamer 'he actually looked squarely into the Cooke lenses of my cameras.' By the end of the voyage, Mills claimed that 'he was calling me by my first name', and showed great interest in the cameras, being 'amazed' by their mechanical craftsmanship.[59] Mills was also to interview him for what became, arguably, Gandhi's first 'talkie'. Filmed in Borsad for Fox Movietone, it shows the Mahatma answering a series of pointed questions, whilst never making eye contact with either Mills or the lens of the camera.

Edwin Emery claims that in the early 1920s, the AP was 'still frowning upon human interest stories, and was so intent upon its strict rules of accuracy and objectivity that it served its members with only strait-laced and factual accounts'.[60] Mills clearly broke this mould with his Indian assignment when his lengthy by-lined features were syndicated in newspapers across the length and breadth of the US, capturing the unfolding drama and its chief protagonist from distant shores. Featuring the story on its front page, the *Sandusky Register* in Ohio, for instance, headlined Mills' assessment of the Gandhi–Irwin pact: 'Peace Returns to India After Year of Revolt', whereby Gandhi agreed, on behalf of the INC, to call off the Civil Disobedience movement in March 1931. Mills contended that the movement had 'defied all the authority of the British Raj, filled the jails of the country and was responsible for millions of dollars of economic loss'.[61] His descriptive prose was allowed full vent when reporting Gandhi's departure late at night after protracted negotiations with the Viceroy:

> Rain was pouring down in torrents upon the vice regal building and a fierce gale was howling through New Delhi's deserted streets. Prowling hyenas and hungry dogs whined through the cold, wet night. Suddenly the puny and whiteclad figure of Gandhi emerged from the huge stone gate... The Associated Press correspondent, the only newspaperman on the spot, asked: 'Will you sign an armistice today?' 'Better ask the Viceroy', replied the Nationalist leader with his habitual diplomacy... With that the crooked-legged little man who brought the British empire to terms started on a six-mile walk over darkened watersoaked roads to old Delhi... In the pelting rain he held a huge black umbrella over his bare head, resembling a lilliputian under a canopy.[62]

The next month, the *Alton Evening Telegraph* in Illinois printed Mills' report on how Gandhi's decision to attend the RTC as the sole INC representative had 'irked' sections of his party and 'added fuel to the flame of his critics who have complained increasingly recently that he was assuming the role of a dictator of the Nationalist movement'.[63] A series of five articles that Mills completed over the summer of 1931 prior to Gandhi's arrival in London provides further revealing insights into his assessment of the man and his mission. In 'The Puzzle of a Pacifist Rebel', Mills elucidated the policy of non-violent resistance and contended that Gandhi was 'no communist. He believes in thrift, reward for personal effort, the life of the individual and the family, the production of goods by cottage industry.... His test is not what a man has, but what he does with it, and a rich man may pass through the needle's eye into the fold of the Gandhi movement if only he devotes himself and his goods to the service of mankind as a whole.'[64]

In another piece printed in the *Aberdeen Evening News*, entitled 'The Lisping Voice That Stirs a Nation', Mills attempted to explain how Gandhi was leader of 'one of the greatest political campaigns in world history', yet possessed 'next to none of the qualities usually associated with popular leadership'.[65] Physically, he could appear strange and forbidding, rarely making eye contact. As an orator he 'would be termed a "washout" by any American audience. His lisp comes through a feeble, falsetto voice. He seldom uses a gesture and has no vigor of declamation.'[66] Instead it was the content of his speech that moved Indian audiences. Mills described the austerity of Gandhi's life, without an office or secretarial retinue, and the 'complete informality' of his surroundings: 'The highest nabob or the poorest beggar may enter his presence at any hour'.[67]

The *Evening Tribune* of San Diego featured Mills' report from Marseilles where in September 1931 Gandhi set foot on European soil for the first time in 15 years, describing how hundreds of reporters 'surged around Gandhi's frail body until he became fearful and pleaded for air, telling them he would meet them in groups of five'. Accompanied by his youngest son Devadas, also a journalist, Gandhi duly answered their questions, 'always smiling and genial even when the queries appeared foolish to him', according to Mills.[68] At the conclusion of the RTC, Mills suggested that Gandhi saw a renewed period of conflict, a story that made the front pages of the *Canton Repository* (Ohio) under the heading 'Gandhi Ready To Face Hell For Freedom'. Accompanying Gandhi on his regular early morning walk through the chilly fog of east London, Mills quoted him as saying: 'There is going to be hell.... we shall take up again our weaponless battle against England.... I came here expecting nothing and I leave with nothing.' Gandhi concluded 'mournfully': 'We must again go through a Calvary of suffering... It seems God's will that we must take up our heavy cross again and carry it to the end.'[69] Gandhi's use of overtly Christian symbolism to describe India's struggle can arguably be characterised as a calculated piece of political rhetoric designed to strike a chord with a western readership. Continuing with this theme, Mills' report as run on the front page of the *Ironwood Daily Globe* (Michigan) claimed: 'Gandhi is Sad as he Sails from England.'[70] In a note for AP scribbled as he left the port of Brindisi aboard SS *Pilsna*, Gandhi wrote: 'I cannot help expressing my sorrow that my stay has been all too brief.' His disappointment with the RTC was somewhat offset, contended Mills, by his two days in Italy where 'Everyone from Premier Mussolini down manifested the utmost cordiality and the fuss pleased him immensely.'[71]

In January 1932, Mills wrote another series of in-depth sketches on Gandhi which once again received wide exposure in US newspapers as from the pen of one who had 'closely followed the activities of this extraordinary son of the east', in the words of the editor of the *Cleveland Plain Dealer*.[72] Mills began the first article on an autobiographical note:

> Just a year ago I climbed over the picket fence surrounding the railway station at Chinchwood, on the Bombay line, and walked down the platform toward a tiny fragment of humanity, shivering in the chill pitch-blue Indian dawn beside a pile of pots and pans, spinning wheels, milk bottles and books.
>
> 'Good Evening, Mr Gandhi, I am from the Associated Press of America', I said.
>
> 'How delightful that the first person to greet me should be an American,' he replied.
>
> Then he gave the first interview of a year which probably was the most important of his career and which marked an epoch in India's history. Only an hour before had he been secretly released from Poona Prison, before whose gates I had been losing sleep for days. In the year that followed I lost much more while I followed him in India, to the conference in London, and back to India again. But in that year I have come to the conclusion of all those, who, like myself, have studied his amazing personality for any length of time that he is one of the most remarkable figures of his age.[73]

Claiming Gandhi's character was 'so bafflingly complex' as to defy complete understanding, he described him as a 'Shrewd lawyer, politician, agitator, reformer' as well as a 'mystic, religious revivalist and dreamer'.[74] Mills alluded to Gandhi's almost 'hypnotic' influence and discussed the 'charlatan *vs* God' debate in emphasising how Gandhi's character was full of 'contradictions' and 'inconsistencies'. He was at once 'artless as a child' yet 'as artful as a wizard'; 'utterly selfless, yet [he] seems to revel in the limelight of fame'. The following morning the second in the series of articles on 'The man Gandhi', was featured on the front page of the *Burlington Hawk-Eye* in Iowa. Mills informed his audience that the 'rebel extraordinaire and mystic unique' was back in prison at the age of 62: 'my last contact with him was a hearty slap on the back as the officers took him away'.[75] This essay described Gandhi's relationship with his disciples, who called him 'Bapu' (Father) and lived in a community in almost 'primitive' fashion. He was fastidious about his diet, wrote letters in long hand, and was 'worshipped' and 'adored' by women who 'prostrate themselves before him. They ask for his blessing. They name their children after him.'[76] Whilst a third article in the *Cleveland Plain Dealer* discussed the Mahatma's disinterest in monetary wealth. Several American movie corporations, radio companies and newspaper publishers had tried to 'attract Gandhi with liberal offers of money' but had been 'turned down cold'.[77] The final piece was introduced by the editor of the *Burlington Hawk-Eye* as from the pen of one who 'knows [Gandhi's] character more intimately than any other newspaper man'.[78] Mills concluded that Gandhi's repeated imprisonments had 'given him the aura of a national hero and martyr'. He was quoted as saying: 'Prison life has no horrors for a man who puts his faith in God and justice.' Though he admitted that the Raj continued to hold 'the upper hand', still the key constituents of Gandhian *satyagraha* were particularly well suited to Indian conditions and the British were 'puzzled what to do with this restless little insurgent. They have confined him to jail, yet his influence is just as strong.' Emphasising once again Gandhi's spiritual leanings, including his 'great debt' to the Sermon on the Mount and to the Quakers, Mills concluded by reiterating his commitment to self-help as symbolised by the spinning wheel: 'It shall constitute the woof and warp of our liberty. I am sure of that liberty as I am of eternity.'[79]

Overall, AP features under Mills' by-line reveal extraordinary and intimate personal insights, impacting on the front pages of newspapers across the US. Mills' expertise on Gandhi was acknowledged and his in-depth assessments, given their wide exposure, helped impact on the general tone of the American media. Much like Reuters *vis-à-vis* the British and empire press, it can be contended that AP (but without its competitor's subsidies) exerted a seminal agenda-setting role for the US media, especially with respect to Gandhian nationalism. Gandhi, for his part, sedulously cultivated public opinion, as will be discussed later, and in his encounters with Mills unfailingly 'ask[ed] about America'.[80] Even after Mills left India he continued to evince a keen interest in that country's fortunes, as Gandhi was to acknowledge at the time of his death in 1942.

Webb Miller and the United Press

Webb Miller was amongst the crop of dashing UP war correspondents who had come to prominence whilst covering the Great War. The UP shunned anonymity and its 'vividly written and interpretative copy attracted attention'.[81] UP had established a subsidiary in the UK (British United Press) which had penetrated the Indian market by 1926. By 1933, UP had established correspondents in Bombay, Karachi, Calcutta, Madras, Rangoon and Ceylon. As a writer in *Fortune* magazine argued,

> it is in the foreign service that UP's professional pride is most brightly reflected. Webb Miller races from his London office to Croydon airdrome, catches a Karachi-bound airliner of Imperial Airways, dashes down the coast to Bombay to direct coverage of Gandhi's salt riots... Measured by the dollar-and-cents value of their yield in cold facts which the provincial, uncritical US public would not have missed, many of these exciting missions may not be worth the money and trouble... [but]... they are the breath of life... [and] help to enhance UP prestige.[82]

The above quotation alludes to the story which was to catapult Miller, by then European News Manager, to international fame and earn UP a global scoop in 1930. It revolved round Miller's explosive testimony of police reaction to unarmed protestors at the Dharasana saltworks – 'the sickening whack of the clubs on unprotected skulls' – a saga which made headlines in the US and throughout the world via syndication in the 1,350 newspapers served by UP.[83] The British Library of Information (BLI) in New York, which was the primary agency enjoined with official publicity in the US and administered by the FO, admitted that 'such despatches as Mr. Miller's could hardly fail to give an undesirable impression of British administration and as might be expected this was exploited to the full by the professional Indian agitators in the United States'.[84]

Having witnessed two riots at the Wadala saltpans near Bombay during May, Miller got information about the biggest peaceful demonstration planned by the INC, which was to boycott the saltpans at Dharasana, 150 miles north of the city. The arduous physical journey, due to its relative remoteness and absence of transport links, was made worse by official attempts to prevent his arrival, including forcibly offloading him from the train before Dungri, which was a considerable distance away.[85] Eventually Miller arrived after trekking the final miles on foot to find himself the only foreign correspondent on the scene. His eyewitness accounts detail the lead-up to the demonstrations, the discipline and organisation of the rank-and-file volunteers, and the stirring exhortations of the leaders, including Sarojini Naidu and Manilal Gandhi, the second son of the Mahatma. The protests involved row upon row of people attempting to walk up to the salt-pans, which were protected by ditches, barbed wire and 400 armed Surat police. 'Though everyone knew that within a few minutes he would be beaten down, perhaps killed, I could detect no signs of wavering or fear ... There was no fight, no struggle; the marchers simply walked forward until struck down.'[86] At times the exercise appeared futile to Miller, who confessed that 'the spectacle of unresisting men being methodically bashed into pulp sickened me so much that I had to turn away'.[87] In another despatch he confessed: 'In eighteen years of reporting in twenty two countries, I have never witnessed such harrowing scenes as at Dharasana.'[88]

What made the story so riveting was not just the dramatic nature of Miller's narrative but the attempts made by the GoI to suppress his telegraphed despatches and deny allegations of a cover-up, details of which took centre stage in subsequent mailed reports which made this UP story doubly damaging for a publicity-conscious Raj. Working on the assumption that up-country telegrams would receive less prominence than ones sent from Bombay, Miller managed to get three out of five reports filed to London from nearby Bulsar immediately after the event. As he had feared, none of his subsequent and longer despatches telegraphed from Bombay made it through, though the GoI denied censorship. Miller threatened to fly to Persia to telegraph his reports. Such persistence paid off, with his stories eventually being transmitted but only after the excision of some passages relating to the police.[89] Miller had the last laugh when he discovered that there was limited censorship of airmail letters. His exploitation of this loophole meant vastly greater costs for the UP as it involved sending lengthy full-rate or deferred-rate messages to the private address of the UP manager in London, messages which were not routinely examined by censors in the belief that as speed was of the essence to a newspaper, all significant news would be sent by telegraph to a newspaper office utilising the press rate which was only one-sixth as expensive.[90] Miller did not experience similarly overt interference during his subsequent tour of Calcutta, Delhi and Simla – where his notoriety notwithstanding, he even managed to interview the Viceroy – the Raj having clearly learnt a valuable lesson about the deleterious consequences of bad publicity.

Despite attempts at professional neutrality, Miller's despatches revealed an underlying condemnation of official policy at Dharasana and by implication of the British claim to be a civilised, democratic nation, which provoked an outcry in political circles. Whilst admitting that he had gone to India 'idealistic to the Congress or Gandhi cause', once in the country he often 'argued with Indians against their cause'.

Miller was assiduous about the factual accuracy of his reports, though his critics often accused him of pandering to sensationalism. However, the validity of his journalism cannot be decried on account of partisanship. Indeed, the opposite might well be argued, since Miller though sympathetic to Indian demands for greater self-government, remained to be convinced that the myriad problems he witnessed within the country could be solved without British rule. 'I could not hold with Indians who wanted complete independence.'[91]

The BLI had to admit, unpalatable as the US press reports were: 'if we judge the American Press by its own standards it cannot be too strongly emphasized that as a whole it has treated British Indian policy fairly in its news columns and during [1929–30] with an unusual degree of understanding in its editorial columns'.[92] Given the paradigm of freedom of speech and expression that bound the British and US media as part of a common liberal democratic tradition, the GoI could ill afford to resort to the more draconian repression that it repeatedly enforced upon Indians. On the contrary, officials were alert to the increasing necessity of securing 'a good press' in the West. Though the Raj attempted to censor foreign wires and newspaper reports, it was helpless beyond a point to completely suppress them. Ironically, such attempts could backfire in spectacular fashion as the case of Miller exemplified, with US news agencies helping to disseminate views through wider networks often beyond the purview of Reuters. It was the presence of the American media – unfettered, interested and aware – that ensured that the story of Gandhian nationalism gained a transnational status which, in turn, contributed to make the Civil Disobedience Movement the most formidable challenge yet faced by the Raj.

Chicago Daily Tribune, McCormick and Overseas Coverage

The *Tribune* enjoyed unrivalled commercial success after the Great War and, despite the economic crisis following the Wall Street Crash, by the early 1930s it boasted a daily circulation in excess of 830,000, with over one million for its Sunday edition, making the latter the US market leader. By 1946 its daily circulation had increased to 1,075,000, the largest of any standard-sized newspaper.[93] Its largely affluent, middle-class, conservative readership was concentrated in the so-called 'Chicago-land', strongest in the metropolitan area, but also in the surrounding five-state region of Illinois, Wisconsin, Indiana, Michigan and Iowa. Yet its political influence was felt across the country and within the corridors of power in Washington, though in many respects its position was out of sync with US foreign policy in the interwar years. Dominating the paper was its Manager-Editor, Robert R. McCormick, or the 'Colonel' as he liked to be called. McCormick began as Manager in 1914 in collaboration with his cousin, Joseph Patterson. (His family's Medill Trust owned the majority shares and controlled the publishing company.) By 1919 he had assumed sole command and exercised great discretion regarding newspaper policy notwithstanding the presence of a managing editor, Edward Scott Beck, *in situ* from 1910 to 1937. The Colonel's international experience was limited to a short wartime stint in France, a tour of Russia in 1915, and annual trips to oversee the Paris edition of the *Tribune*, established in 1917. From the late nineteenth century with the Spanish-American War, foreign, especially war, reporting, was taken increasingly seriously by the *Tribune*'s owners. For McCormick this fulfilled a key aspect of his conceptualisation of the paper's status and is revealed by the *Tribune*'s coverage of the First World War where it was 'at the head of the pack' of US papers.[94] The growing reputation of its main rival, the *Chicago Daily News*, further spurred McCormick's efforts.

Chicago itself was an interesting mix of provincial and international, and provided an ideal setting to nurture foreign coverage in its press. With the second largest population in the US, by 1900, four out of five Chicagoans were foreign or foreign born, including one in five journalists.[95] J. Edwards has argued that the paper's values reflected 'the individualistic values of small town, free enterprise America'.[96] However, McCormick envisioned his paper in much more ambitious and global terms than is suggested by such an assertion. The *Tribune* masthead proclaimed it to be the 'world's greatest newspaper' – and continued proclaiming it as such until 1977 – with its Paris edition labelled as 'Europe's American Newspaper'. By assiduously building up a large and reputable cadre of reporters, the *Tribune* was one of only seven US papers which maintained a dedicated foreign service. This comprised around thirty correspondents, many of them space-rate stringers, scattered over twenty-two offices worldwide, supplemented by news agency copy. In 1930 it was estimated that McCormick was expending $1,000 a day on the *Tribune*'s foreign service.[97] As Shirer noted, the cost of dispatching a story via telegraph from Kabul to Chicago came to a dollar a word.[98] An illustrated full-page advertisement in October 1930 proclaimed the values of its foreign service based on a scoop from Shirer, who was the first western reporter to cover the enthronement of Nadir Khan as King of Afghanistan: 'Only by spreading its own writers over the world can the Tribune make certain of information uncoloured by propaganda or external prejudice. Far-flung, experienced, its staff ensures reliable news from foreign countries.'[99]

At the heart of the *Tribune*'s foreign policy lay 'a spirited chauvinism'.[100] McCormick 'disliked' the major European powers because 'he believed their leadership and social structure were entirely corrupt'. Britain exemplified for him all that was wrong with Europe, 'based on a belief that foreigners, especially the English, were dangerous'.[101] In his opinion, Britain's class system and hereditary monarchy made her socially an oligarchy and, despite wealth accrued from her colonies, she nevertheless owed the US a considerable war debt and made matters worse, in McCormick's eyes, by adopting an air of moral superiority over Americans. Though acknowledging the benefits of imperial rule and by implication British domination, nevertheless the *Tribune* was critical of specific policies and supported Indian demands for future self-government. In practice, therefore, the paper was widely regarded as anti-British since they were 'always the subject of constant sniping' and the *Tribune* 'certainly relished twisting the lion's tail'.[102]

McCormick and India

According to R. N. Smith, Shirer's posting to India allowed him 'to stoke his employer's anglo-phobia at regular intervals'.[103] Based on the evidence of this study, this is rather overstating the case. McCormick was also intrigued by India *per se* and before Shirer's sojourn, the *Tribune* had William Daley stationed there and it was he who covered Gandhi's iconic Salt March. Shirer himself was replaced in January 1932 by Egbert Swenson, whose short tenure was followed in the summer by the visit of Philip Kinsley. The IO Information Officer, Hugh MacGregor, claimed that Kinsley was a 'special confidential representative' whose visit was intended 'not so much for the purpose of writing, as for the purpose of informing Col. McCormick regarding the real situation.'[104] Thus MacGregor reiterated the 'necessity of our ensuring that he leaves India with the most favourable impressions'.[105]

The Colonel encouraged 'the exclusive interview, the dashing exploit, exposes, scoops, something to make big headlines'.[106] The David and Goliath spectacle of Gandhi versus the imperial juggernaut thus provided the ideal setting for his imagination. Referring to the political epic unfolding in the subcontinent, McCormick reminded Shirer: 'Bear in mind that you are in a post considered here to be the most interesting in the world and are watching a development which is unlike what has gone before.' He was also curious to know just how outrageous are the princes who are being trotted out as the saviours of the British empire, to what extent do they starve their peasants and do they tyrannize over all their subjects? Are their harems enormous and extravagant? Are the Indian princes being modernized with their Oxford education or do they merely extract the cultural pleasures from it and carry on as their forefathers?[107]

The crux of the problem, argued a *Tribune* leader, was as a consequence of 'different mentality'. The Englishman was concerned about Pax Britannica, while the Indian was 'thinking much more of his own self-respect'.[108] Indians, like the Chinese, were 'deeply convinced that their culture, their civilization, their fundamental ideals, their way of life, are superior to that of the occident and that only the fact that the west is ruthless and effective in the use of physical force has made it possible for an inferior civilization to impose its will upon the higher'. Though the benefits of British rule were recognised, yet 'any American who remembers the history of the struggle for independence of the American colonies, and especially anyone who is conscious of the difference of eastern and western mentality and morale, must feel that the demand for complete independence will grow and in all human probability must eventually arrive. The present problem is how to prepare for it.'[109] The allusion to the American War of Independence was a frequently utilised historical trope.

McCormick was not averse to the empire: 'there is no doubt in our own western mind that in spite of the great wealth the British have drawn from India ... it has been more than paid for by the benefits which British order and justice have brought to the masses of the Indian peoples'.[110] Nevertheless, in responding to Gandhian nationalism, the *Tribune* was heavily influenced by Shirer's analyses, which McCormick backed without reserve. Taking the lead from him, the nationalist movement was characterised as a 'revolution' and 'revolutionary', whilst the Indians themselves were 'revolutionists'. (The word 'riot' was used occasionally to refer to specific incidents.) There appeared to be no soul-searching as to the constituents of a revolution and no compunction about its frequent use. The connotations associated with the word 'revolution' were apparent in the context of the US's own historic struggle against the British and implicit in such usage was the idea of legitimacy. Additionally, by the comparatively infrequent use of the term 'civil disobedience' – common currency in the British press – the suggestion that the Indians were not being obedient to established legal codes of conduct was neatly circumvented. The *Tribune* did not hesitate to describe British repression as 'atrocities', and the word 'war' was also repeatedly used to analyse the state of affairs between colonisers and colonised – for example, Shirer's piece entitled 'WAR TO FINISH! GANDHI REJECTS BRITISH TERMS' (6 September 1930), or another entitled 'GANDHI HUSHES HIS "LIBERTY FOR INDIA" WAR CRY' (20 August 1931). The strength of the sentiments conveyed by such terminology set the *Tribune* distinctly apart from its Fleet Street counterparts.

Underlying such commentary was the personification of the revolution in the shape of the Mahatma, a process that was imperative in the context of appealing to a popular readership in the American Midwest largely ignorant of India. This is brought out explicitly in the paper's editorials – for instance, on the occasion of the signing of the Gandhi–Irwin pact. 'Gandhi's revolution is like no other great one in history', McCormick claimed. 'It takes its character from the ethics and religion of the mahatma's faith and from his aesthetic adherence to it.'[111] Another editorial on 3 May 1931 summed up the *Tribune*'s position. While India was 'remote, profound, always human, Gandhi is India's voice.' Gandhi was 'clearly the voice of Asia.... In Gandhi Asia is articulate.' Yet admiration often went hand in hand with a reluctance to accept Gandhi's views on modern mechanised civilisation and his repudiation of western industrialisation: 'With his spinning wheel and his all around farm he tries to lead his people back to a distributive society against the encroachments of industrialism.'[112]

W. L. Shirer and India

Shirer's coverage of India can be divided into two phases. The first is the time he spent in the subcontinent which took place over a couple of visits, initially during the summer and autumn of 1930 (August–November), and then from February to June 1931. During these nine months he travelled the country conducting intensive fieldwork and in-depth interviews. He was a prolific correspondent and worked strenuously to build a personal rapport with politicians, both British and Indian, including Jawaharlal Nehru, Sarojini Naidu, Dr M. A. Ansari, Tej Bahadur Sapru, C. Rajagopalachari, Srinivasa Sastri and M. A. Jinnah, but most especially with Gandhi and his private secretaries, Pyarelal Nayar and Mahadev Desai. He was 'greatly impressed' by Nehru, who was, as he noted in his diary, 'by no means wild extremist people repute him to be ... He's modern enough ... but not wild.'[113] In another diary entry Shirer claimed to 'like him better each time ... He has many sound ideas social reforms, but he would not institute communism, as people <u>accuse</u>

him.'[114] He found Naidu to be a 'very amusing & refreshing woman, extreme & bombastic & loose & enthusiastic on every subject. Not consistent for 2 minutes but I like her. She wants an artistic revolution but realizes political upheaval must come first.'[115]

Shirer's contacts spread beyond politicians to include a variety of prominent intellectuals, such as Rabindranath Tagore, and journalists, for instance, on the *Bombay Chronicle* where S. A. Brelvi was instrumental in opening doors to the local nationalist cadres and helping establish his journalistic feet during 1930.[116] Shirer wrote to Jinnah in September 1930: 'I know you are very very busy just now, but perhaps you could give me a few minutes...I have been talking...with such widely differing persons as Shaukat Ali, Sardar Sulleman Kasum Mitha, Mr Bomanji and Professor Shah, and from them I have got an idea or two which I would like to discuss briefly with you.'[117] Mitha helped arrange Shirer's subsequent trip to Afghanistan from where he wrote describing his 'splendid trip' from Peshawar to Kabul and how the anniversary ceremonies of Nadir Shah's coronation were 'a great success and...a beautiful and interesting pageant'.[118] In a letter to Tagore, Shirer requested a message for his readers who would 'greatly appreciate a word from you', emphasising how the 'interest of my fellow-countrymen in the Indian struggle is intense and, I believe, sympathetic'. Though the recent spotlight had focused on Gandhi, 'they have not forgotten you who first introduced them to the poetry and art of your great country'.[119] Similarly, Shirer ensured coverage of the Raj perspective – for instance, recording a long interview with Emerson: 'He had been keen to see me and evidently was anxious to put over the government side.' In the event, Shirer found Emerson to be candid and intelligent, and enjoyed 'getting a decent presentation of the official side'.[120]

During his stay, Shirer witnessed many official crackdowns on civil resistors and, like Mills, with whom his paths crossed on several occasions, he was able to provide detailed first-person accounts of the progress and impact of the Indian 'revolution', thus introducing a US audience to the complexities of the unfolding crisis. Reporting on 28 August 1930 on the arrest of the INC working council, Shirer contended that 'this wholesale move to wipe out the entire governing body' revealed the unwillingness of the Raj to compromise. The next day he described the retaliatory strike: 'India Stops all work as Britain Jails 9 Leaders': 'Robbing the revolutionary movement of practically its entire leadership cast gloom', since as an activist noted: 'We have no more leaders who can sway the masses, and no more nationally known orators to prod them on.' Shirer compared this action to the outcome in 1775 had Britain imprisoned 30,000 Americans, including leaders such as Adams and Jefferson. Their victory would have been impossible. Such references to America's colonial past helped mediate difficult and distant scenarios to a popular readership. Shirer's copy was often syndicated in Indian newspapers, thereby securing a transnational impact (Figure 3.2).

Shirer finally met Gandhi in Delhi during February 1931 after the latter's release from prison. His diary entry of the interview, reproduced here, evokes the instant rapport between the men: 'After all these years of hero-worshipping ... I thought I might be overwhelmed by the man. Not at all. He put me immediately at my ease.'[121] Accompanying Gandhi, he recorded India's euphoric welcome of him, as the railways cut through a large swathe of the country from Delhi to Ahmedabad, then through Kaira and Surat into Bombay between 8 and 16 March. 'Front paged today with my story of Gandhi's triumphal procession through heart of India', read his subsequent diary entry.[122] Shirer was convinced that 'The old slavish Indian mentality is gone. Gandhi has resurrected a proud defiant people.'[123] His diary over the following weeks and months reveals not just his proximity to Gandhi, but also a mature emotional sensitivity to the ebb and flow of imperial politics. Thus an extract from 16 April reads: 'Talked with Gandhi for three quarters of an hour ... He does not look well. ... I missed his usual exuberance and joyful optimism ... and I gather from his manner and what he said he was not very hopeful of coming to a settlement by negotiation ... He divulged for the first time that he has no intention of participating in any preliminary technical committee meetings before the Round Table Conference begins.'[124]

Over the following months, a large proportion of Shirer's efforts, by his own admission, were directed at understanding Gandhi and his brand of mass non-violent resistance. 'I would like to penetrate deeper the mysterious power this modern saint has over these masses', he noted in March 1931.[125] His resultant despatches were models of effective story-telling combined with hard-hitting incisive journalism, all of which was conveyed in elegant prose and with a picturesque turn of phrase. Shirer achieved a consistently sophisticated level of analysis as well as several journalistic coups which were given top billing in the *Tribune*. These accomplishments reflect the fact that he had successfully penetrated the many worlds of Indian nationalism with close access to major players across the political spectrum, whilst simultaneously establishing trust in his impartial credentials as a journalist. Shirer was in a position to demand urgent responses from Gandhi, cabling him as occasion demanded, confident that Gandhi welcomed the opportunity to present his side of the picture and trusted the Iowan to interpret

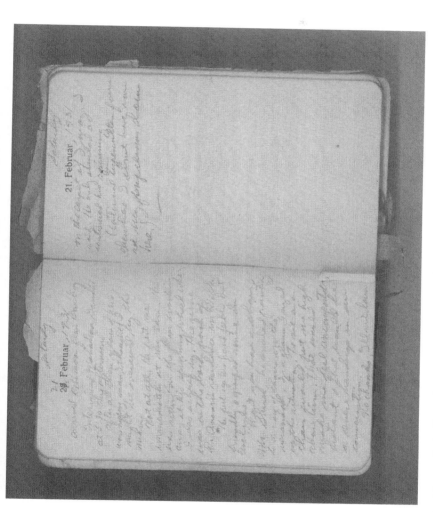

Figure 3.2 Extract from private diary of William L. Shirer, 21 February 1931, reprinted by permission of the Literary Trust of William L. Shirer, George T. Henry College Archives, Coe College, Iowa

his thoughts and ideology faithfully. To cite just one instance in some detail, there is a personal telegram from Gandhi in Bardoli to Shirer in Simla during June 1931, when he broke his long silence and explained the issues surrounding his attendance at the second RTC in London: 'so far as I can see absence communal solution blocks my participation round table conference stop delicate situation Gandhi Irwin settlement makes my immediate leaving India difficult apart from these difficulties I am anxious attend round table conference and take full share deliberations and press congress demand . . .'.[126] This telegram was reproduced in full in the *Tribune* along with an accompanying article, which appeared the next day claiming a scoop: 'Gandhi decides on Peace as Weapon to Free India'. (This story and telegram were also reprinted in several Indian newspapers.) 'He is ready to negotiate for a permanent peace', Shirer informed his readers, and then set out the conditions that Gandhi insisted on for the progress of negotiations.[127] In one stroke, Shirer was able to establish his credentials as a journalist with privileged information and provide a transnational platform for Gandhi's message, thus serving the needs of nationalists, as well as functioning as a conduit of information and dialogue between the nationalists and the Raj. On his departure from India he expressed his gratitude to Gandhi: 'often I must have tried your patience in my hungry quest for news. That you always received me (and my fellow journalists) with kindness, consideration and sympathy is to me only one proof of your greatness. I certainly shall treasure it for a long time to come.'[128] As it transpired, that was not to be the end of their association since Gandhi's decision to attend the RTC enabled Shirer to travel from Vienna to Marseilles and then to London to spend September–October working alongside John Steele, the *Tribune*'s chief correspondent in England.

With Gandhi in England

Shirer's coverage of Gandhi in England was a masterful piece of investigative journalism that received high praise from McCormick. It began auspiciously with Shirer achieving a major scoop in filing a story from aboard the boat train transporting Gandhi from Marseilles to Folkestone, given that Shirer's passage was only secured as a special favour orchestrated by Professor Shah and the entourage of the Nawab of Bhopal. The British had decreed that no 'outsiders' were to be allowed on the train, a thinly veiled attempt to hamper publicity for the nationalists. 'Twenty-five leading American and English correspondents were moving heaven and earth for places on the train', claimed Shirer. At the eleventh hour his friends 'wangled' him a berth utilising the

Nawab's quota of reservations. 'I had been told I was to be Maulana Ali Khan, secretary to His Highness. So I was...when conductors and company officers indignantly demanded what I was doing on the train.'[129] 'Gandhi was good copy', he noted subsequently. 'Chicago and Paris editions front paged it. Gandhi's uncompromising demand for "complete independence" and his blunt refusal to even consider dominion status, which he gave to me exclusively, made a good story.'[130]

The battle for hearts and minds from the perspective of the Raj forms a seminal subtext to the twentieth century. It is thus imperative to understand the convening of the RTCs as primarily an exercise in propaganda by an imperium desperate to seize back the initiative from the INC and help influence the terms of the political debate over the future of India. The conferences represented an attempt to broker a very English deal around the time-honoured table, consulting with Indian representatives carefully chosen on a predetermined political basis, with significant weighting given to minorities and Indian princes, as counterpoise to the INC.

For the INC, too, as Ranajit Guha has aptly noted, the importance of persuasion in the nationalist project under Gandhi was 'an attempt to invest the energies of mass political movements in its bid for hegemonic dominance'.[131] Gandhi had refused to attend the first RTC, but he was persuaded to represent the INC at the second, by Irwin's acceptance of three key principles: that all future development would follow a federal basis, certain safeguards regarding defence and finance would be retained in Government hands, and increased responsibility would be given to Indians in constitutional terms. During these negotiations, Irwin had been criticised by sections of Fleet Street, much to the consternation of even so conservative an observer as George V. The King, who had continued to take an interest in the subcontinent since his Coronation Durbar, 'deprecates as much as you do the attitude of the Conservatives, egged on by die-hards from India, are adopting', noted his private secretary, Sir Clive Wigram, to the Viceroy.[132] However, the subsequent meeting of the King and Gandhi at Buckingham Palace achieved a level of notoriety, with varied versions of the event surfacing in the public domain and in private correspondence. According to Wigram's interpretation, the King was 'very nice' to Gandhi 'but ended up by impressing on him that this country would not stand a campaign of terrorism...His Majesty warned Gandhi that he was to put a stop to this...Gandhi spluttered some excuse, but H. M. said he held him responsible.'[133] The Secretary of State, Sir Samuel Hoare, who advised both the King and Gandhi to maintain a cordiality that the occasion demanded, was, however, of the opinion that Gandhi came out of the encounter rather well. As he recounted to the Viceroy, 'the conversation did not go too badly. Towards the end of it the King told him that civil disobedience was a hopeless and a stupid policy ... Gandhi quite politely replied that he must on no account be drawn into an argument with His Majesty.'[134] Kingsley Martin writing as 'Critic' in the London Diary for the *New Statesman and Nation* (hereafter *New Statesman*) contended that Gandhi would emerge as 'the man who saved the Conference.'[135] The King of Sarila, representing the 250 smaller Princely states at the RTC, observed how it was Gandhi who received the 'loudest cheer' from the crowds lined outside the conference venue and was 'surprised that the British should applaud loudest the person who wanted to snatch from them their most precious jewel'.[136]

Shirer also accompanied Gandhi on his three-day tour of the industrial north of England, where he reportedly enjoyed even greater public acclaim. 'GANDHI INSPECTS HAVOC WROUGHT BY HIS BOYCOTT', was the title of one story on 25 September, referencing the economic consequences of the closure of cotton mills in Lancashire. Gandhi's visit to the weaving mills of Darwen to meet the millworkers and the mayor received prominent coverage: 'GANDHI LIONIZED BY THOUSANDS HE PUT OUT OF WORK' ran the headline of another feature: 'Lean, gaunt, haggard looking men and women stood silently in line awaiting the payment of the dole ... But when they saw the "holy man" from far off India they cheered. "Good old Gandhi. He's all right." '[137] Shirer was convinced that the fundamental economic and class divisions between the north and south-east of England explained the differing nature of the receptions accorded to Gandhi.

> To sophisticated London Gandhi has been more the freak, the butt of jokes in the newspapers, the cause of laughter at the news-reel movies – in short a funny little man who wears a loin cloth and spins and pretends to put demands to the great British Empire. The industrial north, simple and hard-working and not caring much about politics, received him differently ... Lancashire liked him. Cotton magnates and workers sat at his feet and listened to him as he spun and talked. They argued. They questioned. They explained.[138]

Select Themes in Shirer's Coverage

In terms of sheer quantity and depth of coverage, Shirer's reports ranged impressively over a number of issues. Underlying most coverage was a preoccupation with the nationalist movement, and Shirer was 'impressed by the widespread campaign with its efficient organization in a land of many races, languages and quarrelling creeds.'[139] In general his descriptive and evocative prose reflected the need to bring to life a world far removed from the experiences of his American readers. At one level this meant that the more unusual aspects of Gandhi's actions and character were emphasised, with Shirer's reports being supported by Steele's coverage. For instance, before Gandhi set foot on European soil, interest had been built up with regular accounts of his long sea voyage that highlighted details guaranteed to intrigue western readers, building up expectation exponentially as with the serialisation of a good novel. There was the story, for example, of how Gandhi 'scorn[ed] luxuries' and chose to sleep on a wooden bench on the ship's deck and befriended the ship's cat: 'a big black fellow, to whom he feeds goat's milk and with which he shares his bench nightly'.[140] There were other 'strange things for the uninitiated', such as 'the half ton of mud brought from the sacred Ganges' by M. M. Malaviya, a distinguished Congressman. Malaviya, it was claimed 'converts the mud into miniature gods for purposes of worship'. At dusk each evening, Gandhi summoned his 'small flock of followers to prayer ... all squat Buddha like on the deck, hands clasped, heads bowed, eyes closed, in meditation'.[141] On another occasion, *Tribune* readers were informed about the compliment paid to India's 'holy man' by the ship's Captain, who organised a special Christian service when Gandhi's favourite hymn, 'Lead Kindly Light', was sung.[142] Thus the spiritual and the idiosyncratic were combined to reinforce what the average American reader might associate with the East. At a more substantive level, however, many seminal themes were also raised and discussed.

Clothes and the Man

References in the *Tribune* to Gandhi's physical appearance and dress were similar in style to Mill's reports for AP. For instance, in one lengthy feature, Shirer's story was headlined: 'Gandhi explains why he gave up wearing clothes, He seeks to Emphasize Poverty of His People.'[143] His sojourn in England provided further vivid images of the disjuncture between western expectations and Gandhian realities. Gandhi chose to stay in the poor East End of London, and to wear a loin cloth with a shawl and sandals on his bare feet, despite the autumnal cold. Thus a headline on 13 September read: 'London's Slums titter at weird dress of Gandhi.' 'Somehow I feel at home here,' the paper quoted the 'emaciated little holy man ... as he made his way through a crowd of towering Cockney dockworkers'. A front-page headline on 31 October noted how

Gandhi was to go to 'the King's Party in Loin Cloth', which was followed up with the details of the event. 'Gandhi sips Boiled Goat's Milk at Tea given by King' ran another headline, and readers were reminded of his attire: 'The Mahatma's shawl was gossamer, and it had been freshly washed by Miss Madeline Slade, his British born disciple, but his ensemble contrasted strangely with the dazzling silken robes' of the Indian princes and the formality of the monarch's dress.[144] At one level, by focusing on such stories, the *Tribune* was, like other American and popular British papers, concentrating on the less challenging option – the idiosyncratic man – rather than tussling with the complexities of his mission. Gandhi's colourful personality and striking appearance made for easy press and newsreel copy wherein he was mocked for his sartorial inappropriateness.

However, as the analyses accompanying such stories in the *Tribune* indicate, there was, simultaneously, an appreciation of how Gandhi's choice of clothing was a strategic act of political defiance. Attire became a symbolic and actual form of resistance and a statement of difference, which also acted as a powerful metaphor for Gandhi and India's indomitable spirit. Gandhi explained his wardrobe in *Young India*: 'I must, therefore, appear not as the English would have me but as my representative character demands. I represent the Congress because and in so far as it represents Daridranarayana, the semi-starved almost naked villager.'[145] In a lengthy editorial with the headline 'GANDHI'S LOIN CLOTH IN LONDON', the *Tribune* argued:

> The British empire is always a moral force. It does not concede a motive which is not altruistic, but in a half yard of cotton cloth Gandhi is of even greater morality and altruism. He not only does not want anything for himself, but obviously he hasn't anything except six pence worth of his own spinning. If the empire is pious. Gandhi is piety itself... If the empire could get him into a pair of pants, a starched collar, a coat with a few decorations, a high hat, and spats, he might be as easy to handle as an American diplomat.[146]

Thus the *Tribune* succeeded, where many of its contemporaries had failed, in rising above the populist and stereotypical response and explaining how Gandhi's persona dovetailed into his nationalist advocacy.

Violence, Inequity and Religion

One of the more striking images that Shirer conveyed repeatedly through his columns was the violence of British rule as exemplified in the suppression of civilian protests. Here is an evocative and heartfelt passage written in 1930:

> It has been grim war in India the last six months, and it being war, there have been many casualties, brutalities, miscarriages of justice and all the other accoutrements of war... It is an unequal struggle so far as violence goes. For the law has disarmed the Indian, and unarmed citizenry against policemen with guns haven't much of a chance... I defy any Westerner, hardboiled and used to bloodshed though he may be, to watch just an ordinary, routine lathi charge and not come away with the depressed feeling that he had been to some sort of an execution. It is a terrible sight. These little brown men, apparently so frail, squatting in the gutter while a policeman, usually a hefty European sergeant, whacks away at them with his bamboo stick.[147]

Further, the juxtaposition of what Shirer considered the extravagant lifestyle of the British, in the midst of widespread poverty and deprivation prevalent across vast swathes of India, was used as an effective tool to critique the Raj. This is brought out in successive despatches from Simla, the summer capital, where the official elite chose to spend seven months of the year in sanitised, refined elegance, cut off from the harsh economic realities of the country. Or, in his descriptions of the new winter capital at Delhi, juxtaposed with Gandhi's simple existence: 'The medieval and the modern; the East and the West; the magnificent Oriental splendor maintained by a British Viceroy and the rigid, drab asceticism of a half naked Indian Saint Francis of Assissi.'[148]

Religion was identified as a crucial marker of Indian identity and was routinely alluded to in Shirer's analysis of the politics of colonial opposition. He admitted in his *Memoir* that this preoccupation reflected not just the critical importance of religion in the nationalist movement, especially the conflict between Hindus and Muslims, but also his interest in Christianity and comparative philosophy. Another contemporary American journalist, Harold Isaacs, claimed that Gandhi 'pooled religion and politics in a manner disconcerting and eventually frightening to Westerners, who generally think of such a union as ideal but not very practical'.[149] Despite an insatiable curiosity, Shirer was not entirely comfortable in interpreting the philosophy of resistance that underlay Gandhi's technique of revolution, and often elected to allow readers to interrogate Gandhian philosophy directly through the interview technique. Shirer posed searching questions to Gandhi and reproduced the Mahatma's replies verbatim without further comment. 'My method is love and truth, and no force can avail against them', Gandhi is quoted as saying in an interview on 23 March 1931. Another headline ran: GANDHI'S CREED IS TO CONQUER WITH LOVE, wherein he expounded on the 'Law of Love as opposed to the Law of Destruction'.[150] At one level, according to Gandhi, this was a simple extension of the non-violence humans practised towards each other in everyday life: 'All well constructed societies are based upon the law of nonviolence.' However, to apply it as a political creed involved 'a fairly strenuous course of training to attain a mental state of nonviolence. It is a disciplined life, like the life of the soldier.'[151]

Gandhi's Mass Appeal

Notwithstanding Shirer's growing admiration for Gandhi's courage and personal integrity, he did not underestimate his protagonist's political astuteness. Whilst in England, Shirer noted how Gandhi 'bargains in Manchester. "Help us win our political independence and we'll give you preference on your cotton goods." '[152] Gandhi's 'tremendous hold' over India was 'stronger than at any time', and he remained 'the absolute dictator of the Nationalist movement'.[153] Shirer appreciated that the rising strength of the anti-colonial resistance lay in the support of the masses, despite them being unruly and excitable, especially when trying to get a glimpse of the Mahatma. Shahid Amin has shown how Gandhi was treated as a god, and the act of receiving his *darshan* was akin to visiting a holy shrine.[154] This is most emphatically brought out in Shirer's coverage during early 1931, when Gandhi, released from prison, travelled in a triumphal procession through north India. Thus the *Tribune* announced that 'Gandhi rides home in rags a hero'. The ensuing story recounted how at Ahmadabad

> He received a riotous welcome, such as no monarch, modern or ancient, Indian or English, has ever received... A half crazed brown horde took possession of the station... and would not give up until the twentieth century god of theirs appeased them with a simple blessing. The mahatma was moved to tears when the thousands knelt and kissed the earth on which he passed. Finally, after hours of milling in which hundreds had their clothes half torn off and sandals ripped from their feet, the frail little man, hailed anew as India's apostle of peace and liberty, was rescued from the howling mob and spirited away to safer parts on the shoulders of volunteers.[155]

And in this melee to see their modern saint, social distinctions among Hindus were forgotten:

the barriers of a 3,000 year old caste system were obliterated as if by magic. Filthy and perspiring sweepers rubbed sweating shoulders against excited Brahman divines. Untouchables for once did not pollute the atmosphere of their betters by their presence. Corpulent merchant princes, proud nawabs, and rajahs jostled the lowliest servants and the wild scene was enacted over and over in fifty towns.[156]

The train was delayed by several hours as it was frequently stopped while the crew 'brushed off fanatical peasants like locusts'. Similar scenes were repeated the next day when Gandhi addressed the crowds: 'Rescue Gandhi as 100,000 riot to touch India's 'idol', ran one headline.[157] Yet again, the day after, readers were informed how '50,000 women maul Gandhi; 20 hurt in crush'.[158]

The spontaneity of the masses and their frenzied acclaim for Gandhi made an indelible impression on Shirer. Comparing the Indian scenario with what he came to encounter later in Nazi Germany, he argued in his *Memoir* that though Hitler was 'wildly proclaimed by a mass of 200,000 Germans' at a party rally in Nuremberg, 'that meeting was staged, the audience was captive'. The Indian crowds came on their own initiative, were 'unorganised' and sometimes 'disorderly, milling about in their excitement at merely being in the presence of the Mahatma'. The Germans were 'deeply moved by the masterful oratory' of Hitler, yet Gandhi 'scarcely raised his voice and made no gestures. I doubt if the vast majority in the huge crowds I saw ever caught his words. They were fulfilled by the sight of him and especially by receiving his darshan. I witnessed the phenomenon; I cannot say that I fully understood it.'[159]

'A Master Dramatist'[160]: Gandhi and the media

The previous sections have focused on the perspectives of Shirer as a foreign correspondent and the *Tribune* as the featured newspaper, to provide a detailed microstudy of US press association with India in the interwar years. This analysis needs to be situated within two further – and wider – frames of reference. First, it is necessary to reiterate that Shirer and the western media were interacting with a politician who was a prolific journalist and excelled at public diplomacy. James Mills contended that Gandhi was 'a master of the art of propaganda. Whenever his "inner spirit", as he calls it, tells him he has a message for the world, he sends for all the newspaper men.'[161] This made Gandhi more accessible to journalists, but they were faced with an even greater challenge in terms of interpreting him accurately.

Gandhi's relationship with journalism has been noted by contemporaries and historians, and commented upon by the man himself. It is useful to remind ourselves that the bulk of extant Gandhi writings are in fact editorials or short essays from his varied publications. He was a hands-on editor who wrote copiously for four newspapers over his lifetime, beginning in South Africa with *Indian Opinion* and, in India, for *Navajivan, Young India* and *Harijan*. Subsequently Hindi (*Harijan Savak*) and Gujarati (*Harijan Bandhu*) editions of *Harijan* also made an appearance. Gandhi wrote how *Indian Opinion* became 'a mirror of part of my life. Week after week I poured out my soul in its columns, and expounded the principles and practice of Satyagraha as I understood it.' For a decade till 1914 'there was hardly an issue ... without an article from me'.[162] It provided Gandhi with 'a training in self-restraint' and also a crucial channel to friends and supporters. 'Satyagraha would have been impossible without *Indian Opinion*. ... For me it became a means for the study of human nature ... as I always aimed at establishing an intimate and clean bond between the editor and the readers.'[163] The deluge of letters he received from readers made Gandhi 'thoroughly understand the responsibility of a journalist, and the hold I secured in this way over the community made the future campaign workable'.[164]

For Gandhi the 'sole aim' of journalism was 'service': 'The newspaper press is a great power, but just as an unchained torrent of water submerges whole countrysides ... even so an uncontrolled pen serves but to destroy. If the control is from without, it proves more poisonous than want of control.'[165] He came to experience such control from outside in the context of an imperial system that brooked little opposition after he had called off the Non Co-operation movement. Subsequently tried in 1922 under the Press Act of 1910, Gandhi was convicted of sedition and treason based on his writings in *Young India*, and sentenced to six years imprisonment. Yet he was acutely conscious of language: How could ordinary Indians 'be trained in Satyagraha through the medium of English?' The solution was to be found in the Gujarati monthly, *Navajivan*, which was run by Indulal Yajnik and financed by Umar Sobani and Shankarlal Banker.[166] 'Through these journals,' Gandhi recalled, 'I now commenced ... the work of educating the reading public in Satyagraha.'[167]

In earlier sections I have touched upon Gandhi's encounters with prominent Americans. Those that took place during the 1940s have received due notice from scholars. For example, his letter to President Roosevelt in 1942 at the height of the Quit India crisis was smuggled out of the country by the American journalist Louis Fischer, who spent an eventful week at his ashram and later came to pen several acclaimed books.[168] Gandhi informed Roosevelt that he was prepared to cooperate with the Allies and even have them station troops in the subcontinent, but India 'must become free even as America and Great Britain are'.[169] Gandhi also addressed an open letter to the American people, which was sent to the India League and quoted widely, including in *Time* ('Gandhi to America'), in which he exhorted their help in recognising that the grant of Indian independence was an essential wartime measure.[170] Other well-known personalities espousing India's cause at this juncture included Claire Booth Luce, correspondent, activist and wife of the powerful publisher of *Time* and *Life*, Henry R. Luce, as well as John and Francis Gunther. In 1939, *Life* published an admiring account of Nehru and, according to his biographer, Henry Luce, felt that in granting freedom to India the British 'should feel themselves standing on a most magnificent pinnacle of history'.[171] John Gunther was one of the most influential journalists in the US and the couple's championing of Nehru and Gandhi, and the subsequent publication of Gunther's bestseller, *Inside Asia*, caused considerable official consternation.

Yet what is less well appreciated is how Gandhi's American correspondence bag had increased manifold from the 1920s and early 1930s. For instance, Frazier Hunt of the *Tribune* interviewed Gandhi in 1920 and the New York *World* sent a special correspondent to cover his exploits.[172] Prominent amongst his co-correspondents were missionaries (e.g. Rev. Boyd Tucker, Principal of Collins High School, Calcutta), the YMCA (e.g. Rev. Kirby Page), church leaders, most notably Rev. Frederick B. Fisher, Methodist Bishop of Calcutta (1920–30), and Rev. John H. Holmes, Minister of the non-denominational Community Church of New York. In a sermon delivered on 10 April 1922, Holmes proclaimed Gandhi to be the 'greatest man in the world', a message which served to catapult him into general American consciousness. He was later to reminisce about the 'audacity of this declaration':

> A great audience had gathered, for the subject of my discourse was a riddle which titillated the public imagination.... But all was confusion when I named Gandhi, for few had ever heard of this Indian ... But by some strange miracle of fortune, the sermon found its way to India ... This was widely published, even in the native press, and everywhere stirred interest and acclaim.[173]

Holmes became a regular collaborator and was present at Folkestone in September 1931 to welcome 'My Gandhi' to Britain.[174] As editor of the weekly *Unity*, Holmes routinely republished Gandhi's writings from *Young India*, including extracts from *My Experiments with Truth* (subsequently published as a book by Macmillan). He also wrote for *Young India* and *Bombay Chronicle*, with Gandhi reciprocating by contributing special messages for *Unity*. Rev. Fisher wrote regularly for American journals too – for instance, a celebrated sermon in 1930 on Civil Disobedience by him – 'Gandhi before Pilate' – was reprinted in the *Christian Century*.[175] This Chicago-based weekly with its pacifist editor, Charles C. Morrison, was foremost amongst periodicals to publicise Gandhi during the 1930s. Its India correspondent was P. O. Philip, Secretary of the National Christian Council. Such self-motivated and networked supporters also campaigned through public meetings, petitions and letters to American and British politicians helping internationalise Gandhi's message. American newspapers, by far the most effective and accessible means of popular publicity, were increasingly joined by popular magazines which served to reach a more variegated audience. This phenomenon included journals of international repute, such as *Time*, as well as the publications *Literary Digest*, *World Tomorrow*, *Current Opinion*, *The Living Age*, *Survey*, *Commonweal*, *Christian Century*, *Outlook* and the *Catholic World*.

Dalton has argued that Gandhi's influence 'derived in large part from both a professional use of the media and a performer's sense of his audience'.[176] As discussed earlier, nowhere is this brought out more dramatically than in the Dandi March. Gandhi wrote a message for the media immediately upon breaking the salt law, demanding 'world sympathy in this battle of Right against Might'.[177] There was much speculation that Gandhi might finally make it across to the US at the conclusion of the RTC as he had been pressed to do over the years by many of his American admirers, including Fisher and Shirer.[178] Shirer was convinced of the welcome awaiting Gandhi: 'We are a new people and exuberant and enthusiastic but certainly you would not mistake that as "sensational" or "silly". Tagore did not. Mrs Naidu did not. Nor will you.'[179] However, he decided against following his illustrious colleagues across the Atlantic, preferring to concentrate his efforts on the London and English stage where 'drama and organization were welded by Gandhi to bring forth the new weapon of a bloodless war'.[180] Indeed, Gandhi's mere presence in London, a major news hub, was sufficient to ensure that both the man and his mission received greater and more sustained attention in the western media, including the large number of American journalists assembled there, who even threw a special luncheon in his honour at the Savoy.

Shirer did, however, achieve the unthinkable when he convinced Gandhi to record his first and only radio broadcast to the US, a sensational achievement given his reluctance to engage with broadcasting, as discussed in Chapter 4. His general attitude towards technology puzzled western correspondents, such as Margaret Bourke-White, the famous *Time* and *Life* photojournalist in India during 1946–8, who wrote how his

> anti-machine references made at prayers always disturbed me, especially since they were delivered through a modern microphone. When the talk was finished, Gandhi would step off his prayer platform in to the milk-white Packard car belonging to the richest textile manufacturer in India, Mr Birla … Of course Gandhi took nothing for himself, and the members of his ashram lived in austerity. But still I was not satisfied by these inconsistencies.[181]

On a chilly September day in 1931, Gandhi broadcast live through the Columbia Broadcasting service, making a clarion call: 'I have, therefore, no hesitation whatsoever in inviting all the great nations of the earth to give their hearty co-operation to India in her mighty struggle.'[182] The text of the broadcast was carried by AP and reproduced verbatim in many US newspapers, including the *Tribune*, where Shirer's description of the event provides an evocative insight into the interaction of the 62-year-old veteran with cutting-edge media technology. 'GANDHI APPEALS FOR WORLD'S AID IN FREEING INDIA' ran the headline:

> Finally he came, hitching up his loin cloth, and squatted before the microphone. He grabbed the microphone as if it were a toy and for 30 seconds radio officials gritted their teeth nervously. There was a complete silence. Gandhi looked at the microphone fascinated. But not a word came from him … Then hitching his feet up under him, Gandhi started to talk. His sharp eyes stared at the centre of the microphone. His voice was low, but distinct. He later said that he was not nervous in the least, but that the microphone and the idea that it was carrying his frail voice across the ocean to millions he has never seen fascinated him.[183]

Mills, who was present at the recording, described the session as a significant break with tradition: 'Although it was the first time in his eventful life that the mahatma faced an invisible audience of so many millions, he approached the microphone like a veteran actor, betraying no nervousness, never faltering and never having to search for an appropriate phrase.'[184]

Gandhi's attitude to the western press, in particular the British national newspapers, had always been proactive. In 1897, in connection with garnering support for the cause of Natal Indians, he advised his representative travelling to London to liaise not just with MPs but to target Fleet Street editors from across the political spectrum, including conservative papers like *The Times*, *Telegraph*, *Globe*, *Standard* and *St James's Gazette*, and more liberal and radical ones such as the *Echo*, *Star*, *Westminster Gazette* and *Daily News*, as well as *India*, the official organ of the British Committee of the INC. As James Hunt concludes, Gandhi had 'a more realistic perception of where power lay in London'.[185] It can be argued that Gandhi's visit in 1931 was pre-eminently an exercise in propaganda intended to facilitate his reach beyond Westminster and Whitehall. The major international exposure accorded him after his Salt March enabled him to court western public opinion more aggressively. It was an attempt to pressurise the Raj through taxpayers and parliamentary representatives who 'finally called the British tune'.[186] The British Government was 'increasingly sensitive to pressures from world opinion',[187] and were aware of Gandhian tactics, as the Viceroy, Lord Willingdon, grumbled to the Secretary of State in September 1931: 'It does seem that people at home are making a terrible fuss of him. Every movement of his seems to be registered in the Press.'[188] The following month Willingdon again argued that 'you can't rely on him at all. He is too keen on keeping in the limelight, and keeping up the popularity stunt.'[189]

Whilst the RTC negotiations might have failed from the Congress perspective, the Gandhian publicity campaign was eminently successful (Figure 3.3). Upon arrival in London, he proclaimed via a message to *The Times*: 'I want the goodwill of every Englishman and every Englishwoman in the mission of peace that has brought me to England.'[190] The Mahatma undertook nine carefully choreographed trips to the provinces and engaged the attention of disparate social classes. The international, national and local press followed his progress and Gandhi was rarely out of the headlines. He was sensitive to the distress of the English working class, which is revealed in his speeches in Lancashire. He was also careful to laud his supporters: despite a hectic schedule, he took time to visit C. P. Scott, the legendary erstwhile editor of the *Guardian*. The visit served as symbolic recognition of the paper's championing of Indian causes despite the distress caused by INC

A FRANKENSTEIN OF THE EAST.
GANDHI. "REMEMBER—NO VIOLENCE; JUST DISOBEDIENCE."
GENIE. "AND WHAT IF I DISOBEY *YOU?*"

Figure 3.3 'A Frankenstein of the East', cartoon by Raven Hill, 12 March 1930, reproduced with permission of Punch Ltd

economic boycotts amongst its readership in northern constituencies. Further, Gandhi avoided negative publicity by maintaining an ideological middle ground, refusing, for example, to be drawn into the ferment then gripping 1930s Europe. Organisations and protests which might be tainted by the threat of violence or marxist and communist agendas were taboo.[191] Despite such strategies, not every newspaper or interest group was empathetic and the picture painted of Gandhi in some of the popular press was as a dangerous extremist and rebel. Rev. Holmes recalled a conversation about some particularly 'vicious attacks' in the British press, though Gandhi remained stoical: 'No, they do not trouble me, but they pain me terribly. Think of how fully and freely I have talked to the reporters... And yet they print these slanderous lies.'[192] Queried by a reporter just before his departure from London about whether he was sorry he had made the trip, ' "No", he said firmly. "I was only a myth and a mystery to many Britishers until I came." '[193]

British Propaganda and the American Press

The second wider frame of reference was British recognition and growing unease at the increasing American interest in the subcontinent apparent after the Great War.[194] Though considered important to counter anti-British propaganda in the US, attempts were stymied by the lack of funds for large-scale initiatives and infrastructural investments. The BLI acted as the nerve centre of official operations in North America and its Indian section worked in cooperation with the IO Information Office and the FO Press Office, as well as liaising with the DPI in Delhi. The BLI prepared regular summaries of US press coverage divided into distinct categories: despatches from India and those from London, local reports, editorials, special articles and lectures. The Indian section's report for 1929–30 confirmed that these were years of 'greater activity in the public discussion of Indian affairs than at any time in the experience of the Library'. With respect to the US press, the political developments in India were 'bound to receive a good deal of attention, and especially because Mr. Gandhi has for some time been good value as "news" '.[195] What was of additional concern was the use of the public platform, which had been exploited 'for an unusual amount of mischievous misrepresentation and has contributed much to American misunderstanding of Indian governmental policy'.[196] Forums such as the Foreign Policy Association, politics departments of leading universities, discussion clubs, interschool and intercollege debating societies had all registered widespread interest in the subcontinent. The BLI admitted that it was not designed 'to enter the arena of platform oratory' and therefore 'our critics have their best opportunity to damage the good name' of Britain and to 'embarrass those Americans who would think well of us'. The BLI had nevertheless some success in recommending and occasionally securing 'protagonists for the British case on important occasions', as well as distributing book lists and printed material to the general public.[197]

These years also witnessed 'a marked increase' in the number of India-related societies, with the BLI noting fifteen such organisations that were 'either wholly or in part devoted to the advancement of Indian cultures or Indian revolutionary interests'. Radio and film propaganda as well as newsreels were considered less threatening at this juncture, though one newsreel company which was controlled by Hearst, had some limited impact as their 'pictures have been damaging.'[198] 'Ordinarily this multiplication of organized effort might be regarded as a symptom of weakness rather than strength,' concluded the report, 'But the interest in the Indian situation was so widespread and so marked in 1929 and 1930 as to render this interpretation untenable.'[199]

Given such testimony, Whitehall felt it imperative to organise a sustained response. More attention was paid to sending eminent lecturers to the US, with the British journalist S. K. Ratcliffe warning a meeting of the East India Association that the state of American public opinion towards India could no longer be a matter of indifference.[200] Professor L. F. Rushbrook Williams, historian and erstwhile Chief Publicity Officer for the GoI, supported Ratcliffe's observations and travelled to the US in 1930 to deliver a series of pro-Raj lectures, which also received coverage and comment in American journals.[201] Other officials roped in by the British during 1930 included Lord Meston and Sir John Simon, who spoke on numerous public platforms and wrote for the press. Prominent public figures who also responded to the situation, though acting in a private capacity, included Cornelia Sorabjee and Edward Thompson, the latter writing a series of articles for *The Times*. The IO reacted to the increasing number of requests for speakers and information made to it by establishing an unofficial committee under the chairmanship of Sir John Kerr, consisting of Lord Howarth of Penrith, F. H. Brown of *The Times*, representatives of the East India Association, and F. J. Richter, editor of the *Asiatic Review*.[202] The British Embassy's publicity section in Washington undertook enhanced surveillance of Indian visitors, almost all of whom were now viewed as propagandists in the nationalist cause. American interest in such visits was affirmed by Thompson, who wrote how

Gandhi and Nehru (who have neither of them ever been there) are men tremendously admired, Gandhi indeed admired by many hardly on this side of idolatory. The anti-British propaganda is vocal and admirably organised. Having faced anti-British crowds in the largest halls of such cities as Baltimore, Boston, Philadelphia, New York, Chicago, with women distributing anti-British leaflets outside at the doors, I know something about this.[203]

Historically, the attitude of the GoI had been to consider the US as primarily an HMG sphere of responsibility.[204] From the 1920s the DPI had begun contributing not just printed material and official publications but also subsidies to the BLI, spurred by such developments as the purported revival of the Ghadr movement in the US (and in Victoria, British Columbia).[205] Whilst in 1930 the 'importance of countering anti-British propaganda in existing abnormal conditions'[206] was widely accepted, the GoI was 'not prepared to undertake counter propaganda on a considerable scale as a permanent arrangement'.[207] The Secretary of State, however, proposed raising the DPI contribution from $2,200 to $5,500 p.a.[208] The existing DPI funding covered the costs of rent for one room and the salary of one typist at the BLI. The additional monies proposed would double the rooms and typists as well as pay for an India expert.[209] The GoI agreed in principle about the necessity of 'an expert' who could research information, proffer advice or lecture as the need arose. It was the provision of funds that proved the stumbling bloc, 'for it is certain that no money will be voted by the Assembly for a purpose which will be regarded with the utmost suspicion as anti-national'.[210] It would, therefore, need to be sourced from 'Secret funds' in the D.P.I.'s budget.[211]

The ensuing discussions showed the Raj's difficulty. There was concern in Delhi at the reaction of the Legislative Assembly should the secret nature of this funding become public, a possibility made more likely by the fact that the proposed appointee would be expected to intervene in public discussions of policy. The Viceroy was concerned that should even this modest increase in subvention come to light it would 'inevitably attract attention out here, and we should probably have general question of policy raised in Assembly'.[212] He was wary of facing charges from non-official Indian members whose views would 'almost certainly be that propaganda activities, for which money is required, were directly opposed to national aspirations'.[213] Eventually a compromise was arrived at whereby it was agreed to allow 'a non-recurring grant in the abnormal conditions now prevailing' from Secret Service funds, but only for the financial year 1930–1.[214]

In an attempt to utilise these extra funds, the IO proposed the temporary appointment of Lt. Col. A. V. Gabriel (retd. ICS) as a special correspondent of the BLI based in London. Gabriel had considerable experience of American conditions and his help had been utilised on a voluntary basis in the past.[215] He began work in January 1931 with a monthly allowance of £75 plus free passage to and from the US. Gabriel's remit involved 'complying with any requests for information received from the Library and collating information available here in the form required in America',[216] and was to alternate his services with R. Wilberforce, a Director of the BLI, whilst the latter was in London. The permanent continuation of this scheme was considered unfeasible, as the Director of the DPI, R. S. Bajpai, pointed out, since it would involve an expense greater than that requested by the Secretary of State. Further, in view of the impending constitutional changes, the GoI did not wish to make an arrangement permanent which 'is almost certain to be turned down by a Minster responsible to the Indian legislature'.[217] In the event, Gabriel was employed only till the end of February and was replaced by Wilberforce for another two months.

Chicago Daily Tribune and Official News Management

Major Fleet Street dailies such as *The Times*, which had enormous cachet in American political circles, as well as Reuters, often joined the official bandwagon, claiming fundamental misconceptions and oversimplifications in US press coverage of empire, which reflected the lower standards of its journalism and public life. As McCormick was stung to retort to one such charge in 1930,

> Americans who have been in touch with the products of British publicity know that wherever there is news of British origin concerning their own country it is poisoned. The news of America in the London newspapers is mainly of the abnormalities, brutalities, and asininities of American political and social life. By British controlled news agencies it is thrown about the world until the world picture of the United States is one of a half savage people vulgarised by their superstitions and cruelties.[218]

Within the subcontinent, however, the British faced a fundamentally different challenge since curbing the freedom of the US press would expose it to accusations of moral turpitude, as discussed earlier. The fact of suppression could not be concealed. Thus when some of Daley's dispatches in 1930 were censored and delayed to the point of rendering them useless, the *Tribune* lodged strong protests with the IO. MacGregor hastened to clarify that the GoI

> sanctions no censorship over Press messages sent by reputable correspondents to reputable newspapers or news agencies abroad. This is

the present and actual practice and has been in operation since July. The only exception is on the North West Frontier where for military reasons a censorship may be occasionally exercised.[219]

Thus Shirer 'apparently had no trouble', and Steele reassured McCormick: 'I have no doubt at all that the authorities here see the danger in a political censorship and will do all that they can to restrain local officers who may not be so far-sighted.'[220]

John Steele had established a good working relationship with the IO, yet was often at the receiving end of its criticism about what the Raj considered misrepresentation and inaccuracy. Though complaints were routinely lodged with the paper, it was apparent that little substantive could be done to curb the *Tribune's* right to free expression. For example, Wilberforce wrote to Arthur Willert at the FO about the 'unusually hostile character' of the leading article on 12 December 1930 urging that the matter be brought to Steele's attention: 'This would . . . at least show the editor of the Chicago Tribune that we resent such gross misrepresentations being made.'[221] On another occasion, umbrage was taken with one of Steele's articles entitled 'Cost of "White Man's Burden" angers India' (12 January 1931), which asserted that Indians paid $160 million for the privilege of being ruled by the British with the Viceroy receiving $96,000 per annum, which was four times the salary of the British Prime Minister and double what was paid to his Dominion counterparts. In another edition of the paper the same story ran with a more aggressive headline: 'Bare $160 million cost of British mastery of India' where the 'peasantry foots the bill for "White Man's Burden"'. A. S. Fletcher at the BLI demanded facts to verify the story. He was determined to counter the charge and publish a rejoinder, whilst noting privately: 'Would Mr Steele work in China for the nominal pay of a Chinese official?'[222] In the event, officials had to settle for a verbal reprimand expressing grave dissatisfaction.[223] A. H. Joyce (deputy to MacGregor) was particularly incensed by these articles, as he claimed that Steele had been in touch with the IO for guidance and thus his article could only be described as 'a wilful misrepresentation' which had damaged British reputation 'beyond repair'.[224] To take yet another instance, press summaries provided by the BLI for March–April 1932 denounced Swenson's reports, which it argued were 'noteworthy for their sensationalism and their attitude of hostility to the British raj'.[225] Swenson's despatch of 12 March contended that the imprisonment of INC leaders was 'fanning a hot flame of resentment and hatred all over India'. On 29 March, Swenson contrasted the pomp of the Viceregal court with the growing squalor of the masses. On 30 March the *Tribune*'s headlines accompanying his report read: 'British police strip and flog women of India.' Swenson claimed that the Indian press was 'stoutly and with some success resisting strangulation by the ruthless ordinance regime with which the Government is trying to kill the civil disobedience movement'.[226]

However, beyond expressions of dismay and outrage, British officials were powerless to counter critical and potentially damaging interpretations in the *Tribune*. This was particularly galling when news reports were factually incorrect, as with the story in September 1931 that the heir of Maharaja Sir Chandra Jung, Prime Minister of Nepal, who had been studying in London, had been asked to leave Britain.[227] Whilst this caused only a minor diplomatic embarrassment, other reports were considered more insidious, such as one in the Paris edition of the *Tribune* on 13 February 1932 entitled '12 thousand Afridis attack Britain' with heavy resultant casualties. Joyce expostulated that the incident related was 'wholly untrue. Situation on NWF [North West Frontier] is quiet.'[228] This story also ran in the New York *Daily News,* where the headline read: '786 Die in India Battle as Tribe Attacks Britain', claiming that the Raj had been 'caught napping'. Whilst this was hardly surprising given that the *Tribune* and *Daily News* were under the same ownership, it was cause for alarm at the FO where Rex Leeper had to be reassured that Fleet Street had been debriefed and that all US news agencies had issued denials.[229] Once again, the *Tribune*'s attitude was considered particularly galling as Joyce made clear to the London staff: 'I pointed out that the whole story was an invention, and protested strongly that no attempt was made to ascertain the facts by reference to this office ... it was inconceivable that a message of such gravity should have been published without enquiries being made.'[230] Though a contrite Steele was apologetic – 'I can't say how sorry I am that that kind of propaganda, built on half or even less than half truth, was allowed to creep in' – the damage in official eyes was irretrievable.[231]

And what of Shirer and Government propaganda after the Gandhian encounter? Though Shirer's career came to focus on Europe and Nazi Germany after 1931, his interest in India remained undiminished. In addition to print, he used his newfound status as a radio broadcaster in the lead up to, and during, the Second World War to great advantage. Thus, for example, the IO were concerned about Shirer's broadcast over the Columbia Broadcasting system in February 1942, a sensitive moment with the impending Cripps Mission and Roosevelt's concern about the fate of 'subject nations'. A year later, taking the opportunity of a visit by Shirer to London, Jossleyn Hennessy, Publicity Officer with the British Embassy in Washington, wrote to Joyce (now promoted as MacGregor's successor), observing how Shirer was 'friendly except on India. Anything you can do to influence him would be valuable. He is an influential commentator.'[232] Joyce confirmed the difficulty of approaching Shirer who had 'always been very critical of our Indian policy... he was quite bitter about the imprisonment of the Congress leaders'. He did not want Shirer 'to think that we were trying to "get at" him', though that is what the IO did precisely wish to do, keeping an extravigilant eye on the *Tribune* on account of its generally belligerent coverage.[233]

Historians have concentrated overwhelmingly on the 1940s as witnessing the substantive beginnings of US engagement *vis-à-vis* India.[234] Yet the American reading public did not suddenly awaken at their breakfast tables to concerns about India and British imperialism during the course of the Second World War. As this chapter has sought to demonstrate, such claims have been made at the expense of the relative neglect of the interwar years, which were, in fact, seminal in laying the foundation of US popular opinion largely through exposure in the media, with news agencies and mainstream newspapers such as the *Tribune* playing a critical role in this process. Intensified British attempts at monitoring, controlling and directing American opinion during the 1930s clearly reveal that there was much to cause concern in the exponential rise of both quantitative and qualitative American reporting of the Raj.

Concluding Remarks

Today, William Shirer is best remembered for his exposé of Nazism and the Third Reich. However, the maturity necessary for this coverage would not have been possible but for his imperial baptism of fire in India, which provided an invaluable exposure to the human condition – the struggle against inequity, oppression and the indomitable courage to resist – all of which he faithfully chronicled in the pages of the *Tribune*. Unquestionably, this left a defining mark on him as a journalist. That it also profoundly influenced him as a human being was a debt he came to acknowledge in his *Memoir*. His daughter, Linda S. Rae, affirmed to me how 'My father's brief time covering Gandhi in India was transformational for him. His conversations with Gandhi and contact with him profoundly affected and influenced him for the rest of his life. It shaped his way of thinking and viewing the world until his dying day.'[235]

The Indian experience brought about a fundamental questioning of the liberal values Shirer felt he shared with the British and which they claimed underlay the imperial mission. His writings on imperialism go beyond merely reporting the climactic events unfolding in the empire, but involved a seminal twentieth-century journey in his evolution as a critic. The challenging and many-nuanced approach necessary to create accurate, reliable and meaningful images of distant countries, people and events in early 1930s America needs to be underscored. Shirer's intelligence and astute observation was reflected in his detailed but subtle writing, as was his ability to link developments on the ground with larger historical trends. By means of his appraisal of Indian nationalism based on eyewitness testimony, Shirer brought home to Americans the unfolding drama from very distant shores. Yet it should not be concluded from this that he was simply a co-conspirator. Although Gandhi was indeed a special confidante, Shirer also cultivated a range of sources from across the political spectrum, including the Muslim League, right-wing Hindu nationalists and Liberals, and within the ICS (Figure 3.4). Once Shirer's impartiality had been demonstrated in print, he was able to win the trust of the Mahatma's inner circle and his private secretaries 'kept me well informed and in dozens of ways facilitated my work and my understanding'.[236] Describing how he overcame their initial reluctance ('Didn't they want to get their side of the story reported in the world press?'), it is entirely to Shirer's credit that he gauged accurately that what he was witnessing was nothing short of a watershed in Britain's hegemony in the subcontinent. For him the Gandhi–Irwin truce signed on 5 March 1931 'marked a turning point in the Indian revolution'.[237] As he wrote to Nicholas Spykman, an economist at Yale, 'I am not so sure that the British hold on India is secure right now.'[238]

However, he was to candidly admit in his *Memoirs* that his appreciation of the subtleties of imperial control and nationalist response evolved over time, and even at the end of his stint in India he was never totally at ease with the country's social and cultural realities. The full portent and potentialities of the Gandhian revolution took him a while to comprehend, despite occasional tutelage by the Mahatma himself. With disarming honesty, Shirer confessed: 'But I was too sceptical, too ignorant, too much impressed by British power to fully believe him.'[239] What Gandhi was attempting to do 'had not made much sense in the West, where violence was second nature to us and had dominated most of our history'.[240] Yet, by sheer dint of application, Shirer eventually managed to convey the many dimensions of Gandhi as a tireless campaigner, a talented negotiator, an eloquent speaker, a facile editor and a deeply spiritual politician. Of equal significance for the young American was his ability 'to penetrate' the Indian 'mind and soul' and to understand the gulf of hatred that appeared to separate the followers of the two major faiths. That the British had 'often encouraged Hindu-Moslem

120

Figure 3.4 Gandhi and his associates, including Pyarelal Nayar, Mahadev Desai and Sarojini Naidu, 1931 [photograph, copy] by William L. Shirer, reprinted with the permission of the Literary Trust of William L. Shirer, George T. Henry College Archives, Coe College, Iowa

animosity and sometimes fomented it' was for him 'no excuse for the Indians to give in to it'.[241]

Shirer was able to deploy his skills to enrich and challenge US awareness of the wider world and he succeeded, to a large degree, in deconstructing Indian stereotypes and presenting personae that combined western and Indian ideologies. This was a daunting endeavour, as was admitted by no less an authority than Rushbrook Williams, who argued that Indian conditions were

> so complicated that the task with which the American press found itself confronted of explaining this situation to a largely uninformed public has proved of surpassing difficulty. I should like to pay a respectful tribute to the general anxiety of the American Press to elicit facts on the Indian situation and to present them as clearly as possible.[242]

Yet Shirer was not totally immune from the stereotyping and romanticisation prevalent in much US and western media coverage when confronted with the East. To an extent, he was bound by the dictates of the contemporary press culture, and the language and imagery he often employed (like McCormick's editorials) was influenced by the dictates of popular journalism. McCormick demanded nothing if not a dramatic story, and world exclusives were especially welcome. On the whole, one is struck by the descriptive intensity of Shirer's despatches – the people, places, objects and emotions were all conveyed with a vivid physicality. The frailty of Gandhi in his loincloth and gossamer shawl bounding up the steps of Buckingham Palace, the dusty heat of the north Indian plains and the torrential monsoon downpours, the starving thousands riven by caste and class yet united in attending Gandhi's mass rallies, the hundreds clinging precariously to the railway carriage carrying the Mahatma, the large contingents of women in their colourful attire marching on the streets to the nationalist tune, the bloody assaults by the police on peaceful demonstrators – these were all captured in evocative and picturesque language.

Crucially, Shirer was at liberty to express his critique of the Raj in a manner that was difficult for most of his Fleet Street counterparts. Described by him as 'my eccentric publisher', McCormick was often dictatorial but at the same time he respected the integrity and professionalism of his staff.[243] Indeed, Shirer's exposés appeared to strike a personal chord with McCormick, given that his despatches, accompanied by dramatic headlines, repeatedly made the front pages of the *Tribune* and were splashed across the Sunday editions. 'You did some excellent work in India', McCormick commended his foreign correspondent, and despite the acrimonious note on which Shirer's connection with the paper was to end, he remained convinced about the integrity of the *Tribune*'s coverage.[244] Thus upon introducing his successor in India, Shirer was able to reassure the Mayor of Calcutta: 'you can be sure that the Chicago Tribune...will be one newspaper at least which will give the world the real true story now going on in India'.[245]

The pages of the *Tribune* reflected Shirer's sympathy for the cause of the anti-colonial struggle. They also demonstrated a keen awareness of the larger problems ailing Indian society, particularly caste, class and religious tensions, as well as economic inequalities. Simultaneously, Gandhi's 'anti-modern' stance and repudiation of western industrialism came in for criticism in its pages. Despite his profound admiration for Gandhi, Shirer was aware that he was dealing with a 'shrewd bargaining diplomat',[246] and he retained a healthy scepticism on many issues, most critically the admixture of religion in politics which was a cornerstone of Gandhi's political praxis and which Shirer felt contributed in no small measure to the Muslim distrust of INC policy. He also did not condone Gandhi's adherence to traditions such as the caste system.[247]

Finally, this microstudy, juxtaposing event and personality, also provides evidence of the transmutation of the news reporter into the news being reported. Shirer became embedded in the imperial saga he was covering. This was best captured when he was made the subject of a full-page advertisement on 19 September 1931. 'Tomorrow's Tribune', its readers were promised, 'will bring to you another colourful news story by William Shirer...Don't miss this important dispatch by the same Chicago Tribune man whose exclusive interview with Gandhi in Marseilles first gave the world the news that Gandhi's demand from Great Britain would be complete independence for India.' Below this in smaller type the *Tribune* reiterated how Shirer 'told in unbiased, vivid reports...the story of Gandhi's fight for freedom and of the operation of the British policy' and had 'personal acquaintance' with the Mahatma, which 'enables him to obtain first the news of Gandhi's actions and policies'. Thus it was Shirer, and not India, that took centre stage, making explicit the transformation of the foreign correspondent from an eyewitness to making history.

4

'Invisible Empire Tie': Broadcasting and the British Raj in the Interwar Years

Introduction; Radio in India; Commercial Radio Broadcasting; Government of India & Broadcasting; BBC & Indian Broadcasting; The Fielden Years; Broadcasting & Print; Concluding Remarks

> From Earth to Heaven, distance conquered, In Waves of Light... To East and West speech careers, Swift as the Sun, The Mind of Man reaches Heaven's confines, Its Freedom won.
>
> *Akashvani* by Rabindranath Tagore[1]

Introduction

When the Viceroy, Lord Irwin, spoke at the inauguration of the first broadcasting station in Bombay in July 1927, he optimistically claimed that wireless in India would provide an 'invisible empire tie' that would be 'stronger than the strongest cable of woven wire'. Such views were echoed a decade later by Rabindranath Tagore in a poem entitled *Akashvani* (Heavenly Proclamation),[2] composed specially to mark the opening of the first short-wave station in Calcutta. Tagore had always been 'very keen to help' and had recorded several broadcasts from Shantiniketan, 'his name a great draw anywhere in India'.[3] However, such predictions of a spatial world transformed by the medium of radio communication proved rather exaggerated. For the study of the fate of broadcasting under the Raj in the interwar years discloses a reality altogether more prosaic and hesitant, characterised overall by an abysmal lack of creative policy-making. Was this deliberate official instruction, or simply a failure to grasp and exploit the potentialities of broadcasting? Was All India Radio (AIR) ever about all India? What were the roles of key organisations such as the ICS and the British Broadcasting Corporation (BBC), as well as prominent individuals within these organisations? Jean Seaton has argued that individuals in broadcasting 'explain the real story', adding a colour and vibrancy to institutional accounts.[4] The creativity inherent at the heart of programming is also due in large measure to their talent and versatility.

The development trajectory of radio under the British provides fascinating insights into the interplay between the sociopolitical and strategic imperatives of imperial rule, the technological and commercial demands of a new communication medium, the role of personality, experiments in imperial constitutional devolution and the coming of war. The focus in this chapter is on the macrolevel institutional context of radio's development and its impact in the making of the imperial experience during the interwar years, with both structural factors and human agency being considered equally significant in the process. Content analysis of programming and concurrent developments in the Indian states, such as Baroda and Mysore, will not come under scrutiny here, though it is worth noting that the GoI acknowledged early on the implications of a medium that knew no political boundaries and attempts to regulate the operation of wireless telegraphy, telephony and radio broadcasts *vis-à-vis* princely India were *in situ* by 1926.

Radio in India: A potted history

Prior to 1921 the use of wireless was the preserve of the GoI. However, the first radio transmission under private aegis took place in that year and in February 1922 the Indian States and Eastern Agency, a subsidiary of the Marconi Company, was granted the first transmitting licence in British India. The banner of broadcasting was upheld precariously by amateur radio clubs in Bombay, Calcutta, Madras and Rangoon from 1923 to 1924. In 1926 the Government's beam wireless system was inaugurated between Rugby in England and Kirkee, the operation of which was handed over eventually to Imperial and International Communications (the successor to the Marconi Company). In 1927 the Indian Broadcasting Company Ltd (IBC) was granted a licence on lines similar to those under which the BBC operated in Britain, and with an aerial input of 1.5 kilowatts it opened studios in Bombay and Calcutta amid much fanfare: 'Everything went like clockwork', commented the *Indian Radio Times*.[5] Yet within a few years the IBC folded and the GoI was forced to take broadcasting under its wing, assigning it to the Department of Industries and Labour (DIL) on 1 April 1930. By the end of

1931, licences had failed to reach the 8,000 mark and officials expressed doubts as to the viability of the Indian State Broadcasting Service (ISBS), the successor to the IBC. Eventually the ISBS was revamped and rechristened AIR, and in 1936 it began broadcasting from a 20 KW new medium-wave station in Delhi under the direction of its first Controller of Broadcasting, Lionel Fielden who was seconded from the BBC and came armed with a reputation for creative excellence. Also in 1936, AIR was admitted as a regular associate member of the Union Internationale de Radio-diffusion, Geneva.

By the time Fielden relinquished his post in 1940, the outbreak of the Second World War had ensured that both 'the medium and the message', to paraphrase McLuhan's iconic aphorism, were harnessed to the cause of British propaganda. In 1943, AIR's new studios in Delhi created the 'largest centre of broadcasting activity in the East'.[6] A 100 kilowatt transmitter capable of overseas broadcasts was set up in 1944. In 1947, partition of the subcontinent meant that the nine extant AIR stations were divided, with those in Lahore, Peshawar and Dacca going to West and East Pakistan, respectively. The remaining six stations and eighteen transmitters in British India reached only 11% of the population (and covered just 2.5% of the land mass) and were located in Delhi, Calcutta, Bombay, Madras, Lucknow and Tiruchi. However, within a year, 15 stations were in operation, the number rising to 18 in 1949. By the sixtieth anniversary of India's independence, these had increased exponentially to include 231 radio stations and 373 transmitters covering 99.14% of the population and 91% of the landmass.[7] Today, non-news sectors have been privatised and are completely open to Foreign Direct Investment, with over one hundred private channels and cable networks. There are in excess of 240 FM stations and 820 television channels, the latter including over 120 news channels.

Commercial Radio Broadcasting: 1921–30

While interpretations may vary about the role of radio during the Raj, what is not in question is the abject failure of private commercial broadcasting. Like elsewhere, radio proved to be an irresistible medium for keen amateurs who were the first to experiment with it. The Bombay, Calcutta, Madras and Rangoon radio clubs begun in 1923–4 were on a small-scale, operating on medium-wave transmitters loaned from the Marconi Company. The GoI had favoured such initiatives on the grounds that 'a private commercial undertaking ... was far more likely to be sensitive to the changing needs of the public than a Government

department'. Further, the finances of India 'precluded any large outlay of public funds on which the financial return was problematical'.[8]
In September 1924 the GoI decreed that these radio clubs were to receive
75% of the licence fees it collected. By April 1927 there were about
1,000 broadcast receiver licences in force, but the financial arrangements
were temporary until the formal establishment of a private company.[9]
With the IBC commencing operations in the summer of 1927, and with
the BBC's Eric Dunstan appointed as General Manager, it appeared that
commercial radio was off to a good start. The IBC Directors included
businessmen and merchants such as C. N. Wadia, Sir N. N. Wadia,
R. M. Chinoy, Sultan Chinoy, F. E. Rosher, R. D. England, Sir Ibrahim
Rahimtoolah and Raja Dhanrajgiriji Narsingirji, as well as the GoI representative, P. J. Edmunds, the Director of Wireless. The Raja was in
effect a sleeping partner, with the major shareholder being the Indian
Radio Telegraph Company (IRTC). Two-thirds of the issued capital of the
IRTC was held by the Marconi Company, and there was concern at the
potential influence that the latter enjoyed over the IBC.[10]

The GoI and some provincial governments had expressed doubts
about the level of demand for broadcasting and the speed of its uptake,
and voiced the need to provide safeguards against the development
of an unrestricted monopoly. This was a *leitmotif* in the approach of
the DIL summarised in its mantra: 'regulated control is essential to the
success of broadcasting'.[11] Therefore the GoI dictated that the putative
organisation would function as a private monopoly only for the first five
years of its ten-year contract, though the allocated wavelengths and the
sites of broadcasting stations would be subject to official approval. The
IBC would be free to manufacture equipment, levy licences and retain all
profits during this period, after which the GoI would introduce a sliding
scale with respect to the proportion of the fees payable to it. The GoI and
provincial governments retained sole discretion regarding the imposition of censorship, including prebroadcast censorship, with the IBC
forbidden to transmit talks of a political nature and requiring mandatory
prior approval of all speeches. Educational broadcasts aimed at schools
and universities had also to be of 'an entirely non-political nature'.
News bulletins had perforce to utilise Reuters and API as the officially
approved news agencies. Government communiqués and weather fore-
casts accounting for up to 10% of the total programme time would
need to be broadcast free of charge.[12] Overall, as the GoI informed
the IO, 'Provision has thus been made for complete control by the
Government.'[13] However, these sentiments papered over a lack of una-
nimity on several issues between the centre and the provinces. The

governments of Bombay and Burma, for instance, argued that the private companies should not be forced to include official news gratis. Commercially, that would be tantamount to subsidising the general taxpayer at the expense of the licence-holder.

This official stranglehold might arguably help to explain the failure of broadcasting to appear an attractive alternative to print in the public eye or for commercial investors. As it transpired, the Raj need not have feared the power of the medium as handled by the commercial sector. The IBC, with only 7,775 licences after two years, never appeared to come close to achieving what Rahimtoolah claimed would be yet another heroic tie linking India into the worldwide chain of imperial broadcasting. Likewise Irwin's initial euphoria evinced high aspirations for linking the far-flung corners of India through a communications medium which offered 'special opportunities' for entertainment and education. 'I have little doubt that, before many years are past, the numbers of its audience will have increased tenfold.'[14] Unfortunately, these ambitious claims were supported by a severely undercapitalised company. The IBC had issued capital to the value of 6 lakhs, of which 5 lakhs were expended on initial construction and associated costs, leaving only 1 lakh – about £7,500 – as working capital. Dunstan began to remonstrate as early as February 1928 about the 40% reduction in programme allowance and the cutback on daily broadcasting from 5 to 3.5 hours only. In desperation he even tried, albeit unsuccessfully, to raise £65,000 in Britain.[15] 'Thank heavens I have a sense of humour,' he confided to Sir John Reith, Director General of the BBC, 'otherwise I should have committed suicide some time ago.'[16] Severe financial constraints meant low salaries, staff retrenchment, poor output and miniscule outlay on programming, with virtually non-existent publicity or promotion. Combined with poor licence sales, piracy and evasion of fees, this forced the IBC into voluntary liquidation and it ceased broadcasting after 28 February 1930.

Critically there appeared no willingness on behalf of European or Indian entrepreneurs to invest in radio, a situation which can only partially be explained by the general retrenchment of capital investment within India during the interwar years. When broadcasting was initially opened to public tender, the IBC was the 'only one to make a definite offer'.[17] The comparison with civil aviation, which witnessed the proverbial 'take-off' phase in these decades, further highlights the problem. The first flight carrying mail within India (from Allahabad to Naini) is technically dated as early as 1911; in 1920 an air service between Bombay and Karachi was inaugurated. It was in the 1930s, under the aegis of the industrialist Tata that the expansion of the domestic air industry really began. The Tatas launched their first service on 15 October 1932 from Madras to Karachi via Ahmedabad, Bombay and Bellari, and the following year a weekly service began linking Karachi and Calcutta, followed by a Bombay–Trivandrum service (1935) and a Delhi–Bombay service (1937).[18] Commercial air travel between empire and periphery also grew exponentially: 1927 witnessed the beginnings of regular flights to India from England and the first weekly airmail service commenced in 1929. The transimperial network was also flourishing with India a major hub in the Australasian air service.[19] By 1933 the operation of the trans-India air service was spearheaded by Indians who formed the Indian Trans-continental Airways Ltd, which, working in unison with the GoI and Imperial Airways, linked Karachi to Singapore in the England–Australia air service. In December 1933 the Calcutta–Rangoon service was established by Indian National Airways.[20] In stark contradistinction, the failure of private capitalism *vis-à-vis* radio was to lay the foundations for direct state involvement and provides a partial explanation of the scepticism and disregard that characterised the official response to the medium.

The failure of private commercial broadcasting is not, with hindsight, difficult to explain, with a critical factor being the undercapitalised levels of the IBC. The expected take-up from licence-holders needed to shore up working capital, as witnessed in the West, never materialised, with only Europeans and Indian elites inclined to subscribe. There had been little outlay on staff or programming to attract and retain a wider audience. The high cost of the imported sets – about Rs 500 for a four-valve set – as well as an exorbitant 50% import tax put it outside the reach of the masses. Widespread piracy made the collection of fees harder to accomplish. Thus one could empathise with the editor of the IBC's journal, *Indian Radio Times*, who announced gloomily in its farewell issue of 7 February 1930: 'Broadcasting in this country will be dead by the end of this month.'[21] An equally pessimistic outlook pervaded the pages of the *Indian Wireless Magazine*, where the ire was directed chiefly at the IBC. It's 'Special Broadcasting Failure Number' (February 1930) argued that there had been a 'want of business acumen and inability to manage one's own home with available resources'. It was felt that the GoI ought 'morally and legally to step in' given that broadcasting was considered as 'a necessary adjunct to civilization and we cannot conceive how India, a land of 30 crores of people can do without this'. Yet the editorial questioned whether the failure of the IBC should be equated with the failure of broadcasting *per se*. ' "Broadcasting failure" is putting together incompatible words. Broadcasting cannot fail.'[22] Such a response was hardly surprising in a trade journal whose clientele was directly affected by the potential collapse of the industry, but it does also serve to suggest a degree of public despondency.

Government of India and Broadcasting

However, the foretold death of radio was commuted to a life sentence under GoI control. Broadcasting was assigned to the DIL, as noted earlier, and the ISBS was born. The GoI purchased the failed IBC's assets for Rs 3 lakhs with an undertaking to run it for two years. In fact, by October 1931 officials had decided to wash their hands of the enterprise altogether. This decision was met with an outcry from the press and in the legislature, forcing the GoI to finally announce its continuance in May 1932. Concerted attempts were now made to cover the deficit by raising customs duty and economising on costs. During 1930–1 the losses amounted to Rs 1,65,710 and the following year the figure stood at Rs 1,09,506.[23] This was due to a number of factors, chief amongst which were the high cost of the imported receiver sets and the limited range of the stations which reduced the catchment area. A new Wireless Telegraphy Act came into effect from January 1934, licence fees for receivers were fixed at Rs 10 per annum, and customs duties were raised to 12.5%. Small profits were also made from advertising and the sale of radio publications. The end of the financial year 1932/3 saw the service record a profit of Rs 84,000, which increased substantially to Rs 2,34,000 in the following year.[24] Thus, crucially, in less than four years after the Government takeover, and with prudent planning, broadcasting had become commercially solvent and even profitable.

Though licence numbers were still miniscule at about 16,000, and there had been little investment in infrastructure, the potential of the medium was now recognised and it would be reasonable to expect that even sun-dried bureaucrats interested only in the bottom line would enthusiastically push for major expansion. In order to dissect the response of the Raj *vis-à-vis* radio during the 1930s, several overlapping themes need to be considered, including government *mentalité* as well as the bounded political context within which these developments were unfolding. Given that broadcasting was effectively a Government department, the strategies and culture of imperial bureaucratic control perforce played a critical role. The GoI takeover had been necessitated by the considerable pressure brought to bear from vested interests, including existing licence holders, dealers in wireless equipment, the press and legislators. There was also concern at the implications were the medium to fall by default into opposition hands – 1930 was, after all, when Gandhi's Salt March had galvanised the masses, making Indian nationalism the cynosure of domestic and international eyes, as discussed in Chapter 3.

Thus the GoI found itself the residuary legatee of a failed private enterprise and a fledgling broadcast service. Without a policy blueprint for its development or any budgetary provision to fund future initiatives, broadcasting was assigned to the DIL, a move which neatly symbolised official attitudes – radio was viewed as an industrial undertaking rather than as a creative sociocultural service in the public interest. It was affirmed as such by John Coatman, Director of the Department of Public Information (DPI) and later Chief News Editor at the BBC, who acknowledged how the DIL 'took no effective interest in broadcasting' and the Home Department 'has not yet [in 1934] seriously considered <u>its</u> interests', regarding broadcasting 'as primarily an industry'.[25] Indeed, the Director of the DIL accepted this charge, admitting that 'there were no real developments of any kind' by that stage.[26] This reluctance to acknowledge the status of broadcasting is also revealed by the fact that despite the creation of a separate Department of Communications in November 1937, its staff were retained on temporary contracts, and 'in theory liable to have their services terminated on a month's notice, and with no claim to pension or provident fund'.[27] It was only in 1943 that a Ministry of Information and Broadcasting was established and the permanent value of broadcasting was now reflected in fixity of tenure for its staff. Yet 'this feeling of insecurity', as Seth Drucquer, an AIR broadcaster, noted, 'permeated broadcasting in its early years and its effects [would] take some time to wear off'.[28]

As Harold Innis has persuasively argued, the space and time bias of modern communications ensured their seminal value for far-flung European empires, and indeed the strategic importance of wireless in defending so large a territorial empire as India was appreciated early on. However, it was apparent soon after the end of the First World War that financial retrenchment was putting the upkeep of wireless and relay stations under considerable strain. Economic factors had underlain moves in the early 1920s to decommission several 'inefficient' stations. The Home Department resisted such demands and was eventually successful in allocating Rs 4 lakhs to recondition the eight existing stations. Its arguments in support of wireless reveal the critical role of communication technology in underpinning the very fabric of imperial rule. James Crerar at the Home Department recalled the dire situation in the aftermath of the Amritsar Massacre, when telegraph and railway communications were successfully breached by Indians effectively paralysing the official response.[29] And it was believed that in any future large-scale disturbance 'the destruction of communications would be the first item in the programme'.[30]

Thus it was that the GoI, utilising its unparalleled technical, legal and financial resources, ensured that the Indian opposition had no access to the airwaves. No party political broadcasts or propaganda were permissible, and annual sessions of the INC were not given airtime. This became a difficult line to hold as the political dynamics of the 1930s altered and became more confrontational. In the run-up to the elections in 1937 (under the GoI 1935 Act), this ruling came increasingly under censure in the Central Legislative Assembly. S. Satyamurti, for instance, questioned whether parties would be 'allowed to use the broadcasting stations for political propaganda, as is done in England, especially on the eve of elections'.[31] Likewise, M. Asaf Ali wondered if the different political parties would be allowed to broadcast 'at least one speech each during the election campaign'.[32] Responding to these charges, Sir Frank Noyce, head of the DIL, reiterated that 'no election manifestoes or speeches or extracts therefrom' could be sanctioned. He was also forced to acknowledge that though during British elections 'there was a relaxation of the strict rule in regard to political speeches', this was impossible in India since 'conditions in this country are not similar'.[33] Lionel Fielden was also keen to utilise the dynamics of these elections to help energise AIR and make radio more appealing and relevant to a larger constituency, convinced that it did not pose a threat to the Raj: 'Hostile mobs will <u>not</u> rush into rebellion at the sound of Gandhi's voice!'[34] He was also concerned to alleviate the suspicions of the INC regarding official intentions and to pre-empt moves by nationalists to establish independent provincial stations outside GoI purview. However, his requests were firmly turned down by the Home Secretary, M. G. Hallett, who contended that 'it is going to be a delicate matter to draw the line between legitimate electioneering... and propaganda intended to be subversive to Government... By broadcasting election speeches we might in effect be using machinery set up by ourselves for disseminating sedition.'[35]

At one level, such an official response to political content in broadcasting grew organically from the traditions of media surveillance and repression of dissent by which the British in India had tempered their utilitarian liberalism from the nineteenth century. Thus when emergency powers were reimposed in the early 1930s it was merely a case of extending punitive control to the airwaves and was achieved relatively seamlessly. The thinking behind Government action can be explained by the Lazarsfeldian 'two-step flow of communication' and hence of media influence: 'ideas, often, seem to flow *from* radio and print *to* opinion leaders and *from them* to the less active sections of the population'.[36] Thus Indian broadcasters would influence, in the first instance, those opinion-forming elites with access to the medium, who would in turn be the harbingers of change in their respective constituencies. Someone with Gandhi's stature could, of course, appeal directly to the masses and work on a national and even transnational stage, as evidenced by his successful appeal to international opinion during the Civil Disobedience movement, as discussed in Chapter 3. However, nationalists were also concerned at incurring the wrath of the Raj. Replying to Fielden's request to broadcast on AIR, Gandhi explained:

> My dear Fielden, you know and I know that if I do so I shall increase the number of your listeners by four or five millions overnight: if I knew you were going to stay in India, I might do it; if you don't, I shall merely increase the strength of my enemies.[37]

What also needs underscoring is that this official reluctance to explore the potentiality of radio was at odds with the British state's previous enthusiasm for exploiting and developing the beacons of technological modernity in the shape of the most advanced media available. Driven from the mid-nineteenth century by an agenda of defence, propaganda and the advancement of private capitalist enterprise, it had routinely underwritten commercially unviable projects, like the laying of undersea cable networks in their remoter possessions for political and security ends. The British had also supported telegraph monopolies and subsidised news agencies, especially Reuters and API.[38] Why should the imperium now appear reluctant to develop broadcasting as the newest addition to the pantheon of modern communication?

A recurrent official defence was advanced on the grounds of financial stringency. A cash-starved bureaucracy in an adverse economic climate – the constriction of the world economy and an increasing disengagement of capital investment in India – could not justify the public funds for an outlay such as that required by broadcast technologies and associated externalities. Further, as the failure of the IBC demonstrated, there was little guarantee that any such outlay would yield appreciable dividends. Yet the financial facts appear to cast doubt over such a justification of state inertia, with the evidence demonstrating how the GoI had managed by 1932–3 to make broadcasting not just solvent but even profitable, a success that was acknowledged in the Indian press.[39] Instead, as will be argued in this chapter, the impetus for change was to come primarily from the metropolis and the BBC. Another aspect of this imperial perspective deserves to be highlighted: the rapidly evolving political context of 1930s India, where any large-scale state investment in new technology might well have been perceived as an exercise in futility. During these years the Raj was grappling with the transnational effects of the Great Depression combined with the rising tide of nationalist discontent coalescing around a resurgent INC. These difficulties were combined with further British attempts at constitutional devolution with the eventual passage of the GoI Act of 1935. Additionally, with failures in European diplomacy reaching a critical stage, war clouds appeared to threaten the imperial *status quo* in the East which in turn had an inevitable strategic impact on the planning of a radio network.

Two further and related issues merit attention. First, the evolving Raj ideology *vis-à-vis* propaganda and the role assigned to radio within it. Second, and more specifically, the issue of provincial autonomy under the 1935 Act and its potential impact on broadcasting. As analysed in *Reporting the Raj*, the Great War and immediate post-war years were critical in coalescing official attitudes regarding the necessity to encompass publicity, propaganda and news management as legitimate weapons of governance. The primary motivator was Edwin Montagu, Secretary of State, who was convinced that public opinion needed to be cultivated and, indeed, often created, in support of official measures as the atmosphere within which the Raj functioned was equally critical to its success and longevity as the quality of its governance. Successive Viceroys and Secretaries of State during the interwar years appeared to embrace this shift in imperial *mentalité*, and the need to improve both the organisation and the scope of publicity was acknowledged in the face of an energised opposition under charismatic leadership. Yet, for the British, the political liberalism embraced at home was hardly reconcilable with the principles underlying imperial governance, and, as Dipesh Chakrabarty notes, her Indian policy was 'forever haunted by this contradiction'.[40] Whilst frequently presenting their Raj as a progressive and liberalising force for the benefit of the governed, and exporting a free press tradition, the British were confronted with an increasingly critical media furthering the campaigns of nationalist opponents.[41] In keeping with the Montagu strategy of persuasion, as witnessed in the lead up to the GoI Act of 1919,[42] and with the passage of its successor in 1935 fast approaching, officials felt that the revival of the Press Act 1910 (rescinded in 1922) would send out the wrong signals. British rhetoric of provincial autonomy would sit uneasily with a renewed drive to curtail freedom of expression. However, imperial ideology was nothing if not ambiguous. To counter the challenges posed by civil disobedience, the Press Ordinance was passed in May 1930 which allowed for the suspension of newspapers. In defending his decision, Irwin claimed that in the face of the breach of the peace by the nationalists, he had little choice but to arm the Government with special powers, the use of which in normal circumstances would be indefensible. Under his successor, Willingdon, the Press (Emergency Powers) Act made it to the statute book in 1931. Though intended for the duration of one year, it could be extended *ad infinitum*, and the onus of proving innocence fell upon those who were being prosecuted.

It has often been observed that propaganda and censorship are but two sides of the same coin, and, given the heightened politicisation of these years, the former now assumed a greater resonance. Secretary of State Sir Samuel Hoare, as noted in Chapter 1, was convinced that the right atmosphere was essential for the success of the constitutional reforms and offered to engage with British journalists and claimed some success:

> The press here has really been admirable. We took a great deal of trouble about it. I myself saw the more prominent people from the British and American press and the Office dealt effectively with the London and provincial press generally.[43]

Hoare was concerned, however, with a relative lack of institutional infrastructure within the subcontinent: 'I am made the more nervous', he confessed, 'about our inadequate propaganda in India and the great disadvantage in which we now find ourselves in getting our case across the country and the world.'[44] He was cognisant with British methods of political manipulation, having honed his skills whilst Treasurer of the Conservative Party and through witnessing both Downing Street and the FO in action.[45] Hoare cultivated a progressive outlook *vis-à-vis* imperial communications as embodied in his flamboyant support for civil aviation, travelling on the inaugural flight to India in 1927 whilst Minister of Air and subsequently authoring several books on the subject. In contrast, at 65, Willingdon was the elder statesman, with a wealth of Raj experience having previously been Governor of Bombay and Madras, and seemingly entrenched in the civil service ethos.

As the Hoare–Willingdon correspondence makes apparent, the two were 'never very close', only meeting in person in 1934.[46] Yet

Willingdon readily accepted the necessity for change at this juncture, citing an instance during an Assembly session where 'a strong Congress Opposition backed by the nationalist press emphasised the necessity of taking more effective steps to put our views across'.[47] 'I entirely agree', wrote the Viceroy, 'that this is where we fail sadly in this country, and I am going seriously into the matter to see if we cannot do something much more active at this juncture.'[48] One result of this reappraisal was the secondment of A. H. Joyce from the IO Information Department to help restructure the DPI, then under the directorship of Ian Stephens, who was to achieve eminence subsequently at the *Statesman*, first as assistant editor (1937–41) and later as editor (1942–51). Joyce's recommendations included direct, indirect and unofficial attempts to cultivate the press and the urgent necessity of training Indian staff, but, revealingly, broadcasting was excluded from such strategising.

Thus, though the propaganda function had, by the 1930s, become encoded in imperial governance, nevertheless broadcasting remained the elephant in the room. The GoI's stance throughout these years was marked by a conspicuous absence of any detailed discussion involving radio or an acknowledgement of its potential for political publicity. So it was that Irwin wrote to Lord Sykes, Governor of Bombay, about the necessity for improved official publicity to oppose 'the extreme and universal hostility to Government displayed by the Indian edited press'.[49] Consequently the need to bolster support from British-owned and -edited papers was felt even more keenly; as Irwin confided to the Secretary of State on the death of Sir David Yule, proprietor of the *Statesman*, it was 'very desirable' that the paper 'should not fall into irresponsible hands, and I wondered whether you might have been able to put a word in, at the right moment and in the right quarter, to prevent this happening'.[50] Yet neither Irwin nor Sykes (who in 1923 had overseen the grant of the BBC charter and was centrally involved with formulating broadcasting strategy) made any allusion to the potential of radio, and Irwin's extreme reluctance to engage with the BBC will be discussed in a later section. Given the critical timeframe of Irwin's Viceroyalty, it is revealing that his biographers make no mention of radio or broadcast policy.[51] Astonishingly, even four years after the GoI takeover of the IBC, his successor, Willingdon, admitted to Reith that broadcasting had 'never been discussed in the Executive Council'.[52]

Official memoranda in the lead-up to the passage of the GoI Act of 1935 state unequivocally that the chief formative elements in public opinion were the press and platform with no mention of broadcasting. Willingdon's successor, Lord Linlithgow, appeared to be aware of the new medium, especially in enhancing the Viceregal voice; nevertheless, much like his predecessors, he remained preoccupied with newspapers and Reuters. This is clearly evidenced in his inaugural speech, which, ironically, was also broadcast by AIR on 18 April 1936, a first in the annals of the Raj. The Secretary of State commended the broadcast as 'admirable' and felt certain that 'it will have produced a favourable atmosphere at the very start of your reign'.[53] Fielden played a critical role in bringing this about, with the speech being translated into several Indian languages and also transmitted via the BBC through the personal intervention of Reith.[54] Linlithgow acknowledged that this radio operation had been 'a very great success'. 'I feel not the least doubt', he added, 'that it is of really vital importance to get broadcasting organised here on the soundest and widest basis possible, and I propose not only to take a close personal interest in all developments, but to do my utmost to encourage them.' Linlithgow was keen to secure assistance from Reith, acknowledging that he could 'rely on Fielden in whose energy I have the greatest confidence'.[55] Reith, in reply, noted how it was 'the first time that a Viceroy's inaugural address had been heard in England' and confirmed that Fielden was 'almost inarticulate with delight', hopeful that the event would give 'an immense impetus' to Indian broadcasting.[56] This broadcast was also subsequently relayed via cinemas in Calcutta, and through loudspeakers erected on the beach in Madras where officials claimed 'very large numbers, estimated at 10,000, listened to it with close attention'.[57] Linlithgow also admitted privately to the Secretary of State that this response had made him aware that broadcasting could be 'an even more potent instrument of propaganda in this country, whether for good or mischief, than I had thought'. He was 'a little apprehensive' at the discretionary powers over radio given to the provinces through the new 1935 Act and was determined to ensure that 'no unreasonable advantage is taken of that discretion'.[58] Fear of the power of the airwaves to whip up provincial ardour was evident throughout the 1930s.

What is remarkable, however, is that despite such avocations, Linlithgow made no mention of AIR, broadcasting or, indeed, its Controller, in his inaugural speech. Instead he paid due deference to the powers of the press, accepting that if the Indian papers were to 'discharge their responsible duties towards the public, and to comment effectively upon current affairs, they require, whatever their editorial policy, to be informed as far as practicable upon the facts at issue'.[59] The lack of any reference to wireless can arguably be interpreted as a deliberate omission, an impression confirmed through a perusal of subsequent

Viceregal correspondence throughout his tenure, which reveals little evidence of concerted action to incorporate broadcasting into the Government agenda or to encourage creativity in its growth. Unlike print, there were few official attempts to develop broadcast publicity. To some extent the GoI's blinkered vision *vis-à-vis* radio might well have reflected the uncomfortable reality that they were hoist on their own petard having reiterated that the medium would be apolitical and non-partisan. Utilising it for overt political propaganda now would make it impossible for the Raj to maintain neutrality, balance the needs of speakers and vested interests, and not be accused of impropriety given that radio was a government monopoly. The BBC model, which the GoI expressly wished to emulate, had managed this balancing act with some success and its experience could have served as a convenient guide. Therefore it becomes pertinent to question how far this self-denying ordinance regarding radio in India became in effect a convenient excuse to ignore or delay developing the medium.

Just as the BBC's worldwide reputation is acknowledged to have been consolidated by the Second World War, so it was the impetus of large-scale conflict that galvanised a more spirited use of the radio in India in ways which are reminiscent of the impact of the Great War on attitudes towards the press.[60] The Viceroy broadcast from Delhi on 3 September 1939 that 'India is awake and armed'. During the war, the Commander in Chief frequently addressed the country – for instance, from the newly opened Simla station in May 1940, appealing for 'unity, courage and faith', and Tagore expounded on the horrors of war from Calcutta.[61] AIR devoted the week commencing 11 June 1940 to 'talks, discussions and plays bearing on the situation created by Italy's participation in the war and the collapse of the French army'. A month later a series of fortnightly talks entitled 'News from Berlin' was started from Lahore 'to counter German propaganda'.[62] By this stage, measures were undertaken, though not entirely successfully, to control listener habits by criminalising the act of receiving and publicising enemy broadcasts by private and commercial licence holders.[63] Meanwhile the war also provided an opportunity for nationalists to engage in a limited underground propaganda offensive through Subhas Chandra Bose's 'Azad Hind Radio'. Bose also infamously broadcast from Berlin in May 1942. The Quit India movement in 1942 saw the emergence of a short-lived clandestine wireless network with bulletins in English and Hindi/Hindustani aired under the signature line: 'This is the Congress Radio calling from somewhere in India.'[64]

Issues unconnected to the conflict were also covered. Thus Linlithgow inaugurated a series of talks entitled 'Tuberculosis in India' on 5 July 1940.[65] The Cripps mission in 1942 received considerable airtime, with Sir Stafford broadcasting on 30 March, arguing that 'it is for the Indian people and not for any outside authority, to discuss and decide their future constitution'. AIR also launched a campaign backing Professor Reginald Coupland's report into the future of constitutional reforms. The GoI defended such transmissions on the grounds that they served a legitimate public interest of popular education. Therefore it does beg the question, yet again, whether earlier inaction represented to a far greater degree than hitherto acknowledged official inertia as well as ineptitude to integrate broadcasting within an imperial service agenda. Indeed, it is difficult to refute the allegations made in 1937 that even a decade after the inauguration of the IBC, 'as a medium of instruction and propaganda, the influence of the radio [had been] potential rather than real'.[66]

Unsurprisingly, the BBC also had numerous programmes geared towards India and the war effort, including daily Hindustani broadcasts,[67] and 45 minutes were devoted every day to a series of more 'literary' General Talks in English, overseen by Zulfikar Bokhari, featuring a range of British cultural icons and Indians drawn from across the political and social spectrum. George Orwell was keenly associated with these broadcasts and defended their use of English, claiming that though the numbers reached were only about 5% of the Indian population, these programmes also appealed to other educated groups distributed across South and South East Asia as well as in the West. The participants included E. M. Forster, T. S. Eliot, Stephen Spender, Rebecca West, Professor Gordon Childe, Wickham Steed, Mulk Raj Anand and Narayana Menon. Their topics reflected an eclectic range from 'China's Literary revolution', 'Science and Magic', 'Tolstoy's Birthday', 'Microfilms' and 'The Man in the Street'. In addition, there was a range of more political programming, such as Princess Indira of Kapurthala's analysis of parliamentary debates in a weekly series entitled 'The Debate Continues', and 'Hello Punjab', involving contributions from Indian soldiers stationed in Britain. The widening reach of the English-language Indian press also served to add value to such initiatives.

Compared with the GoI, the IO had always been more enthusiastic about the rich potential of imperial propaganda via broadcasting. The Secretary of State urged Irwin in 1929:

> The more I think of it, the more important it seems to me, to develop broadcasting in India for political propaganda purposes. If it cannot

be made to pay, ought not the government to undertake it? How otherwise is the government case ever going to be heard?...before very long there will be a good deal of propaganda to be done when...the new reforms have been decided on. Is it not worth your while to try to have some machinery perfected in time?[68]

Similarly, in December 1931, Hoare wanted Willingdon to seriously consider the continuation of the Calcutta and Bombay stations despite their financial difficulties, 'for I am sure that if once broadcasting can be put securely on its feet, there is a great future for it in India, and if, in time, it makes sufficient progress to enable it to penetrate into the villages, it will provide an invaluable medium for propaganda'.[69] Likewise, Hugh MacGregor observed to Fielden: 'I can see you and your wireless doing more for India by broadcasts than Stephens or I singly or in combination.'[70] Writing in the preparatory stages of the 1935 Act, MacGregor presciently analysed its impact on broadcasting, contending that while hitherto policy had been determined largely by financial needs, under the reformed Constitution, politics would be the 'chief controlling factor'. While every effort had been made to ring-fence the powers of the Viceroy administratively,

we have done nothing officially to secure his position in relation to Indian opinion on which...the maintenance of the whole structure...must depend....there merely exists a vague idea that under the provisions made for his personal Staff he may be able to appoint a Press Secretary. This is applying a pill to an earthquake. Under the White Paper he is left as a super-Prime Minister without a Party to support his views and policies and without machinery to propagate his views, for the existing publicity machinery will automatically pass under the control of the Indian Ministry. Such a set of conditions demands for the success of the Reforms Scheme an acquiescent India, which we know does not exist and is unlikely to be evolved in the future. It is therefore imperative that the Governor General's position should be strengthened in relation to public opinion...[71]

One of the measures MacGregor considered seminal was the creation of a broadcasting system under the control of the Viceroy that would provide a crucial link to public opinion, especially in an emergency. He opined that the most efficacious system would be an Indian version of the BBC, politically independent but controlled by the Viceroy and its Charter. The needs of the provinces could be met, as in Britain, by the establishment of regional stations. MacGregor's plans offered one of the most astute insights into the broadcasting dilemma, and elements of this approach were to colour planning of the broadcasting structure under Fielden, though significant changes in official publicity strategy in peace times had to await Lord Mountbatten's arrival on the scene, as is discussed in Chapter 5.

The choice in the mid-1930s thus boiled down to central control with devolution or provincial control with cooperation and coordination. How provincial governments would be prevented from using the wireless for partisan politics became a pressing concern. Many were convinced that broadcasting would 'certainly be used as a political weapon if it is entirely controlled' by provincial ministries and utilised for 'anti-imperial purposes'.[72] The increasing impetus towards centralisation thus reflected official recognition that radio might become a battleground between the Centre and the provinces, as well as between different regional interests. Thus the need to institute centralised control became an imperative in the revisions to the 1935 Act. Since education, entertainment and information were already transferred subjects, the GoI could not force provinces into a central scheme of broadcasting against their will. Via Section 129 of the revised Act, broadcasting now became reserved in the federal list, ensuring control over its maintenance and development. The Centre would not 'unreasonably refuse' to entrust to a provincial government or federated state 'such functions with respect to broadcasting as may be necessary to enable them – a) to construct and use transmitters in the Province or State; [and] b) to regulate, and impose fees in respect of, the construction and use of transmitters and the use of receiving apparatus'.[73] The Federal government would not transfer control over the use and maintenance of extant transmitters but there was nothing to prevent provinces from establishing new ones. It was reiterated that policy was to be firmly the preserve of the Governor General, who also had final discretionary authority to act 'for the prevention of any grave menace to the peace or tranquillity of India … or as prohibiting the imposition on Governments or Rulers of such conditions regulating matter broadcast as appear to be necessary to enable the Governor-General to discharge his functions'. Despite provinces being bound by such sweeping central regulations, Section 129 also confirmed that it would 'not be lawful' for the Federal government to 'impose any conditions regulating the matter' broadcast by provincial ministries or Indian rulers.[74] Thus control over the content of programming was to be retained by the provinces, a situation which was inherently contentious but, given the context of devolved

Table 4.1 Growth of Radio Licences in British India, 1927–39

Year	Number of licences
1927	3,594
1928	6,152
1929	7,775
1930	7,719
1931	8,056
1932	8,557
1933	10,872
1934	16,179
1935	24,839
1936	37,797
1937	50,680
1938	64,480
1939	92,782

Source: Compiled from Broadcasting in India, pp. x–xiv.

government, probably inevitable. There was also a desire to encourage provinces to develop and finance their local services, addressing the problem of major linguistic differences which would make it virtually impossible for a central organisation to undertake programming for all India. Overall, whilst the service had to be developed under the circumstances of the new Constitution, there were no moves to delink direct government control (as opposed to overall supervision) of AIR, which remained firmly part of the formal institutions of the Raj (Table 4.1). (For a provincial distribution of licences, see Appendix II.)

The BBC and Indian Broadcasting

Reith and India

This section seeks to highlight the influence of the BBC under John Reith upon the development of Indian broadcasting. Inevitably, this will also involve a discussion, albeit brief, of BBC broadcasting to India as well as its broadcasts about India to a domestic audience in Britain, a theme we also return to later in the chapter when discussing BBC periodicals and Indian coverage (Figure 4.1).

From the early 1920s there had been interest expressed at the BBC, chiefly in the person of Reith, to explore the potentialities of broadcasting in India. Reith admitted in 1923, when Managing Director of the British Broadcasting Company, that 'I should like to organise Indian

Figure 4.1 Sir John Reith, director general of the BBC, leaving the annexe of Westminster Abbey, London, after superintending the broadcast arrangements for the coronation service, 3 May 1937, reproduced by permission of Associated Press Corporate Archives, London and New York, AP photo

broadcasting from here.'[75] Asa Briggs has argued that this reflected his 'international ambition ... to develop Empire broadcasting'.[76] Later, as Director General of the BBC, Reith expended heroic efforts to encourage the development of a viable Indian system, his interest being infused by a desire to include her within the ambit of the imperial family: as Malcolm Frost, the BBC representative visiting India in 1933 to gauge the reception of the BBC Empire Service (ES), argued, 'the practical justification was the establishment of a sentimental link between residents in the overseas dependencies and the Mother country and the fostering of British propaganda using the word in its widest sense'.[77] As a passionate advocate of empire (though he referred to himself as a Gladstonian liberal), Reith was convinced of the desirability of imperial unity. From the mid-1930s the expansion of broadcasting was also urged, according to Briggs, on the grounds that this unity was being threatened 'not so much by the natural development of movements towards self-government inside it as by the machinations of other great powers'.[78]

Indian listeners had to be insulated against foreign encroachment by stealth. Whilst within Britain, as John MacKenzie has noted, Reithian broadcasting attempted to 'educate the public to a national consensus which included a royal and imperial ethos as part of an immutable order'.[79]

Yet while these issues were indisputably vital, it was also the case that Reith saw in the wireless a weapon to establish a new order of cultural modernity helping in the process to address the vast problems besetting the subcontinent due to mass illiteracy and poor communications. He was convinced that broadcasting could be 'the determining factor in the future of India – the integrator'.[80] His perspective was infused with a Christian zeal, reinforced by the example of his brother Douglas, a missionary and English teacher at Hislop College, Nagpur, during 1907–12. It is significant that Reith's views reflected not just faith in the imperial enterprise and a passion for broadcasting, but also an abiding interest in India *per se* (though he had turned down the job of General Manager for a Scottish engineering firm in Bombay in 1919).[81] Reith was frequently consulted by the IO to evaluate its broadcast policies, as will be discussed later,[82] and had even contemplated taking over the radio helm directly, in response to a request from Willingdon in 1934.

It was the Viceregal job, however, which Reith coveted as 'one of the very few in the world really worth having',[83] an ambition that never quite left him. He entertained little self-doubt as to his suitability for the post but there is no evidence that he was ever a serious contender. Reith's views about the seminal importance of India were made apparent to Fielden in a farewell letter before the latter's departure: 'You certainly realized the supreme responsibility which is committed to you and what you have it in your power to do. I don't know that anyone – not excluding the Viceroy – can do for India what you can.'[84] Reith's own passage to India did eventually materialise a decade later when he flew from Ceylon to Delhi on his way back from the Antipodes: 'It was extraordinary to be flying over India – India!'[85] He spent a week as the Viceroy Lord Wavell's guest and was much impressed by the imperial grandeur on offer. The subsequent announcement of Britain's imminent departure was a personal blow:

> What upset me far more than their decision to evacuate by June 1948 was that Mountbatten had been made viceroy . . . So that is the job I most wanted on earth gone for good. It is not just a cleaning up. More can be done by the viceroy in the next year than in the last hundred.[86]

Reith's final visit to north India and Pakistan took place during the winter of 1963, where in Delhi he met with President Radhakrishnan, remarking: 'one wished all Presidents were such as he, with his tremendous background of philosophical learning'.[87]

Yet, whilst at the helm of the BBC, Reith's relationship with the GoI had been less than sanguine. In 1924 and 1925 during a visit to London, the Viceroy Lord Reading was invited to explore broadcasting potentialities with the BBC but turned the offer down.[88] Earlier, when Lord Chancellor, Reading had 'unwittingly got involved in a scandal about pushing the shares' of the Marconi Company of which his brother Godfrey Isaacs was Joint Director, and Parathasarathy Gupta has argued that this made him wary of further involvement.[89] Similar overtures to the IO during the 1920s were also politely rebuffed. Frustrated Reith confided to his diary:

> There is neither vision nor recognition of the immense potentialities of broadcasting: no ethical or moral appreciation; just commercialism. It is an unparalleled opportunity for service in India, but they have let the chance go.[90]

Reading's successor was approached in 1931 with the suggestion that he broadcast a short series of talks on contemporary developments. Yet Irwin prevaricated, contending that he 'felt worried; doubted if it would be advisable; thought on the whole he had better not'.[91] This overall lack of enthusiasm was deeply frustrating, for whilst the BBC's 'aid and advice' had been widely sought by other countries, 'there has been little or nothing of the sort from official India where, perhaps above all countries, the beneficent power of this service might most be felt'.[92] Tellingly, even after the establishment of the ES, there was 'no official discussion of the larger issues of a proper service' within the subcontinent.[93]

Reith claimed the ES was the 'most spectacular success' in the history of the BBC, with Cecil Graves as its director and J. B. Clark as his deputy.[94] Briggs contends that few departments 'enjoyed such autonomy in their early years. Few also enjoyed such outside influence.'[95] Though this area has received scholarly attention, nevertheless India has been largely sidelined in these studies. In terms of the future of broadcasting in the subcontinent, the ES represented something akin to 'the Dame Nellie Melba moment' in Britain when her opera broadcast from the Marconi Works in Chelmsford in June 1920 became 'a turning point in the public response to radio. It caught people's imagination.'[96] The ES was to prove equally popular, India taking part for the first time when the King's speech was relayed to the subcontinent at Christmas 1932. At the same time a special half-hour programme was broadcast from Bombay to England and the US comprising a short speech by the Governor, some Indian music and a running commentary relaying street scenes. The ES became a lifeline for Europeans and Indian elites as evidenced in the rush to purchase new sets, which, given an import duty of 50%, also helped boost funds for official coffers. Customs revenue rose from Rs 56,000 in 1932 to Rs 4 lakhs in 1934, an expansion 'mainly due to improved reception of programmes from the BBC rather than improved programming within India'.[97] The rise in the number of licences tells its own story: from 8,557 at the end of 1932, it doubled in two years to 16,179 and reached almost 25,000 in 1935. In addition to covering India-related stories in Britain, the BBC also commissioned programmes such as the 'Matters of Moment' series beginning in October 1937, which featured such distinguished commentators as Edward Thompson and Sir Philip Chetwode.

Despite a frustratingly slow rate of progress, the BBC continued to engage with Indian issues in the 'hope that some far greater activity may be planned'.[98] This was made more challenging by the lack of a coherent national policy or a 'national' broadcasting authority in India. BBC staff corresponded regularly with their counterparts in the fledgling provincial stations, proffered advice and technical expertise, carried out detailed surveys and extended the services of a succession of its employees to senior management and technical posts.[99] In an attempt to locate some overarching themes permeating the BBC's response, it is productive to use the Reithian framework of public service broadcasting as enunciated in his *Broadcast over Britain* and developed further in his memoirs, *Into the Wind*. From the beginning it was felt, given the size and diversity of India as well as the enormous potential of the medium, that central control and coordination were essential for utmost efficiency. Around the same time as *Broadcast* appeared, the Sykes Committee had concluded that 'the control of such a potential power over public opinion and the life of the nation ought to remain with the state, and that the operation of so important a national service ought not to be allowed to become an unrestricted commercial monopoly'.[100] It is revealing to note how several key members of this Committee, in addition to Reith, came to be directly associated with India: its Chairman, Major General Sir Sykes became Governor of

Figure 4.2   Broadcasting House, BBC Headquarters, London, 6 June 1936, reproduced by permission of Associated Press Corporate Archives, London and New York, AP photo

Bombay; Viscount Burnham, Chairman of the Newspaper Proprietors Association, was appointed to the Indian Statutory Commission; and J. J. Astor, who as President of the EPU had, as I have argued elsewhere, a continuing preoccupation with the development of the Indian press.[101]

Astor and Burnham were also proprietors of *The Times* and the *Telegraph*, respectively.

For Reith, state control was not the ideal option, preferring instead a private–public partnership such as the form of institutional experiment inaugurated by the BBC of a 'public corporation'.[102] However, by the early 1930s it was apparent that conditions in India were too markedly different for this ever to materialise and the BBC reluctantly concluded that it did not 'now feel so sanguine that a self-supporting system' could be organised there. Broadcasting would perforce need to be a government subsidy but, notwithstanding this, the BBC maintained that an efficiently organised service could yet be developed.[103] A centrally controlled institution, as epitomised in the rebranding of the ISBS as AIR, and with headquarters in the capital, served to embody this change of perspective.

It is useful to underline the fact that discussions over radio within the Raj were marked by the absence of a detailed policy framework regarding broadcasting or the role of an officially owned and controlled service. Given the bureaucratic propensity of the imperial mind, this lacuna is puzzling. Was the service to optimise commercial returns or to function as a public subsidy with moral responsibilities? And who was the service intended for? Was AIR ever about all India? Underlying the Reithian conception was a strong sense of uniting the nation behind a common and shared cultural experience. According to Reith the IBC appeared to reveal little sign of 'moral or ethical responsibility which is, or ought to be, inherent'. He was convinced that broadcasting 'might exercise a great influence in India; it might even be a determining factor in the future state of the country'. Nevertheless, it was necessary 'to have high regard to public service obligations'.[104] Yet was this possible, even if desirable, in British India?

Some assessments along these lines have been offered in the previous section which focused on the response of the Raj. However, what was the BBC's own input? Some of the first in-depth policy papers emanating from Savoy Hill on India were produced at the behest of Lord Burnham, who was 'enormously interested' in the light of his impending role on the Indian Statutory Commission.[105] Dated 26 September 1928, the resultant memorandum reveals strategic lines of thought pertinent to appreciating contemporary attitudes as well as the developing relationship between the BBC and the Raj. India, claimed the BBC, was 'essentially a country (or continent) of village communities, and therefore, adapted to communal listening'. The challenge of reaching the masses was more akin to that of Russia than Europe. Russian broadcasting stations enjoyed 'an implicit government backing' with the output directed at the 'village loudspeaker, which thus becomes a focus of the life of the community'.[106] However, the main difference with India was that 'the hand of the Government must not be obvious', with 'popular confidence' being an 'absolutely indispensable factor' in the success of broadcasting.[107] A purely government service with an obvious official agenda would struggle to achieve the level of confidence needed for success. This ideology of popular acceptance, even within an imperial context, was a critical aspect of the BBC's critique, and a concern with popular sensibilities is reflected throughout these years in its approach to the subcontinent.

Five years later, when Frost visited India he noted that whilst talks were the best form of 'direct propaganda', these could not become 'too obvious' as the 'obvious glorification' of the empire was 'likely to cause irritations'. 'Desirable' talks could include descriptions of English life and institutions, country and historic buildings, as well as general political and economic topics, but these should be 'of a simple elementary nature'. There was a widespread impression in India that the BBC standard was 'definitely too specialised', with the talks 'directed by experts to experts'. Instead, Frost contended that the 'standard of the Daily Mail or Pearsons Magazine was more suitable than that of the Times!'.[108] In institutional terms, it was suggested that the GoI should create 'an all-India organisation catering for the masses, which it can influence and possibly underwrite, but need not openly direct or subsidise'.[109] As developments in the 1930s demonstrate, and as the analysis of Fielden's tenure below will highlight, such an approach in the imperial context proved a challenging proposition, and one which the GoI was reluctant to pursue. Yet this position *vis-à-vis* broadcasting stands in stark contrast to official attitudes towards print. Despite a long history of repression coupled with various strategies to achieve a good press, as I have discussed elsewhere, the GoI never seriously attempted to set up and run its own national newspaper.

Another significant BBC-inspired debate which had a significant impact on the development trajectory of Indian broadcasting took place during 1936 and involved two of its senior technical experts, H. L. Kirke and Cecil W. Goyder. Kirke was Head of BBC Research and had been seconded from January to May 1936 to assist Fielden with the setting-up of the New Delhi operations. Goyder replaced Kirke and was appointed Chief Engineer of AIR, remaining *in situ* for a decade till Independence. The main issues concerned the nature of the service as well as its primary audience. Kirke worked in close cooperation with Fielden

and his Report had the full assent of the Controller, such that its recommendations can be taken as a joint production. They considered it
crucial to regard the ISBS as 'more or less a commercial undertaking
and not as a social service'. This in turn raised the issue of its audience. Was radio to be directed primarily towards urban centres which
might provide licence revenues, or to the rural areas that arguably 'are
more in need of broadcasting' but where the ability to participate in the
listening process was stymied by comparatively greater poverty? Could
not a compromise between the two publics provide the ideal solution,
with the costs of the rural service being offset, to an extent, by the revenues derived from the urban fee-payers? However, in order to proceed
on either account, it was important to establish a self-supporting service. As the Report affirmed, 'If broadcasting is to develop as it should,
the Service must have a life of its own and strength to survive budgetary fluctuations. In the early stages at least, vitality can come only
from the body of sophisticated listeners who are prepared to pay for
their entertainment.'[110] Goyder's views differed from Kirke's Report with
respect to the rationale for the expansion of broadcasting. Goyder maintained that the primary need was to make AIR truly all India in coverage.
Limited funds dictated that initially 'at least a second grade service'
for all India should be provided, to be supplemented later with 'a first
grade medium wave service at important centres'. Thus Goyder envisaged a two-tier system of expansion and was against the use of only
medium-wave transmitters to provide a high-quality but restricted service. Eventually the essence of Goyder's vision prevailed and laid the
basis for the further expansion of AIR. New transmitters came into operation in Lahore and Delhi in 1937 and in Bombay, Lucknow, Madras
and Calcutta in 1938.

Meanwhile, Reith had managed, eventually, to cajole the GoI to
undertake a major overhaul of broadcasting, and during the summer
of 1934 under his directive a detailed memorandum was produced for
the IO. Many of its key recommendations were subsequently adopted in
spirit, if not in every detail, with one of the most important being Reith's
insistence on centralised control – both 'technical control' and 'control of policy' – as 'very desirable in the interests of both efficiency and
economy'.[111] As discussed earlier, whilst centralisation was instituted in
1935, it was tempered by having to allow significant provincial autonomy regarding programming. The best that the GoI could hope for was
some form of coordination by consent.

At this juncture, and contrary to Reith's prior disappointing encounters with Viceroys, Willingdon turned out to be 'most pleasant and

intelligent and very much interested'.[112] During meetings in London in the summer of 1934, and whilst admitting that he had not hitherto taken 'much interest', Willingdon now appeared energised, promising to make amends: 'You and I together will pull this through', he reassured Reith.[113] Later that autumn, and largely as a result of Viceregal initiative, plans for creating the post of Controller of Indian Broadcasting began to materialise. 'As you deliberately aroused my enthusiasm for broadcasting,' Willingdon admitted to Reith, 'I would like to have ... the guidance of one of your best lieutenants.' What was required was a 'superman' who would need 'great tact, and a complete sympathy with the Indian point of view', as well as having to 'make the best' of a department which 'has been badly starved in the past'.[114]

However, despite Willingdon painting on a broad canvas, in reality we witness the limited perspective of an imperial bureaucracy which envisaged merely 'an Administrative Expert' to control the Delhi station as well as to 'advise' the GoI on the future of broadcasting.[115] As is apparent from the ensuing protracted negotiations, there was considerable ambiguity about what precisely was being envisaged, with officials clearly uneasy and swimming in uncharted territory. D. G. Mitchell, Secretary to the GoI, explained to the Indian High Commissioner, Sir B. N. Mitra, in November 1934 that the Controller would be 'expected to make suggestions' to GoI and local governments regarding 'the most suitable means' for developing broadcasting, and that he would need to have 'a more intimate knowledge of broadcasting, particularly on the programme side'. However, at the same time, since the service would remain an official undertaking, 'the general lines of policy' would be laid down by the GoI.[116] This attitude provoked Reith to confide to his diary that Willingdon's earlier correspondence 'gave quite an inaccurate picture of what they require. Instead of the superman which he asked for ... all they want now is a man to run the New Delhi station' and to 'supervise' the ones at Bombay and Calcutta.[117] Reith was unable to accept the Viceroy's invitation to visit India in this connection due to other pressing commitments, but he did offer the BBC's South African blueprint as a model to consider for India.[118] For Reith and the BBC a longer-term programme of growth was essential but, without a clearer sense of what the future of Indian broadcasting was to be, it proved difficult to suggest nominees for the post of Controller: 'The responsibility is so great and so much depends on having the right man.'[119] Further, the BBC's approach, however amenable to Willingdon, appeared to cause concern amongst the ICS cadres:

The BBC seem to contemplate a broadcasting dictator; but what we want is an expert head of a technical department, who will do the usual spadework. We have plenty of ideas about general policy, and so have local Governments, and we can supply all the local knowledge needed and keep the expert on the right lines in these matters.[120]

Yet between the summer of 1934 and the spring of 1935 there appeared to have been a discernible shift in official *mentalité*. Sir Frank Noyce, Head of the DIL, affirmed in 1934: 'This expert will be the keystone of the whole structure.'[121] And a year later when questioned in the Legislative Assembly about the process of selection of the new Controller, Mitchell himself, now Noyce's successor, supported the views that the incumbent would be 'the expert' with the GoI on programmes and a general adviser. In explaining why the post was not advertised in India, Mitchell argued that they wanted to 'take advantage of the enormously greater experience' of the BBC which was 'generally admitted to be the most successful broadcasting institution in the world'.[122] He also emphasised that it was the Government's 'intention' to run the ISBS 'on the same lines and principles' as the BBC.[123]

Thus from the vantage position of the BBC, when Fielden set sail for India, the winds of change had begun to blow, however gently, in its favour. Official pronouncements now suggested that Reith's previous misgivings regarding the remit of the post had been replaced by a conviction that what was finally on offer was the opportunity to achieve a much more ambitious programme of creative growth on the BBC model. Ever eager to take the accolade for such developments, Reith confided in his diary: 'Apparently I made a great impression on him [the Viceroy] and everything that is happening about broadcasting in India seems to be due to me.'[124] Characteristically, he also took entire credit for the amendment to the Bill (eventuating in the GoI Act 1935) establishing federal control over broadcasting: 'that is certainly due to me. I had been told by the India Office that it would be quite impossible'.[125]

The Fielden Years, 1935–40

The *Statesman* published a fulsome eulogy of Fielden upon the publication of the first official *Report on the Progress of Broadcasting in India*, which was largely written and compiled by him. Fielden had 'done his job superlatively', claimed the paper, and had succeeded in 'putting India on the Radio Map of the world', ignoring the irony that several months before the article's publication his contract had been terminated early and he had conceded defeat to his *bête noire*: the GoI.[126] In his memoir Fielden conveyed a different picture of his Indian tenure, which he likened to being caught in the middle of 'an Asiatic rugby scrum': 'Malice and intrigue and lack of reliability on the Indian side, a tepid, even obstructive attitude on the Government side', combined with his own 'perhaps excessive impatience and enthusiasm reduces me at times to the last stages of irritation'.[127] While home on leave during July 1937, he had published two anonymous and damning critiques of the state of Indian broadcasting in *The Times*, which the paper followed up with a supportive editorial. Fielden also complained to the Secretary of State that 'his enthusiasm met with little encouragement from higher authority'.[128] He was to bemoan similarly to Frost: 'Things here seem to be moving more slowly and with greater difficulty than ever. I almost despair of the possibility of establishing anything like an efficient broadcasting service in this country.'[129] Two years later, Fielden remained as dissatisfied, writing to Sir Cecil Graves, Director of the Empire Department at the BBC,

> It is all a case of here lies the man who tried to hurry the East and there is not much to be done about it...I find it very difficult to be happy when I am completely divorced as I have to be from all aesthetic interests...Most of my time is taken up by fighting desperately for money, adjusting budgets, looking after publications, trying to build up an organisation which may be reasonably secure against dictators, whether bureaucratic or otherwise, and endeavouring to conduct publicity without a publicity department.[130]

Even accounting for Fielden's flair for the dramatic, his analysis offers unique insights into the institutional and policy context of broadcasting as well as the interplay of structure and human agency in an imperial setting.

Fielden was born on 15 May 1896, educated at Eton and Oxford, saw active service in Gallipoli, Egypt and Palestine during the Great War, and afterwards worked for the FO as interpreter at the League of Nations and with the High Commission for Refugees in Greece and Turkey. He joined the BBC in 1927 and succeeded almost immediately in impressing senior staff, such as Hilda Matheson, Director of General Talks, who wrote how Fielden had 'shown himself peculiarly suited to our work and to our requirements...He is particularly tactful and therefore particularly successful in his personal dealing with speakers.'[131] Later backing him for promotion, she made another ringing endorsement: 'He is exceptionally intelligent and ready with sound and original ideas. His past work experience... as well as his interests and his contacts, have been extremely useful to us.... he has good judgement and a good manner with people of varying kinds.'[132] Promoted to work as special assistant to Charles Siepmann at the end of 1929, his remit involved providing 'ideas' for Talks programmes, producing 'special Talks features and stimulating and criticising the content and execution of Talks throughout the Branch'.[133] He received glowing reports after only a month in the new post: 'He has a freshness of outlook and a standard of criticism as high as it should be... and he combines this with peculiar gifts for handling speakers.'[134] Two years later, Matheson had again nothing but high praise: 'He is much more than an "ideas merchant"... I would always trust his judgement on the right lines for any given talk, its handling and presentation and its implications.'[135]

With the passage of time, such ringing commendations were tempered by an acknowledgement that Fielden was 'not by temperament or constitution an office worker', though he had managed 'to combine a high degree of imaginative inventiveness with a considerable volume of routine work'.[136] However, Fielden remained 'the outstanding original mind' within Talks, where he was 'irreplaceable and a tower of strength for us'.[137] As an 'originator' Fielden deserved the 'highest praise', yet he was 'not a good head of a department. He is dangerously high strung.' It is imperative to underline, nevertheless, that Siepmann followed this critique by concluding that this was 'the price we must pay for exceptional originality of mind', acknowledging how Fielden was 'ruthless in his expectations of himself and in his concern for BBC standards... on balance we win hands down by his services'.[138] By early 1935, Siepmann had reason to be more optimistic, concluding that Fielden had 'matured a lot. His judgement is more sober and more reliable. He has shown an increasing capacity for handling people and for inspiring them with his own flair for broadcasting. I regard him as ripe for more senior office and responsibility.'[139] Such an evaluation assumes greater significance given that it was made independently, at a time when Fielden was being considered for the post of Indian Controller. Overall, therefore, the BBC recognised Fielden's exceptional talent, acknowledged his development as a broadcaster, admitted his shortcomings but expressed an unequivocal willingness to work around them.

Ironically, Fielden's arrival at the BBC had coincided with Dunstan's departure for India, and he had 'envied' the latter's experience of, as he put it rather flippantly, 'transmitting barbaric music on bejewelled instruments to a population of Indian princes in the intervals of holding profound converse with sages of charms and infinite wisdom'.[140] Eight years later, when searching for pastures anew, Fielden became 'bitten with the Indian idea'. The allure of organising broadcasting for an entire subcontinent proved irresistible, though he was mature enough to appreciate that his enthusiasm was in marked contrast to his lack of specific expertise: 'I did not know India, or any Indian language, my knowledge of broadcasting was lop-sided.' Tellingly, he also admitted to be

> fatally undecided whether Broadcasting in India was Fun or Mission.... Emotion and vanity told me that I was a Saviour, speeding to the rescue of poor black people, to whom I should be frightfully nice ... Ambition told me that I was capable of creating a much better service than the BBC. I was in a constant state of falling between all these stools.

Fielden spent months diligently attempting to acquire engineering skills, Urdu and Sanskrit grammar – he was a gifted linguist, being fluent in French, German and Italian – as well as acquainting himself with imperial policy by perusing the mighty tome of the GoI Act 1935. He was staggered to discover that despite the complexity of issues tackled therein, there was little that engaged specifically with the exciting opportunities thrown up by broadcasting: 'Surely, in this immense, sprawling, illiterate country, broadcasting could educate, unify, and direct as no other medium could. The spoken word could run like fire once again through India.' He read the Act's views on broadcasting, much like Reith had, less as inaugurating a new vision and far more as an attempt to preserve the *status quo*. Potentially the most worrisome aspect for Fielden was that it portended not a unified broadcasting network but quite the opposite: 'Every Government and every Prince could cash in on the new medium ... unless Indian broadcasting could, within the next year or two, acquire, so to speak, an All India Personality, which would hold it together.'[141]

Reith had backed Fielden for the job and shared some of the same drive – he had been 38 (compared with Fielden's 39) when he became Director General. Reith was aware that his protégé, though 'brilliant', was not a run-of-the-mill administrator, and worried about adverse reactions from sun-dried civil servants. In a farewell letter, Reith had issued a prescient warning 'to tread very delicately, and to be very wary ... Its therefore not just temperament but your temperament conditioned and controlled that is wanted.'[142] Fielden corresponded weekly with Reith, as Dunstan had before him, and Reith admitted that he 'encouraged him to blow off steam on me and I do the best I can to help him, writing him long letters which sometimes seem to me rather sermonising, but which, apparently, are helpful to him'.[143] Fielden was grateful for Reith's 'constantly cheer[ing] me with wise letters';[144] however, even the optimistic mentor began despairing as the years progressed and Fielden failed to grapple with the complexities of the Raj.[145] Thus at a meeting in London during July 1937, Reith confided in his diary: 'Told him not to trail his coat, not to fraternize so much with Indians, not to make rackets about things which don't matter...and such like advice – all of which he said he would take.'[146] Unfortunately, as discussed below, Fielden was temperamentally unsuited for a patient long game, working within an imperial juggernaut where control and conformity rather than creativity were the watchwords.

Fielden's enthusiasm took an early blow, both metaphorically and physically, in the heat of the monsoon soon after disembarkation at Bombay at the end of August 1935. He was appalled at the primitive state of its broadcasting centre where the 'atmosphere', he claimed, resembled that of 'a bankrupt brothel', and the three main requirements for studio purposes – silence, ventilation and acoustics – were conspicuous by their absence.[147] Fielden was equally disappointed by the lacklustre approach of the Indians during his tours of inspection around the country in the first few months of his term. Understaffed, underfinanced, lacking in training or creative sense of purpose, it became apparent why, despite the potential for millions of listeners, its broadcasting service had only about fifteen thousand. Low investment in programming meant lower standards of output, which was intrinsically deleterious to the growth of a medium which required for its success to attract and retain the enthusiasm of a growing audience. He also formed an entirely unflattering opinion of the ICS with respect to its general attitude to Indians but also specifically in its disregard for the creativity of broadcasting. Thus Fielden's sense of mission was up against formidable obstacles from the start in terms of poor infrastructure and equipment, as well as the prevailing civil service mindset.

Fielden reluctantly came to accept the catalytic role of political patrons within the gargantuan bureaucratic system that was the Raj: 'To get the ear of the masses, and pour into that ear the wisdom of its own great men...that was the first, the crucial, point.' In order to accomplish this he needed to 'get the ear' of the Viceroy without which 'I was done for. I felt sure that, under a benign Viceregal eye, Indian broadcasting could begin to flourish: without it, never.' Willingdon was 'genial, kind and sympathetic' and approved Fielden's plans: 'I had an entrée to the Viceroy's house at any hour.'[148] To such high-profile support, Fielden could add that of Lord Brabourne, Governor of Bombay and later of Bengal. Unfortunately, the first few months of Fielden's tenure were also Willingdon's last, and Brabourne was to die suddenly in Calcutta. Linlithgow, by contrast, was taciturn and remote, 'a rather old fashioned British aristocrat, with a public school boy's sense of duty, but lacking in "political imagination" and "sensitiveness"'.[149] A stickler for protocol, he was guided almost entirely by successive Members of his Council, all with questionable degrees of enthusiasm for radio. Fielden confirmed to Reith how Linlithgow's secretary 'has written me a polite note to say that I "must not discuss cases with him directly, but through the Departments"'.[150] Personal factors also appeared to cloud official judgement. Clow's fervent Presbyterianism made him hostile to rumours of Fielden's homosexuality.[151] Such homophobic undercurrents were not, of course, the preserve of the Raj. Francis King, a young writer visiting Fielden after the Second World War at his villa in Antella, recalled how 'a homosexual, even a charming, intelligent, Rolls-Royce-owning, English one, tended to be mal vu in Florentine society'.[152]

Linlithgow's assessment of Fielden after just a year's infrequent acquaintance bears testimony to the blinkered vision which bedevilled the civil service approach to both the man and the medium. The Controller was 'by no means an easy problem', claimed Linlithgow, having

> precisely the qualities of imagination, and the capacity for planning ahead, which are in my view so essential at this stage for the development of broadcasting in India. These qualities unfortunately are counter-balanced by a very marked incapacity to submit to the control of Government and of the official machine and a very marked deficiency on the administrative side.[153]

Linlithgow also asserted that Fielden did not inspire those around him and provided little support as a mentor – claims that are contradicted by the successive assessments at the BBC referred to earlier. To accuse Fielden of lacking the bureaucratic skills of an experienced civil servant, as Linlithgow did, was not just unfair but also revealed the crux of the ICS hostility. Though the Viceroy was forced to admit that there was 'no one in the official world at the moment who could take his place' and that Fielden had exceptional qualities of 'imagination and capacity for taking a broad view', less than two years into Fielden's five-year contract, Linlithgow was already contemplating his successor.[154] 'It is an awful pity', Reith remarked, 'that the Viceroy is not friendly to him.'[155] Reith, in his turn, often wrote in unequivocal support of his protégé – for example, in October 1937, affirming to Linlithgow how 'He had done excellent work here and as far as we were concerned would have been with us still had he not gone to India.'[156] Such views, supported by several other personal testimonies from contemporaries within India, paints a compelling picture supporting Fielden's recurrent laments that he lacked encouragement and support from the Viceroy and his entourage.[157]

The success of any enterprise must also depend on the quality of supporting staff, and unfortunately the low pay and poor morale were monumental disadvantages. The small wages meant inevitably that recruitment was limited to the lower echelons of the education ladder. Whilst the fact that it was a state enterprise afforded a modicum of stability, it also meant that broadcasting was subject to any economies that the GoI might see fit to impose. Before Fielden's arrival, broadcasting had been delivering a profit, yet operating within the DIL meant that he did not have access to the full budget or control over how it was allocated. Most critically, not all the profits derived from broadcasting were ploughed back into its development, and only a small proportion made their way into Fielden's hands. Inevitably, he began to 'skirmish with Authority':

> The studio premises were appalling, the rates of pay were enough to degrade any organisation, and the whole business of building up a broadcasting network was generally regarded as wasteful and unnecessary. I had to fight for every penny.[158]

Exceptional amongst the ranks of the ICS was the Finance Member, Sir John Grigg, who oversaw the largest single dose of capital injected into broadcasting – 40 lakhs or about £300,000 during 1936. Nevertheless, this represented but a drop in the ocean. Kirke argued that this sum was 'negligible' when compared with England, where the expenditure amounted to 'well over 100 lakhs for transmitting stations alone', whilst within Europe – which in size was more akin to the subcontinent – there were over 100 stations operating at a cost of around ten crores.[159] Further, the DIL and Home Department's attitude to hiring new staff indicated a disregard for the specific needs of broadcasting. This was well exemplified by its treatment of news.

Whilst the GoI had given assurances at his appointment that Fielden would have in place 'an adequate staff under him at Delhi',[160] in reality this never materialised. Fielden's aim to build a professional news service with a strong editorial team for AIR seemed legitimate given the major expansion envisaged with the setting-up of the flagship studios in Delhi. Yet his demands were met with scepticism, as Hallett admitted: 'I am possibly unduly cynical about Broadcasting and sceptical as to the pace with which it will develop.'[161] The ISBS had utilised Reuters and API both organisations being considered 'generally reliable'; more importantly, as Hallet acknowledged, 'we have established a fairly effective control over them'.[162] (The Viceroy noted how 'we give a good deal of financial help to Reuters and to the API'.)[163] Advocating the continuance of this system, Hallet contended that as far as 'news' was concerned, 'it seems to me pure waste of money to employ an experienced journalist'.[164] Confronted with such attitudes, MacGregor could sympathise with Fielden's predicament, noting how the essential prerequisites of selection and compression of news fit for broadcast were 'amongst the most skilled in journalism' and helped impart the 'right tone' to the news. Thus a professional news editor 'can influence opinion to an important degree without any possible charge of propaganda or any proved charge of unfairness'.[165] The GoI further suggested that if such appointments became inevitable, the Public Service Commission ought to carry out the recruitment, despite the organisation patently having no experience and little awareness of the requirements of radio, and the fact that, as Fielden noted, broadcasting required 'rather a combination of qualities than a set of qualifications'.[166] Eventually he managed to secure a skeletal staff at Delhi – Charles Barns from London was recruited as News Editor in 1937 and was to remain in post till just after Independence – but appointees continued to be poorly paid, on temporary contracts and forced to operate within a miniscule budget. Thus Fielden's despondency knew no relief, as demonstrated by his correspondence with MacGregor later that year: 'The whole picture is gloomy in the extreme. I don't really know what the Government of India wants, but, between their obstructionism and Indian offensiveness ... I cannot feel that broadcasting will make any headway whatsoever.'[167]

Broadcasting needed to construct its own frames of reference, but this was considered neither feasible nor desirable by the Raj. The perennial conflict between creative imagination and administrative efficiency was further complicated by the politics of communalism in the 1930s. The need to maintain a balanced communal intake when hiring Indians was paramount, and appointments were regularly scrutinised by Indian members of the Assembly – a system which militated against the requirements of creativity and aptitude as selection criteria. The output of AIR, serving an audience of mixed communities had also to 'preserve a strictly non communal attitude'. For instance, despite the fact that stations at Lahore and Peshawar serving an essentially Muslim audience 'cannot help reflecting the kind of culture which predominates', a concerted attempt was made to avoid exclusively Muslim or Hindu modes of presentation. Readings from the Quran, or naats and qawwalis which were recognised as distinct Islamic forms of music, were balanced by bhajans and kirtans considered its Hindu and Sikh counterparts, and festivals of all communities were marked in equal measure.[168]

The regulations and circumlocution proscribing the functioning of the Raj were also at odds with the demands of a fast-paced and flexible broadcasting scenario; instead it served to stifle initiative and multiplied routine correspondence. 'I must have covered positively miles of paper with facts,' recalled Fielden, but the process 'never in the least helped me to decide what the dickens Indian broadcasting was *for*'.[169] Any suggestion of speed was eschewed by the ICS: 'They had to pass the baby around, and sometimes to let it quietly die ... I therefore went in person to badger officials ... and they did not like it.'[170] The demands of official scrutiny meant, for instance, having a programme schedule fixed weeks if not months in advance, a virtually impossible task given the nascent state of broadcasting and the paucity of resources. Fielden eventually confessed failure: 'I could not stop the growth of red tape or the accumulation of a deadly routine.'[171]

Censorship was imposed with a fanaticism that left little scope for originality. With scope for wide and rapid transmission, radio had, from its inception, justified prebroadcast censorship in imperial eyes, since, as Coatman remarked, it was going to be 'an infinitely more powerful agency for good or bad' than the press, hence the 'vital importance of starting and keeping it on the right lines'.[172] Irwin had been insistent that the GoI would 'retain very wide powers of supervision and control' over the IBC and could impose 'special directions' regarding programme content. His justification of the process was that it would ensure a 'high standard and an elevating tone'.[173] Nevertheless, it is significant that when in 1927 the GoI's proposal for banning all political broadcasts had first been mooted, not all provincial administrations had concurred. The governments of Madras and Burma argued that, provided material was not prohibited on the grounds of public interest, political speeches and announcements should be permitted.[174] Further, as the Governor of Assam pointed out, 'in dealing with political matter it is impossible to draw the line between what is reasonable and what is not, and...therefore, the alternatives are either to bar all political matter, including Government propaganda, or to allow everything which does not constitute a breach of the criminal law'.[175] The ban was eventually approved, and the GoI reserved emergency powers to disseminate information or combat misrepresentation in 'exceptional or critical circumstances'.[176]

Despite legislation banning the use of broadcasting to further specific political agendas, in practice it became notoriously problematic to judge what constituted unacceptable political content. Seeking guidance from the precedents established at the BBC, and its handbook for controversial topics, Fielden explained how in 1938, with the newly elected INC ministries in control of seven provinces, the situation was 'particularly difficult and delicate'. On the one hand the GoI was 'excessively bureaucratic & cautious & nervous'; on the other, the Indian ministers, 'unless they are lulled into some sort of belief that they are not excluded from the radio, are likely to take steps to build their own stations & thus ruin the central control altogether'.[177] However, unlike in Britain, officials 'won't speak and if they won't speak its difficult to allow Congress ministers to speak and thus we are getting into a vicious circle of doing nothing at all which is not only very bad for our development, in a country which thinks & breathes nothing but politics, but also dangerous...'.[178] (The National Planning Commission, established by INC and chaired by Jawaharlal Nehru, began deliberations in 1939, with the Committee on Communications headed by Sir Rahimatullah Chinoy, however its report was only published in 1948.)

The idea of civil servants appearing before the microphone was a cause for concern given that such broadcasts could be taken to represent official statements. Payment for such services was also problematic. Was a salaried government official to receive an additional payment to talk on a government owned service? How far could an official distinguish between his job and his broadcasting? Civil servants were, therefore, proscribed from broadcasting without prior clearance, which was often delayed and sometimes denied, further reducing the pool of accessible talent available to fill radio schedules. When Stephens, for example, was invited to talk about the DPI, he refused, worried about the possible adverse impact of publicity – this coming from a department whose *raison d'être* was official publicity. To MacGregor the situation was inexplicable: 'Why the Dickens shouldn't you broadcast about the Bureau?', he remonstrated with Stephens. 'It seems to me an excellent opportunity to make it up with the public, enlist its sympathies and get rid of some of the suspicion that has attached to the Information Bureau in the past.'[179]

No aspect of radio's creative freedom was immune from government interference. To take the innocuous example of instrumental music, though initially allowed to be broadcast without censorship, in 1937 the Home Department decreed that all such broadcasts also needed prior authorisation. An acute sensitivity to external and foreign policy dictated even the content of book-review programmes. For instance, a review of recently published books on Russia, which was scheduled to air on 26 April 1938, was banned since the broadcaster had used 'juicy extracts' critical of the government. Even third-party opinion presented as a book review was deemed politically 'unsuitable', since radio was 'controlled and financed' by the GoI, 'it could be justifiably regarded...as officially inspired propaganda against Stalin and his system'. Yet the ambiguities inherent in such actions were obvious even to the censor who acknowledged that the talk 'does not publish any new facts but merely quotes from books, which have been published and are being probably widely read. Had it therefore appeared as an article in a privately owned and controlled journal or review I do not think that the Soviet Government or the Government of India could have taken any exception to it.'[180] In the aftermath, a lengthy reprimand was sent to Fielden enjoining him to remind all station directors of their 'responsibilities' given that their output was 'propagated by an organisation which is completely under Government's ownership and control'.[181] In another case reflecting domestic sensitivities, censors refused to pass a book review unless the words 'the PM of Patiala' were replaced by the more generic 'an Indian state'. The context was a reference to the Prime Minister (an ally of the Raj) who, upon 'hearing an account of riots in London asked if the rioters were still alive, and being told they were, simply remarked, "Bad management!" '.[182]

Fielden's political sympathies also brought official opprobrium, making a difficult job often impossible. He had gauged that the balance of power within India was shifting, but was frustrated in attempts to reflect this in AIR programming. Drawn to the nationalists, particularly the INC high command, whom he found to be urbane, witty and intelligent, Fielden made many friends and went 'quite often to see Gandhi'. He also corresponded with Nehru and was particularly fond of Sarojini Naidu, who 'became, for a time, a fast friend'.[183] He made no attempt to disguise such sentiments, later confessing that between 1939 and 1943 he was 'obsessed with the idea of immediate Indian independence'.[184] During the Second World War, working briefly under Sir Malcolm Darling at the Ministry of Information, Fielden helped organise Indian broadcast propaganda and also wrote for the national press – for example, in the *Observer* in support of Cripps' mission. He also went on lecture tours on behalf of the Indian Freedom Campaign, which was run on a shoestring by Fenner Brockway. Out of this grew his impassioned critique of the Raj, *Beggar My Neighbour*, in 1943, which was promptly banned.

Despite such pro-nationalist credentials, whilst Controller Fielden had been unable to rely on the support of the INC. Gandhi accused him of being 'a milk and water liberal...this country is an armed camp, and you must be on one side or the other'.[185] To Fielden's expostulation that his job as a broadcaster was to remain neutral, Gandhi is reported to have responded: 'Then both will throw stones at you.' On another occasion, replying to Fielden's plea for help, Gandhi is claimed to have said: 'But why should I help a machine which will be used against me?'[186] (In the event, the sole occasion on which Gandhi was to visit an AIR studio took place in Delhi on 12 November 1947 when he addressed refugees in Kurukshetra camp on the occasion of Diwali.)[187] Jim Mills of AP, who was allowed exceptional access to Gandhi during the 1930s and had against the odds managed to film him extensively (as discussed in Chapter 3), affirmed that he 'hates everything mechanical – cameras, photographs, radios, typewriters, railroads, automobiles – machinery of all kinds. His theory is that machinery is the curse of modern civilization.'[188] Gandhi's attitude to broadcasting reflected his aversion to modern technology as emblematic of western industrialisation, and hence a tool of imperial oppression and economic exploitation.[189] Similarly, Fielden's friendship with Nehru often led him to act as the latter's intermediary with officials like Clow, but in his turn Nehru, though sympathetic, appeared unwilling to stand up and be counted on Fielden's behalf. Likewise, Naidu failed to be persuaded about the benefits of rural radio, exclaiming: 'The villager doesn't want your beastly wireless: he wants food and soap.'[190] Fielden recounts yet another instance where, whilst on a visit to Madras to meet Pandit Rajagopalachari, the Prime Minister, 'in order to obtain his collaboration, or at least his blessing' for the establishment of two radio stations in the presidency, the ensuing conversation developed into an argument about the merits of eastern versus western civilisation. Rajagopalachari, according to Fielden, claimed that 'broadcasting was entirely foreign to Indian life, because the personal touch was essential. Irritated, I pointed out that he had a telephone on his desk and that he had come to the office in a car.'[191]

Such political proclivities were combined with a general disregard for the niceties of Anglo-Indian society. Fielden distanced himself from British colleagues, did not join the European Club and refused a Government-allotted house. Given that for the Raj AIR was not about all India but much more about targeting safe constituencies, unsurprisingly he became 'extremely unpopular' and was accused of disloyalty: 'They began to think...that under my guidance broadcasting might develop not only into a great nuisance, but also into a great danger.'[192] That there was little love lost between employer and employee is clearly brought out when Fielden came to London on sick leave during 1939. The lack of enthusiasm for his return was communicated in confidence to the IO: 'They would probably feel little regret if he decided to cut adrift, but presumably do not particularly wish to give him any ground for saying that they and <u>not</u> he broke his contract', which did not expire until August 1940.[193] Yet by the summer of 1939 it had been decided not to renew his contract, as Linlithgow noted privately to Lord Zetland:

> I have reached the conclusion on Clow's advice...I cannot resist the weight of evidence that while he has, in the highest degree, the qualifications of imagination, of wide technical experience, and of high intellectual quality, he is no administrator...Fielden has passed through the hands of a somewhat unusually good succession of departmental Chiefs...and without exception...they found him difficult to a degree so far as organisation and the handling of his department was concerned.[194]

In the event, Fielden's tenure was terminated early in April 1940, with hindsight perhaps inevitably given how he had been consistently identified as the single point of systemic risk.

Despite his many travails, Fielden did, however, manage to record a small measure of success: 'I was king of my growing dunghill', he noted, and AIR as it came to exist by 1940 was shaped to a substantial extent by his hand. The acronym AIR and its display over a map of India, which was the logo adopted as the new emblem of Indian broadcasting, was, in fact, conceptualised by Fielden who envisaged radio as a truly representative and encompassing institution. He describes in his memoirs how, in order to have his design passed, he employed verbal subterfuge and let Linlithgow take the credit for it. A particularly valuable contemporary assessment of his career came from Grigg, who was amongst only a handful of ICS able to fully appreciate Fielden's role in a balanced perspective. Grigg claimed that if one were to juxtapose what had been achieved within very difficult conditions, the epithet 'miraculous' would not be an exaggeration.[195] When compared with the millions of pounds expended by the BBC, these achievements were undertaken with a combined annual capital outlay in 1939 – that is, on administration, engineering, maintenance and programmes – of less than £200,000. Nine transmitting stations and fourteen new transmitters had been erected, the nucleus of a properly trained staff had begun to take shape, and there were improvements in programming quality. Output now varied between 8 and 12 hours daily and in at least two languages, though occasionally transmitting in as many as four from one centre alone. Interstation relays were begun in early 1939, and after the outbreak of war, AIR was issuing 27 news bulletins in eight languages over its network. In addition to the complexities of language, poverty, lack of inexpensive receivers, communalism and political unrest, there was also the difficulty of 'touch[ing] upon any single activity of national life without arousing embittered controversy or rancour'.[196] Indians such as H. R. Luthra, who had worked with Fielden, including as Director of Programmes at Lahore, wrote appreciatively about how he 'encouraged new ideas and experiments with new techniques ... he built up a nucleus of programme men dedicated to broadcasting as a distinct art calling for high professional skills. He set up standards and created traditions which survived him by many years.'[197]

Undoubtedly Fielden's chronic mood swings, political sympathies and deep-seated impatience of office routine – in short, a combination of emotional and professional factors – made his experience especially difficult. The lack of opportunity to contribute at a creative level was deeply frustrating too: 'I find it very difficult to be happy when I am completely divorced as I have to be from all aesthetic interests ... to sit and write on files all day long with scarcely ever a visit to a studio is, I find, a soul-wearing business.'[198] But Fielden was also tainted, to a degree, by prejudices similar to those he claimed afflicted his countrymen:

> I hated Indian inefficiency ... inferiority complex ... noise, and ... dirt, just as much as I hated British cruelty ... patronage ... complacency, and ... bad taste. And so, loving nobody, I found myself, so to speak, in the middle of an Asiatic Rugby scrum in which I kicked everybody and everybody kicked me.[199]

Fielden's criticisms of Indian broadcasting ruffled many feathers, yet it is crucial not to view his professional opinions in isolation. His was but one of several voices raised in critique of official ineptitude and lack of empathy. Goyder complained likewise that 'the only reward for two years unbroken toil is, on the unofficial side carping criticism and, on the official side, the creation of needless difficulties'.[200] V. A. M.

Bulow, who had worked for the IBC and as Advisor to the Madras presidency on secondment from the BBC, argued similarly in 1941 that it was 'only too evident' that the GoI was 'lethargic and lacking in initiative. What has been accomplished now, could have been accomplished years ago but for the short sighted policy of the Central government and its advisers.'[201] Such concerns were echoed within the ICS too from the likes of Seth Drucquer, Special Officer in charge of Civil Defence Publicity during 1941–2, who accused Government departments of not being 'receptive to new ideas', with the consequence that 'throughout its early years, broadcasting had to struggle for funds for development against the arguments of persons not trained or educated to realize its potentialities'.[202] Similarly, Luthra claimed that Fielden was 'right in continually fighting the establishment to get them to recognise that broadcasting was not just like any other government activity'.[203] Even Willingdon was gracious enough to admit to Reith that 'There is unfortunately in our administration a good deal too much of the close corporation business, and the bringing in of an outsider is not always very well received.'[204] It was left to Grigg to make the most public condemnation of Indian conditions via a BBC broadcast which also included a frank assessment of AIR's first Controller, and thus serves as a worthy epitaph of the Fielden years:

> he found the pretensions of the 'heaven-born' irksome and said so very loud and clear; some of his staff were disloyal, others were incompetent... and even those... to whom he succeeded in imparting some of his own enthusiasm, suffered from their inexperience... worst of all, he had to endure a great deal of personal vilification from those – politicians, newspaper editors and others – for whose relations and protégés he had refused to make or do jobs... Some of his troubles were of his own making. He never learnt or even tried to learn to circumvent difficulty or obstruction; he charged straight at it and often bruised himself in the process. He had no time or inclination to try to get his way by judicious flattery... And if he was often tiresome to those he considered his enemies and sometimes so to his friends, this ought to have been a very small price to pay for his genius and his abounding vital energy.[205]

Broadcasting and Print

One of the more interesting aspects of the radio story in India was the establishment of specialist broadcasting periodicals, which along with the BBC's journals provide insights into wider perceptions and illuminate transnational linkages. With striking resemblance to Northcliffe's *Mail*, which sponsored the first live broadcast of Dame Nellie Melba in 1920, it was the *Times of India* in association with the Department of Posts and Telegraphs that responded to a request from the Governor of Bombay, Sir George Lloyd, to help make the first known broadcast of music a year later during August 1921. The larger dailies marked the key milestones in broadcasting and helped put pressure on a reluctant GoI to persist after it announced its intention to wind up the ISBS in 1931. Newspapers were also a growing avenue for radio advertisements and featured schedules of domestic and BBC output, though, as radio programmes were subject to copyright, the press were not allowed to publish more than two days' output at a time.

Yet, overall, it is indicative of the lacklustre state of broadcasting that it hardly appeared to excite or capture the attention of the Indian press in a sustained fashion, and any fears of competitive rivalry only began to surface in the late 1930s when there seemed to be a semblance of rejuvenation in the fortunes of radio. The main issues causing concern to the press were the reorganisation of AIR news services with more frequent and better-produced bulletins, threatening the value of their daily product, as well as the advent of privately sponsored programmes which began on an experimental basis in 1934. Under the heading 'Prostituting Wireless', the *Statesman* expostulated that in departing from British practice and veering towards the American model, the Raj was 'selling the wireless over the public's head for the sake of revenue'.[206] These sentiments were echoed by the *Amrita Bazar Patrika*, which claimed that the daily news broadcasts had 'already deprived newspapers of much of their interest and novelty'. The commercialisation of broadcasting with advertisement-led programming would thus be a double body blow.[207] The *Times of India*, labelling the scheme 'Broadcasting to Let', argued that the financial benefits would be far outweighed by the 'serious loss of morale such a principle involves in so essentially a public utility service'.[208] All papers agreed that it was the 'thin edge of a wedge which, if permitted entry, will prove difficult to dislodge'. Indian broadcasting 'would be shackling itself with chains from which escape might well become impossible'.[209] Newspaper deputations lodged protests with the GoI and with Fielden, who managed to reassure journalists that their interests would not be compromised.[210]

BBC Periodicals

The significance of the precedent established by the BBC in this sphere is unquestionable. Reith had always maintained the critical need for a flagship publication, and for wireless and print to be yoked together in its public service traditions. Thus the *Radio Times*, a title chosen by Reith, was launched on 28 September 1923 and was immediately successful, with its second number recording sales of a phenomenal 285,000 copies.[211] By 1947 its circulation had risen to 7 million copies weekly. *The Listener* followed in 1929, but not before Reith had to overcome considerable opposition from the British press, which raised the cry of 'unfair competition'. As *The Times* argued, 'it is a plain question of equity; a State-protected enterprise clearly should not be brought into competition with others'.[212] *The Listener* was intended as a more weighty weekly publication featuring reports of broadcasts, often accompanied by evocative photographs.

The Listener reveals an eclectic BBC outlook towards Indian coverage. For instance, copiously illustrated features on travel during 1936 included Eric Linklater's 'A Scot Abroad' series on the NW Frontier (20 May); 'Trains, Tombs and Elephants' (27 May) and 'Clubs and Cows' (10 June). Sir Stanley Reed compared 'Delhi: Today and Yesterday' (23 December) and E. O. Lorimer had an evocative series on the relatively obscure peasants of Hunza in the Karakoram mountain range who were 'the jolliest, happiest lot of people I have ever met'.[213] 'What Caste Means in India' was subjected to scrutiny by Professor J. H. Hutton (20 October 1938); her 'disappearing wildlife' concerned Lt. Col. C. H. Stockley (27 October 1937); and Dhanvanthi Rama Rau, wife of the Deputy High Commissioner, spoke about the 'Women of India' (9 September 1936). Rural broadcasting also received airtime with, for example, *The Listener* devoting its front page on 21 June 1933 to highlight the launch of 'A Scheme for Broadcasting in Rural India', published under the auspices of the Indian Village Welfare Association, at a meeting in London chaired by Sir Francis Younghusband. *The Listener* commented: 'We ought not to be backward in using this instrument for the benefit of the largest peasantry in the world.' Amongst British campaigners backing this initiative was Lt-Col H. R. Hardinge, who urged British radio manufacturers to invest since 'Even a small percentage of the half-million or so villages in India surely offers a sufficient incentive.'[214] Inevitably the concurrent constitutional changes received more attention in BBC programming, and were reflected in the pages of *The Listener*. Thus Coatman discussed the significance of the Indian General Election (5 March 1937), while later that month the Marquess of Lothian broadcast on 'The New Indian Constitution'.[215] Viscount Samuel reflected upon the notion of 'Democracy on Trial in India' (6 April 1938), Sir M. Zafrullah Khan, member of the Executive Council, talked about 'India's Place in the Commonwealth' (26 May 1937), and afterwards, as the newly elected Minister of Commerce in the Central Government, he was interviewed by A. Weyworth (22 September 1937).

Indian Radio Publications

Following in the footsteps of the Reithian experiment, the IBC began publication of the *Indian Radio Times* from July 1927. Issued twice monthly from Bombay at 1 anna, it featured a skeletal diet of programme listings, short essays, radio advertisements and a few talks. Yet it returned a profit after only two issues and by September was 'paying for itself'.[216] It was joined in 1929 by *Betar Jagat* in Bengali, published in Calcutta but at half the price, with both being continued by the ISBS. In 1935 the *Indian Radio Times* was renamed the *Indian Listener* and doubled in price and scope. It had a modest circulation in 1932–3 of around 4,500, but nevertheless recorded a net profit of Rs 2,187. Circulation rose to over 13,000 by 1934–5.[217] *Betar Jagat*'s profits were Rs 851 from a circulation of about 2,000.[218] The growth in popularity of these publications paralleled the increase in radio licences in the 1930s and provided an avenue for enterprising Indian journalists to migrate between media. Thus Nirad C. Chaudhuri, the well-known cultural critic and memoirist, began his career in 1936 writing features in *Betar Jagat* on an *ad hoc* basis before moving to work full time as a news broadcaster in Delhi from 1942, where he also supervised war bulletins and commentaries: 'I wrote the scripts in English for translation into the major Indian languages, and I myself translated them into Bengali and broadcast them.'[219]

Concerted attempts were made to cater to the linguistically diverse clientele with the establishment of *Awaz* (Urdu) and *Sarang* (Hindi), as well as *Vanoli* (Tamil), to coincide with the inauguration of the Delhi and Madras stations of AIR in 1936 and 1938, respectively. Despite limited budgets, these publications were profitable and provide an interesting perspective on the early years of broadcasting. A. N. Bhanot, a graduate of Punjab University, became Joint Editor of the *Indian Listener*, *Awaz* and *Sarang*, and urged government departments for more advertisements, emphasising how 'a single insertion... is equivalent in value to 15 insertions' in a newspaper, given its wider readership per copy. 'They are turned half a dozen times during the daily broadcasts by each member of more than 30,000 families.... missing no class, creed or political section of the community.'[220] By mid-1939, official estimates claimed that these journals combined reached about 47% of the total number of radio owners and were distributed as follows – *Indian Listener*, 21,250; *Awaz*, 5,000; *Sarang*, 2,500; *Betar Jagat*, 3,100; *Vanoli*, 1,250 – though readership per issue would have been substantially higher. Their reach also extended beyond Indian shores – for example, the *Indian Listener* and *Awaz* circulated in Burma, Ceylon and Afghanistan.[221] Fielden concluded that these journals would act as 'a force making for the cultural unification' of India.[222] Much more research is needed to verify the lasting significance, if any, of such claims.

Concluding Remarks

At the outbreak of the Second World War, neither the structural and institutional framework, nor a culture of radio, had succeeded in establishing themselves in British India. Despite its pretensions to greatness, AIR had a considerable distance to traverse before fulfilling its potential to become a service fit for all India. A decade earlier the BBC had shown remarkable prescience in predicting that it was unlikely that the total of individual licences in India would 'ever greatly exceed 100,000', and therefore the political and cultural purposes for which it was 'desirable and necessary' to promote broadcasting would not be served by addressing so small a percentage of the population.[223] In 1939 this figure stood at 92,782 and Fielden was to deliver his *coup de grace*:

> Four years of hard labour had produced fourteen transmitters and a competent staff – and in four years the four hundred million people of India had bought exactly eighty five thousand wireless sets. It was enough to make a cat laugh. It was the biggest flop of all time.[224]

The imperial narrative of liberal modernity – the traditions of which can be traced back to the debates of the 1830s – did not, a century later, extend to incorporating this latest innovation in communication. Instead it sought, if anything, to isolate the majority of Indians such that 'the invisible Empire tie' that Irwin had eulogised so fulsomely in 1927 remained, for the most part, truly invisible. This stillbirth coincided with broadcasting's efflorescence in Britain, the US and Europe. By 1938–9 there were 8.95 million licensed radios in Britain which amounted to one in five of its population.[225] P. J. Edmunds, the Director of Wireless, had acknowledged that broadcasting was 'a very sensitive thing and it is doubtful if it would ever obtain the confidence of the public in India if entirely worked by Government'.[226]

The Raj's early failure to engage with radio stemmed to a significant degree from prejudice. Dunstan, Manager of the fledgling IBC, had confided to Reith that the GoI 'as yet looks on broadcasting as an uninteresting toy, which, if it cannot stand straightaway on its own feet, must remaining lying until it can: they are not going to help'.[227] When its hand was forced, the Raj had, as Grigg was later to admit, taken on the service 'reluctantly' and continued it 'rather grudgingly', routinely starving it of capital, with poorly paid staff retained on temporary contracts. The creative vision, such as it existed, was primarily a metropolitan effort, with key personalities associated with British broadcasting playing a stellar role despite the fact that Reith's vision for Indian radio, fashioned on the BBC model of a high-minded and unbiased medium of public enlightenment, struggled to get off the ground. This contrasted with successful developments in Australia and Canada during the 1930s, a phenomenon that Tracey has termed 'the public service broadcasting project'.[228]

The interwar years provide little evidence to counter the charge that the Raj had neither the inclination nor the imagination to pursue the broadcasting dream. The initiatives required for successful institution-building appeared largely dormant or comatose, and proactive policy-makers were conspicuous by their absence. With a virtual monopoly over the airwaves, broadcasting remained an adjunct of the state, run by a small coterie of imperial administrators who worked within a traditionally hierarchic institutional structure bent on maintaining the *status quo*. Despite utilising wireless for strategic purposes, the collective spirit of the ICS militated against exploiting its social, political and cultural potential. For the Raj, broadcasting was an untested medium whose relationship with the public was, unlike with the press, still a matter of negotiation. Even with newspapers, the GoI had been slow to undertake any meaningful and organised approach to media management with the critical impetus only coming with the advent of the mercurial Edwin Montagu to the IO during the Great War.[229] However, much GoI press propaganda was essentially reactive in origin; with the nationalists effectively muzzled with respect to broadcasting, there appeared no need for firefighting. The battle between strategic control and freedom of expression was over before a single shot had been fired. The imperial mindset was essentially risk averse and chose not to respond to the creative potential of this new medium during the interwar years. As Philip Graves writing in *The Times* concluded, even after taking into account the numerous challenges posed by distance, poverty, illiteracy and atmospheric conditions: 'Yet, in spite of all these impediments, the finances of Indian broadcasting are in a fairly healthy condition. The chief obstacle both to an increased demand for wireless broadcasting and to its extension lies in its absolute control by the Government of India.'[230]

5
'Operation Seduction': Mountbatten, the Media and Decolonisation in 1947

Introduction; The Mountbatten Factor; Freedom at Midnight: The Foreign Media; British National Press; Broadcasting & Newsreels; Indian & Anglo-Indian Press; Concluding Remarks

Introduction

14/15 August 1947 has become seared in imperial consciousness as the date of the first major decolonisation of the twentieth century, altering forever the lives of millions. As John Keay writes, 'For the Indian subcontinent, as for the rest of the colonial world, the twentieth century peaked at Independence.'[1] But what were the popular perceptions of this defining event at the metropolitan heart of empire, particularly as interpreted in the British national media, including the press, radio and newsreels? How did the Raj stage-manage this last act of the imperial drama, and did the British media play a part in furthering the official line on decolonisation? To better appreciate the 'constitutive impact' of empire on Britain requires moving beyond generalisations to 'analysing specific contexts', claims James Epstein, and this chapter attempts to offer a more empirically sensitive portrayal of one such context to help tease out the ways in which the end of empire was explained to a popular audience.[2] It will be argued that the conceptualisation and orchestration of the 'Raj decolonisation project' under the guidance of the Viceroy, Lord Louis Mountbatten, was seminal to this endeavour. Such an approach also serves to shine a light on the transformed context within which the public mediation of these events played out. Indeed, as Maria Misra has noted, 'Whilst partition itself was about blood and violence . . . in Delhi both Mountbatten and Nehru were determined that Independence would be a celebration.'[3]

In 1947 a widespread British perception of the loss of India was to view it as an orderly and planned transfer of power that not only involved the minimum of disruption but also served as the fulfilment of long-cherished nineteenth-century Macaulayite ideals that underlay the very establishment of the imperium. As the wider imperial superstructure unravelled in the post-war decades, there persisted a notion that the British 'understood empire' and were thus well equipped to 'end our dominion over palm and pine relatively amicably and successfully'.[4] Further, as Cannadine has argued, since the empire 'existed and endured as a pageant, it was at least consistent with that element of caparisoned theatricality that it ended and expired in a succession of valedictory rituals, which were ... deliberately made up and self-consciously invented'.[5] As this case study will seek to demonstrate, Mountbatten deserves credit for helping establish the template for such an approach to 'independence' ceremonials, in their conceptualisation if not in every detail, for the majority of British colonies and dependencies in the decades that followed 1947.

The British media played a key role in establishing and perpetuating such perceptions. Newspapers were seminal in creating the first draft of the history of decolonisation, and served to imprint images and attribute significance to the process for posterity. In any discussion of print and empire the bounded context is pre-eminently important, for though Fleet Street prided itself on its Fourth Estate privileges, the constraints of coercive subjugation that underlay the Raj threatened always to impinge upon the extent and nature of its coverage. However, with the British national press reaching circulations of 15.5 million daily, government officials were not in a position to underestimate its potential to influence the voting public. By mid-1947 the combined circulation of national and provincial dailies in Britain had risen to 28,503,000.[6] In London there were nine national morning papers and three evening dailies. Amongst the 25 provincial morning newspapers, England could boast of 18 papers, with six in Scotland and one in Wales. The evening provincial press was also far more numerous in England, which had 64 papers compared to nine in Scotland and two in Wales.[7]

After the Second World War, and despite the handicap of extended wartime restrictions, commercialism and advocacy continued to be comfortable bedfellows in the national press, most of which were private enterprises run by a combination of powerful proprietors and influential editors, proclaiming their freedom to make political choices. Amongst the few espousing an overt commitment to a party or movement were the *Daily Worker* (funded by the Communist Party of Great Britain) and *Reynolds News* (owned by the Co-operative movement), whilst the labour *Herald* was controlled by a commercial–trade union partnership. The operation of ownership chains linking national, provincial and the local press ensured the circulation of fact and comment throughout the country, a process especially marked in relation to foreign and imperial news. The war years also helped consolidate and enhance the reputation of the BBC manifold both domestically as well as overseas. The BBC's reach encompassed virtually one hundred percent of the domestic audience, and hence its potential to inform and influence was virtually unsurpassed. In 1940 its ES was renamed the Overseas Service and it began to broadcast in Hindi. British journalists also continued to be lured to the subcontinent to work on not just the Anglo-Indian but increasingly the Indian-run papers, thus consolidating transnational news linkages.[8]

The Mountbatten Factor

The contrast between the last two viceroys of British India could not have been more striking. In 1943, Lord Wavell was promoted by Winston Churchill from Commander in Chief of the Indian Army to Viceroy, a move endorsed by the British press in recognition of his war record. However, it was acknowledged, not least by Wavell himself, that his was a 'stopgap' Viceroyalty.[9] His relationship with Whitehall, particularly after the war, has been described as 'disastrous', evidenced in the progressively 'sour' correspondence with the new Labour Prime Minister, Clement Attlee, which indicated 'not the break-up of a friendship' but 'merely a removal of the political niceties'.[10] Further, while aware of the role of public opinion, Wavell did not feel the necessity to cultivate the media on a systematic footing. Ian Stephens, editor of the *Statesman*, contended that he came across as 'reticent, enigmatic' and with 'no particular liking for social events and wholly lack[ing] interest in or capacity for self-display'.[11] Wavell did, however, reserve special regard for *The Times*, whose correspondents, Alexander Inglis and James Holburn, 'understood how Governments work...and could be relied upon to give a balanced view. They were also most discreet and did not misuse inside information.'[12] 'Delhi has become an acute problem', noted Ralph Deakin, *The Times* Foreign Editor, in 1945, when conveying both Wavell's and Leo Amery's request for his reinstatement to Holburn: 'there is some compensation in the keen desire that high authority has displayed to have you back'.[13]

A biographer has recently claimed that Attlee's two major contributions regarding India were 'setting a withdrawal date and appointing Mountbatten to find agreement between the parties'.[14] Mountbatten brought a new and dynamic approach to the style as well as the substance of imperial governance. He was 'extrovert and sociable', and functioned 'in a blaze of publicity', with a legendary capacity for self-promotion.[15] While being filmed for an ITV series in the 1970s, he insisted on directing the lighting and camera angles himself since 'it was important for him to be shot from 6 inches above his eye line'.[16] He also had a genuine fascination with technology and communications, an interest stimulated early, graduating from the Naval Signal school in 1925 and a year later from the Institution of Electrical Engineers at the Royal Naval College in Greenwich. This preoccupation was in evidence throughout his life as he invested in innovation – for instance, in 1959 backing Colin Cockerell, the inventor of the Hovercraft – while in 1966 his interest in computers was rewarded with the Presidency of the British Computer Society.[17] When delivering the first Mountbatten Lecture to the National Electronics Council in London, the septuagenarian argued that 'Technology advances only so far as man will allow it. Invention and innovation tend to upset ways of living to which people have become accustomed and so, to a very large extent, progress depends on overcoming prejudice – indeed fear.'[18] His own career demonstrates how he sought to work with new technologies and overcome any fear.

Mountbatten wanted 'always to simplify, to popularise, and in particular to photograph', with a firm belief in the necessity of 'developing and using an image'.[19] Such proclivities were in evidence when he visited India as the Supreme Commander, Combined Operations, South East Asia in 1943. Stephens reminisced about attending a garden party in Delhi organised at Mountbatten's behest 'mainly to let him meet war correspondents... I was immensely impressed... he seemed an absolute winner.'[20] He was convinced that Mountbatten's 'glittering personality' had its desired impact on the assembled media at a challenging moment in the conduct of the Second World War. Max Desfor, the famous AP photographer, corroborated such testimony: 'he was very photogenic... he knew what was a good picture'.[21] Desfor claimed that the press 'were always kept well informed' and noted the assistance he received from Mountbatten, now Viceroy, in facilitating his assignments to Burma and the Northwest Frontier in 1947: 'Everything was arranged, and I became a member of the party, and went right with him.' Desfor claimed that he came to know Mountbatten 'very well' during the two years he was stationed in the subcontinent, and considered him to be 'one of the greatest men I've ever known'.[22] A similar impression was conveyed to the young Narendra Singh, Prince of Sarila, at another testing moment during negotiations on 25 July 1947 to discuss the post-Independence fate of two-fifths of the subcontinent ruled by Indian princes.

> Suddenly there was a hubbub and I saw a tall handsome man with black hair mounting the rostrum in an English admiral's white uniform and an imposing array of military and civil orders and decorations that would have outshone even the most jewelled potentates who confronted him. For a few minutes Lord Mountbatten was caught in a blaze of flashbulbs as photographers took pictures; he was very upright, but moved his head slightly to the left and the right in perfect showmanship.[23]

Describing the speech that followed, which was essentially a British abdication of responsibility, Mountbatten nevertheless 'succeeded in creating the impression that he was a friend who was trying to help the princes and his bearing and enthusiasm was infectious'.[24] The following month, Sarila was invited to another reception at the Viceregal residence: 'The business for which we were there was being relentlessly pursued. Princes who had not yet decided to sign the instrument of accession were taken in batches to sit with the viceroy for a friendly chat.' Observing the cut and thrust of statecraft, Sarila was struck by the 'smooth performance' of the ADCs who 'introduced each one of us by name and title – and we were more than 150 guests – to the viceroy without referring to any list or paper'. It was a combined Indo-British propaganda operation *par excellence*, with Sarila being equally impressed by Sardar Patel – the Home as well as Information and Broadcasting Minister in the interim government – who first 'flattered' the princes as 'scions of a race that had fought for centuries to protect India's integrity and honour and then asked abruptly whether they would let India down now when it was approaching freedom'.[25]

Mountbatten transformed the traditional approach to the office by appreciating the extraordinary demands of the situation: as Lord Ismay remarked, India in March 1947 'was a ship on fire in mid-ocean with ammunition in the hold'.[26] Against precedent, Mountbatten handpicked a new public relations team to accompany him, one of the key appointments being Alan Campbell-Johnson OBE, who was the first (and only) press attaché appointed to the Viceregal staff. With a background in the Royal Air Force, Campbell-Johnson had worked closely with Mountbatten at the Combined Operations headquarters and was in a unique position to witness him as a 'communicator'. This team would work alongside the administrative and secretarial staff *in situ* in Delhi, a decision which was controversial even for the usually supportive Attlee. As Mountbatten was later to admit, 'No one saw the point...If it had gone wrong, we would have had the most awfully tough time.'[27] However, as discussed below, it turned out to be an astute decision, with Campbell-Johnson acting as the lynchpin assisting to orchestrate the stage-management of the Mountbatten handover of power and help create the mythic dimensions of his personal role in the process.

Such synergy was apparent in the negotiations prior to the departure of the Viceregal party for India. It was considered imperative to develop a more proactive strategy *vis-à-vis* the Indian press and Campbell-Johnson liaised extensively with the IO Information Department and his counterpart, the veteran A. H. Joyce, as well as with Sudhir Ghosh, the newly appointed Press Officer at the Indian High Commission in London. By early March, Mountbatten had met Christopher Chancellor, General Manager of Reuters, for 'a most useful meeting', and, Joyce had supplied Campbell-Johnson with a list of important journalists in India, including members of the Indian and Eastern Newspaper Society.[28] Though the principal Muslim League papers had elected not to join the Society, this did not diminish its importance in official eyes. He advised Campbell-Johnson to establish '*personal contact* with these papers as soon as possible after your arrival'.[29] Joyce also singled out a few editors who were 'of outstanding importance in influencing all-India opinion', including Stephens (*Statesman*), Sir Francis Low (*Times of India*), Devadas Gandhi (*Hindustan Times*), Kasturi Srinivasan (*Hindu*), Geoffrey Tyson (*Capital*) and S. P. Lokanathan (*Eastern Economist*).[30] The consensus was weighted against any regular question-and-answer sessions with the Indian press since the danger of misrepresentation was felt to outweigh any potential benefits. A fully representative coverage would also necessarily involve over two hundred journalists. Instead it was planned to have 'an editorial tea-party' soon after Mountbatten's arrival, to be followed by informal meetings with Indian as well as British, American and other foreign representatives.[31] Ghosh, who had 'very strong contacts with all the Congress leaders', agreed that it would be far more effective to get the Viceroy's views across through private consultations which were not entered into the Court Circular.[32] Campbell-Johnson was therefore able to organise 'a social meeting with selected editors' within only a few days of touching down in New Delhi (Figure 5.1).[33]

Figure 5.1 Lord and Lady Mountbatten at the Viceregal Swearing in Ceremony, Durbar Hall, Viceregal Lodge, New Delhi, 24 March 1947, reproduced by permission of Associated Press Corporate Archives, London and New York, AP photo

More formally, Mountbatten set the ball of his diplomatic charm offensive rolling by breaking with protocol to make a speech at his inauguration, which he later admitted was 'pretty cheeky... really a bit of an impertinence'.[34] Mountbatten stressed how his was 'not a normal' Viceroyalty, and that he sought 'the greatest goodwill of the greatest possible number' of Indians.[35] The Mountbattens were also determined to raise their office to new sartorial heights and create a vivid first impression of ceremonial splendour. He adorned himself with every conceivable decoration, including the Viceroy's heirloom jewel in diamonds, and, accompanied by a suitably resplendent Edwina, displayed 'a form of panache which was entirely lacking before.... it struck a new note from the beginning'.[36] Importantly, for the first time, 'film cameras whirred and flash bulbs went off' in the previously sacrosanct Assembly Hall, to capture the swearing-in ceremony on celluloid.[37] It is revealing to note the marked difference from Wavell's inauguration in 1943, when AIR was allowed to relay proceedings 'provided the voices of the principal speakers were not included'.[38] The decision meant that listeners could only hear the recording of a description of the scene, and incidental sounds.

The fact that Mountbatten had 'come out and declared his policy within one minute of becoming Viceroy'[39] seems to have had the desired impact upon the Anglo-Indian and the Indian-run press, where he appeared to have got off to a flying start. Newspapers commented upon his engaging frankness and charm of manner (*Hindustan Times*), his readiness to take quick decisions (*Pioneer*), and his embodying 'that combination of natural authority and progressive spirit which characterises the British Royal House' (*Statesman*).[40] The *Tribune* argued that Mountbatten would need to do his utmost to 'enable transfer of power to keep India united', while the *Sind Observer* urged a firm hand and not vague generalities. *Dawn* was convinced that Mountbatten had 'great and unprecedented responsibilities' but would 'doubtless be wooed and fawned upon, cajoled and alternately threatened, a time honoured Congress way'.[41] Within Britain, too, the inauguration was given 'prominence' in the principal papers as 'an innovation appropriate to the special circumstances'.[42]

Mountbatten described his approach to political negotiation as a process of 'open diplomacy', which he claimed was the 'only one suited to the situation in which the problems were so complex and the tension so high'.[43] Even when he was pressed for time, Mountbatten would conduct meetings by asking the 'social sort of question first...very much like an after-dinner conversation, never any atmosphere of business, no pressure. In fact, I wouldn't even let people bring in bits of paper with notes on what they wanted to say...and it really disarmed them.'[44] He insisted on dictating a summary immediately afterwards so that a record was available for review by his team.[45] The social dimension to high politics – the wining and dining of diplomacy – was also taken to new heights under the Mountbattens, who entertained on an industrial scale: 'We did it much better than the Wavells,' boasted Mountbatten, 'I mean, really laid on everything, we went to town.'[46] Phillips Talbot was impressed at how the couple always 'managed a warm smile and firm handshake even for the last hundred guests'.[47] Talbot was foreign correspondent for the *Chicago Daily News* but had earlier spent several years in India as representative of the New York-based Institute of Current World Affairs. Another significant departure was that Mountbatten insisted on at least half of any guest list being composed of Indians: 'we were determined to bring Indians into the Viceroy's House who had either never been asked, or who would never even have dreamt of accepting if they had been asked'.[48]

Social gatherings served to establish camaraderie and create trust. These were also an integral part of Viceregal interventions, designed to curtail censorious comment or to smooth ruffled editorial feathers that could potentially derail imperial negotiations. For instance, on 10 July the Mountbattens gave an 'At Home' to the Standing Committee of the AINEC and the Central Press Advisory Committee, about thirty journalists who represented the 'most powerful managerial and editorial interests' in the non-Muslim press. The Viceroy gave 'an informal talk and listened to many of their reactions' to the 3 June and Cabinet Mission Plans.[49] The atmosphere was tense at the start but by the end, the minutes noted, bonhomie had been restored, with even the usually critical Devadas Gandhi welcoming Mountbatten's new role as Governor General of independent India.

A perusal of the minutes of almost every staff meeting demonstrates how systematically press comment was scrutinised and how keen an interest Mountbatten took in cultivating journalists: proffering advice, correcting mis-statements and being available to lunch as occasion demanded. During the second such meeting, for instance, Lord Ismay singled out *Dawn* and *Hindustan Times* as needing to be cautioned. Abell pointed to the difficulties of this process given that these newspapers were effectively controlled by the League and INC respectively. At the end of March, it was decided to invite Stephens for a meal, whilst Campbell-Johnson took Nehru to lunch, in part to ascertain his connections to the pro-INC press. In early April, Campbell-Johnson was asked to raise awareness in the press of non-political events, such as Edwina's visit to a nursing college, to help create a more balanced appreciation of the Raj. At another meeting in April, the leak in the *Hindustan Times* regarding the defence bill was discussed, and it was suggested that the source might well be Sardar Patel himself, forcing Mountbatten to quip that he was 'beginning to feel that it might be necessary for him to use the medium of the World Press to shed an impartial limelight on events in India'.[50] At a meeting with Nehru, Mountbatten referred to yet another article in the same newspaper about official negotiations to secure a truce between the various parties. 'Is there anything we can do to prevent for the future the embarrassment that is caused by press reports of this kind?' he queried Nehru. 'It does seem to me an intolerable state of affairs that the press should be allowed to obtain confidential information which they put out without any consideration of the public interests.'[51]

The apogee of such interaction came at the Viceroy's press conference in Delhi when he expounded the Plan of 3 June which granted Independence but with Partition. Mountbatten was to note privately how

> for two and a quarter hours I was under violent cross-fire on every conceivable subject... I luckily knew my subject pretty well... and feel I was able to answer all the questions to most people's satisfaction. At all events the follow-up in all sections of today's press has been more favourable than the most sanguine of us could have hoped for.[52]

Campbell-Johnson enthused that the event had been 'a tremendous success' and had done 'much to clarify and stabilise the situation and control the whole tone of press comment'. The reactions of the three hundred correspondents present were 'quite the most enthusiastic I have ever experienced'.[53] The Viceroy demonstrated a command over the subject which moved Stephens to claim: 'For sheer intellectual range and vigour, for assured grasp of minutiae, yet brilliant marshalling of the main lines of a long, difficult argument, it was an extraordinary performance.'[54] Andrew Mellor of the *Herald* was 'stunned' by the performance, while Eric Britter of *The Times* called it a *'tour de force'*.[55] Talbot agreed that it had been a 'spectacularly successful' conference which had also 'won over the usually critical Indian press'.[56] Only two major Indian newspapers – the *Hindustan Times* and the *Indian News Chronicle* – were hostile to plans for what they considered to be the Balkanisation of the subcontinent, but significantly even they did not question the Viceroy's credibility.

Whilst monitoring the Indian press debates in the weeks following this meeting, Campbell-Johnson informed Joyce that though the response had been 'extremely factious' reflecting communal and/or party affiliations, and with the issues of Dominion Status and the position of the princely states eliciting the most critique, yet there had been 'no major eruption'. He recounted a telephone conversation on the subject with Devadas Gandhi, who

> went out of his way to draw my attention to a Reuter's report... which referred to the creation of 'two new nations'. He said that this 'new nation' theory was most repugnant to the Congress conception of things and had very much distressed his father who had stressed his objection at a prayer meeting. His father had added that in so far as the report came from Reuter's it was inevitably

Government inspired. I was, of course, at pains to explain that I was sure the story in question did not really carry all the meaning he had read into it, as a subsequent Reuter's report on the same subject referred to the 'two Dominions'.

Given the 'extreme sensitiveness' of Indians, Campbell-Johnson advised Joyce 'to give some private guidance that reference to the two new nations is distasteful and may cause a certain amount of embarrassment out here'.[57]

Meanwhile the BBC's coverage of the announcement was considered to have been 'magnificent', with the Corporation being regarded as a seminal tool by Mountbatten, who attached the 'greatest importance to clear transmission in England and America'.[58] AIR prepared special bulletins, provincial governors had transcripts translated for wider distribution, and British representatives in London, Washington, Canberra, Toronto, Singapore, Rangoon and Shanghai each received copies in time for a near simultaneous release.[59] Mountbatten was also keen to have the 'widest broadcast publicity' for the speeches on AIR that followed his own announcement and that were delivered by Nehru, Jinnah and Baldev Singh (Defence Minister in the interim government). For official policy to be endorsed publicly by the INC, Muslim League and Sikh leadership respectively was considered advantageous in creating positive public perceptions of government policy.[60] These English broadcasts were followed by translations in Hindi read by AIR announcers, except for Nehru, who 'spoke, with the English script in front, improvising the translation as he went along'.[61] Similarly, on 6 July, Mountbatten sent feedback to the Secretary of State, Lord Listowel, on the Indian Independence Bill from newspapers including the *Hindustan Times*, *Indian News Chronicle, Statesman* and *Dawn*: 'First reactions are extremely favourable . . . while newspaper leaders are critical of certain details . . . the British have on the whole come out well.'[62] Listowel was in a position to appreciate Indian conditions, having served as Under Secretary of State from November 1944 to May 1945, during the course of which he had established a good working relationship with nationalists, including Nehru.[63]

The Viceregal staff operated within an imperial context that set enormous store by image and presentation. Campbell-Johnson helped implement a rigorous schedule of media management, paying close attention to detail, frequent press conferences, informal press briefings and overall attempts to personalise the government–media dynamic, which in the final analysis bore handsome dividends. 'By dint of giving up some of the hours of the day,' he wrote, 'and sacrificing some of the paper work, I have managed to achieve fairly good relations with most of the correspondents here. I am sure it pays to be available even if one has not a lot to say, and the Indians undoubtedly react favourably to minor courtesies which the European correspondents might take for granted.'[64]

Via letter and occasional face-to-face meetings, Campbell-Johnson also advised Fleet Street editors, foreign journalists and London representatives of Indian papers. The latter were a substantial presence in the metropolis and were represented by the Indian Journalists Association (IJA) established in 1947. The IJA served as a liaison with Fleet Street and government departments, and established 'long distance relations with the Indian newspaper world which we serve'.[65] The IO arranged for Indian journalists to have separate weekly press conferences from May to August in lieu of the fact that they had a special interest to serve, and their quota in the parliamentary press gallery was supplemented for special debates. Officers at the IO should, claimed Campbell-Johnson, also follow his lead, 'which is to meet Indian correspondents socially and privately, entertaining them at one's house and club'.[66]

The IO Information Department had matured over the interwar years and was, at this juncture, exceptionally well led by Joyce, who had the added advantage of understanding the workings of the Indian central publicity organisation, as discussed in Chapter 1. He was able to reassure Campbell-Johnson that despite severe newsprint shortages, which meant that international news 'suffers to an appalling extent...You can always rely...on our giving the fullest possible prominence' to Mountbatten's statements and to his 'efforts to bring HMG's policy to a successful issue'.[67] In pursuance of this strategy of media management, Joyce invited, for instance, editors of several prominent provincial newspapers, including the *Guardian*, *Yorkshire Post*, *Birmingham Post*, *Glasgow Herald* and the *Scotsman*, to meet the Secretary of State, who 'would be glad to have the opportunity of a private talk with you regarding Indian affairs'.[68] That such consultations were welcomed is revealed by the alacrity with which the invitation was taken up by these journalists. Another constituency targeted by Joyce was the representatives of the US press in London, as noted in Chapter 4. Many American journalists were grateful for such support – such as William White and Honor Balfour of *Time* and *Life*. Thus Balfour wrote to Joyce in May 1947: 'I thought you would like to know that my cable last week on the position in India was based entirely on our chat. Thank you so much for all your help and for giving me such excellent guidance. Once I locate you, I know I never have to worry any more!'[69]

Overall, throughout the tense summer of 1947, Campbell-Johnson and Joyce were able to maintain harmonious working relations with both the foreign and the Indian media. Mountbatten was to admit later: 'God, if I hadn't had Campbell-Johnson to soften up the Press...They were absolutely eating out of our hands in the end.'[70] The smooth workings of the London–New Delhi media operation – what Campbell-Johnson referred to as 'a good piece of teamwork from 7,000 miles range' – was based on the personal commitment and shared vision of administrative elites such as Joyce and Campbell-Johnson, and lay at the heart of the successful implementation of imperial policy during these months.[71]

In concluding this section, however, it is pertinent to emphasise that such intensive persuasion campaigns did not altogether allay the anxiety of the GoI, specifically with regard to the incitement of communal disturbances by the Indian press. Under Wavell, special punitive legislation had been imposed from January 1947 which continued into the summer and included the Press (Special Powers) Ordinance, enacted to deal with what were judged to be inflammatory writings and speeches, and their dissemination via the media. Such actions, it was believed, contributed to tensions between the main religious communities and hindered the return to normality in riot-torn areas. The Ordinance was enforced in the capital, where a general precensorship order was imposed on all dailies from 24 March to 7 April. The *Tribune* noted in May how the Punjab Government's censorship continued in force: 'We are therefore unable to comment on the situation in the province.'[72] During May and July, three Urdu newspapers in Delhi, for example, faced precensorship orders. R. N. Bannerjee, Secretary, Home Department, noted that though there had not been widespread enforcement of the Ordinance, 'mainly because of the shifting political atmosphere', yet its mere existence 'has had a salutary and deterrent effect on writings tending to incite communal hatred'.[73] Under Mountbatten, Indian newspapers were served with repeated warnings to give them 'some locus paenitentiae', before the imposition of legal restrictions. However, officials were in no doubt about the continuing danger from reactionary elements, contending that 'effective control must obviously be maintained over the Press for some time to come'.[74]

It is also necessary to reiterate that such official news management was being undertaken within a political context in which Indian politicians and parties, especially the INC and the Muslim League, were not averse to utilising the weapon of propaganda, and engaged in systematic publicity, largely through the press. Often this involved no more than preaching to the converted. Low claimed that by the 1940s 'pro-Congress newspapers...constituted by far the greater portion of the Press of the country both in English and in Indian languages'.[75] The long tradition of nationalist-inspired and controlled press, as discussed in previous chapters, continued apace and included prominent INC leaders. Gandhi's political creed was inseparable from his journalism, as discussed in Chapter 3, a trait inherited by Devadas, his youngest son, who was Managing Editor of the *Hindustan Times* as well as Chairman of AINEC. Jinnah helped establish *Dawn* as the mouthpiece of the Muslim League and was a wily manipulator of the foreign media. For instance, his controversial proposal to establish a corridor across the breadth of the subcontinent to link the proposed geographical areas of East and West Pakistan was first made public in an interview with Doon Campbell of Reuters, in the certainty that it would be the surest way to achieve the greatest impact in Britain. Apparently, as soon as Reuters released the story, Jinnah's secretary rang up foreign correspondents in Delhi to draw their attention to it. 'BBC and Times representative told me', Mountbatten wrote to Listowel, 'they propose to play the story down and consider most of their colleagues will do the same.'[76] In India the two newspapers to make significant capital out of the issue were predictably *Dawn* and the *Hindustan Times*. The Viceroy admitted that though political and press reactions to the interview were 'not as strong as might be expected...London coverage was likely to be heavy with Reuters imprint on it. Interview aimed primarily at London'.[77]

Freedom at Midnight: The Foreign Media

The Indian subcontinent became the cynosure of international media attention during the summer of 1947, with journalists congregating in the capital just as they had in 1911, though anticipating now the establishment of a new India. The two hotels they favoured – the Imperial and the Cecil – became *de facto* media headquarters. Both US news agencies were represented: the UP, which also had representatives in Bombay, Calcutta and Karachi, and the AP, which had significantly strengthened its position in 1945 with the establishment of a new office in Delhi headed by Preston Grover, Chief of Bureau in India and China. Its headquarters continued to be located in Bombay, with sub-bureaus in Lahore, Calcutta and Madras. Both agencies worked increasingly with local correspondents, acknowledging their contribution, especially in times of rising violence, as they could 'get around in places where an American or Englishman would be set upon with little chance of surviving long enough to get the news'.[78] Several Indian newspapers had begun subscribing to these American agencies in the interwar years, as a preferred option to Reuters, much to the chagrin of the Raj. As a commentator in *Forum* weekly argued, these agencies were 'a real headache to "Reuters" who have ruled the roost on this side of the world for decades, aligning with the Raj and broadcasting its Imperialist voice. A.P.A. and U.P.A. can now smash "Reuters" racket in the East'.[79] In 1945, AP was subscribed to by 16 newspapers and radio stations in India, with daily reports of 4,000 words being sent in cipher from London to Bombay and then redistributed throughout the country.[80] Desfor was assigned to the Delhi office, joining a four-strong staff in February 1946, and was to remain till April 1949, recording the major turning points in the lead-up to decolonisation and the nascent beginnings of the new nation-state. His photograph of Gandhi and Nehru sitting together during the INC annual conference in Bombay in 1946 became an overnight sensation and was to achieve iconic status when reissued as a stamp by the GoI in 1973.[81] Amongst other international agencies present in Delhi were the Agence France Presse, Tass and the Chinese Central News Agency. Newspapers with special correspondents included the *New York Post, New York Times, New York Herald Tribune, Life, Time, Chicago Daily News, Chicago Herald Tribune, Christian Science Monitor* and the *Sydney Morning Herald*. These correspondents had also organised themselves into an effective lobby in the shape of the Foreign Correspondents' Association, with the redoubtable Desfor as President (Figure 5.2).

The British networks of communication included Doon Campbell of Reuters (supported by a host of reporters across the country), Robert (Bob) Stimson, Donald Edwards and Gordon Mosley from the BBC, and over fifteen Fleet Street special correspondents representing quality dailies such as *The Times* and the *Telegraph* (which had absorbed the *Morning Post* in 1937), as well as popular papers such as the *Express, Mail* and *Herald*. Necessitated by the post-war financial climate, some British newspapers also supplemented their traditional reliance on Reuters by establishing news-share syndicates, such as 'The Times and Manchester Guardian Service'. There were also collaborations between national and provincial papers – for instance, the *Telegraph*'s Colin Reid also functioned as the *Scotsman*'s special correspondent, while Lt. Gen. H. G. Martin likewise served as military correspondent for both. Further, Fleet Street had well-established links with Anglo-Indian newspapers, including the *Statesman*, the *Times of India, Pioneer* and the *Civil and Military*

Figure 5.2   Max Desfor, photo by author, 2014

Gazette (CMG).[82] Thus, for example, the editor of the *Statesman* acknowledged how, despite 'strong occasional policy-differences, especially over
Hitler's menace' in the 1930s, they had a long-established 'entente' with
The Times since 1875. The paper held the Indian copyright for *Times*
articles, and its editor and resident director were '*ipso facto* its Calcutta
and Delhi correspondents'.[83] Likewise Indian journalists were recruited
as correspondents for British dailies, such as Shiva Rao of the *Hindu*,
who wrote for the *Guardian*, U.N. Sen, who represented the *Herald*, and
Lanka Sundaram of the *News Chronicle*. Tough wartime newsprint restrictions continued into peacetime and further curtailed the amount of
space allocated to foreign news. However, there was a lack of uniformity
across India in terms of both the quality and the range of British media
coverage. The north-west was historically a problematic area for recruit-
ing reliable local correspondents, as witnessed by the travails of even
a well-established a paper such as *The Times*, a factor which assumed
special significance in the context of widespread communal clashes during 1947. Large centres like Peshawar remained unrepresented, whilst
others, such as Karachi, were covered by *The Times*'s Bombay representative, Low of the *Times of India*, on the basis that the timelag between
Karachi and Bombay was less than that between Karachi and Delhi,
and that Sindh was insufficiently important to warrant a permanent
correspondent.[84]

British National Press

On the day, how did the British press choose to interpret the end of empire? In terms of presentation, with the exception of *The Times* and the *Guardian* (both of which still continued the tradition of not featuring news on the cover), newspapers accorded the story pride of place on their front pages, with no expense being spared typographically to make features and headlines bolder and bigger than usual. Coverage extended into editorials, in-depth features and by-lined reports from special correspondents. In terms of column inches *The Times* and the *Guardian* led the way, followed closely by other dailies, such as the *Telegraph*, the *News Chronicle* and the *Herald*, with the *Daily Mirror* bringing up the rear, devoting only 14 lines or 66 words on its front page to the story.[85] Prospective maps of the new nations were produced in the *Mail* and *The Times*, even though the recommendations of Radcliffe's Boundary Commission were only published three days after Independence. The following headlines capture some of the spirit of the coverage (Table 5.1).

Flags – both old and new – captured an iconic image of change. For the Raj, one photograph took centre stage. While Nehru and Mountbatten had agreed that newsreels were not to film the lowering of the Union Jack, Fleet Street remained at liberty to photograph it. One prominent instance of this took place on the ruined ramparts of the Residency in Lucknow, from where the *Telegraph* correspondent informed its readers it 'had never been lowered since recapture of the town after the siege of

Table 5.1   Headlines of the British national press at Indian Independence

'Power is handed over in India', 'Lord Mountbatten on a friendly parting', 'The End of an Era' (*The Times*)

'India Is Now Two Dominions', 'Power Transferred at Midnight' (*Daily Telegraph*)

'India is pledged to peace' 'Midnight guns greet two new Dominions', 'An Accidental Empire ends' (*Daily Herald*)

'Farewell and Hail', 'Curious Apathy in Karachi', 'Delhi Rejoices and Mr Gandhi Fasts' (*Manchester Guardian*)

'Freedom day', 'The New Beginning' (*News Chronicle*)

'India: 11 words mark end of an empire' (*Daily Mail*)

'Indians Link Arms – Greet Freedom' (*Daily Mirror*)

'India greets dawn of Independence' (*Daily Worker*)

'India's Flags Unfurled' (*Star*)

'India: the end of an epoch' (*Spectator*)

'The Raj Passes' (*Observer*)

1857'. The *Illustrated London News* (ILN) devoted the entire front page
of its Independence number on 23 August to a photograph of this view,
noting how the flag was 'symbolic of a great era'.[86] Now it had been
replaced by the Indian tricolour at midnight, 'secretly and without ceremony', noted the *Mail*.[87] The *Contemporary Review* had a detailed feature
some months later entitled 'A Flag Hauled Down', where A. F. Fremantle
quoted Wordsworth's lament over the fall of a great city: 'And what if
she had seen those glories fade, Those titles vanish, and that strength
decay; Yet shall some tribute of regret be paid.' Fremantle offered his
'tribute of regret' in the form of an account of the fall of the Residency
and what it 'means still, to those who have known it and something
of its history'.[88] For the British this served as a poignant and symbolic
reminder of the heroic sacrifices of empire, and its inclusion in the
Independence celebrations is not without significance. LeMahieu's contention that the British press from the interwar years became both an
image- and a word-driven medium as a result of technological advances
and being forced to compete with the popularity of other media, like
cinema and newsreels, was epitomised at this juncture by newspapers
such as the ILN, whose Independence number had page upon page
devoted to views of the ceremonies in India, Pakistan and London,
providing a fulsome visual record of events and personalities.[89]

The flag symbolism was also carried through in newspaper features
recording the hoisting of the tricolour from the IO and the Pakistani
flag from Lancaster House, with the popular London evening daily, *The
Star*, noting how the western avenue of Aldwych 'sparkled with all the
colour of an Indian scene' at the flag-hoisting ceremony.[90] The radical weekly *New Statesman* under the editorship of Kingsley Martin had
been a consistent champion of anti-imperialist causes. Writing in his
acclaimed column 'London Diary' under the pseudonym 'Critic', Martin
was euphoric on Independence Day: 'To see the Indian flag hoisted at
Aldwych was a wonderful cure for cynicism. Few aspirations for the
good have succeeded in our time, and we are so accustomed to worthy
defeat and barren victories that a victory that fulfils a worthy aspiration
deserves all the emphasis we can give it.'[91] Throughout the 1930s and
1940s, Martin had 'worked continuously' with the India League run by
Krishna Menon, a man he felt was of 'extraordinary ability'.[92] According to his biographer, he also became 'greatly attached' to Nehru and
Mountbatten,[93] made frequent visits to India, was present at the time
of Gandhi's assassination, and also wrote a regular column for *The Illustrated Weekly of India*. One of his greatest disappointments was, as he
admitted in his autobiography, 'the discovery that peoples who had

been held together under Imperialist rule would not cooperate with each other when they were free'. India was the 'most unhappy case of all', where Muslims and Hindus had 'everything to gain by remaining friends'.[94] The *Telegraph* and the radical *Reynolds News* profiled Krishna Menon upon his installation as the new Indian High Commissioner in London, but from markedly opposing perspectives. The former contended that the appointment 'may be received with mixed feelings', since Menon, as a Socialist member of the St Pancras Borough Council, was not *'persona gratissima'* in Whitehall. By contrast, Peter Yorke in the *Reynolds* ('This man saw his dream come true') extolled the sacrifice and achievements of Menon and his compatriots.

While Fleet Street was unanimous in extending the 'universal goodwill' of Britain (*Spectator*) and promises of 'unstinting' support (*Telegraph, News Chronicle*), one compelling characteristic of this coverage was its self-congratulatory tone. Witnesses to history in the making, journalists of both quality and popular papers from across the political spectrum portrayed the peaceful 'transfer of power' as the 'fulfilment of the British mission'.[95] Victor Thompson in the labour *Herald* appeared to encapsulate press sentiment when he contended that 'The empire which began as an accident has ended on purpose.'[96] Macaulay's 1833 dictum on Britain's 'proudest day' was widely quoted giving the lie, argued the conservative *Mail*, 'to those on the other side of the Atlantic and elsewhere who proclaimed us oppressors'.[97] This theme was echoed by the liberal press too – for example, the *Guardian* emphasised how 'freedom by a voluntary transfer of power [was] unique in history'.[98] Indians, its editorial noted, were able to 'rejoice at achieving their independence without the prelude of country-wide civil war to which some months ago many had resigned themselves'.[99] Similarly, Norman Cliff, the *News Chronicle*'s special correspondent, contended: 'Never has a great Imperial Power surrendered its proud domain or freedom been acquired by subject millions by so peaceful and friendly a transition.'[100]

The *Guardian* stressed how Britain went to India 'not to conquer but to trade. Events not intention created the British Raj.' Indeed, it was the Raj that by enabling 'contact with the outer world' facilitated the 'recovery of a vitality and self confidence' by the Indians. 'As soon as this happened, the political changes now being completed could only be a matter of time, for Great Britain had neither the desire nor the ability to rule a people which had recovered the will to rule itself.'[101] Having acquired the empire, the civilising agency of the Raj came to the fore, the fruits of which were now the abiding legacy for Indians. Independence was for the *Guardian* not an abdication but the 'fulfilment of the

British mission'.[102] The *Observer* was similarly convinced of the 'moral and material benefits' that the Raj had brought to India, which for *Times* leader writer H. M. Stannard included 'the strength and adaptability of the British tradition of political freedom', 'political ideas and constitutional methods for reconciling liberty with order' and 'a new conception of public service'.[103] *The Times* praised the 'quiet, persistent work, maintained for generations, of British men and women who under the Indian sun and the sacrifice of domestic happiness did their duty unflinchingly before God and man'.[104] Institutions singled out for universal commendation included the Indian Army and the ICS. Sir George Schuster claimed that the ICS had displayed 'such integrity, such single hearted devotion, such thoroughness and accuracy' that it had left behind 'a priceless heritage'.[105] Sir Malcolm Darling, whose involvement began in 1904, recorded a touching tribute, 'An ICS farewell to India', though he took care to also give due regard to the struggle waged by the INC.[106]

The Times editorial declaimed loftily that the 'British official in India was like the British climate, more than trying at times but very healthy to live with'. Like the Romans, it argued, British 'adventurers from their gusty island constructed a bridge between East and West... if the bridge but hold, there is opportunity for a reverse movement and the new India, quickened by acquired political sanity and a zeal for human welfare, can give to the West, storm-crossed by circumstance, something of her tranquil wisdom and her sedulous pursuit of eternal verities'.[107] The *New Statesman* admitted that at the moment of departure, nostalgia would 'tug at the hearts', but, despite these 'last-minute looks over the shoulder', Indians and Europeans were beginning to enjoy a friendship between equals.[108] It was also the case that in Pakistan, Britons continued to occupy key posts, with six out of nine Government departments under their supervision.

In true media tradition, there was a strong tendency to personalise politics. Taking the lead from Attlee, Wavell was all but forgotten, the press instead hailing Mountbatten as India's saviour. The *Guardian* noted how, less than a century after Victoria, her great-grandson stood as the freely chosen constitutional head of a free state.[109] Mountbatten's charismatic personality, good looks and royal connections no doubt played a large part in feeding this press adulation. In the words of the *Mail*, 'By his own remarkable powers of personality he brought the Indian leaders together and achieved in less than five months what others for more than a decade had sought in vain to do.'[110] Attlee, too, was praised 'for the firmness of his Indian policy' (*Mail*), with the *Guardian* reminding readers that his statecraft 'was the culmination of years of devotion' to India, beginning with his membership of the Simon Commission in 1927.[111] Even erstwhile critics of the Prime Minister, such as the *Spectator*, acknowledged his 'courage' in committing himself to 'a great act of faith'.[112]

Indian protagonists did not, however, fare as well. While Nehru's 'tryst with destiny' speech was quoted by several papers and he was the recipient of a few positive, though passing, references, what many from across the political spectrum (including the *Express*, *Mail* and *Telegraph*, as well as the *Herald*) chose to reiterate was the gratitude expressed by Indian leaders towards the British, selecting excerpts from their speeches in the Constituent Assembly to emphasise the point. The front page of the *Telegraph* headlined its main story from Colin Reid – 'Indians Praise Britain' – wherein Sarvapalli Radhakrishnan was quoted as saying: 'When we see what the Dutch are doing in Indonesia and the French in Indo-China, we cannot but admire the sagacity and genius of the British people...As from midnight tonight we can no longer blame the Britisher. '[113] Similarly, Rajendra Prasad, the Assembly's President, maintained that freedom was the 'consummation and fulfilment of the historic traditions and economic ideals of the British race'.[114] The imagery of the grateful imperial subject/student and the wise and benevolent colonial master/teacher was a recurrent underlying motif. *Punch* made this explicit in its inimitable style with a cartoon featuring 'Dr Bull's Imperial Academy', where the solar-topee-wearing eponymous hero is bidding farewell to three pupils, each holding a degree scroll inscribed with a different word – 'Moslem', 'Sikh' and 'Hindu'. The caption reads: 'Good-bye and good luck – and don't forget there's quite a flourishing Old Boys' Society you might care to join.'[115]

Notable also by its absence was any detailed discussion of Indian nationalism or the freedom struggle. The few references that were made came predictably in the quality papers. The *Guardian*, like *The Times*, alluded to the key personalities of the INC, quoted from Nehru's speech, and in its editorial on 15 August chose to emphasise the vast challenges facing post-colonial India: 'But Indians have not fought for Independence in the belief that it was a bed of roses. They have claimed, naturally and rightly, the honour of confronting and fighting the dangers with which their country is faced.' Its Independence Day edition also featured a long essay by Sir George Schuster entitled 'The Future of India, Tasks that Face the Two Dominions'. Over the summer the *Guardian* had published reports on different political constituencies, such as the Gurkhas, the Sikhs and the Indian Left, which included the Communist Party, the Socialist Republicans and the Radical

Democrats, along with their principal advocates, such as Sarat Chandra Bose and M. N. Roy.[116] Likewise, Martin in the *New Statesman* stressed how 'We should not forget that this is a victory for the idealists, for Gandhi and Nehru and countless others who suffered for their persistence with long periods in stifling gaols.'[117] Victor Thompson in the *Herald* also made a passing reference to the Indian struggle and the consequent 'bitterness and violence' between the Hindus and Muslims.[118] However, even he attributed the rise of the nationalist movement to the seeds sown by British liberals, who 'continually questioned British rule, insisted that self-government must always be the eventual goal, [and] forced the authorities to proceed with the Indianisation of administration and services'.[119] When Gandhi was mentioned he was invariably portrayed as aloof from the celebrations: 'His creed rejected, his dream of a united India shattered, the architect of India's freedom is a sad, lonely figure on this day of official rejoicing.'[120] Gandhi could not 'reconcile himself to violence and division' although he had been forced to accept the reality of Pakistan.[121]

Partition was widely regarded as a misfortune. Stanley Reed, now knighted and a Conservative MP, referred to it as 'a tragedy' (*Spectator*). The 'fissures' between Hindus and Muslims had 'continuously developed with the transfer of power', beginning with the award of separate electorates in the GoI Act of 1909. Reed reiterated the sentiments expressed in many papers when he referred to the 'astute leadership' of Jinnah in consolidating a feeling of inferiority and cultural difference amongst Muslims.[122] Cliff claimed that the Hindus were 'more likely to deplore the partition of their country than to rejoice at its liberation'.[123] The veteran *Times* correspondent Ian Morrison stressed how the unavoidable Balkanisation of the subcontinent had 'come in a way that has been a disappointment to many Indians who have devoted their lives to the struggle for independence. The vision which they have always had of a strong united India has proved impossible of attainment. Partition has brought sadness to many, and joy in the ceremonies... is not unalloyed.'[124]

While Jinnah was not universally championed, there was a pro-Muslim, anti-Sikh and anti-INC position taken up by, for instance, Sir Evelyn Wrench writing in the *Spectator*, who claimed authority on the basis of personal acquaintance with Jinnah. 'Englishmen can remember with gratitude', claimed Wrench, 'the fact that he refused to embarrass' the Government during the war whereas the INC had launched the Quit India movement in 1942.[125] Amongst detractors of Jinnah was the radical H. N. Brailsford, who found a congenial home in the *New Statesman* but also wrote for periodicals such as the *Contemporary Review*, where he argued that Jinnah had worked 'at every turn to widen the breach' and 'fought only for his own community, in the feud which he has steadily embittered, without a thought for the good of India'.[126] The *News Chronicle* likewise contended that Partition was 'largely the creation of one man, and all indications are that at the outset it will be mainly under his personal rule'. The British were more or less absolved of blame. As 'Sagittarius' wrote in the *New Statesman* (in homage to the Kipling classic 'White Man's Burden'):

> They would not be united
> According to your plan –
> You frowned upon partition
> But yielded Pakistan[127]

Similarly the *Observer*'s editorial position was that while the new Dominions 'should have been born without the pangs of war is good; it is for the two Indias to sustain the peace'.[128] Even the *Guardian*, long the stalwart of Indian nationalism, maintained: 'We have handed over India to the Indians: they have chosen what ... seems a second best – a divided India. But it is their choice; if they come together well and good, but their destiny is in their own hands.'[129]

There also appeared to be a consensus in Fleet Street not to dwell on the communal troubles on Independence Day; but there were a few exceptions where reports of celebrations were juxtaposed with those of massacres. *The Star*'s headline for one report read: 'India Celebrates as Thousands Riot' Meanwhile the *Herald* declared: '120 Killed as India Riots and Feasts'.[130] 'High Death Roll in Punjab', 'Fierce Communal Battles' ran a *Times* story. 'Lahore Ablaze' reported Ralph Izzard, the *Mail*'s special correspondent. The triangular communal situation in the Punjab, where Sikh sentiments were embroiled in the general Hindu–Muslim antipathies, was discussed in the weeks leading up to Independence in *The Times*, *Guardian*, *Telegraph* and *Observer*. Special mention was made of the fraternisation on the streets of Calcutta where 'Hindus and Moslems linked arms' (*Mirror*) and 'drove round the city roaring their joint welcome to independence' (*Daily Worker*). Several papers also singled out what the *Guardian* claimed was the 'Curious Apathy' in Karachi on 14 August, a lethargy that was in sharp contrast to the next day when India erupted with festivities.[131] The *News Chronicle* argued that the Muslims 'show more delight at release from Hindu than from British domination'. For the *Times* correspondent this could be explained by a combination of factors, including the 'lethargic temperament of the ordinary Sindhi', the fact that the majority of Karachi's population were Hindus and a general realisation of the 'tremendous problems' that Pakistan now faced. Only the *Herald*'s Mellor and the newsreel footage from Paramount and Gaumont seemed to contradict this somewhat subdued impression. Mellor referred to Karachi as 'The City of Flags', where 'Cars hooted and bumped each other, people climbed lamp posts and stood on roofs or got jammed in the dense masses in the roads.'

However, Fleet Street was unanimous in highlighting what it regarded a dereliction of British duty towards the princely states. Long the bulwarks of conservative imperialism in the face of rising nationalist agitation, their special relationship with the Raj came to an abrupt end with Independence. 'That Britain should have had to default in its obligations to the Princes is deeply to be regretted', argued the *Spectator*. 'Nothing could be more repugnant to public opinion in Great Britain than any enforced severance from the Commonwealth of rulers who have, in many cases, given loyal support to it in war and in almost all cases value their British connection highly.'[132] The *Contemporary Review* featured a survey of this new constitutional status by V. S. Swaminathan,[133] while, in the *Express*, Sydney Smith chose to give prominence to the largest of these, Hyderabad, where there were no celebrations on 15 August. Alongside a photo of the Nizam who 'insists on maintaining independent relations' with Britain, Smith informed readers that its ruler had a yearly income of £3 million, yet spent barely £5 a month on himself and 'prefers to live on a verandah with a pet goat as companion'. It is unclear how this image of an eccentric rich potentate was meant to endear him to a British audience or help consolidate his claim for an independent status within the Commonwealth. Another *Express* staffer who developed an enviable reputation as an India expert was James Cameron. Charles Foley, the paper's Foreign Editor, allowed Cameron great latitude: 'my relationship with the newspaper could be likened only to that of a very remote and insignificant curate to the Holy See: I accepted their authority and paid no attention at all to their doctrine'.[134] Cameron claimed that this system worked well during his reportage of 'the lengthy and tormented process' of the negotiations for India's independence with 'every manifest enthusiasm for their success, without any real appreciation of the fact that Indian independence was of all things the one Lord Beaverbrook most earnestly opposed'.[135] Cameron admired Nehru, which was

vigorously reflected...in all I wrote, without regard to or even realization of the fact that of all the many *bêtes noires* in the *Express*
catalogue of anathema Mr Nehru stood highest. At no time was there
any secret that any political beliefs I had were socialist, and most
especially anti-Imperialist; for some reason it never occurred to me
that it should have been professionally helpful to remember, if only
occasionally, that I was writing for an organization most articulately
dedicated to the cause of Empire. In retrospect I am still surprised
that this state of affairs went on for so long.[136]

The journalistic freedom enjoyed by Cameron serves as testimony to
Beaverbrook's assertion that, despite his undiminished admiration for
the empire, he allowed the expression of diverse opinion and did not
routinely dictate the political line of the *Express*. As Kevin Williams has
recently emphasised, not even the most active press barons exercised
absolute control over the content of their papers, but left an enormous
amount of discretion to the editors.[137]

Finally, whilst most of Fleet Street echoed the optimism expressed by
the *New Statesman* that the Indians were 'not a bitter, or an unforgiving
race...they will not allow memories of the past to vitiate the potentialities of the future',[138] there was an overwhelming acknowledgement that
a new balance of power needed to be created in the East and that British
foreign policy would have to be reassessed. 'The substitution of such a
balkanised system for the unity which existed before can hardly fail to
increase international tension', worried the *Guardian*.[139] Other underlying anxieties were exposed by the caricaturists' pens. *Punch* portrayed
Mountbatten as the cameraman attempting to orchestrate a picture of
an unstable triumvirate made up of a smiling British Lion flanked by
two ferocious tigers on either side representing the two new dominions,
with the caption: 'Tria Juncta in Uno' (Figure 5.3). And a cartoon in the
News of the World depicted a conversation between a fruitseller and a
flower girl beneath a statute of Disraeli as Lord Beaconsfield, who had
been central to the project of making India the jewel in Britain's crown,
with the caption: 'Egypt gone, and India. Blimey 'e wouldn't 'arf 'ave
used some unparliamentary language!'[140]

The role of the Commonwealth was considered critical though there
was some doubt about whether both new Dominions would join the
association. The *Spectator* was convinced, as was the *Guardian*, that
'By severance from the Commonwealth they can gain no freedom which
is not theirs already; by association with it they will ensure a coiper-
ation that must inure in every way to their advantage.'[141] There was

TRIA JUNCTA IN UNO
"Hold that!"

Figure 5.3 'Tria Juncta in Uno', cartoon by E. H. Shepard, 23 July 1947, reproduced with permission of Punch Ltd

also a sense that India and Pakistan, with their ancient civilisation and traditions, were uniquely placed to act as mediators between the East and West in ways which, the *Mail* argued, 'may profoundly affect the future of the world. Their statesmen now have the power, if they use it right, to bridge the gap between East and West; to make us both, in a true sense, one world.'[142] In addition, the significance of the creation of Pakistan as 'the leading State of the Muslim world' meant, according to *The Times*, that Karachi had emerged as 'a new centre of Muslim cohesion and rallying point for Muslim thought and aspirations'.[143] This was a prescient sentiment indeed, given the context of contemporary geopolitics.

Broadcasting

During the 1930s the BBC under Reith and Fielden had taken a keen interest in Indian broadcasting, as analysed in Chapter 4. However, it was only with the outbreak of the Second World War that the medium was consistently exploited in India for official propaganda. By 1944 there were 189,096 radio receiver licences in British India, with an output of 60,000 transmission hours.[144] In September 1943 the Department of Information and Broadcasting set up a Publicity Planning and Coordination Board consisting of publicity advisers to the GoI. AIR now employed increasingly large numbers of Indians in editorial and senior news positions, and an important innovation saw several of them posted abroad as war correspondents, including B. K. R. Kabad, Pran Chopra and Gohl Obhrai in China, Indonesia and Japan, respectively.[145] In 1943 the new post of Director General was created and A. S. Bokhari became the first incumbent. As noted earlier, it was only in March of that year that AIR was converted into a permanent organisation.[146] Bokhari's brother, Zulfikar, was Fielden's protégé and Director of the Bombay station; largely at the latter's recommendations he had also been seconded to the Ministry of Information in London covering Eastern programming during 1940–1. During the final months of the Raj, under the watchful supervision of Sardar Patel and in close liaison with Mountbatten, AIR was utilised on an unprecedented scale with radio being especially influential since its multilingual output could reach millions outside the purview of the English-language press.[147] In the AIR Independence Day programme it was envisaged that the assumption of power ceremonies would take centre stage in the first transmission. However, in the second and third transmissions there were to be a number of broadcasts by outstanding personalities, including Rajendra Prasad, Sarojini Naidu, Nehru and M. A. K. Azad – all in English, Patel in Hindustani and Baldev Singh addressing primarily the Sikh constituencies. Vijaylakshmi Pandit, Sucheta Kriplani and Kamladevi Chattopadhyay were to participate in a special women's programme in Hindustani, and there was also to be a rural programme and a feature on 'Free India', devised and produced by Aubrey Menen.[148]

However, the reputation of AIR suffered on account of its continued identification with British control, and it was viewed as 'part of a vast propaganda organisation forming one substantial wall of the palisade'.[149] BBC staffers felt, much like Lionel Fielden had a decade earlier, that the 'highly dynamic' profession of broadcasting was 'ill-adapted to the narrow bureaucratic methods'. 'My impression, as a very frequent visitor to the headquarters of the AIR,' claimed Donald Stephenson, 'is that one finds there far too many buff-covered files and far too little constructive programme planning.'[150] As its organisation continued to evolve through the 1940s, Stephenson was appointed as Director of the BBC's Delhi office in February 1944, joined a month later by Percival Fearnley as its first Press and Public Relations Officer. Over time the responsibilities of the Director also came to encompass an element of audience research. Stephenson acknowledged that the 'status and repute' of the BBC gave him 'great facility of access' not only to senior Government officials but also Indian political leaders.[151] In a revealing appraisal of his functions at this sensitive juncture, he highlighted four key areas. The first two involved the 'purely managerial and office' functions together with the daily routine of broadcasting. The third and fourth roles were directed at 'making and maintaining political and military contact on the higher level ... Luncheon and dinner invitations are, on the whole, a curse, but they have to be faced.' In addition there was the 'long term planning' for the future of the Delhi office and of BBC operations in, from and to India.[152] Stephenson also stressed the challenge faced by journalists trying to operate in isolation from politics: 'It is necessary, though extraordinarily difficult, to keep one's sphere of activities within the legitimate province of broadcasting. In this country everyone seems to take a hand in politics, and the man who concentrates on his own job seems to be a rare phenomenon.'[153]

The increasingly volatile nationalist context necessitated reappraisals of the status, output and viability of the BBC within an India hurtling towards Independence. Stephenson identified the ambiguous response to the BBC from Indians – that is, why there should be dissatisfaction despite the fact that 'it is listened to with surprising frequency and with much good-will'. First, he suggested, it was because BBC broadcasts 'addressed directly to the Indian people originated as a political expediency dictated by the outbreak of war'. Second, there was 'a profound sense of disappointment' that the BBC, like AIR, 'is bound by the "sealed lips" policy on the more controversial details of India's grievances'.[154] Yet while the BBC's inability to engage in public controversy might well have frustrated political elites, its reputation and ability to reach a transnational audience ensured that it remained an attractive medium for officials and nationalists alike.

After further soul-searching about its future – for instance, by another BBC staffer C. J. Pennethorne Hughes[155] – the Director General, Sir William Haley, concluded in July 1946 that careful deliberations and high-level consultations with experienced colleagues and a longer-term perspective were essential since 'Feeling in India in the coming months is likely to be such that whatever we do will be hailed with suspicion. Immediate Indian reaction can therefore I think be discounted in decid-ing our future course of action.'[156] Finally the decision was made to continue with a revamped Delhi office since it was considered inappro-priate at the moment of decolonisation 'to strike our flag in India – or even to lower it to any appreciable extent'.[157] In 1946, Donald Edwards replaced Stephenson, and Haley informed him that his ignorance about India was 'an advantage' since it would 'make the Indian problem clear to your own simple mind and so to the audience'. He added, somewhat cryptically, that should Edwards 'get in trouble with the authorities', he would have Haley's support provided he 'deserve[d] it'.[158] However, at the same time, Bob Stimson, an established journalist with the *Times of India*, was also appointed as overall Manager, his knowledge of local conditions being considered valuable at the moment of political transi-tion. Edwards reached Delhi 'one blazing noon': 'I winced as my hand touched a wall hot as a furnace door... at my hotel a mob of hungry men clamoured to be my servant... By midnight on the first day I had had six baths.'[159] Professionally, things proceeded more smoothly and Edwards found that the mere mention of the BBC opened doors every-where. He recorded an interview with Nehru on condition that Nehru was given access to the transcript before broadcast, a precaution made necessary by the delicacy of the impending negotiations of the Cabi-net Mission Plan. In the interests of impartiality, he also interviewed Jinnah.[160] However, Edwards was to reminisce that of all his encounters with nationalists, the most seminal was with Gandhi, to whom he was allowed unprecedented access, due in part to the reputation established by Edwards's uncle who lived in Poona as head of a theological college and 'knew and admired' the Mahatma. Edwards was deeply shocked by the religious fervour of Indians, which he witnessed at one of its darkest moments during the great Calcutta killings in 1946, an issue he dis-cussed at some length with Gandhi. Like William Shirer, as analysed in

Chapter 3, he found that when discussing religion 'I did not grasp all that Gandhi said. It was like catching bubbles in the air.'[161]

The BBC's adherence to balance, reliability and political neutrality was thus established before Independence, and has continued, with some notable disruptions, ever since. Campbell-Johnson was pleased with the BBC coverage of the 3 June announcement, describing it as 'magnificent', affirming how it was 'good to see that they have at last woken up to the full importance of India and are laying on ambitious programmes to cover the transfer of power'.[162] He also had 'long talks' with Gordon Mosley, one of the BBC representatives in Delhi, who was returning for consultations in London. It was considered advantageous to acquaint head office with 'some of the local problems in the light of the latest political developments here'.[163] Not leaving it to chance, Mountbatten met with Haley and secured his commitment to provide 'very full attention to the period of the transfer of power'. The BBC thus despatched a dedicated team of veteran news reporters to cover events, including Wynford Vaughan Thomas, Edward Ward and Richard Sharp, along with two distinguished feature writers, Francis Dillon and Louis MacNeice. Thomas had recently covered the royal tour to South Africa, and Sharp had reported from the South East Asia Command during the Second World War, though neither had been to India before (Figure 5.4).

Armed with three mobile recording units, their brief was 'to report fully in this country and all over the world the progress of transfer from August onwards and further most importantly to provide material for programmes describing the British record of achievement in India'.[164] The news team was to convey comprehensive eyewitness accounts of day-to-day events, whilst the writers were to collect recordings from a variety of locales. Sir Reginald Coupland, Professor of Colonial History at Oxford, was to act as adviser and historical consultant. While there was approval of measures to cover events just before and after 15 August, there was concern, as articulated by Listowel, that, should there be continued communal violence after the transfer of power, the BBC's aim of emphasising British achievement might give unintentional offence as 'we should appear to be trying to emphasize awful consequences of abandonment of power'.[165] Mountbatten concurred: 'It would be far better to let the new Dominions find their own feet within the Commonwealth, rather than overstress the whole business at the start.'[166] However, the Viceroy remained confident that 'in the end we shall be able to get the right stand on things'.[167]

The issue of the BBC's *Listener* magazine to cover Indian (and Pakistani) Independence featured large photographs of the two flags

202

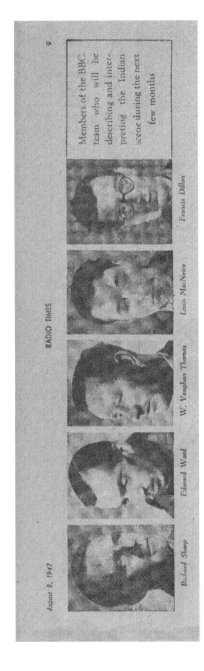

Figure 5.4 BBC India Team for Independence coverage, the *Radio Times*, 8 August 1947, reproduced by permission of the *Radio Times*

on its front page, and a short editorial likewise entitled 'Under Two Flags' (interestingly the former IO building was shown to have both the Union Jack and the Indian tricolour aloft its flagpole).[168] The day's news bulletins reported on the transfer of power, and the *Listener* featured a photomontage depicting critical scenes in the history of the Raj as well as reproducing the text of General Sir William Slim's broadcast, 'A Tribute to the Indian Army'.[169] Meanwhile the BBC's onsite team were duly involved in a range of broadcasts, arriving in Karachi on 8 August where they were witness to the Viceregal pomp and circumstance on display during Pakistan's Independence Day on 14 August. The BBC's proclaimed objective was 'to record and report the impact of this great change in their destiny on the peoples of India at the moment of its happening'. The resultant programmes were based on impressions taken from both the 'streets and bazaars' as well as the 'council chambers', transmitted to London via air mail and radio telegraphy. At Broadcasting House these were rearranged into weekly features and aired on the Home Service during the Sunday evening prime-time slot (6.10–6.40 p.m.) as the 'Report on India'. From the BBC's finest team, on what was considered a 'responsible and arduous assignment', these broadcasts continued for two months.[170] The technical challenges involved were accentuated by the hot climatic conditions, and Stimson claimed that the melting of discs during outside recordings was a serious possibility. AIR shared its high-powered transmitter in Delhi to allow daily BBC transmissions to London for speedy editing. The discs were flown from Karachi, reaching within 48 hours, whilst the topical reports were cabled.[171]

The tapes and transcripts for the first three Reports, covering the lead up to and the moment of Independence, have not been preserved in the BBC's archives. However, the fourth, aired on 31 August, has, and it reveals the imprint of official choreography as well as a judicious attempt to present a balanced and positive picture of the new nation despite the emerging horrors of Partition. Stories from Stimson and Thomas focused on the Punjab and the plight of the Sikhs, whom Stimson considered 'the unhappiest people in the Indian subcontinent today'.[172] Thomas spoke frankly: 'This is a horror story, unpleasant to listen to and even more unpleasant to relate. But unless you listen to this story you can't really understand the wave of terror that is spreading on both sides of the line in Pakistan and in the east Punjab.'[173] However, these narratives were followed by a lengthy report from none other than Lady Mountbatten, who began by suggesting that

In listening to Indian news, it must have occurred to you that the great statesmanship shown by the Indian leaders has sometimes been overshadowed by the story of the communal struggle, poverty, fanaticism, squalor and sudden death. During the past five months, I have had a unique opportunity of seeing for myself the other side of the picture, the struggle against disease and destruction. It has not, perhaps, quite the same news value. It's a battle, however, which is being fought by individuals, services and institutions, grappling with medical relief and other humanitarian problems.[174]

Edwina went on to relate several such positive stories. And to further paint a more optimistic picture, her input was followed by Richard Sharp's recordings from Calcutta, wherein he corroborated such optimism, claiming that 'in other parts of India, this faith in the ability of the people to work together has been justified. In striking contrast to the tragedy of the divided Punjab, has been the news of friendly demonstrations in the other divided province, Bengal, where the presence of Mr Gandhi in Calcutta seems so far to have served as a rallying point for the forces of tolerance.'[175] Stimson emphasised the grave economic problems facing the new nation, arguing that there were similarities between India and Britain after the Second World War, 'for we too are faced with a major economic crisis. But here in India, our crisis is only just beginning to be front pages news.' The last word was predictably given to the Vicereine, who reiterated the needs of the common man and how 'An early revolution in health, education, housing and general standard of living is vital, if the Indian people are to have a fair chance of benefitting from their newly-won independence.' Concluding on an uplifting note, she declared: 'But on all sides, I have found the stirring of a new spirit.'[176]

This series was followed by more in-depth documentaries broadcast during 1948, composed and produced by MacNeice and Dillon, and with two guest presenters, Francis Watson and Phillip Woodruff, both prominent ICS-wallahs. MacNeice was an accomplished poet and BBC features writer, and was given enormous creative freedom by his producer, Laurence Gilliam, who encouraged his staff to travel and obtain the first-hand knowledge necessary to compose authentic documentaries. MacNeice claimed India to be 'the most foreign country' he had ever visited.[177] Before and during the war, he had met Indian writers and intellectuals in London, including Mulk Raj Anand, with whom he had struck up a friendship. Now, along with his colleagues, MacNeice travelled the length and breadth of the subcontinent, visiting Kashmir and the Khyber Pass in the north and north-west, Hyderabad, Madras, Mahabalipuram and Cape Comorin in the south, as well as taking in the Ajanta and Ellora Caves in the west, and travelling east to Benaras and Calcutta. His documentary-feature that resulted from this lengthy sojourn, 'India at First Sight', was broadcast on 13 March, followed by two further pieces, 'Portrait of Delhi' (2 May) and 'The Road to Independence' (23 May). MacNeice, though clearly moved by the striking contrasts of poverty and plenty, nevertheless displayed a remarkable sensitivity to Indian sentiment, choosing not to dwell exclusively on the atrocities accompanying Partition, but interpreting the difficulties in the birth pangs of modern statehood with an even-handed panache. Coulton claims that MacNeice's documentaries were inherently personal accounts, and 'this tends to reduce objectivity, and occasionally to introduce a note of sentimentality'.[178] Yet, as has been persuasively argued by David Hendy, to remove emotion and empathy from the creative process would arguably have devalued its impact.[179] In the case of India, such emotion served to provide for the ordinary British listener a valuable account of decolonisation as well as a flavour of the nascent Indian nation, which was as legitimate a perspective as any contained within an official despatch.

Over the following months, the BBC in London also continued to engage with the aftermath of Independence, inviting a range of speakers to share reminiscences on air. Prominent amongst these was the architect of the Partition boundary, Sir Cyril Radcliffe, who emphasised, much like Fleet Street journalists, that 'The gifts we brought were Roman: peace, order, justice and the fruits that those things bring. Men are apt to prize them the less the longer they enjoy them'. But in a frank admission, he also accepted that 'such gifts are not everything. They are the structure, but not the heart or the brain in the life of a people. It may be that somewhere on our course we mistook the means for the end and, absorbed in our practical tasks, we failed to penetrate to the heart or soul of India.'[180]

Newsreels

As Independence approached, and despite their hectic schedule Mountbatten and Campbell-Johnson made sure that when in London they also prioritised meetings with newsreel representatives. Mountbatten was 'anxious that all important phases of the ceremonies, should be covered by newsreel men',[181] but was 'appalled' at the 'indifference' of the major companies who, apart from the American financed Paramount and Movietone (who employed two Indian stringers), had no plans to cover the event.[182] It is a sobering thought that were it not for Mountbatten's personal intervention, it is doubtful whether there would be any substantive cinefilm records of the British handover of power. Indeed, it was only with three weeks to go that John Turner of Gaumont-British News was hastily appointed as the official representative of the Newsreel Association to work on a rota agreement. Long-Maddox, the Association's secretary, vouched for Turner 'as a reputable and responsible person' who had a distinguished war record.[183] Turner was to remain in the subcontinent till the summer of 1948, capturing Mountbatten's term as Governor-General. Mountbatten was assiduous in ensuring that the GoI paid for Turner's domestic travels, even though he was not attached to the Viceregal staff. Instead it was emphasised that he was 'to publicise India and not the Viceroy'.[184]

Turner had barely time to prepare to film 'a world story', arriving in Delhi on 10 August and flying out to Karachi with the Mountbattens three days later.[185] His schedule was dictated by the engagements of the Raj, which were faithfully recorded. Turner was greatly aided by the practical and logistical assistance he received from the aforementioned Indian stringers – Ved Prakash (Paramount) and his brother Mohan (Movietone) – as well as liaising with Desfor of the AP, covering several stories together. Turner also captured the mood of the crowds – 'I could not help but be infected by everyone's cheerful spirits' – as well as more informal events, such as the Mountbattens' walkabout, accompanied by daughter Pamela, at a children's playground during the afternoon of 15 August. Working amongst the 'chaos with screaming, pushing youngsters' did provide 'good pictures', Turner reminisced, but it was 'hard work'.[186] This story of the transfer of power appeared in the newsreels of 21 August and was despatched back to Delhi where it was screened on 24 August. According to Mountbatten, the audience 'were much impressed by the excellence of the photography and the competence of the commentary'. He felt that Turner had 'got off to a good start and his presence here should lead to a great improvement in the hitherto meagre film material on India'.[187] Campbell-Johnson claimed that the film rota agreement worked well, resulting in 'excellent newsreels',[188] However, historians have argued that the overwhelming emphasis of the coverage was on eulogistic accounts of the official ceremonies, with key Indian and Pakistani protagonists often sidelined or ignored.[189] This was inevitable to some degree, given that the Independence events were choreographed to revolve around the British, especially the Mountbattens. However, Turner's subsequent newsreel footage did reveal the horrors of Partition, and the precarious conditions for millions of refugees.

Indian and Anglo-Indian Press

Though not the principal focus of this case study, it is, nevertheless, useful in this context to note the response of the English-language Indian press on Independence Day, including some of the major Anglo-Indian and Indian-owned publications.[190] Most papers brought out special Independence supplements, helped by the lifting of paper rationing for the occasion, wherein events, photographs, personalities and comment jostled for space along with advertisements for all manner of Raj- and Independence-related memorabilia marketed as 'mementoes for the most memorable day'.[191] Business services and product advertisements emphasised their 'national' and 'Indian' credentials, with the link between patriotism and quality seamlessly drawn. So an advertisement for the 'Radio Corporation of India Ltd' claimed it to be 'A Gigantic Concern but purely national'.[192] Another for 'The People's Set' purported to be the first Indian-made radio available for only Rs 95 and with most components produced in India.[193] Dunlop (India) proclaimed its tyres were '10 years Made in India', whilst 'Little's Oriental Balm Co' contended that while the freedom fight was begun in 1886 [sic], the 'blessings of Freedom from Pain was enjoyed by its people from 1885' through its product.[194] From a perusal of advertising it would appear to be business as usual for British manufacturers, including such prominent brands as Ponds, Rennies, Cussons, Vaseline, Brylcreem and Johnson's.

Given the size of the country, newspapers reflected inevitably upon the particularities of their regional position as well as their political and economic connections. Thus the *Bombay Chronicle* had an interesting feature on the cinema industry: with the exception of Lahore, the majority of films were produced in Bombay and indeed, in independence week itself, four new titles were released.[195] Its leading article entitled 'Jai Hind' claimed how India's Independence was 'an event of importance to the world'. 'Freedom at last! India, this ancient, beloved land of ours released after hundred and fifty years of the agony and humiliation of slavery, is free to-day.'[196] The *National Herald* unsurprisingly gave Nehru a prominent place on its front pages, on 12 August featuring his assurances to minorities juxtaposed with Patel's call for a united front, while on 13 August it captured Nehru's arrival at the Lucknow aerodrome from his ancestral home in Allahabad. The paper's coverage on Independence Day concentrated on local celebrations and dignitaries, noting how 'Lucknow Goes Gay, City a Riot of Colour'.[197]

Amongst the key pillars of the Anglo-Indian press were the *Statesman* and the *Times of India*. The *Statesman*'s euphoric front page proclaimed

'Political Freedom for One-Fifth of Human Race'. Its leader claimed that 'Britain's sincerity, Lord Mountbatten's speed and skill, and the ideals, statesmanship and eventual practical capacity for compromise of this country's leaders have made August 15 1947 the greatest day in modern Indian history... The speed with which during this final brilliant Viceroyalty... the transfer of power has been achieved is almost stupefying.' The *Times of India* reflected upon the 'Frenzied Enthusiasm in Bombay' and featured photographs of Nehru, Mountbatten and Jinnah. Its editorial, simply entitled 'Freedom', with the subtitle 'One Era ends: A new begins', followed the line of Attlee's peroration in Parliament, and discussed the speed and goodwill with which power was 'transferred' to the new Dominions. It acknowledged 'those Giants of the Past' who had made Independence possible; however, it is revealing that these 'Giants' were predominantly Indian moderates, including Dadabhai Naoroji, Pherozeshah Mehta, Tilak, Gokhale, Besant, W. C. Bonnerjea, Surendranath Bannerjea, C. R. Das and Motilal Nehru. Partition was blamed on 'all parties', though the paper was thankful for freedom 'without a violent and bloody upheaval' and felt that the future was 'pregnant with immense possibilities'.[198]

Indeed, a general sense that the day marked but the opening act of a long drama pervaded the columns of many newspapers. Hope was combined with trepidation, given the enormity of tasks that lay ahead for the new nation. The *Pioneer*'s editorial argued that there was 'a sense of both weariness and disappointment... we at least must not fail to measure up to our independence'.[199] The *Bombay Chronicle* noted how 'the past is still with us' and that 'there is no peace'.[200] The *National Herald*'s leader, entitled 'To the Fallen and To the Free', claimed that 'Nothing less than an epoch is dying and nothing less than a civilization is being re-born', and that this represented 'not merely the liberation of the flesh but also of the mind'. This liberation was from 'alien rule, thought, speech and manners' that represented 'the tyranny of mind over mind'.[201]

Despite such sentiments, noticeable space in the Indian-owned press was also accorded to analyses by British journalists and political commentators, as well as to messages of congratulations from overseas covering details of celebrations in London, Washington, New York, Moscow, Cairo, Switzerland, Johannesburg, Saigon, Canberra, Singapore, Tokyo and so on.[202] The *National Herald* featured a long essay entitled 'From Annexation to Liberation', which quoted with approval Macaulay, Gladstone and Burke. The *Bombay Chronicle* placed in its gallery of photos Britons such as A. O. Hume, W. Wedderburn, Alfred Webb and

George Yule. The *Pioneer, Bombay Chronicle* and *Statesman* all printed versions of the same essay by Arthur Moore (former editor of the *Statesman*) entitled 'Appointment with Freedom'. 'Now is the appointed day. Now is the day of salvation', proclaimed Moore. 'On every one of us who lived in India...there is a personal responsibility to start this day with our thoughts right...To me such a day was to be fitting climax of the intertwined story of Britain and India, the fulfilment of Britain's mission.'[203]

Apart from universal adulation heaped upon the 'freedom fighters', what is also noticeable is how the 'history of Indian Independence' was considered to be 'in a large measure the history of Congress'.[204] Substantial space was devoted to Gandhi by all newspapers. The *Bombay Chronicle*'s Independence supplement was dedicated to the Mahatma, and its 15 August leader declared him to be 'the father of our nationalism and the architect of our freedom', a sentiment echoed in the *National Herald, Times of India* and *Statesman*, amongst others. Like several of their Fleet Street counterparts, these papers also emphasised how Gandhi, instead of celebrating in Delhi, was living in the 'shambles' of Calcutta 'amidst the raging fire that is consuming not only houses and bodies but hearts and souls'.[205]

A preoccupation with communal violence in the months leading up to Independence also served to display the ideological stance of various publications. Thus the *Pioneer*, now in its 83rd year, exhibited a marked tendency to lay the blame at the door of the Muslim League. In a leading article published a week before Independence, it noted: 'There can be no security for either India or Pakistan if the dangerous theory that Muslims in India and Hindus in Pakistan serve as mutual hostages is not discredited by all responsible leaders.'[206] The League, the paper contended, 'roused Muslim fanaticism to fever pitch', whilst the INC 'kept harping on the virtues of nonviolence', which did little to stop the 'senseless' rioting. 'There is no use disguising the fact that the riot honours went to the League.'[207] *Dawn*, unsurprisingly, took the opposite stance. In the final days prior to Independence, it repeatedly expressed doubts about whether the Muslims in India would receive a fair deal under the INC. The paper took umbrage at the fact that whilst India automatically achieved membership of the United Nations organisation as the successor state to British India, Pakistan was regarded as 'a mere separatist State breaking away from the Indian dominion'.[208] *Dawn*'s Independence Day number and supplement were dominated by the Muslim experience and insisted on referring to India as 'Hindustan' in an attempt to underline distinctions based on religion. 'The Story of the Muslim Struggle for Independence' was how editor Altaf Husain characterised the final decade of the Raj, while another essay from the pen of Ishtiaq H. Quraishi recounted the 'The Story of Indian Muslims' across the millennia.[209]

The anguish over communal killings and riots was understandably more visible in the journals based in the regions directly affected, but overall it was not a marked feature of Independence Day press coverage *per se*. A pertinent example of the former was the CMG based in Lahore, whose pages were replete with news of communal killings, destruction of property and lawlessness. On 9 August its editorial was captioned 'Dying Lahore'. The CMG criticised all leaders who took an extreme political stance – for instance, singling out V. D. Savakar's comment: 'As we never accepted the rule of the British, we will never accept the existence of Pakistan.' The paper compared this unfavourably to comments by Sardar Patel who, though opposed to the vivisection of the country, hoped for mutual cooperation.[210] On 14 August the CMG proclaimed in a bold and big display that 'Murder and Arson Reach new Peak' and 'Ancient Walled City a Veritable Wall of Flames', with 111 killed and 116 injured the day before. Its leading article was captioned 'Vendetta' and argued that 'Tomorrow the sun of Independence will rise for India, but for the Punjab it will be a cheerless dawn. The partition announcement was hailed with the relief which greets the end of indecision; but the hope then born of the opening of an era of constructive activity has not been able to survive the chaos which partition in practice has produced.'

The *Tribune* was another longstanding and reputable newspaper published in Lahore with strongly nationalist rather than sectarian credentials. However, its management was forced to flee after Partition to Ambala and later Chandigarh, and its premises and personnel subjected to arson and attack, as it was identified in Pakistani eyes with Sikh and Hindu sympathies. Its coverage over the summer of 1947 inevitably reflected a concern with the division of its primary readership constituency. A leader in May accused Jinnah of being 'committed to the cult of vivisection', and 'first trotting out the preposterous theory that Hindus and Muslims were two disparate nations'.[211] It further argued that the 'solicitude that he has exhibited for the welfare of the minority communities has left them cold; they read something sinister in that solicitude'. The *Statesman*, too, was sympathetic to the Hindu position, contending that the fact that they 'should be less pleased than the Muslims with the manner in which independence has come about may be readily understood ... it is natural that Hindus should hope and even work to upset it'.[212] There was, however, a marked difference in tone when the situation in Calcutta on 15 August was discussed. Here in the Hindu–Muslim amity was cause for celebration. There were 'Amazing scenes of popular enthusiasm', noted the *Statesman*'s staff reporter. 'The exuberance of the people knew no bounds. The beflagged streets were packed with hilarious crowds, men, women and children participating in the festival.'[213]

Finally, what is noticeable is the distinct lack of rancour towards the erstwhile colonial officials, especially the Mountbattens, who were universally praised. The *National Herald*'s leading article entitled 'Power' commended the Viceroy, who had carried out an intricate plan.[214] The *Pioneer* featured extracts from a speech by Krishna Menon paying 'tribute to that great, gallant and noble Englishman, Lord Mountbatten'.[215] The Anglo-Indian press echoed the *Statesman*'s claim that his new post was 'shining proof of the unparalleled personal esteem attained by Lord Mountbatten among Congressmen and Leaguers alike during four short dramatic months'.[216] The Mountbattens themselves released a letter apiece to the Indian press especially composed for the historic occasion. The Viceroy paid his 'tribute': 'Upon the Press has fallen the heavy responsibility for keeping the public well informed about one of the most complex political and administrative operations in history … By upholding fair comment and accurate reports, it has an equally vital part to play in the future. There can be no finer guarantee to a nation's welfare than a free Press in the service of a free nation.' Edwina claimed to have 'seen for myself what a valuable contribution the Press has made to the great events we are now celebrating, and I have also been most impressed by the space and treatment given to all those activities affecting the health, education and social welfare of the people'.[217] Not to be outdone, India's new ruling elite also used the media to reach the masses. Nehru's 'messages to the nation' declaimed how 'The Appointed Day has come – the day appointed by destiny, and India stands forth again, after long slumber and struggle, awake, vital, free and independent.' Rajendra Prasad reiterated the importance of the tasks ahead: 'India Must Conquer Privation, Disease and Hunger.' Sardar Patel echoed such sentiments, pleading for 'universal co-operation': 'Let us not forget in the joy of the hour, the stupendous responsibilities and obligations which freedom has brought in its wake.'[218]

Concluding Remarks: 'It was a close race, we just pulled it off'

This chapter has had two primary foci: first, the British media: the national press, the BBC and newsreels, and the diverse arguments put forth into contemporary popular debate about the end of empire; second, the powerful government propaganda machinery in New Delhi and the IO, and their evolving relationship with the communication-media under the direction of the publicity-savvy Mountbatten, who played a seminal role in mediating the public image of decolonisation. Expressions of mutual admiration abounded between nationalists and the Viceroy, and the fraternisation between colonisers and colonised on the day itself, as witnessed in Delhi, was a remarkable display. The 'flood of popular emotion... has borne all along with it', contended the *Statesman*. 'Extraordinary manifestations' of it occurred in Delhi, where Mountbatten 'became a popular figure to an extent never possible for any Viceroy in living memory'.[219] Even *Dawn* on 14 August headlined in bold its front-page story: 'Qaed-E-Azam's Tribute to British People', referring to Jinnah's toast to the King at the state dinner for the Mountbattens in Karachi, during which he also praised Queen Victoria as 'a great and good Queen', as well as the British Government, which despite 'many acts of commission and omission' had managed an 'absolute transfer of power unknown in world history'. Such fraternisation was no doubt, in part, motivated by *welt-politik*, but the atmosphere that allowed such fraternisation was also manufactured by a well-conceived and clever publicity campaign masterminded by Mountbatten over several months.

Overall, Campbell-Johnson argued that the Independence celebrations had gone off 'very well from the publicity viewpoint', and the reception accorded to the Mountbattens in both Delhi and Bombay 'was quite extraordinary'.[220] Despite last-minute preparations, the newsreel film-rota agreement had worked successfully. The BBC had devoted considerable resources and some of its best talent to covering the end of empire, with its overall laudatory message supporting the official image Mountbatten desired to convey. After Independence, the Corporation strove to provide a balanced picture of the new India: coverage of Partition massacres in the Punjab, for instance, being juxtaposed with those of the celebrations uniting Hindus and Muslims on the streets of Calcutta; or a discussion of the problems facing the new democracy being presented alongside a picture of an ancient civilization with enormous potential. The British national press was in a particularly influential position – its journalists enjoyed unprecedented access to the locus of imperial power and to primary news sources. Special correspondents were deployed in large numbers, and its leader writers were men of ability and longstanding experience of the East, such as L. F. Rushbrook Williams, who wrote the majority of the leaders in *The*

Times and had been successively Fellow of All Souls College, Oxford, Professor of History at Allahabad University, Chief Propaganda Officer to the GoI during the Great War, and Adviser at the Ministry of Information during the Second World War, as well as Colin Reid, the *Telegraph's* Special Correspondent, whose expertise lay in coverage of the Muslim diaspora.[221] Other high-profile contributors included Kingsley Martin, Malcolm Muggeridge, Desmond Young, James Cameron, Arthur Moore and Stanley Reed, all with exceptional reputations in British journalism, their commentaries adding *gravitas* to the official proceedings. The Anglo-Indian press followed a line similar to Fleet Street but was markedly more sympathetic to the new India and its aspirations. Taking the lead from their political leaders in the Constituent Assembly, the Indian press on Independence Day displayed little overt rancour towards either the British or the outgoing Viceroy. Criticism, where it existed, was muted and generalised as critiques of the colonial *mentalité*, with an occasional focus on specific events, such as the Amritsar Massacre or the Quit India movement. Overall there were no sustained recriminations; instead, a significant number of Britons, both official and non-official, were singled out for praise, with several also invited to contribute to its pages on Independence day itself.

Although the majority of Fleet Street had broadly supported the imperial project, they appeared to reach, with only a few murmurings of regret, a remarkably consensual verdict on the loss of the proverbial jewel in the British Crown. India was 'willingly relinquished' by the imperial nation, the Labour *Herald's* special correspondent concluded, as 'a shining act of faith and justice'.[222] Distinctions between papers of different political persuasions, so marked in domestic politics and indeed in the lead-up to Independence, appeared to dissolve in the moment of its realisation. The extent to which this reflected a pragmatic response to what was perceived as an inevitable change given the political consensus at Westminster, or was influenced by new international pressures operating in a post-war world and specifically from the self-proclaimed leader of the free world, the US, is debateable. There is less doubt, however, that sophisticated systems of information management and propaganda were deployed by the Raj anxiously looking towards the world's stage for approval and keen to maintain productive ties with the new nations of the East. British enterprise and capital investment 'dominated' India's private foreign sector in 1947. By the end of the 1950s, this was 'well above the 1948 level'.[223] Britain still had a powerful stake in India economically and strategically, and the official priority was to protect this scenario.

It would be difficult to deny that what *The Times* referred to as Mountbatten's 'high powered diplomacy of discussion', and Pamela as her father's 'Operation seduction',[224] had an impact in fashioning the story conveyed to the reading public, though it is more problematic to gauge the specific extent and nature of this influence across the spectrum of the political press. What is also of import is the impact of Fleet Street coverage within the subcontinent and transnationally, where it was taken to reflect a wider British popular opinion. However, what is open to much less debate is that this honeymoon period in press reportage of the subcontinent was over almost as soon as it began. And herein lay the paradox. The narrative as structured on Independence Day was one of the fulfilment of the Raj's imperial destiny: Macaulay's dream in the 1830s. The press were able to portray Independence as a British achievement – as something arising almost organically out of her long-term policy and vindicating her rule. Yet, within a few days, sections of the British press (particularly the conservative press), as well as some US newspapers, began to reassess and question the capacity for self-governance of the Indians. The consequences of Independence were increasingly seen as bearing out the warnings of those like Winston Churchill who had seen the empire as necessary for good governance and stability within India – the so called Pax Britannica. Therefore both the act of Independence and its aftermath – though for very different reasons – were seen as justifying imperial rule. Thus the *Observer*'s leader writer argued on 31 August that 'the Punjab massacres are a sad commentary on India's attainment of independence, barely a fortnight old'.[225] It blamed the 'fanatical hatred of the Sikhs for Moslems long recklessly fanned by Sikh leaders [that] has exploded uncontrollably' since the Boundary Commission's decisions and the Boundary force itself had failed 'miserably'. The *Telegraph*'s headlines highlighted the 'civil war' that engulfed the disputed areas of the Punjab, with Reid arguing that Radcliffe's award had been deliberately 'withheld during the Independence celebrations because of the volcanic situation and for fear of immediate repercussions'.[226]

As part of the official response to the post-Partition crisis, a special Public Relations Committee was established in Delhi with Unni Nayar (seconded from the *Statesman*), B. L. Sharma (representative of the Press Information Office) and Campbell-Johnson as its members. They convened a daily press conference, and information bulletin boards were set up at the Imperial Hotel, and the offices of the *Hindustan Times*, the *Statesman*, AIR and API. A continuing problem was the lack of facilities for correspondents in east and west Punjab, which was 'one of the causes of badly balanced reporting'.[227] The mass of the foreign correspondents were also based in Delhi, further directing the critical spotlight on the Indian government and imposing, in effect, a news blackout from Pakistan. The blame for the communal troubles was laid, in some quarters, almost unequivocally at India's door, a sentiment reinforced when Delhi was engulfed in the crisis during September. Delhi 'fears Mob Rule "Volcano"' claimed the *Observer*. 'Communal flames from the Punjab holocaust have spread to the heart of the Indian capital itself... Delhi today is a badly scarred city... perched precariously on the edge of a communal volcano.'[228] *Punch* depicted a large snake resembling a boa constrictor representing the 'Punjab massacres', strangling a hapless deer named 'Minority' in its deathly grasp.[229]

According to Campbell-Johnson, after Independence there was 'a marked decline' in the relations between the GoI and the British and overseas press corps. Contributing to this fracture were a few British and American correspondents who had been

> somewhat 'trigger happy' in their coverage, and one does not have to come very far to nose out horrific incidents. What is much more difficult is to view the whole Punjab crisis in perspective and in doing so to decide where the story begins. Objectivity in this communal tit for tat is very difficult to come by and not readily accepted by opinion on either side of the border.[230]

An enraged Nehru mounted 'a strong attack on the foreign press' at a conference on 28 August, threatening to impose censorship, though he was ultimately dissuaded from doing so by, among others, Mountbatten and Campbell-Johnson, the latter claiming that his relationship with journalists was 'unimpaired', enabling him to act as 'a mediator'.[231] One repercussion from this crisis was to give the signal to Indian newspapers to launch attacks on their overseas counterparts. The *Hindustan Standard* in a leader entitled 'A Base campaign' argued that 'Highly coloured and tendentious accounts of the disturbances in India continue to be flashed in the Tory press in the UK and their yellow counterpart in the US.'[232] The paper deplored the 'almost ghoulish delight' with which they attacked the GoI. 'We do not want that a veil should be drawn over the dark happenings in this country,' the editorial contended, 'But, equally, we cannot permit a deliberate distortion of the truth. We cannot advise our Government to sit quietly while our country and its administration are being hit below the belt by a band of alien slanderers with falsehood as their chief weapon. Their own linen is not half as clean as that of India.'[233] Lord Ismay appreciated the irony of the situation: 'Whenever one complained about outrageous reports... one was met with the rejoinder that India and Pakistan were democratic states, and that the Press was free to say what it liked. But the British Press was apparently expected to observe different standards, and we were bombarded with protests about the sometimes highly-coloured stories of the massacres which had been published in England.'[234] In the circumstances, Ismay travelled to London 'to try and put matters in the right perspective... to the Cabinet and the Press'.[235]

These sentiments of the Indian press resonated, however, with some sections of Fleet Street. Thus for the *New Statesman* this 'deliberate press campaign designed to convince the British public that the end of British rule in India has thrown the entire country into a state of anarchy is as wicked as it is misleading. Every incident in the Punjab tragedy indicative of local breakdown in administration is exaggerated and distorted to give the impression of nation-wide collapse.' Citing the example of the *Express*, wherein, the *New Statesman* contended, 'No effort is spared to hold up the Governments of two Member states of the British Commonwealth to contempt and ridicule and to label them after three weeks as unfit to rule.'[236] The *Express* stance might well have reflected, to some extent, the personal proclivities of its proprietor, Lord Beaverbrook, who was passionately pro-empire. He also disliked Mountbatten, whom he felt was acting like Santa Claus giving away Britain's prized possession.[237] While acknowledging that the suffering and killings were immense, the *New Statesman* maintained that even this provided 'no justification for the silly suggestion in some newspapers that the Indian settlement was a mistake'. And while these massacres were 'a ghastly by-product of painful re-birth' in India, they were 'much less serious' than, for instance, the great Indian famine in 1943, which was 'barely reported in England when one and a half million died'.[238]

Thus there emerged two main accounts of Indian Independence: a pro-empire version apparently coexisting with a celebration of decolonisation. In other words, press comment vindicated British rule for achieving a peaceful transfer of power, and at the same time British rule was also vindicated by the subsequent violence that engulfed the new nation-states. How do we explain this apparent dichotomy? Perhaps one could suggest that both approaches contained essential truths about the British imperial experience. The British had always been divided as to the meaning of its Indian Raj – either a paternalist despotism in the name of superior Christian civilization or a progressive programme of improvements leading to eventual self-rule. Of the two the former had deeper roots in the mainstream British press and helps to explain the reversion to this kind of coverage in the post-independence period. What requires explanation, therefore, is why the more optimistic view prevailed in the lead-up to and during August. To a substantial extent this can be attributed to the Mountbatten–India Office media operation. Both Mountbatten and the decisive plan he enunciated inspired confidence. He provided a narrative for Independence that seemed to render it a progressive British achievement. The positive newspaper reportage was not entirely unexpected, and in following the official position on empire in 1947 it was consistent with its coverage during the 1930s, when the bulk of the press backed a policy of appeasing nationalists through the devolution of self-government.

In a sense, therefore, Mountbatten reaffirmed this position with his skill in imperial choreography, his role being to dramatize a script that was already largely written and in so doing to provide the imagery that would fix how the world saw 15 August then – and how we see it now. Mountbatten was very conscious of his role in making history, and reminisced how on that fateful morning in Delhi: 'We started off with the utmost pomp of which we were capable, and I was determined that we'd go down with colours flying very high, and the whole works were turned on.' And at the end of a very long day he was to conclude: 'This was the great moment... We'd got there. It was a close race, we just pulled it off. The people were so overjoyed, they shouted... "Mountbatten ki jai! Lady Mountbatten ki jai! Pamela Mountbatten ki jai!"...'.[239]

Such overwhelming public displays of joy were corroborated by most western journalists, including Talbot, who toured the country during August. For him, two 'astonishingly bright threads' were a marked feature everywhere: 'a sudden, unpredicted return to Hindu-Muslim amity and a warm outflowing of friendly expressions towards Britain'.[240] Whilst the Mountbattens had received 'a satisfying welcome' in Karachi, it paled in comparison to that in Bombay, made more remarkable by the fact that 'Eighteen months ago the American flag was ripped down during the Royal Indian Navy mutiny... This week, however, instead of "Death to Englishmen" and "Britishers Go Back", Bombay crowds raised the shout "Hail England".'[241] Though Talbot admitted that 'Spontaneous enthusiasm is not necessarily... either deep-rooted or long lasting', it appeared to him that 'the Attlee concept of giving India independence to save her as an associate of the English-speaking world stands a chance of bearing fruit'.[242]

Mountbatten always claimed to have great affection for Indians and India, going back to when he had first travelled to the subcontinent accompanying the Prince of Wales in 1921–2, and during which he had also become engaged to the beautiful heiress, Edwina Ashley, in Delhi.[243] Comparing his own position as Viceroy favourably to that of his predecessors, especially Linlithgow, who Mountbatten contended was 'always perfectly correct, [but] never had any warmth for anybody...We came out and it changed. That's what really did the trick. They could not afford to bypass my own role because I could go out and get as much of a following for what I was going to say as for what they were going to say.'[244] Even accounting for Mountbatten's insatiable ego and the fact that he 'never lost an opportunity for self-congratulation',[245] there does exist substantial evidence to support claims for the couple's general popularity. It is useful to acknowledge the role of personality and charisma, in the Weberian sense, as a significant tool in the Raj arsenal. Talbot felt moved to declare: 'Tall, with a cleanly chiselled face, broad shoulders and an air in wearing uniforms that could hardly be matched by Clark Gable, the admiral promptly on arrival loosed a story-book personality that is apparently equally effective with Hindus and Muslims, men and women, and politicians and pressmen. In no time he was the talk of Delhi dinner tables.'[246] And Keay concluded how the Viceroy's 'legendary charm would ensure that two hundred years of colonial exploitation ended with warm smiles and hearty handshakes'.[247] Yet while the success of this imperial charm offensive is undeniable in impacting upon the lead-up to and the Independence project itself, it could hardly be sustained in equal measure when faced with the communal bloodbaths that accompanied Partition. These events helped to create deep faultlines within Fleet Street itself, as well as between the foreign and the Indian press and political opinion, fracturing trust in western perceptions of the new post-colonial realities.

6
Concluding Remarks

In *The Media and Modernity*, the sociologist John Thompson hoped 'to shed some light on our contemporary, media-saturated world while avoiding a myopic preoccupation with the present'.[1] As a historian, I am rather fortunate in that my research also has continuing and, arguably, heightened contemporary relevance in a globalised world. Perhaps this isn't altogether surprising, given that these areas encompass communication and political culture, power and protest, and are intrinsic to how we define ourselves. Whilst history does not repeat itself, trends can be highlighted and impacts reconsidered. Overall, the significance of the interests engaged within the confines of this volume go beyond what I believe to be the intrinsic value of illuminating the historical past and reinforce how important historical context is to the understanding of contemporary events.

To take a prominent example, I was struck by the fact that the Egyptian revolution which began in 2010, had at its inception the work of a young Google employee and internet blogger, Wael Ghonim, who is largely credited with energising the anti-Mubarak, pro-democracy demonstrations and whose websites were replete with exhortations to emulate Gandhi's mobilisation techniques. Gandhi's 'triumph in the face of the British Empire assured me', wrote Ghonim, 'that great battles could be fought and won without violence...Gandhi is certainly one of my heroes.'[2] Quotations from Gandhi frequently came up on 'Kullena Khaled Said' ('We are all Khaled Said'), the Facebook page he launched in protest at the unprovoked and brutal murder of an innocent young man by secret police in Alexandria. Ghonim, based in Dubai at the time, used his skills as Head of Marketing for Google Middle East and North Africa to successfully exploit social media on behalf of the oppressed, writing informally and in the colloquial Egyptian dialect that was more relevant to young Egyptians, and eventually linking up with other internet protest pages.[3] He exhorted his Facebook group to watch Richard Attenborough's 1982 film on Gandhi and also translated verbatim a scene wherein Gandhi proclaimed: 'They may torture my body, break my bones, and even kill me. Then they will have my dead body – not my obedience!'[4]

Ghonim's Facebook page was built on a vision of participatory democracy: 'Engagement was the page's core concept and was certainly far more important to the page than activism.'[5] This virtual world became a 'critical alternative for promoting the cause', enabling Ghonim – much as print had Gandhi – to argue that Khalid's treatment was not exceptional: 'Torture is both systematic and methodical at the Ministry of Interior, I said.'[6] Under the Raj, both legal and administrative fiat as well as force were used routinely to suppress dissent. There are divergences between imperial India and twenty-first-century Egypt, yet what linked the Indian and Egyptian responses was an approach to protest that, at its core, had an intrinsic engagement with, and exploitation of, extant media as well as the importance of engaging the masses. The Egyptian 'Silent Stands' parallel Gandhi's non-cooperation and civil disobedience strategies; the reliance on social media and the internet compares well with Gandhi's use of the press, microphone and mass rallies. For both movements, political engagement and social protest utilising extant communication channels through participatory mass action were considered as important as attaining the ultimate goals of national liberation or the overthrow of a violent dictatorship.

The case study of the American press and Gandhian nationalism (Chapter 3) also helps draw attention to another significant contemporary development in international affairs: the high-profile US engagement with the subcontinent in evidence since the year 2000, symbolised by the fact that from then on every US president has undertaken a state visit to India, including Bill Clinton, George W. Bush and Barack Obama. The salience of this development is underlined when we note that this equals the sum total of all presidential visits previously undertaken over the half-century since 1947. Historically, the groundwork for political and popular involvement with India was facilitated via print and electronic media coverage with the roots of this process going back to the interwar years and well before the more conventionally accepted watershed of the Second World War. Such a perspective has received corroboration recently from Giovanna Dell'Orto's study of the American press from the mid-nineteenth century to the contemporary period wherein she argues that in general the US 'press has been a crucial factor – an irreplaceable mediator – in international affairs, historically and currently, by functioning as the public arena where meanings for things literally foreign become understandable realities that, in turn, serve as the basis for policy and action'.[7] This chapter further serves to reiterate the transnational popularity of Gandhi and demonstrates just how synonymous with Indian nationalism the wider world perceived him to be.

Within Britain, during 2011–12, we witnessed how the issues raised in the Leveson Inquiry into the press had not altered substantively from when the first Royal Commission on the Press deliberated in 1947–9, or, indeed, since the rise of the mass popular press in the late nineteenth century. The Inquiry was established to examine the 'culture, practices and ethics of the press and, in part, the relationship of the press with the public, police and politicians'.[8] The complex, and frequently incestuous, relationship between newspapers and governments in the pursuit of political influence lies at the heart of both imperial and contemporary Britain. But what has been their legacy in post-colonial India? The *Statesman* in a leader entitled 'After Freedom' (6 August 1947) referred to Prime Minister Attlee's description, during one of the last parliamentary debates on India, of the INC and Muslim League as the successor authorities to the Raj. Yet despite their immense popularity, said the *Statesman*, these parties did not represent the totality of their peoples, and to characterise them as 'successor authorities' carried with it 'totalitarian implications'. Though the newspaper conceded that the 'initial prospect of virtually unopposed one-party rule' did indeed loom large for both India and Pakistan, 'Newly won power often proves a heady intoxicant, and for some while after August 15, both in India and Pakistan, much intolerant pressure against would-be dissidents or existing minorities is a possibility with sharp resentment of criticism.'[9]

How prophetic these words were in 1947, and how prescient they turned out to be, can be gauged from the striking continuities in government ideology and practices *vis-à-vis* press freedoms with their concomitant emphasis on censorship and information control, between the colonial and post-colonial eras. This was brought out graphically even before Independence in the approach of Sardar Patel, Minister of Information and Broadcasting and Home Minister, both posts which he continued to hold till his death in 1950. Addressing a meeting with prominent newspaper editors and members of the AINEC in October 1946, Patel claimed how 'We shall scrupulously respect the freedom of the Press: in fact, we shall help it to exercise its legitimate functions; and we have every confidence that the Press for its part, will assist us in administering the affairs of the country.'[10] In what became the *leitmotif* for the independent Indian nation, Patel adumbrated the Government–press relationship unequivocally as a symbiotic one: 'The Press must have unfettered freedom in the presentation of news and expression of views, but it also has the obligation to preserve the integrity of the state and support the legitimate activities of a popular Government. It must, when occasion demands, help the Government in defeating the forces of disruption.'[11]

In response, the *Hindustan Times*, which had marked INC sympathies and was a prominent member of the AINEC, accepted without question such an assessment of the role of the media, emphasising how the press 'should not shrink from the unpleasant task of enforcing discipline on its own members'.[12] *Dawn* led the countercharge on behalf of a group of 16 Muslim papers in Delhi, which were not members of the AINEC, and rejected the organisation's right to formulate an agreement with the GoI to undertake to 'suppress the liberty of the press'.[13] Though *Dawn*'s motivations were linked far more with the ensuing political power struggles, its opposition serves to highlight the uncomfortable collusion between sections of the press and the government of an independent and democratic India.

The Nehruvian years, and not only they, also reveal marked similarities with the Raj *mentalité* in the sphere of legislative control, as I have argued elsewhere, further bearing out the *Statesman*'s prognosis.[14] Soon after Independence, Wavell's Ordinance (as discussed in Chapter 5) was passed as Act XXXIX or the Press (Special Powers) Act 1947, which was intended to remain in force for two years. Even before the passage of the Act, and as affirmed by the Chief Commissioner of Delhi, there were a large number of precensorship orders imposed on English-, Urdu- and Hindi-language newspapers, including *Dawn*, *Hindu Weekly*, *Jung*, *Wahdat*, *Alaman*, *Naya Daur*, *Aj* and *Baljit*. *Naya Daur* forfeited its security of Rs 500 and warnings were also issued against the *Indian News Chronicle*, *Liberator* and *Panjam*. And this represented merely the list for the first half of October 1947.[15] The Constitution of the Indian Republic came into force in January 1950, borrowing as many as 250 articles from the GoI Act of 1935, thus ensuring a significant continuity in ideological and institutional terms. It is instructive to note that the Indian Constitution did not explicitly guarantee freedom of the press. Instead it was subsumed under the general directive of freedom of speech and expression, which was protected legislatively as a Fundamental Right. The communal and political tensions in post-Independence India were used to justify the introduction by Nehru in May 1951 of an amendment to the Constitution intending to severely restrict the freedom of the press, which provoked widespread public outcry but was eventually passed in a modified version, to be followed a year later by a new Press Act. As Norman Brown has argued, 'The situation was admittedly a bad one, but it is doubtful if the solution was good either.'[16]

A firm grasp on the new communication technology of broadcasting was apparent in the imperial relationship with AIR, as analysed in Chapter 4, which was continued by Indian ministries and was also reflected in the stranglehold exercised over television, wherein state-owned Doordarshan became the sole television network for most of the twentieth century. Nirad C. Chaudhuri, who worked for ten years at AIR (split equally between the colonial and immediate postcolonial regimes), wrote of his concerns about having to compromise his integrity despite the attainment of Independence: 'I felt nervous that under the new regime my superiors might now ask me to write commentaries supporting its policies and extolling the achievements of the Congress, which in most cases I could not do without doing violence to my convictions and becoming an opportunist.'[17] Chaudhuri noted how, for example, he was asked to write about the Quit India movement. This meant, he claimed, that he was 'to glorify it ... The Indian bureaucrat always justified that sort of trimming by putting forward the well-known plea that the Civil Service must serve every government.'[18] Though for the most part Chaudhuri worked undisturbed, 'I had, however, to be careful. All India Radio was a Government Department, and its broadcasts were regarded as expressions of sympathy and policies of the Indian Government.' Overall, he claimed to have been able to 'reconcile truthfulness with policy' under both administrations, but his story illustrates the continuing pressures operating on broadcasters.[19] This view has received corroboration from others, including Sir Mark Tully, the veteran BBC broadcaster and journalist whose Indian career spanned most of the post-Independence decades and who is still active today. During a Nehru Memorial Lecture delivered in 1991, Tully quoted Nehru's opinions on broadcasting, expressed during debates in the Constituent Assembly: 'My own view of the set-up for broadcasting is that we should approximate as far as possible to the semi-autonomous corporation. Now I think that is not immediately feasible.' As Tully argued, four decades later, Indian broadcasting had failed to achieve even the semiautonomous condition Nehru had alluded to. The liberalisation of the Indian economy and professionalisation of official attitudes towards communications and the media only began to change substantively in the mid-1990s.

Another evocative illustration of continuity is afforded by the commemorations within Britain and the far-flung Commonwealth during 2012, marking the Diamond Jubilee of Queen Elizabeth II, the vivid echoes of which can be found a century earlier at the Coronation Durbar of her grandfather in Delhi, as described in Chapter 2. We witness a preoccupation with the monarchic symbolism of British influence, whether it be in early twentieth-century India – a land steeped with reverence for royalty and ritual – or in the Commonwealth of the twenty-first century, with members of the Royal Family undertaking extensive tours to distant shores. The intensive media coverage of these developments and the apparent public appetite for them can be further linked to the general fascination with political 'spectacle' and 'media events' that continue to dominate much of our contemporary lives, but which have significant historical roots, as demonstrated in the cases discussed here.

This approach is tied into another overarching theme of the book – namely, empire as spectacle, a conceptual framework most keenly associated with the genre labelled 'new imperial history' and epitomised in MacKenzie's book series, 'Manchester Studies in Imperialism', as well as in the work of scholars such as Cohn and Cannadine. In Chapter 2, this methodology was applied to consider the Delhi Durbar as a 'media event', utilising the theoretical propositions advanced by Dayan and Katz. These perspectives can also be usefully directed to other developments discussed in the book – for instance, Gandhi's Salt *satyagraha* in Chapter 3 or Mountbatten's stage management of decolonisation in Chapter 5. Images of Lord and Lady Mountbatten, resplendent on the Viceregal thrones in the Constituent Assembly hall in August 1947, bear striking resemblance to those of George V and Queen Mary at the Durbar amphitheatre in December 1911. This was no coincidence. Mountbatten envisaged Edwina's role as reminiscent of Queen Mary's, and acknowledged: 'But of course in the case of the transfer of power, like the King and Queen, she had her own place. We had a separate throne for her.'[20] The notion of 'media spectacle' has also been used by Doug Kellner to study twenty-first-century developments. He defines the phrase to mean 'media constructs that present events which disrupt ordinary and habitual flows of information, and that become popular stories which capture the attention of the media and the public'.[21] Acknowledging the influence of Dayan and Katz and earlier social theorists, such as Guy Debord, Kellner contends that spectacles are 'technologically mediated events' in which the media 'process contemporary historical events and

struggles in a spectacular form'.[22] Such spectacles circulate through contemporary communication networks, including television, the internet
and mobile phones, much as they did, I would argue, a century earlier
through imperial ones.

Ultimately, media events and spectacles are *a priori* based on relationships: among elites – political, social, cultural; the media – press
journalists, cinefilm makers, photographers, broadcasters, internet blog-
gers; and the audience – including wider-reading and viewing publics
not physically present at events, which Thompson refers to as 'a public without a place'.[23] Undoubtedly, imperial-media events discussed in
this book were seen as reinforcing the power structure of the Raj through
direct and indirect means, as well as allowing nationalists to fight their
political corner and garner wider support. In this, both parties appear
to have had some success. However, we need to be cautious about the
extent of influence attributed to the media as well as the degree of control exercised by political elites over the Fourth Estate. Further, these
relationships were not necessarily linear but often 'circular and systemic,
as much contractual and hegemonic'.[24] To a substantive degree, their
success was predicated on compromise and cooperation.

This goes to the salience of context as a key determining variable
in the imperial-communication experience. Thus, with the advent of
Mountbatten and his successful Independence project, we are reminded
of the ability of the media to fix an image of decolonisation for posterity. Nye has argued that 'Charisma produces soft power, for better and
for worse.'[25] We witness how Mountbatten, who exemplified the ideal
of charismatic authority, helped provide the blueprint that served as
the choreographic template for successive moments, marking colonial
independence from the British during the second half of the twentieth
century. Or, to take the case of broadcasting, it was the stranglehold of
the Raj during the interwar years that ensured the stillbirth of the Indian
radio industry at the precise juncture which witnessed its take-off phase
in Europe and the US.

Each of the case studies have also served to demonstrate the seminal
role of agency through the contribution of key individuals including
Chirol, Fraser, Grigg, Stephens, Reed, Mills, Miller, McCormick, Shirer,
Reith, Fielden, MacGregor, Joyce and Campbell-Johnson, as well as various imperial proconsuls and prominent nationalists. These members of
the political and professional elites came to play a critical part in providing the impetus, as well as shaping the process, of imperial change
over the course of the twentieth century, a process which culminated in
the retreat from empire. Dulffer and Frey make a similar case for other

European empires, arguing that such elites were 'vital in mediating and driving the complex processes which ultimately led to decolonisation'.[26]

Technological change and the rapidly evolving processes of communication have never been more ubiquitous than they are in the twenty-first century. Indeed, taken together with the mantra of globalisation, they serve as markers of our contemporary world. Yet this preoccupation is hardly novel. The imperial response to communication institutions and new media, as discussed in this book, highlights how technological innovation underlay the British imperial experience, providing both the infrastructural and cognitive sinews of hegemony. It helped make the empire truly global. The crucial role of technology in this context has been reinforced from various intellectual perspectives over the past several decades. For instance, it has been opined that the European empires in the nineteenth century were 'economy empires', facilitated by the exploitation of new and cheaper technologies, a process which was reversed in the twentieth when they ceased to be as financially viable. 'In the process, they unbalanced world relations, overturned ancient ways of life, and opened the way for a new global civilization.'[27] Going back earlier in time, technology theorists have attributed seminal effects emanating from the impact of new media – such as print contributing to the Protestant Reformation, and the rise of science and the newspaper press as an important ingredient in European nationalism.[28] However, we must beware of the tendency towards technological determinism inherent in such an approach which in 'focusing so positivistically on the ways in which technology shapes society, ignores the simple fact that society shapes the definition and uses of technology'.[29] As revealed in these case studies, the imperial experience under the Raj provides us with ample evidence to justify such caution.

Further, utilising Nye's analysis of contemporary politics (and as discussed in Chapter 1), what the Raj was attempting to do was 'to combine hard and soft power into an effective strategy' which he labels '*smart power*'.[30] Nevertheless, the exercise of imperial smart power also served to reveal the ambivalence that lay at the heart of British governing strategies with respect to communication technology and media, reflected, for example, in its hybrid perceptions of the press both indigenous and foreign. Print in India was about imperial control as well as an expression of the freedom of the press, and as such subject to nationalist appropriation. Likewise, it is apparent in the GoI's commitment to control broadcasting (discussed in Chapter 4), within the context of the liberalising agenda for the devolution of responsibility to Indians on their road to self-government, embodied in the GoI Act of 1935.

Studies of the gathering crisis of the British empire in the twentieth century have failed to give due attention to the critical context of the new communication environment within which elite and subelite opinion was formed. The Raj was an organisation driven by the twin ideologies of modernity and cultural imperialism. International telegraphic news agencies and networks, the British press and Indian print culture, wireless and broadcasting, all had a significant impact upon governing *mentalité* and praxis. The British attempted to forge a symbiotic relationship with these communication technologies and media institutions, through complex formal and informal strategies utilising coercion (hard power) and persuasion (soft power). However, events during these decades also reveal the degree to which the Raj's information strategy was being undermined from within India as well as challenged transnationally. The transforming context of media within Britain and the subcontinent, and the expansion of communication networks linking Britain and India, were all key catalysts for change in the first half of the twentieth century. The consequences of these developments were varied, impacting as they did on the nature and institutions of imperial politics and journalism, on popular culture and the growth of nationalism. I hope, in conclusion, that this book will go a little way towards providing important linkages between the historical processes of empire and colonialism, on the one hand, and the renewed contemporary interest in the impact of communication, new media and globalisation, on the other.

Notes

1 Communications, Media and the Imperial Experience: Perspectives and Perceptions

1. *The Times*, India and the Durbar, 1911, pp. 1, 5.
2. M. P. Roth, *Historical Dictionary of War Journalism*, Westport, CT, 1997, pp. 267–268.
3. S. Gopal, *British Policy in India*, Cambridge, 1965, p. 304.
4. ToI, 15 August 1947.
5. J. Osterhammel, *Colonialism*, Princeton, 1997, pp. 64–66.
6. J. Hartley, *Popular Reality: Journalism, Modernity, Popular Culture*, 1996, p. 33.
7. Sir S. Hoare, *India by Air*, 1927, p. 98.
8. Viscount Templewood, *Empire of the Air*, 1957, p. 170.
9. J. S. Nye, Jr., *Soft Power*, New York, 2004, p. 5.
10. *Ibid.*, p. 6.
11. *Ibid.*, pp. 6–7.
12. *Ibid.*, p. 1.
13. C. Kaul, *Reporting the Raj: The British Press and India, 1880–1922*, Manchester, 2003, New York, 2004.
14. *Ibid.*, p. 139.
15. Joyce to Matters, 28 March 1941, L/I/1/1422, India Office Library and Records (IOLR), British Library, London hereafter L/I.
16. Nye, *Soft Power*, p. 12.
17. V. A. Smith (with Percival Spear ed. and rewritten, Part III), *The Oxford History of India,* Delhi, 4th edn., 1995, p. 834.
18. B. Anderson, *Imagined Communities*,1983; J. Habermas, *The Structural Transformation of the Public Sphere*, Cambridge, Mass., 1989 English translation (Thomas Burger), German first edn. 1962. For responses, see, e.g., C. Calhoun (ed.), *Habermas and the Public Sphere*, 1992; J. B. Thompson, *The Media and Modernity*, Cambridge, 1995.
19. See Bibliography for an exhaustive list of such books.
20. Cited in A. Mathur, *The Indian Media*, New Delhi, 2006, p. 16.
21. There is a detailed discussion about British approaches to First World War propaganda and the press in Kaul, *Reporting the Raj*, pp. 119–134.
22. See C. Kaul, 'Media, India and the Raj', in A. S. Thompson (ed.), *Writing Imperial Histories*, Manchester, 2013, pp. 188–215.
23. Kaul, *Reporting the Raj*, pp. 31–98.
24. *National Herald*, 'The Press cartels', 8 August 1947.
25. D. Read, *The Power of News*, Oxford, 1999. pp. 316–317.
26. M. Barns, *India Today and Tomorrow*, 1937, p. 101.
27. *Ibid.*
28. See M. Israel, *Communications and Power*, Cambridge, 1994, pp. 127–155.

29. The bibliography contains a list of relevant books in this connection.
30. S. Banerjea, *A Nation in Making*, 1927, p. 262.
31. N. Owen, *The British Left and India*, Oxford, 2007.
32. Kaul, 'Media, India and the Raj', pp. 188–215.
33. N. Krishnamurthy, *Indian Journalism*, 1966, p. 103.
34. For establishment and early development of the IO Information department, see Kaul, *Reporting the Raj*, pp. 151–54.
35. 14 August 1937, L/S&G/8/28, IOLR, hereafter L/S&G/.
36. *Ibid.*
37. *Ibid.*
38. *Ibid.*
39. *Ibid.*
40. A. H. Joyce Memo on Government Publicity, 4 October 1937, Home Political, 16/46/38, National Archives of India (NAI), Delhi, hereafter HPoll.
41. *Ibid.*
42. Viceroy (V) to Secretary of State (S/S), 14 August 1932, Viscount Templewood (Sir Samuel Hoare) papers, MSS Eur E240/5, IOLR, British Library, hereafter TC/.
43. S/S to V, 17 December 1931, TC/1.
44. S/S to V, 8 January 1932, TC/1.
45. S/S to V, 1 July 1932, TC/2.
46. *Ibid.*
47. *Ibid.*
48. S/S to V, 29 July 1932, TC/2.
49. *Ibid.*
50. Sykes to Irwin, 22 May 1929, F 150/1, Sykes Collection, IOLR, hereafter SC/.
51. 'Note by Mr Coatman on the tone of certain sections of the press and the policy to be adopted towards it', 178/29, 1929, HPoll.
52. I. M. Stephens, *Monsoon Morning*, 1966, p. 279.
53. For more details, see C. Kaul, 'India, the Imperial Press Conferences and the Empire Press Union', in C. Kaul (ed.), *Media and the British Empire*, Basingstoke, 2006, 2013, pp. 125–144.
54. See Appendix III.
55. Sir F. Low, 'Present Day Journalism in India and Pakistan', *Asiatic Review*, December 1948, p. 518.
56. *Ibid.*, pp. 518–519.
57. See Kaul, *Reporting the Raj*, pp. 199–229.
58. See Stephens, *Monsoon Morning*; correspondence in Lord Linlithgow and Lord Zetland collections, IOLR.
59. 5 February 1948 cited in *Homage to Mahatma Gandhi*, Information and Broadcasting Ministry, New Delhi, 1948, p. 35.
60. Stephens, *Monsoon Morning*, p. 7. See also E. Hirschmann, *Robert Knight*, Delhi, 2008.
61. Stephens, *Monsoon Morning*, p. 7.
62. J. Natarajan, Survey of the Policy of Newspapers in India since the Introduction of Provincial Autonomy, encl. in J. Hennessy to J. A. Thorne, 8 October 1938, 53/2/38, HPoll.

2 Coronation, Colonialism and Cultures of Control: The Delhi Durbar, 1911

NB: All press references are to 1911 unless specified otherwise.

1. 'The Durbar, from the Crowd', *Blackwood's Magazine*, Vol. CXCI, February 1912, p. 289.
2. D. Cannadine, *Ornamentalism*, 2002 edn., p. 111.
3. TT, 18 December.
4. TT, 2 December, leader by Chirol, 'The King's Arrival in India'.
5. See the distinction made by J. M. MacKenzie (ed.), *Imperialism and Popular Culture*, Manchester, 1986, p. 2.
6. TT, 3 October.
7. Grigg to Northcliffe, 2 February 1911, WDM/1/32, Grigg Papers, Times Newspapers Ltd Archive, News UK & Ireland Ltd, London, hereafter TNL.
8. Sir A. H. Watson, 'The Growth of the Press in English in India', *Journal of the Royal Society of Arts*, January 1948, p. 124.
9. Manager to Grigg, 17 May 1912, Manager's Letter Book 56, TNL.
10. Kaul, *Reporting the Raj*.
11. *Ibid.*, p. 58.
12. See C. Kaul, 'Popular Press and Empire: Northcliffe, India and the Daily Mail, 1896–1922', in P. Catterall *et al.* (eds.), *Northcliffe's Legacy*, 2000, pp. 45–69.
13. Cited in H. Caldwell Lipsette, *Lord Curzon in India*, 1903, p. 121.
14. *Ibid.*, p. 122; emphasis mine.
15. *Ibid.*, p. 123.
16. Cited in Lord Ronaldshay, *The Life of Lord Curzon*, 1928, Vol. II, p. 230.
17. Lipsette, *Curzon*, p. 133.
18. *Ibid.*, p. 141.
19. D. Ayerst, *Garvin of the Observer*, Kent, 1985, p. 87.
20. Kaul, *Reporting the Raj*, p. 87.
21. Garvin to Tina, cited in Ayerst, *Garvin*, p. 49.
22. Observer, 12 November; emphasis mine.
23. D. Dayan and E. Katz, *Media Events the Live Broadcasting of History*, Cambridge, Mass., 1992.
24. M. Weber, *From Max Weber: Essays in Sociology*, New York, 1946.
25. Dayan and Katz, *Media Events,* p. 16.
26. *Ibid.*, p. 15.
27. *Ibid.*
28. *Ibid.*, p. 20.
29. For other imperial debates, see J. D. Startt, *Journalists for Empire*, Westport, CT, 1991.
30. Dayan and Katz, *Media Events*, p. 7.
31. *Ibid.*, p. 8.
32. *Ibid.*, p. 12.
33. Dayan and Katz, *Media Events*, p. 22.
34. *Ibid.*, p. 19.
35. Guildhall speech as cited in W. J. Makin, *The Life of King George the Fifth*, 1936/1937, p. 162.

36. ABPatrika, 10 May, 1910; see also *Statesman* 8 May; *Bombay Gazette, ToI, Advocate of India, Daily Post,* all for 9 May, 1910.
37. GV to Morley, 8 September 1910, RA/PS/PSO/GV/C/N/293/1.
38. *Ibid.*
39. Morley to GV, 12 September 1910, RA/PS/PSO/GV/C/N/293/2.
40. *Ibid.*
41. K. Rose, *King George V,* 1983, p. 132.
42. TT, 17 November 1910.
43. TT, 18 November 1910.
44. See Crewe-Hardinge correspondence, Crewe Collection, MSS Eur Photo Eur 469, IOLR, hereafter CC; S/S to V, 2 February 1911, CC.
45. 'Correspondence and Papers respecting the visit of their Imperial Majesties King George V and Queen Mary to India', 1912, p. 278, RA/F&V/VISOV/IND/1911–1912.
46. S. Bottomore, 'Have you seen the Gaekwar Bob?': filming the 1911 Delhi Durbar', *Historical Journal of Film, Radio and Television,* Vol. 17, No. 3, 1997, p. 314.
47. S/S to V, 27 January 1911, CC.
48. Bikaner to George V, 7 December 1910, RA/PS/PSO/GV/C/N/563/1.
49. J. Pope-Hennessy, *Lord Crewe,* 1955, p. 97.
50. Lord Hardinge, *Old Diplomacy,* 1947, p. 192.
51. V to Richmond Ritchie, IO, 2 February 1911, CC.
52. See, for instance, C. Kaul, 'Monarchical Display and the Politics of Empire: Princes of Wales and India 1870–1920s', *Twentieth Century British History,* Vol. 17, No. 4, 2006, pp. 464–488.
53. S/S to V, 27 January 1911, CC.
54. V to S/S, 15 December 1910, CC.
55. V to S/S, 25 January 1911, CC.
56. V to S/S, 16 February 1911; also 22 February; CC.
57. Cited in H. Butler, *India Insistent,* 1931, p. 70.
58. *Ibid.,* p. 72.
59. Frykenberg cites Jenkins as the originator of the scheme in 1911. However, both ideas had been floating around in official circles for several years. See R. E. Frykenberg, 'The Coronation Durbar of 1911: Some Implications', in R. E. Frykenberg (ed.), *Delhi Through the Ages,* Delhi, 1986, pp. 369–390.
60. Lord Hardinge, *My Indian Years,* 1948, pp. 38–39.
61. V to G V, 23 August 1911, RA/PS/PSO/GV/C/P/522/11.
62. *Ibid.*
63. *Ibid.*
64. Hardinge, *Indian Years,* p. 50.
65. Pioneer, 1 December.
66. S/S to V, 13 January 1911, CC.
67. R. G. Irving, *Indian Summer, Lutyens, Baker and Imperial Delhi,* New Haven, 1981, p. 5.
68. Hardinge, *Indian Years,* p. 43; S/S to V, 27 October 1911 with reference to Hardinge's account 3 October 1911, CC.
69. MG, 11 December.
70. E. A. Philp, *With the King to India,* Plymouth, 1912, p. 13.
71. *Ibid.,* p. 58.

72. As cited in Kaul, *Reporting the Raj*, p. 109.
73. V to S/S 3 November 1911, 'Correspondence and Papers respecting the visit of their Imperial Majesties King George V and Queen Mary to India', 1912, p. 347, RA/F&V/VISOV/IND/1911–1912.
74. *Ibid.*
75. Kaul, *Reporting the Raj*, p. 235.
76. Bottomore, 'Gaekwar Bob?', p. 317.
77. 6 January 1912, p. 436, RA/GV/PRIV/GVD/1912.
78. Pioneer, 27 November.
79. ToI, reproduced in S. Reed, *The King & Queen in India*, Bombay, 1912, p. 113.
80. See I. J. Kerr, *Building the Railways of the Raj 1850–1900*, Delhi, 1997; D. Arnold, *Science, Technology and Medicine in Colonial India*, Cambridge, 2000; various fictional works by R. Kipling.
81. MG, 11 November.
82. *Coronation Durbar Official Directory Delhi 1911*, Calcutta, 1911, p. 107.
83. Pioneer, 1 December.
84. ToI, reproduced in Reed, *King & Queen*, p. 116.
85. TT, 13 November; MG, 11 November.
86. ToI, reproduced in Reed, *King and Queen*, p. 114.
87. H. Nicolson, *King George the Fifth*, 1952, p. 510.
88. Macmillan to Manager, 31 July 1911, TT/FOR/VC/3, TNL.
89. TT, 23 October.
90. See, for instance, MPost & D. Graphic, 1 April; Vanity Fair 5 April; D. Chronicle 6 May; D. Sketch & Manchester Dispatch 12 July; MG 25 August; MPost 20 September; D. Sketch 19 October, 10 November; D. Telegraph & Sheffield Telegraph 10 November; D. Graphic 11 November.
91. See MG, 13 November.
92. MG, 4 December.
93. See TT, 26 October; also 11 November.
94. TT, 11 November, p. 9.
95. See also MPost, 13 November.
96. Cited in TT, 11 November.
97. TT, 11 November.
98. Observer, 12 November.
99. DM, 11 November.
100. TT, 13 November.
101. *Ibid.*
102. TT, 2 December.
103. *Ibid.*
104. TT, 4 December.
105. MPost, 4 December.
106. MG, 4 December.
107. *Ibid.*
108. DM, 2 December.
109. DNews, 2 December.
110. Reuters telegram, 4 December, Bombay, published TT, 5 December.
111. TT, 8 December, p. 9.
112. 7 December, p. 405, RA/GV/PRIV/GVD/1911.
113. Cited in F. R. H. Du Boulay, *Servants of Empire*, 2011, p. 106.

114. J. Fortescue, *Narrative of the Visit to India of their Majesties King George V and Queen Mary*, 1912, p. 121.
115. Reed to Northcliffe, 26 January 1912, enclosed in Northcliffe to Stamfordham, 12 February 1912, RA/PS/PSO/GV/C/N/293/3–4.
116. K. Rose, *King George V*, 1983 p. 134.
117. DM, 8 December.
118. 'Pageant of the Durbar', DExpress, 8 December, p. 1.
119. 9 December, p. 407, RA/GV/PRIV/GVD/1911.
120. 11 December, p. 409, RA/GV/PRIV/GVD/1911.
121. See Box 1, RA/F&V/VISOV/IND 1911–12; MG, 14 December.
122. 5 January, p. 435, RA/GV/PRIV/GVD/1912.
123. 5 January, RA/QM/PRIV/QMD/1912.
124. 10 January, p. 439, RA/GV/PRIV/GVD/1912.
125. Chandavarkar to Lord Reay, Bombay, 27 January 1912, RA/QM/PRIV/CC115, Vol. III.
126. *Ibid.*
127. DExpress, 9 December.
128. TT, 8 December, p. 9.
129. *Ibid.*
130. TT, 11 December.
131. TT, 8 December.
132. Reuters report TT, 11 December.
133. *Ibid.*, TT, 11 December.
134. TT, 8 December, editorial.
135. TT, 13 December.
136. For the new crown, see DM, 15 December.
137. TT, 13 December.
138. *Ibid.*
139. S/S to V, 23 December 1910, CC.
140. 7, 8, 9 December, pp. 405–407, RA/GV/PRIV/GVD/1911.
141. B. N. Ramusack, *The Indian Princes and their States*, Cambridge, 2004, pp. 128–129.
142. 1911 Indian Census.
143. Hardinge, *Indian Years*, p. 52.
144. DM, 13 December.
145. Spectator, 16 December, 1061. See also C. Kaul, 'Washing Dirty Linen in Public: Imperial Spin Doctoring, the British Press and the Downfall of Lord Curzon, 1905', in C. Kaul (ed.), *Explorations in Modern Indian History and the Media*, Media History special issue, Vol. 15, No. 4, November 2009, Routledge, pp. 385–406.
146. Spectator, 16 December.
147. TT, 14 December.
148. DM, 13 December.
149. MG, 13 December.
150. *Ibid.*
151. See papers for 13–14 December.
152. MG, 13 December.
153. Butler, *India Insistent*, p. 69.
154. 'India and her Sovereign', EReview, July 1912, p. 9.

155. *Ibid.*, p. 13.
156. V. Chirol, *India Old and New*, 1921, p. 128; TT editorial, 14 December.
157. TT, 14 December, p. 10.
158. Spectator, 16 December.
159. Butler, *India Insistent*, pp. 71–72.
160. MG, 18 December.
161. Hardinge, *Indian Years*, p. 53.
162. Spectator, 16 December.
163. B. Porter, *The Lion's Share, a History of British Imperialism 1850 to the Present*, 2012, 5th edn., p. 173.
164. Spectator, 16 December.
165. Dayan and Katz, *Media Events*, p. 189.
166. *Ibid.*, p. 190.
167. *Ibid.*, p. 191.
168. *Ibid.*
169. Dayan and Katz, *Media Events*, p. 192.
170. *Ibid.*
171. *Ibid.*, p. 193.
172. *Ibid.*
173. S. Bradley, *An American Girl at the Durbar*, 1912, pp. 140, 162–163.
174. *Ibid.*, pp. 196–197.
175. *Ibid.*, p. 199.
176. See Cannadine, *Ornamentalism*.
177. Dayan and Katz, *Media Events*, p. 201.
178. *Ibid.*, p. 203.
179. *Ibid.*, p. 204.
180. *Ibid.*
181. Observer, 17 December.
182. DM, 13 December.
183. TT, 12 January 1912.
184. *Ibid.*
185. Cleveland to Sec. Home Deptt., GoI, 10 October 1911, 'Correspondence and Papers respecting the visit of their Imperial Majesties King George V and Queen Mary to India', 1912, p. 273, RA/F&V/VISOV/IND/1911–1912.
186. Spectator, 3 February 1912.
187. 'India and her Sovereign', EReview, July 1912, p. 7.
188. *Ibid.*, p. 19.
189. Spectator, 3 February 1912, also 10 February 1912.
190. Lords coverage, TT, 13 December, p. 12.
191. *Ibid.*, p. 12.
192. TT, 13 December.
193. Sir Austen Chamberlain's exhortation as recorded in his book, *Politics from Inside*, 1936, p. 410.
194. TT, 14 December, p. 10.
195. Hardinge, *Old Diplomacy*, pp. 243–244.
196. Spectator, 10 February 1912, p. 216
197. Porter, *Lion's Share*, p. 209.
198. V to Stamfordham, 3 March 1912, RA/PS/PSO/GV/C/N/323/1.

199. Reed to Northcliffe, 26 January 1912, enclosed in Northcliffe to Stamfordham, undated, RA/PS/PSO/GV/C/N/293/3–4.
200. H. P. Mody, 'The King-Emperor's visit: A new epoch', *East and West*, Vol. XI, No. 124, February 1912, Bombay, pp. 105–106.
201. 'The Durbar, from the Crowd', *Blackwood's Magazine*, Vol. CXCI, February 1912, p. 289.
202. *Ibid.*, p. 293.
203. Chirol, *India Old and New*, p. 127.
204. Lord Nicholson to Lord Stamfordham, 19 June 1912, RA/PS/PSO/GV/C/N/244/7.
205. Chirol to Dawson, 13 November 1912, TT/ED/GEB/1/2/2–3, TNL.
206. 12 December, p. 410, RA/GV/PRIV/GVD/1911.
207. Cited in D. Judd, *The Life and Times of George V*, 1973, p. 103.
208. 10 January, p. 440, RA/GV/PRIV/GVD/1912.
209. 11 January, p. 441, RA/GV/PRIV/GVD/1912.
210. Cited in Fortescue, *George V*, p. 244.
211. Judd, *George V*, pp. 103–104.
212. Frykenberg, 'Coronation Durbar', pp. 369–390.
213. R. J. Moore, *Liberalism and Indian Politics*, 1966, p. 103.
214. B. R. Nanda, *Gokhale*, Delhi, 1977, pp. 375–376.
215. Rose, *George V*, p. 136.
216. B. S. Cohn, 'Representing Authority in Victorian India', p. 209; and D. Cannadine, 'The Context, Performance and meaning of Ritual', pp. 101–164, both in E. Hobsbawm and T. Ranger (eds.), *The Invention of Tradition*, Cambridge, 2005 edn., 1st edn. 1983; see also Cannadine, *Ornamentalism*.
217. Pope-Hennessy, *Crewe*, pp. 102–103.
218. C. Percy and J. Ridley (eds.), *The Letters of Edwin Lutyens to His Wife Lady Emily*, 1985, p. 228.
219. C. Hussey, *The Life of Sir Edwin Lutyens*, Woodbridge, Suffolk, 1984 edn., 1st edn. 1950, p. 237.
220. Rose, *George V*, p. 135.
221. Many papers carried some discussion of this issue. See, for instance, MG, 19 December.
222. Major General Sir Harry Watson, 'My Memories of King George V', p. 24, RA/GV/Add/Copy 116.
223. TT, 18 December.
224. W. R. Black, *Dispatches from the World*, Bloomington IN, 2012, p. 95.
225. Bottomore, 'Gaekwar Bob?', p. 334.
226. Hardinge, *Indian Years*, p. 51.
227. *Ibid.*, p. 52.
228. Observer, 4 February 1912.
229. Lipsette, *Curzon*, p. 123.
230. DM, 13 December.
231. TT, 18 December.
232. Spectator, 16 December.
233. DM, 13 December.
234. MG, 18 December.
235. 'India and her Sovereign', EReview, July 1912, p. 17.

236. TT, 11 November.
237. Kaul, *Reporting the Raj*, p. 81.
238. *Ibid.*, p. 109.
239. MacKenzie, *Imperialism and Popular Culture*, p. 8.
240. DM, editorial 13 December.
241. ToI, reproduced in Reed, *King & Queen*, p. 113.
242. TT, 18 December.
243. Observer, 17 December.
244. TT, 14 December. Tragedy was not fully averted as this trauma contributed to the death of the ailing duke shortly afterwards.
245. Chirol, *India old and new*, pp. 129–130.
246. Reed to Northcliffe, 26 January 1912, encl. Northcliffe to Stamfordham, 12 February 1912, RA/PS/PSO/GV/C/N/293/3–4.
247. See Chapter 9 in Kaul, *Reporting the Raj*, pp. 230–256.

3   India as Viewed by the American Media: *Chicago Daily Tribune*, William Shirer and Gandhian Nationalism, 1930–1

1. W. L. Shirer, *Gandhi A Memoir*, New York, 1980, p. 13.
2. *Ibid.*, p. 18.
3. *Ibid.*, p. 14.
4. *Ibid.*, p. 16.
5. *Ibid.*, p. 244.
6. M. Twain, *Following the Equator*, New York, 1897, Vol. 2, p. 16.
7. C. Seshachari, *Gandhi and the American Scene*, Bombay, 1969, p. 35.
8. See NYT, 13 March, 10 July 1922.
9. As quoted in M. Jha, *Civil Disobedience and After*, Delhi, 1973, p. 25.
10. E. S. Reddy (ed.), *Mahatma Gandhi Letters to Americans*, New Delhi, 1998, p. 24; Seshachari, *Gandhi*, p. 38.
11. See Kaul, *Reporting the Raj*, pp. 199–229.
12. L. Rai, 'Need for Publicity Abroad', Tribune, Lahore, 4 September 1919.
13. Lal and Gould have recently provided stimulating insights into the growth of the South Asian community in the US: V. Lal, *The Other Indians*, New Delhi, 2008; H. Gould, *Sikhs, Swamis, Students, and Spies*, 2006.
14. M. V. Kamath, *The United States and India 1776–1976*, Washington, DC, 1976, pp. 110–113.
15. G. P. Pradhan, *Lokamanya Tilak*, New Delhi, 2008 reprint, p. 130.
16. M. Sinha (ed.), K. Mayo, *Mother India*, Michigan, 2003, p. 4; sales figure cited in Seshachari, *Gandhi*, p. 51; see also T. Weber, *On the Salt March*, New Delhi, 2009.
17. E. Thompson, *The Reconstruction of India*, 1931, 2nd edn., p. 11.
18. *Ibid.*, pp. 157–159.
19. See Chapter 4.
20. TT, 7 March 1930.
21. 223/1930, HPoll.
22. T. Ryan, Joint Secy, DIL to G. V. Bewoor, Postmaster-General, Bombay, 7 April 1930, 223/1930, HPoll.
23. *Ibid.*
24. Bewoor to Ryan, 9 April 1930, 223/1930, HPoll.

25. *Ibid.*
26. Sir F. Sykes, *From Many Angles*, 1942, pp. 383–384.
27. S. Gopal, *The Viceroyalty of Lord Irwin*, Oxford, 1957, p. 60.
28. D. Dalton, *Mahatma Gandhi*, New York, 1993, p. 107.
29. L. Fischer, *The Life of Mahatma Gandhi*, 1962, p. 292.
30. *Prajabandhu,* 16 March 1930, cited in J. Tewari, *Sabarmati to Dandi*, Delhi, 1995, pp. 129–130.
31. Time, 'Pinch of Salt' 31 March 1930, p. 25; also 'Saint's Progress', 7 April 1930, pp. 24–25.
32. Time, 5 January 1931, p. 14.
33. W. Durant, 'Portrait', in N. Cousins (ed.), *Profiles of Gandhi*, Delhi, 1969, p. 11.
34. NYT, 7 April 1930.
35. NYT, 11 May 1930.
36. S. Kapur, *Raising up a Prophet: The African-American Encounter with Gandhi*, Boston, 1992, p. 160.
37. See 'To the American Negro. A Message from Mahatma Gandhi', *Crisis*, Vol. 36, July 1929; also *Harijan* 'Two Negro Visitors' (14 March 1936) and 'Non Violence and the American Negro' (20 March 1937).
38. V to S/S, 28 September 1930, 48–11/1931, HPoll.
39. Emerson Note, 26 September 1930, 48–11/1931, HPoll. Emphasis mine.
40. Emerson to H. W. Haig, 9 October 1930, 48–11/1931, HPoll.
41. Read, *Power of News*.
42. Israel, *Communications and Power*, p. 116.
43. Read, *Power of News*, 1992, pp. 81–82.
44. *Ibid.*
45. K. Cooper, *Barriers Down*, 1969, p. 239.
46. *Ibid.*, p. 238.
47. Read, *Power of News*, p. 172.
48. Cooper, *Barriers Down*, p. 268.
49. Associated Press Annual Report, 31 December 1945, p. 90, Associate Press Corporate Archives.
50. Personal data on Mills, unless attributed otherwise, is referenced from James A. Mills, Biographical Reference File, Associated Press Corporate Archives.
51. Mills to Willert, 10 September 1930, 17/1931, HPoll.
52. R. H. A. Carter to W. H. Emerson, 23 September 1930, 17/1931, HPoll.
53. *Ibid.*
54. Emerson to R. H. A. Carter, 16 October 1930, 17/1931, HPoll.
55. 468/1930, HPoll.
56. Cunningham to Mills, 24 February 1931; Emerson to Mills, 24 February 1931, 17/1931, HPoll.
57. J. Davidson, 'Between Sittings with Gandhi', in Cousins (ed.), *Profiles*, pp. 18–19.
58. See O. Gramling, *AP-The Story of News*, New York, 1969 reissue, 1st. edn. 1940, pp. 358–359; and Biographical Reference File, Associated Press Corporate Archives.
59. James. A. Mills, 'Filming Mahatma Gandhi', *Filmo Topics*, Chicago January 1932, Vol. 8, No. 1, pp. 1–2, by courtesy of Associated Press Corporate Archives.

60. E. Emery, *The Press and America*, NJ, 1962, 2nd edn., p. 554.
61. Sandusky Register, Ohio, 4 March 1931.
62. *Ibid.*
63. Alton Evening Telegraph, Illinois, 6 April 1931.
64. State Times, 20 August 1931, p. 6.
65. Aberdeen Evening News, 3 September 1931, p. 8.
66. *Ibid.*
67. *Ibid.*
68. Evening Tribune, San Diego, 11 September 1931, p. 6.
69. Canton Repository, Ohio, 30 November 1931, front page.
70. Ironwood Daily Globe, 15 December 1931, front page.
71. *Ibid.*
72. Cleveland Plain Dealer, 28 January 1932, p. 2.
73. *Ibid.*
74. *Ibid.*
75. Burlington Hawk-Eye, 29 January 1932, p. 1.
76. *Ibid.*
77. Cleveland Plain Dealer, 30 January 1932.
78. Burlington Hawk-Eye, 2 February 1932, pp. 1, 4.
79. *Ibid.*
80. Decatur Daily Review, 26 January 1931, p. 1.
81. Emery, *Press and America*, p. 555.
82. 'The United Press' by Stephen Vincent Benet, Fortune, May 1933, p. 10, in L/I/1/395.
83. W. Miller, *I Found No Peace*, 1938, p. 184.
84. Report of the Indian section, BLI 1929–30, 76/1931, HPoll.
85. Miller, *No Peace*, p. 181.
86. *Ibid.*, p. 184.
87. *Ibid.*
88. Cited in B. Krishna, *Sardar Vallabhbhai Patel*, Delhi, 1995, p. 148.
89. Miller, *No Peace*, p. 189.
90. *Ibid.*, p. 190.
91. *Ibid.*, pp. 208–209.
92. Report of the Indian section, BLI 1929–30, 76/1931, HPoll.
93. Emery, *Press and America*, p. 725.
94. J. M. Hamilton, *Journalism's Roving Eye*, Baton Rouge Louisiana, 2009, p. 140.
95. Hamilton, *Roving Eye*, pp. 162–163.
96. Cited in J. Edwards, *The Foreign Policy of Col. McCormick's Tribune*, Reno, 1971, p. 36.
97. Edwards, *Foreign Policy*, p. 27.
98. W. L. Shirer, *20th Century Journey the Nightmare Years, 1930–1940*, Boston, 1984, Vol. II, p. 14.
99. Tribune, 29 December 1930.
100. Edwards, *Foreign Policy*, p. 45. Hamilton, *Roving Eye*, p. 163.
101. M. Emery (late), E. Emery, N. L. Roberts (eds.), *The Press and America*, Needham Heights, MA, 9th edn., p. 307.
102. Edwards, *Foreign Policy*, p. 54.
103. R. N. Smith, *The Colonel*, New York, 1997, p. 305.

104. MacGregor to R. S. Bajpai, 20 July 1932, L/I/1/392.
105. *Ibid.*
106. Edwards, *Foreign Policy*, p. 27.
107. McCormick to Shirer, 2 July 1931, William L. Shirer Papers, George T. Henry Archives, Coe College, hereafter SP; see also McCormick to Shirer, 17 November 1930, cited in Smith, *Colonel*, p. 305.
108. Tribune, 24 August 1930.
109. *Ibid.*
110. *Ibid.*
111. 4 March 1931.
112. 'An Agreement in India', Tribune, 4 March 1931.
113. 22 February 1931, Shirer Diary entry, SP.
114. *Ibid.*
115. *Ibid.*
116. See, for instance, Brelvi to J. Nehru, 11 September 1930, SP.
117. Shirer to Jinnah, 22 September 1930, SP.
118. Shirer to Mr Mitha, Kabul 22 October 1930, SP.
119. Shirer to Tagore, 2 May 1931, SP.
120. 26 February 1931, Shirer Diary entry, SP.
121. 21 February 1931, Shirer Diary entry, SP.
122. 10 March 1931, Shirer Diary entry, SP.
123. *Ibid.*
124. 16 April 1931, Shirer Diary entry, SP.
125. 10 March 1931, Shirer Diary entry, SP.
126. Gandhi to Shirer, 1 June 1931 cable, SP.
127. Tribune, 2 June 1931.
128. Shirer to Gandhi, 21 July 1931, SP.
129. 11 September 1931, Shirer Diary entry, SP.
130. *Ibid.*
131. R. Guha, *Dominance without Hegemony*, Harvard, Mass. 1997, p. 151.
132. Cited in Nicolson, *King George*, p. 507.
133. *Ibid.*, p. 509.
134. S/S to V, 6 November 1931, TC/1.
135. Cited in C. H. Rolph, *Kingsley*, 1973, p. 191.
136. N. S. Sarila, *Once a Prince of Sarila*, 2008, p. 59.
137. Tribune, 26 September 1931.
138. 26 September 1931, CTFS Manchester, Shirer despatch, originals, SP.
139. *Ibid.*
140. Tribune, 4 September 1931.
141. *Ibid.*
142. Tribune, 7 September 1931.
143. Tribune, 2 June 1931.
144. Tribune, 6 November 1931.
145. Young India, 9 July 1931, cited in *Collected Works of Mahatma Gandhi*, Ahmedabad, 1971, Vol. XLVII, 120, hereafter *CW*.
146. Tribune, 20 September 1931.
147. *Ibid.*
148. Shirer despatch, Delhi undated, SP.
149. Harold R. Isaacs, *Scratches on Our Minds*, New York, 1958, p. 297.

150. AP feature reproduced in Tribune, 21 September 1931.
151. *Ibid.*
152. 17 October 1931, Shirer diary entry, SP.
153. Tribune, 16 March 1931.
154. S. Amin, 'Gandhi as Mahatma: Gorakhpur District, Eastern UP, 1921–22', in R. Guha (ed.), *Subaltern Studies III*, New Delhi, 1989, pp. 1–61; S. Amin, *Event, Metaphor, Memory: Chauri Chaura 1922–1992*, Berkeley, 1995.
155. Tribune, 10 March 1931.
156. *Ibid.*
157. AP report in Tribune, 11 March 1931.
158. Tribune, 12 March 1931.
159. Shirer, *Memoir*, pp. 75–76.
160. F. B. Fisher, *That Strange Little Brown Man*, New York, 1932, p. 30.
161. 'Gandhi of India', Aberdeen Evening News, 3 September 1931, p. 8.
162. M. K. Gandhi, *An Autobiography or the Story of My Experiments with Truth*, Ahmedabad, reprint 1994, 1st edn., 1927, p. 239.
163. *Ibid.*
164. *Ibid.*
165. *Ibid.*
166. *Ibid.*, pp. 394–395.
167. *Ibid.*, p. 395.
168. L. Fischer, *A Week with Gandhi*, New York, 1942, and *The Great Challenge*, New York, 1946.
169. Gandhi to Roosevelt, 1 July 1942, cited in Cousins (ed.), *Profiles*, p. 227.
170. *Time*, 16 November 1942.
171. Cited in R. E. Herzstein, *Henry R. Luce*, New York, 1994, p. 271.
172. F. Hunt, *The Rising Temper of the East*, Indianapolis, 1922.
173. J. H. Holmes, *My Gandhi*, New York, 1953, as cited in H. A. Jack (ed.), *The Gandhi Reader*, New York, 1956, p. 396.
174. The reference is to the title of his book.
175. See Christian Century, 16 April 1930.
176. Dalton, *Gandhi*, p. 108.
177. 5 April 1930, cited in *CW*, Vol. XLIII, pp. 179–180.
178. Fisher, *Brown Man*, p. 30; Shirer Memo for Desai, 30 September 1931, SP.
179. Shirer to Gandhi, 21 July 1931, SP.
180. Fisher, *Brown Man*, p. 30.
181. M. Bourke-White, *Portrait of Myself*, New York, 1963, pp. 278–279.
182. Tribune, 14 September 1931, p. 9.
183. Tribune, 14 September 1931.
184. *Evening Tribune*, Albert Lea, Minn, 14 September 1931, p. 7.
185. J. D. Hunt, *Gandhi in London*, New Delhi, 1993 rev. edn., p. 41.
186. J. M. Brown, *Gandhi and Civil Disobedience*, Cambridge, 1976, p. 257f.
187. J. M. Brown, 'The Role of a National Leader', in D. A. Low (ed.), *Congress and the Raj*, 1977, p. 152.
188. V to S/S, 22 September 1931, TC/5.
189. *Ibid.*
190. TT, 14 September 1931.
191. See Hunt, *Gandhi*, p. 199.
192. Cited in Holmes, *My Gandhi*, 1954, p. 44.

193. As quoted by Mills in Canton Repository, 30 November 1931.
194. Kaul, *Reporting the Raj*, pp.124, 129–130, 151–152, 206, 216.
195. Report of Indian section of BLI, 1929–1930, 76/1931, HPoll.
196. *Ibid.*
197. *Ibid.*
198. *Ibid.*
199. *Ibid.*
200. See S. K. Ratcliffe, 'India and the United States', *Asiatic Review*, London, 26 January 1930.
201. See, for example, New Republic, 20 August 1930, Vol. LXIV.
202. M. C. Seton to W. H Emerson, 24 December 1930, 88/1931, HPoll.
203. E. Thompson, *Enlist India for Freedom*, 1940, p. 96.
204. See Home Dept. to S/S, 30 July 1925, F311/1925, HPoll.
205. See 235/II, 1926, HPoll.
206. *Ibid.*
207. Telegram V (Home Dept.) to S/S, 6 November 1930, 88/1931, HPoll.
208. S/S to V, 17 October 1930, 88/1931, HPoll.
209. *Ibid.*
210. Memo, DPI 20 October 1930, and R. Bajpai memo 21 October 1930, 88/1931 HPoll.
211. *Ibid.*
212. *Ibid.*
213. *Ibid.*
214. Memo, DPI 23.10.1930, 88/1931, HPoll.
215. M. C. Seton to W. H Emerson, 24 December 1930, 88/1931, HPoll.
216. *Ibid.*
217. Bajpai to Emerson, 23 February 1931, 88/1931, HPoll.
218. *Tribune,* 17 August 1930.
219. MacGregor to Steele, 29 December 1930, SP.
220. Steele to McCormick, 31 December 1930 and Steele to McCormick, 2 January 1931, SP.
221. R. Wilberforce to A. Willert, 16 December 1930, L/I/1/392.
222. A. S. Fletcher to A. Willert, 15 January 1931, L/I/1/392.
223. MacGregor to Fletcher, 21 February 1931, L/I/1/392.
224. Joyce to Dawson, 3 February 1931, L/I/1/392.
225. BLI 'Survey of the USA press', 8 April 1932, L/I/1/392.
226. *Ibid.*
227. MacGregor to Wilberforce, 9 October 1931, L/I/1/392.
228. Joyce to Fletcher, 17 February 1932, L/I/1/392.
229. Joyce to Rex Leeper, 22 February 1932, L/I/1/392.
230. Joyce Note, 17 February 1932, L/I/1/392.
231. Steele to MacGregor, 26 February 1932, L/I/1/392.
232. J. Hennessy to Joyce, 14 July 1943, L/I/1/1514.
233. Joyce to R. J. Cruickshank, 17 July 1943, L/I/1/1514.
234. See, for example, G. R. Hess, *America Encounters India, 1941–1947*, Baltimore, 1971; Isaacs, *Scratches on our Minds;* M. S. Venkataramani and B. K. Shrivastav, *Quit India: The American Response to the 1942 Struggle*, New Delhi 1979; K. J. Clymer, *Quest for Freedom*, New York 1995; A. Weigold, *Churchill, Roosevelt and India*, New York, 2008; H. A. Gould, *The South Asia Story*, New Delhi, 2010.

235. Linda S. Rae to author via email, 7 June 2012.
236. Shirer, *Memoir*, p. 43.
237. *Ibid.*, p. 55.
238. Shirer to Spykman, 5 February 1932, SP.
239. Shirer, *Memoir*, p. 61.
240. *Ibid.*, p. 17.
241. *Ibid.*, p. 23.
242. L-F Rushbrook Williams, 'Indian Unrest and American Opinion', *Asiatic Review*, July 1930, p. 489.
243. Shirer, *20th Century Journey*, p. 14.
244. McCormick to Shirer, 30 December 1932, SP.
245. Shirer to Sen Gupta, 7 January 1932, SP.
246. Tribune, 27 September 1931.
247. See his *Memoir*.

4 'Invisible Empire Tie': Broadcasting and the British Raj in the Interwar Years

1. See Appendix I for the full poem.
2. My thanks to Professor Minoti Chakravarty-Kaul for this translation.
3. See, for example, Dunstan to Reith, Good Friday April 1927, E1/897/2, WAC.
4. J. Seaton, 'Writing the History of Broadcasting', in D. Cannadine (ed.), *History and the Media*, 2004, pp. 155–157.
5. *Indian Radio Times*, 29 July 1927, Vol. 1, No. 2, p. 22, E1/897/2.
6. Undated official memo, L/I/1/445.
7. K. M. Shrivastava, *Radio and TV Journalism*, New Delhi, 1989, p. 19.
8. DIL to S/S, 28 April 1927, 60/27, HPoll.
9. *Ibid.*, pp. 2–3.
10. Further Note on Broadcasting by the Director of Wireless, 5 August 1927, 22/7/27, HPoll.
11. DIL to V, Memo 17 August 1926, 22/7/27, HPoll.
12. 1927, F 120, HPoll.
13. Contract of Agreement between IBC and S/S, 13 September 1926, pp. 714–721, annexure A. encl. in C. McWatters, GoI, to Under S/S, 27 January 1927, L/PJ/8/118, IOLR, hereafter L/PJ/.
14. Irwin's speech cited in *Report on the Progress of Broadcasting in India*, GoI, New Delhi, 1940, p. 1, hereafter *Broadcasting in India*.
15. Dunstan to Reith, 14 & 22 February 1928, E1/897/3, WAC.
16. Dunstan to Reith, 5 July 1928, E1/897/4, WAC.
17. Note on Broadcasting by the Director of Wireless, 1 July 1927, 22/7/27, HPoll.
18. A. K. Singh (trans. S. Das), *India Post*, New Delhi, 2009, p. 174.
19. See D. Cryle & C. Kaul, 'The Empire Press Union and the Expansion of Imperial Air Services 1909–1939 with Special Reference to Australia, New Zealand & India', *Media History*, Vol. 15, No. 1, February 2009, pp. 17–30.
20. *Moral and Material Progress and Condition of India, 1933–34*, GoI, 1936, pp. 115–116.

21. Cited in *Broadcasting in India*, p. 161.
22. *Indian Wireless Magazine*, Calcutta, February 1930, Vol. II, No. 4; also January 1930.
23. Sir Frank Noyce, Legislative Assembly proceedings, 7 April 1934, L/PJ/7/754.
24. Note on the Development of Broadcasting in India, 1927–33, encl. in D. G. Mitchell to Under S/S, 28 February 1934, L/I/1/445.
25. Note by Coatman on 'Broadcasting in India', 28 July 1934, pp. 1–2, L/PJ/8/118.
26. Director DIL to Stewart, IO, 27 August 1934, L/PJ/8/118.
27. S. Drucquer, *Broadcasting*, Bombay, 1945, p. 22.
28. *Ibid.*
29. For a detailed discussion of Government propaganda and the Amritsar Massacre, see Kaul, *Reporting the Raj*, Chapter 8.
30. Note by J. Crerar, 29 August 1924, Communication and Wireless Proceedings, 1926, HPoll.
31. Official Report, Legislative Assembly debates, 1 September 1936, L/PJ/8/118.
32. *Ibid.*, 24 September 1936, L/PJ/8/118.
33. *Ibid.*, 1 September 1936, L/PJ/8/118.
34. Memo, Broadcasting in India, January 1937, encl. B, p. 1, E1/896/3, WAC.
35. M. G. Hallett to Fielden, 5 August 1936, L/PJ/7/754.
36. See E. Katz & P. F. Lazarsfeld, *Personal Influence*, New Jersey, 2006, p. 32.
37. Cited in L. Fielden, *The Natural Bent*, 1960, p. 196.
38. See Kaul, *Reporting the Raj*, Chapter 2.
39. Statesman, 2 August 1934; ABP, 27 July 1934.
40. D. Chakrabarty, *Habitations of Modernity*, Chicago, 2002, p. 85.
41. For 1870s–1922, see Kaul, *Reporting the Raj*.
42. See Kaul, *Reporting the Raj*, Chapter 7, pp. 165–198.
43. Hoare to Willingdon, 19 August 1932, TC/2.
44. *Ibid.*
45. S/S to V, 29 July 1932, TC/2.
46. J. A. Cross, *Sir Samuel Hoare*, 1977, p. 143.
47. V to S/S, 17 June 1935, Zetland collection, Mss Eur D 609/6, hereafter ZC/.
48. V to S/S, 16 July 1932, TC/5.
49. Irwin to Sykes, 23 March 1929, SC/1.
50. V to S/S, 13 October 1928, Irwin Collection, Mss Eur D 703/6, hereafter IC/
51. See Gopal, *Lord Irwin*; Glendevon, *Viceroy*.
52. 'Reith's diary entry 30 July 1934', in C. Stuart (ed.), *The Reith Diaries*, 1975, p. 331, hereafter *Reith Diaries*.
53. S/S to V, 27 April 1936, Linlithgow collection, Mss Eur F 125/3, hereafter LC/.
54. 20 April 1936, Reith Diary, S 60/5/4/3, WAC.
55. Linlithgow to Reith, 23 April 1936, E1/896/3, WAC.
56. Reith to Linlithgow, 5 May 1936, E1/896/3, WAC
57. V to S/S, 22 April 1936, LC/3.
58. *Ibid.*
59. L/I/1/1442.
60. See Kaul, *Reporting the Raj*, chapters 5 and 6.

61. Report by S. N. Roy, GoI, to Under S/S IO, 26 August 1940, 52/1/40, HPoll.
62. *Ibid.*
63. See 60/2/40, HPoll.
64. For transcripts and brief history, see S. Sengupta & G. Chatterjee (eds.), *Secret Congress Broadcasts and Storming Railway Tracks during Quit India Movement*, New Delhi, 1988.
65. Roy to Under S/S IO, 16 December 1940, 52/1/40, HPoll.
66. M. Barns, *India Today and Tomorrow*, 1937, p. 251.
67. See *The Listener*, 28 September & 23 November, 1939; 11 April, 13 June, 17 October, 28 November 1940.
68. S/S to V, 17 January 1929, cited in H. R. Luthra, *Indian Broadcasting*, Delhi, 1986, p. 52.
69. S/S to V, 17 December 1931, TC/1.
70. MacGregor to Fielden, 16 March 1936, L/I/1/445.
71. MacGregor's note 1934, p. 424, L/PJ/8/118; see also MacGregor to Peel, 5 May, L/I/1/445.
72. Coatman on 'Broadcasting', p. 3.
73. GoI Act 1935 extract, p. 222, L/PJ/8/118.
74. *Ibid.*, p. 223.
75. *Reith Diaries*, 27 November 1923.
76. A. Briggs, *The Birth of Broadcasting*, 1995, Vol. 1, p. 322.
77. Frost Memo as cited in Stephens to MacGregor, 20 September 1933, L/I/1/445.
78. A. Briggs, *The Golden Age of Wireless*, 1995, Vol. 2, p. 360.
79. J. M. MacKenzie, *Propaganda and Empire*, Manchester, 1984, pp. 10–11.
80. J. C. W. Reith, *Into the Wind*, 1949, p. 207. See Willingdon to Reith, 7 September 1934, L/PJ/8/118.
81. I. McIntyre, *The Expense of Glory*, 1993, p. 95.
82. See, for example, F. Stewart to Reith, 12 April 1934, L/PJ/8/118.
83. Reith, *Into the Wind*, p. 206.
84. Reith to Fielden, 13 August 1935, cited in Fielden, *Natural Bent*, p. 147.
85. *Reith Diaries*, 18 February 1945.
86. *Ibid.*, 20 February 1947.
87. *Ibid.*, 9 November 1963.
88. Reith to S/S, 4 June 1925 and reply 9 June 1925, E1/897/1, WAC.
89. P. S. Gupta, *Radio and the Raj: 1921–47*, CSSS lecture series Calcutta, 1995, p. 4.
90. *Reith Diaries*, 10 April 1926.
91. Reith, *Into the Wind*, p. 142.
92. Comments dated 8.5.34 on report accompanying GoI dispatch, 28 February 1934, L/I/1/445.
93. *Ibid.*
94. Reith, *Into the Wind*, p. 169.
95. Briggs, *The Golden Age*, p. 357.
96. Briggs, *Broadcasting*, Vol. 1, p. 47.
97. Drucquer, *Broadcasting*, p. 6.
98. 28 February 1934 BBC Memo, L/I/1/445.
99. See E1/897/1 & 2, WAC.
100. *Broadcasting Commission Report*, August 1923, HMSO, p. 6, SC/8.

101. See C. Kaul, 'India, the Imperial Press Conferences and the Empire Press Union: The Diplomacy of News in the Politics of Empire 1909–46', in C. Kaul (ed.), *Media and the British Empire*, Basingstoke, 2006, pp. 125–144. Also Kaul, 'Media, India and the Raj', in Thompson (ed.), *Writing Imperial Histories*, pp. 188–215.
102. Briggs, *Broadcasting*, Vol. 1, p. 237.
103. Frost memo, encl. in Stephens to MacGregor, 20 September 1933, L/I/1/445.
104. Reith to Sir William Bull, 22 April 1926, E1/897/1, WAC.
105. Reith to Dunstan, 19 September 1928, E1/897/4, WAC.
106. BBC Memo on Indian Broadcasting, 26 September 1928, L/I/1/445.
107. *Ibid.*
108. Frost memo, encl. in Stephens to MacGregor, 20 September 1933, L/I/1/445.
109. BBC Memo on Indian Broadcasting, 26 September 1928, L/I/1/445.
110. E1/896/3, WAC.
111. Sir F. Stewart, IO to Sir F Noyce, 13 July 1934, L/PJ/8/118.
112. *Reith Diaries*, 17 July 1934.
113. *Ibid.*, 30 July 1934.
114. Willingdon to Reith, 7 September 1934, cited in Reith, *Into the Wind*, p. 207.
115. R. Peel, Minute Paper, 30.1.35, L/PJ/8/118.
116. Mitchell to High Commissioner, 13 November 1934, L/PO/3/3d.
117. 30 November 1934, Reith Diary, S60/5/4/2, WAC.
118. 28 January 1935, Reith Diary, S60/5/4/2, WAC.
119. Reith to S/S, 21 December 1934, L/PO/3/3d.
120. Mitchell to A. M. Green, IO, 13 November 1934, L/PO/3/3d.
121. Noyce to Stewart, 3 September 1934, L/PJ/7/754.
122. Legislative Assembly debates official report, 17 September 1935, L/PJ/8/118.
123. *Ibid.*
124. 1 April 1935, Reith Diary, S60/5/4/2, WAC.
125. *Ibid.*
126. *Statesman*, 22 July 1940.
127. Fielden to J. Thomson, 20 October 1937, L/I/1/445.
128. S/S to V, 19 July 1937, L/PO/3/3d.
129. Fielden to Frost, 23 September 1937, E5/33, WAC.
130. Fielden to Graves, 20 January 1939, L1/144/1, Fielden Staff file, WAC, hereafter FSF.
131. Matheson Memo, 18 January 1928, FSF.
132. *Ibid.*
133. Internal Memo, 27 August 1934, no. 277, as cited in Briggs, *Golden Age*, p. 138.
134. Siepmann Memo, 5 February 1930, FSF.
135. Matheson Memo, January 1932, FSF.
136. Siepmann Memo, February 1931, FSF.
137. Siepmann Memo, January 1934, FSF.
138. *Ibid.*
139. Siepmann Memo, January 1935, FSF.
140. Fielden, *Natural Bent*, p. 127.
141. *Ibid.*, pp. 124,135,146,143, 145.
142. Reith to Fielden, 13 August 1935, cited in Fielden, *Natural Bent*, p. 147.

143. Reith to Sir Eric Mieville, Buckingham Palace, 13 April 1937, E1/896/3, WAC.
144. Fielden, *Natural Bent*, p. 184.
145. See Reith Diary for 1937–8, WAC.
146. 21 July 1937, Reith Diary, S60/5/5/1, WAC.
147. Fielden, *Natural Bent*, p. 160.
148. *Ibid.*, pp. 147, 158, 175.
149. Cited in G. Rizvi, *Linlithgow and India*, 1978, p. 4.
150. Fielden 29 June, Memo, Broadcasting in India, 1937, encl B, p. 4, E1/896/3, WAC.
151. *Ibid.*, p. 188.
152. F. King, Obituary of Lettice Cooper, *The Independent*, 27 July 1994, accessed online.
153. V to S/S, 2 August 1937, LC/4.
154. *Ibid.*
155. Reith to Sir Eric Mieville, Buckingham Palace, 13 April 1937, E1/896/3, WAC.
156. Reith to Linlithgow, 21 October 1937, E1/896/3, WAC.
157. See Reith Diary for 1934–8, WAC.
158. Fielden, *Natural Bent*, p. 186.
159. Kirke, 'Report on the Proposed Development of Broadcasting Stations in India', p. 143, 1936, L/PJ/8/118.
160. D. G. Mitchell to Indian High Commissioner London, 13 November 1934, L/PO/3/3d, IOLR.
161. Hallett to Stephens, incl. in note from Stephens to MacGregor, 12–13 December 1935, L/I/1/445.
162. *Ibid.*
163. V to S/S, 17 June 1935, ZC/6.
164. *Ibid.*
165. MacGregor to Stephens, 3 January 1936, L/I/1/445.
166. Fielden 31 October, Memo, Broadcasting in India, 1937, encl B, p. 3, E1/896/3, WAC.
167. Fielden to MacGregor, 6 October 1937, L/I/1/445.
168. S. N. Roy, Sec. GoI to Under S/S, IO, 8 February 1938, L/PJ/8/118.
169. L. Fielden, *Beggar My Neighbour*, 1943, p. 19.
170. *Ibid.*, p. 190.
171. Fielden, *Natural Bent*, p. 201.
172. Note by Coatman, 31 May 1927, 240/1927, HPoll.
173. V to Sir W. Bull, 20 May 1926, E1/897/1, WAC.
174. See 240/1927, HPoll.
175. *Ibid.*
176. Letter from GoI, 3 December 1927, cited in Luthra, *Indian Broadcasting*, pp. 43–44.
177. Fielden to Sir Stephen Tallents, 1 April 1938, E1/885, Controller of Broadcasting 1935–47, WAC.
178. *Ibid.*
179. MacGregor to Stephens, 16 January 1936, L/I/1/445.
180. Memo by Metcalfe 28 April 1938, 52/5/38, HPoll.
181. J. A. Mackeown to Fielden, 5 May 1938, 52/5/58, HPoll.

182. 21 June 1938, Home Department to AIR Delhi, 52/4/38, HPoll.
183. Fielden, *Natural Bent*, p. 181.
184. *Ibid.*, p. 215.
185. Fielden, *Neighbour*, p. 54.
186. *Ibid.*
187. *Hindustan Times*, 13 November 1947.
188. Mills, 'Filming Mahatma Gandhi', p. 1.
189. Most biographers discuss these themes and his *CW*s also contains similar testimony.
190. Fielden, *Neighbour*, p. 73.
191. *Ibid.*, p. 52. The Madras stations were established the following year.
192. Fielden, *Natural Bent*, p. 191.
193. Memo, Communication Deptt, GoI to A. Dibdin, Under S/S IO, 26.9.39, L/PJ/7/2934.
194. V to S/S, 16 June 1939, L/PO/3/3D.
195. Sir J. Grigg, 'Broadcasting in India', *The Listener*, 2 January 1941, Vol. XXV, No. 625, p. 25.
196. *Broadcasting in India*, pp. 18–19.
197. Luthra, *Indian Broadcasting*, pp. 154–155.
198. Fielden to Graves, 20 January 1939, FSF.
199. Fielden, *Natural Bent*, p. 147.
200. C. Barns to A. H. Joyce, 31 August 1938, L/I/1/445.
201. V. A. M. Bulow, letter to editor, *The Listener*, 23 January 1941, No. 628, p. 132.
202. Drucquer, *Broadcasting*, p. 5.
203. Luthra, *Indian Broadcasting*, p. 146.
204. Cited in Reith, *Into the Wind*, p. 233.
205. Grigg, 'Broadcasting'.
206. Statesman, 2 August 1934.
207. ABP, 27 July 1934.
208. ToI, 18 July 1934.
209. *Ibid.*
210. Fielden to Nixon, 15 July 1937, E 1/877/1, WAC.
211. *Reith Diaries*, 7 October 1923.
212. TT, 5 January 1929.
213. *The Listener*, 15 July, also 22 & 29 July, 5 August, WAC.
214. H. R. Hardinge, 'Broadcasting in India', *The Empire Review*, October 1938, pp. 235–326.
215. *The Listener*, 7 April 1937; broadcast 29 March.
216. Dunstan to Reith, 23 September 1927, E1/897/2, WAC.
217. E. M. Jenkins to Under S/S, P&J. Further report on the Progress of Broadcasting, 9 January 1936, L/I/1/445.
218. Undated official memo, L/I/1/445.
219. N. C. Chaudhuri, *Thy Hand, Great Anarch!*, 1990, pp. 405, 687.
220. 33/7/39, HPoll.
221. *Broadcasting in India,* pp. 80, 164.
222. *Ibid.*, p. 162.
223. BBC Memo on Indian Broadcasting, 26 September 1928, L/I/1/445.
224. Fielden, *Natural Bent*, p. 204.

225. Cited in MacKenzie, *Propaganda*, p. 93.
226. Note by Director of Wireless, 1 July 1927, 22/7/27, HPoll.
227. Dunstan to Reith, 21 January 1928, E1/897/3, WAC.
228. M. Tracey, *The Decline and Fall of Public Service Broadcasting*, Oxford, 1998, p. 38.
229. See Kaul, *Reporting the Raj*, especially Chapter 5.
230. TT, 27 July 1937.

5 'Operation Seduction': Mountbatten, the Media and Decolonisation in 1947

NB: All press references are to 1947, unless otherwise specified.

1. J. Keay, *India A History*, 2000, p. 509.
2. J. Epstein, 'Taking Class Notes on Empire', in C. Hall & S. Rose (eds.), *At Home with the Empire*, Cambridge, 2006, p. 274.
3. M. Misra, *Vishnu's Crowded Temple*, 2007, p. 253.
4. D. Cannadine, 'Independence Day Ceremonial in Historical Perspective', in R. Holland, S. Williams & T. Barringer (eds.), *The Iconography of Independence*, Abingdon, 2010, pp. 2–3.
5. *Ibid.*
6. *Royal Commission on the Press 1947–1949 Report*, 1949, p. 5.
7. *Ibid.*, p. 188.
8. See Kaul, *Reporting the Raj* for a detailed discussion of this process.
9. R. J. Moore, *Churchill, Cripps and India 1939–45*, Oxford, 1979, p. 138.
10. I. Glynn, 'An Untouchable in the Presence of Brahmins' Lord Wavell's Disastrous Relationship with Whitehall during His Time as Viceroy of India', *Modern Asian Studies*, Vol. 41, No. 3, Cambridge, 2007, p. 658.
11. I. M. Stephens, *Pakistan*, Middlesex, 1964, p. 148.
12. Wavell to Leo Amery, 20 December 1944, L/I/1/267.
13. Deakin to Holburn, 11 January 1945, Foreign Editors file, TNL archives.
14. N. Thomas-Symonds, *Attlee*, 2010, p. 180.
15. Stephens, *Pakistan*, p. 148.
16. Cited in B. Hoey, *Mountbatten the Private Story*, 1994, p. 4.
17. J. Terraine, *The Life and Times of Lord Mountbatten*, 1980, p. 179.
18. Earl Mountbatten, *First Mountbatten Lecture*, National Electronics Council, 1978, p. 9.
19. A. Campbell-Johnson, *Mountbatten in Retrospect*, South Godstone, 1997, pp. 49–50.
20. Stephens, *Monsoon Morning*, p. 199.
21. M. Desfor interview with author, 15 April 2014.
22. M. Desfor, 6 June 1997, AP 20, Oral History Collection, Associated Press Corporate Archives, p. 28; also Max Desfor interview with author, 15 April 2014.
23. Sarila, *Prince of Sarila*, p. 206.
24. *Ibid.*, pp. 206–207.
25. *Ibid.*, pp. 207–208.

26. Lord Ismay cited in A. Campbell-Johnson, *Mission with Mountbatten*, 1951, p. 221.
27. L. Collins & D. Lapierre, *Mountbatten and the Partition of India*, Manchester, 1982, Vol. 1, p. 6.
28. Joyce to Johnson, 11 March 1947, L/I/1/1467.
29. *Ibid.*, emphasis mine.
30. Joyce to Johnson, 11 March 1947, L/I/1/1467.
31. Johnson to Mountbatten, 14 March 1947, Mountbatten Collection, Mss Eur F 200/114, hereafter MC/.
32. See report of 14 March 1947 meeting at IO between Frank Owen, Joyce, Charles Eade and R J Cruikshank, MC/114a.
33. Johnson to Joyce, 25 March 1947, L/I/1/1467.
34. Collins & Lapierre, *Mountbatten*, p. 26.
35. L/I/1/1467, p. 162.
36. *Ibid.*, pp. 24–25.
37. Johnson, *Mission*, p. 42.
38. As cited in H. R. Luthra, *Indian Broadcasting*, New Delhi, 1986, p. 141.
39. Collins & Lapierre, *Mountbatten*, p. 26.
40. *Hindustan Times*, 23 March; *Pioneer*, 24 March; *Statesman*, 23 March.
41. Observer, 21 March; *Dawn*, 23 March.
42. Joyce to Johnson, 31 March 1947, L/I/1/1467.
43. Earl Mountbatten, *Time only to Look Forward*, 1949, p. 64.
44. Collins & Lapierre, *Mountbatten*, p. 77.
45. *Ibid.*, p. 27.
46. *Ibid.*, p. 30.
47. P. Talbot, *An American Witness to India's Partition*, Delhi, 2007, p. 305.
48. Collins & Lapierre, *Mountbatten*, p. 30.
49. V's Personal report 12, 11 July 1947, p. 90, L/I/1/1467.
50. V's Personal reports, March–April 1947, MC/114 a.
51. *Ibid.*
52. V's Personal Reports 5 June 1947, cited in Collins & Lapierre, *Mountbatten*, pp. 146–147.
53. Johnson to Joyce 5 June 1947, MC/114.
54. Stephens, *Pakistan*, p. 148.
55. Cited in Johnson, *Mission*, p. 110.
56. Talbot, *American Witness*, p. 304.
57. Johnson to Joyce, 25 June 1947, L/I/1/1456.
58. Johnson to Joyce, 1 June 1947, MC/163.
59. Memo by Johnson, 27 May 1947, MC/114.
60. Johnson to Joyce, 3 June 1947, MC/163.
61. Luthra, *Indian Broadcasting*, pp. 168–169.
62. V to S/S, 6 July 1947 and Nicholls to Joyce, 6 July 1947, MC/114b.
63. Of Irish descent, he succeeded to the title in 1931 with a seat in the Lords, becoming a Labour whip a decade later, and was Postmaster General prior to taking over at the IO in 1946.
64. Johnson to Joyce, 25 June 1947, L/I/1/1456.
65. IJA Executive Committee Annual Report 1948, 9 December 1948, cited in K. P. V. Ayyar *et al.* (eds.), *The Indian Press Year Book 1948*, Madras, 1948, p. 79.

66. Johnson to Joyce, 25 June 1947, L/I/1/1456.
67. Joyce to Johnson, 31 March 1947, L/I/1/1467.
68. Joyce to Wadsworth and others, 1 May 1947, L/I/1/1443.
69. H. Balfour to Joyce, 14 May 1947, L/I/1/400.
70. L. Collins & D. Lapierre, *Mountbatten and the Partition of India*, Manchester, 1982, Vol. 1, p. 6.
71. See L. P. Chester, *Borders and Conflict in South Asia*, Manchester, 2009, for discussion of stage management of the Boundary Commission and Partition award.
72. Tribune, 23 May.
73. Summary, R. N. Bannerjee, 22 July 1947, 30 January 1947, 1947 HPoll.
74. *Ibid.*
75. Low, 'Present Day Journalism', p. 517.
76. V to S/S, 22 May 1947, MC/114.
77. V to S/S, 23 May 1947, MC/114.
78. AP World, Autumn issue 1946, p. 23, Associated Press Corporate Archives.
79. Forum weekly, 11 March 1945, p. 22, Charles A Grumich Papers, AP 21.24, Associated Press Corporate Archives.
80. AP World, March 1945, p. 12, Associated Press Corporate Archives.
81. Max Desfor, Interview with author, 15 April 2014.
82. For a discussion of the development of Fleet Street links with the Indian press, see Kaul, *Reporting the Raj*.
83. Stephens, *Monsoon Morning*, p. 62.
84. Britter to Deakin, 31 December 1946, Foreign Editors file, TNL archives.
85. The *News Chronicle* represented the amalgamation of three iconic liberal papers – the *Westminster Gazette*, *Daily News* and *Daily Chronicle*.
86. ILN, 23 August.
87. DM, 15 August.
88. ContR, January 1948, Vol. CLXXIII, pp. 14–16.
89. D. L. LeMahieu, *A Culture for Democracy*, Oxford, 2002 edn.
90. Star, 15 August.
91. NS&N, 23 August.
92. K. Martin, *Editor*, 1968, p. 162
93. C. H. Rolph, *Kingsley*, 1973, p. 295.
94. Martin, *Editor*, pp. 326–327.
95. MG, 11 July.
96. Herald, 15 August.
97. DM, see also TT, MG, Chronicle, Herald.
98. MG, 11 July.
99. MG, 15 August.
100. Herald, 'Freedom Day', 15 August.
101. MG, 15 August.
102. MG, 11 July.
103. Observer, 10 August; MG, 15 August; TT, 15 August.
104. TT, 15 August.
105. Cited in MG, 15 August.
106. MG, 16 August.
107. TT, 15 August.
108. NS&N, 16 August.

109. MG, 16 August.
110. DM, 15 August.
111. MG, 16 August.
112. Spectator, 18 July; NS&N, 14 June.
113. DM, Express, Telegraph, 15 August.
114. Quoted in Herald, 16 August.
115. Punch, 11 June.
116. MG, 7 August.
117. NS&N, 23 August.
118. Herald, 15 August.
119. *Ibid.*
120. Herald, 15 August.
121. Chronicle, 15 August.
122. Spectator, 15 August.
123. Chronicle, 15 August.
124. TT, 15 August.
125. Spectator, 22 August.
126. ContR, June, p. 21.
127. NS&N, 16 August.
128. Observer, 17 August.
129. MG, 15 August.
130. Herald, Star, 14 August.
131. *Ibid.*, p. 5.
132. Spectator, 18 July.
133. ContR, August, pp. 82–87.
134. J. Cameron, *Point of Departure*, 1967, p. 82.
135. *Ibid.*
136. *Ibid.*
137. K. Williams, *Read All About It!* 2010, pp. 166–170.
138. NS&N, 23 August.
139. MG, 9 August.
140. NOTW, 24 August.
141. Spectator, 15 August.
142. DM, 15 August; also MG, 15 August.
143. TT, 15 August.
144. Drucquer, *Broadcasting*, p. 32.
145. Luthra, *Indian Broadcasting*, p. 137.
146. *Ibid.*, p. 141.
147. See V-Patel correspondence, 22 and 20 April 1947, MC/114a.
148. Listings as published in NHerald, 13 August.
149. Memo, The BBC and India, by D. Stephenson, August 1944, E1/908/1, WAC.
150. *Ibid.*
151. *Ibid.*
152. Stephenson to Clark, 29 March 1944, E1/908/1, WAC.
153. *Ibid.*
154. *Ibid.*
155. Note by Pennethorne Hughes on the future of the Delhi office, 8 July 1946, E1/908/1, WAC.

156. Hailey to Controller, OS, 22 July 1946, E1/908/1, WAC.
157. Stephenson to Controller, OS, 13 August 1946, E1/908/1, WAC.
158. Cited in D. Edwards, *The Two Worlds of Donald Edwards*, 1970, p. 56.
159. D. Edwards, 'A Walk with Gandhi', in W. Crawley (ed.) *A Broadcasting Partnership*, Indo-British Review, Madras, 1994, p. 113.
160. Edwards, *Two Worlds*, pp. 59–60.
161. *Ibid.*, pp. 60–63.
162. Johnson to Joyce, 25 June 1947, L/I/1/1456.
163. *Ibid.*
164. Haley to V, 14 June 1947, MC/114.
165. Listowel to V, 13 July 1947, MC/114.
166. V to Listowel, 15 July 1947, MC/114.
167. V to Listowel, 1 August 1947, MC/163.
168. *The Listener*, 21 August, Vol. XXXVIII, No. 969, pp. 281, 292.
169. *The Listener*, 21 August, Vol. XXXVIII, No. 969, pp. 290–291, 285–287.
170. *Radio Times*, 8 August, p. 9. 'Report from India', BBC Home Service Sundays, 6.10–6.40 p.m. broadcast on 8 August, 17 August, 24 August, 31 August, 7 September, 14 September, 21 September, 28 September, 5 October.
171. *Radio Times*, 8 August, p. 9.
172. 'Report from India', 31 August, transcript, WAC.
173. *Ibid.*
174. *Ibid.*
175. *Ibid.*
176. *Ibid.*
177. Cited in B. Coulton, *Louis MacNeice in the BBC*, 1980, p. 98.
178. *Ibid.*, p. 102.
179. D. Hendy, 'Biography and the Emotions as a Missing "Narrative" in Media History', *Media History*, Vol. 18, Nos. 3–4, 2012, pp. 361–378.
180. BBC Broadcast 2 October as cited in his book, *Not in Feather Beds*, 1968, p. 5.
181. V to Listowel, 14 July 1947, MC/114
182. J. Turner, *Filming History*, 2001, p. 114.
183. Long-Maddox to Joyce, 17 July 1947, L/I/1/1467.
184. V to S/S, 16 July 1947, MC/114.
185. Turner, *Filming History*, p. 115.
186. *Ibid.*, p. 119.
187. Mountbatten to Castleton-Knight, as cited in Turner, *Filming History*, p. 120.
188. Johnson to Joyce, 24 September 1947, L/I/1/515.
189. See P. Wood in Kaul (ed.) *Media and the British Empire*, pp. 145–159.
190. For a short survey of select Indian press editorials, see S. Kamra, *Bearing Witness*, Calgary, 2002.
191. Pioneer, advt, 9 August.
192. Pioneer, 15 August.
193. See NHerald, 14 August.
194. Pioneer, 15 August.
195. BChronicle, 9 August.
196. BChronicle, 15 August.
197. NHerald, 16 August.
198. ToI, 15 August.

199. Pioneer, 15 August.
200. BChronicle, 15 August.
201. NHerald 16 August.
202. See Pioneer, 16 August; CMG, 19 August; BChronicle, 15 August.
203. See Statesman, 15 August
204. BChronicle, 15 August.
205. *Ibid.*
206. Pioneer, 7 August.
207. Pioneer, 9 August.
208. Dawn, 14 August.
209. Dawn, 15 August
210. CMG, 13 August.
211. Tribune, 23 May.
212. Statesman, *Leader*, 13 August.
213. Statesman, 18 August.
214. NHerald, 16 August.
215. Pioneer, 10 August.
216. Statesman, 11 July.
217. See, for example, Statesman, 15 August.
218. *Ibid.*
219. Statesman, *Leader*, 19 August.
220. Johnson to Joyce, 24 September 1947, L/I/1/515.
221. Johnson, *Mission*, p. 68.
222. NHerald, 15 August.
223. M. Lipton & J. Firn, *The Erosion of a Relationship*, 1975, p. 86
224. P. Mountbatten & I. Hicks, *India Remembered*, 2007, p. 66.
225. Observer, 31 August.
226. Telegraph, 17 August.
227. Johnson to Joyce, 24 September 1947, L/I/1/515.
228. Observer, 7 September.
229. Punch, 3 September 1947.
230. Johnson to Joyce, 24 September 1947, L/I/1/515.
231. *Ibid.*
232. Hindustan Standard, Calcutta, 21 September.
233. *Ibid.*
234. Lord Ismay, *The Memoirs of General Lord Ismay*, 1960, p. 442.
235. *Ibid.*
236. NS&N, 6 September.
237. Cited in A. Chisholm & M. Davie, *Lord Beaverbrook a Life*, New York, 1993 edn., p. 455.
238. NS&N, 6 September.
239. Collins & Lapierre, *Mountbatten*, p. 80.
240. Talbot, *American Witness*, p. 314.
241. *Ibid.*, p. 315.
242. *Ibid.*
243. For an analysis of the tour, see C. Kaul, 'Monarchical Display & the Politics of Empire: Princes of Wales and India, 1870s–1920s', *Twentieth Century British History*, Vol. 17, No. 4, 2006, pp. 464–488.
244. Collins & Lapierre, *Mountbatten*, pp. 22–23.

245. S. Bose and A. Jalal, *Modern South Asia*, 1998 edn., p. 198.
246. Talbot, *American Witness*, p. 304.
247. Keay, *India*, p. 502.

6 Concluding Remarks

1. Thompson, *Media and Modernity*, p. vii.
2. W. Ghonim, *Revolution 2.0 A Memoir*, 2012, pp. 107–108.
3. *Ibid.*, p. 61.
4. *Ibid.*
5. *Ibid.*
6. *Ibid.*, p. 63.
7. G. Dell'Orto, *American Journalism and International Relations*, New York, 2013, p. 1
8. http://webarchive.nationalarchives.gov.uk, p. 1.
9. Statesman, 6 August 1947.
10. Cited in Hindustan Times, 14 October 1946.
11. *Ibid.*
12. Hindustan Times, 15 October 1946.
13. Dawn, 16 October 1946.
14. For more, see Kaul, 'Media, India and the Raj', in Thompson (ed.), *Writing Imperial Histories*, pp. 188–215.
15. Chief Commissioner of Delhi fortnightly report, 25 October 1947, 30/1/1947, 1947 HPoll.
16. W. Norman Brown, *The United States and India, Pakistan, Bangladesh*, Cambridge Mass, 1972, p. 306.
17. Chaudhuri, *Great Anarch*, p. 886.
18. *Ibid.*, p. 887.
19. *Ibid.*, p. 888.
20. Collins and Lapierre, *Mountbatten*, p. 82.
21. D. Kellner, *Media Spectacle and Insurrection, 2011*, 2012, p. 3.
22. *Ibid.*, p. 8; see also his *Media Spectacle*, 2003.
23. Thompson, *Media and Modernity*, p. 126.
24. Dayan and Katz, *Media Events*, p. 225.
25. J. Nye, *The Powers to Lead*, Oxford, 2008, p. 53.
26. J. Dulffer and M. Frey, *Elites and Decolonisation in the Twentieth Century*, Basingstoke, 2011, p. 2.
27. D. R. Headrick, *The Tools of Empire*, New York, 1981, p. 209.
28. See, amongst others, Innis, 1950 & 1952, Eisenstein, 1979 & 2011, McLuhan, 1964, Goody and Watt, 1968, Carey, 1989.
29. Dayan and Katz, *Media Events*, p. 230.
30. Nye, *Powers to Lead*, p. 43.

Appendices

Appendix I

Akashvani*

by Rabindranath Tagore (1938)

Hark to Akashvani up-surging
From here below
The earth is bathed in Heaven's glory
Its purple glow
Across the blue expanse is firmly planted
The altar of the Muse
The lyre unheard of Light is throbbing
With human hues
From earth to heaven, distance conquered
In waves of light
Flows the music in man's divining
Fancy's flight
To East and West speech careers
Swift as the Sun
The mind of man reaches Heaven's confines
Its freedom won

---

*Translated from Bengali by Tagore, cited in H. R. Luthra, *Indian Broadcasting*, New Delhi 1986.

Appendix II

Provincial Distribution of Wireless Receiving Licences in British India, 1938*

Province	Number
–	–
Bombay	19,569
Bengal	15,540
Punjab	7,625
Madras	5,535
United Provinces	5,498
Sind	2,384
Delhi	2,322
Bihar and Orissa	2,002
Central Provinces	1,816
NWFP	1,113
Assam	1,076
–	–
Total: 31 December 1938	64,480

*Compiled from Legislative Assembly Answer to Question, 3 February 1939, L/I/1/445, IOLR, British Library, London.

Appendix III

Indian and Eastern Newspaper Editors Society, March 1947*

Amrita Bazar Patrika	*Janmabhoomi*
Ananda Bazar Patrika	*Jugantar*
Ananda Vikatan	*Leader*
Andhra Patrika	*Lokamanya*
Bharat Jyoti	*Mail*
Blitz	*National Call*
Bombay Chronicle	*Navshakti*
Bombay Samachar	*Pioneer*
Ceylon Daily News	*Pravasi*
Ceylon Observer	*Samyukta Karnataka*
Civil & Military Gazette	*Sanj Vartman*
Daily Gazette	*Silumina* (Ceylon)
Dhinamani	*Sind Observer*
Dinamina (Ceylon)	*Statesman*
Evening News of India	*Sunday Statesman*
Free Press Journal	*Swadesamitran*
Hindu	*Swajya*
Hindustan Standard	*Times of Ceylon*
Hindustan Times	*Times of Ceylon* (Sunday Illustrated)
Illustrated Weekly of India	*Times of India*
Indian Express	*Tribune* (Lahore)
Janavani	

*L/I/1/1467, IOLR, British Library, London.

Bibliography

Primary Sources

Manuscript Sources

India Office Library and Records, British Library, London
European Manuscripts (Eur Mss)

Earl of Birkenhead
Lord Brabourne
Sir H. Butler
Lord Crewe
Malcolm Hailey
Lord Halifax
Lord Hardinge
Lord Irwin
Sir Walter Lawrence
Lord Linlithgow
Lord Listowel
Lord Lytton
Lord Morley
Lord Mountbatten
Lord Sykes
Viscount Templewood (Sir Samuel Hoare)
Lord Willingdon
Sir Guy Fleetwood Wilson
Lord Zetland

India Office Records
Series: L/P&J; L/PO; L/I; L/S&G

Cambridge University Library
Lord Crewe collection
Lord Hardinge papers

Times Newspapers Ltd Archive, News UK & Ireland Ltd, London
The Times collection

Royal Archives, Windsor
Correspondence, Diaries and Photographs: George V and Queen Mary

BBC Written Archives Centre, Caversham
Subject Files, Staff Files and Related Memoranda
Diaries of Lord Reith
Files of *Radio Times* and *the Listener*

George T. Henry College Archives, Coe College, Iowa
William L. Shirer collection: correspondence, papers and photographs

Associated Press Corporate Archives, New York & London
Subject and personal files, oral transcripts and photographs

National Archives of India, Delhi
Home Political series
Home Foreign series

Nehru Memorial Museum and Library, Delhi
Manuscripts and microfilmed copies
Aruna Asaf Ali
Prem Bhatia
Frances Gunther
Kincaid-Brown
Lord Mountbatten
Sardar Vallabhbhai Patel
B. Shiva Rao

National Gandhi Museum, Delhi
Photographic Archives

Oral Sources

Interview with Max Desfor, Silver Springs, Maryland, 15 April 2014.

Printed Primary Sources

Newspapers and Periodicals

(British Library Newspaper Library, Colindale & British Library, London;
Nehru Memorial Museum & Library, Delhi; University Library, St Andrews;
Swem Library, College of William and Mary; New York Public Library;
online)

British Newspapers and Periodicals

Dailies

Daily Chronicle
Daily Express
Daily Herald
Daily Mail
Daily Mirror
Daily News (merged with *Daily Chronicle* to form *News Chronicle* 1930)
Daily Telegraph
Daily Worker
Manchester Guardian
Morning Post (absorbed by *Daily Telegraph* 1937)
Star

The Times
Westminster Gazette (merged into *Daily News* 1928)

Weeklies and Periodicals

Blackwoods Magazine
Contemporary Review
Edinburgh Review
Graphic
Illustrated London News
Nation (merged with *Nation* to form *New Statesman and Nation* 1931)
New Statesman
News of the World
Nineteenth Century and After
Observer
Punch
Quarterly Review
Reynolds' Newspaper
Spectator
The Listener

US Newspapers and News Magazines

Aberdeen Evening News
Alton Evening Telegraph
Burlington Hawk-Eye
Canton Repository
Chicago Herald Tribune
Cleveland Plain Dealer
Decatur Daily Review
Evening Tribune (San Diego)
—— (Albert Lea, Minn)
Ironwood Daily Globe
Life
Morning Oregonian
Nation
New York Times
Sandusky Register
State Times
Sunday Oregonian
Time

Indian Newspapers and Periodicals

Amrita Bazaar Patrika
Bombay Chronicle
Civil and Military Gazette
Dawn
Englishman (incorporated into *Statesman* 1924)

Hindu
Hindustan Times
Indian Listener
Indian News Chronicle
Indian Radio Times
National Herald
Pioneer
Sind Observer
Statesman
Times of India
Tribune

Reports, Diaries and Memoirs

(Place of publication is London unless stated otherwise)

Reports

Broadcasting Commission Report (Sykes Commission) (HMSO, 1923).
Coronation Durbar Official Directory Delhi 1911 (Government of India, Calcutta, 1911).
P.E.P., *Report on the British Press* (1938).
Report on the Progress of Broadcasting in India (Government of India, Delhi, 1940).
Moral and Material Progress and Condition of India reports (HMSO, 1920s and 1930s).
First *Royal Commission on the Press* reports (HMSO 1949).

Diaries and Memoirs

Banerjea, Sir, S., *A Nation in Making* (1927).
Bourke-White, M., *Halfway to Freedom* (New York, 1949).
——, *Portrait of Myself* (New York, 1963).
Bradley, S., *An American Girl at the Durbar* (1912).
Buck, E. J., *Simla, Past & Present* (Bombay, 1925, 2nd edn.).
Burne, O. T., *Memories* (1907).
Burnham, Lord, *Peterborough Court* (1955).
Butler, Sir H., *India Insistent* (1931).
Byron, R., *An Essay on India* (2011 reprint, 1st pub. 1931).
Cameron, J., *Point of Departure* (1967).
Campbell-Johnson, A., *Mission with Mountbatten* (1951).
Chamberlain, Sir A., *Politics from Inside* (1936).
Chirol, V., *Indian Unrest* (1910).
——, *India, Old and New* (1921).
——, *India* (1926).
——, *Fifty Years in a Changing World* (1927).
Coatman, J., *Years of Destiny* (1932).
Collins, L. & Lapierre, D., *Mountbatten and the Partition of India* (Manchester, 1982), Vol. 1.
Cooper, K., *Barriers Down* (1969 edn., 1st edn., 1942).

Edwards, D., *The Two Worlds of Donald Edwards* (1970).

Fielden, L., *The Natural Bent* (1960).

Finnemore, J., *Delhi and the Durbar* (1912).

Fisher, F. B., *That Strange Little Brown Man* (New York, 1932).

Fischer, L., *A Week with Gandhi* (New York, 1942).

Fortescue, J., *Narrative of the Visit to India of their Majesties King George V and Queen Mary* (1912).

Fraser, L., *India under Curzon and After* (1911).

Fyfe, H., *Sixty Years of Fleet Street* (1949).

Gandhi, M. K., *Collected Works of Mahatma Gandhi* (Ahmedabad, multi vols. 1971–).

——, *An Autobiography or the Story of my Experiments with Truth* (Ahmedabad, 1994 reprint, 1st edn., 1927).

Ghonim, W., *Revolution 2.0* (2012).

Halifax, Earl, *Fullness of Days* (1957).

Hardinge, Lord, *Old Diplomacy* (1947).

——, *My Indian Years 1910–1916* (1948).

Holmes, J. H., *My Gandhi* (New York, 1953).

——, *I Speak for Myself* (1959).

Homage to Mahatma Gandhi, Information & Broadcasting Ministry (New Delhi, 1948).

Ismay, Lord, *The Memoirs of General Lord Ismay* (1960).

Lawrence, W. R., *The India We Served* (1929).

——, *Fifty Years, Memories and Contrasts* (1932).

Mansergh, N. (ed.), *Transfer of Power, 1942–1947* (multi vols. 1970–83).

Martin, K., *Editor* (1968).

Miller, W., *I Found No Peace* (1938 edn.).

Moon, P. (ed.), *Wavell, The Viceroy's Journal* (1973).

Mountbatten, Earl, *Time Only to Look Forward* (1949).

Mountbatten, P. & Hicks, I., *India Remembered* (2007).

Nevinson, H. W., *The New Spirit in India* (1908).

O'Dwyer, M., *India as I Knew It* (1925).

Philp, E. A., *With the King to India* (Plymouth, 1912).

Pioneer, *The Coronation Durbar* (Allahabad, 1912).

Radcliffe, C. Sir, *Not in Feather Beds* (1968).

Rao, V. R. A., *Coronation Durbar 1911* (Guntur, 1914).

Reed, S., *The King & Queen in India* (Bombay, 1912).

——, *The India I Knew 1897–1947* (1957).

Reith, J. C. W., *Into the Wind* (1949).

Sarila, N. S., *Once a Prince of Sarila* (2008).

Shirer, W. L., *Gandhi A Memoir* (New York, 1980 edn.).

——, *20th Century Journey,* Vol. II (Boston, 1984).

Spender, J. A., *The Public Life* (1925).

——, *The Changing East* (1926).

——, *Life, Journalism and Politics* (1927).

Stead, W. T., *A Journalist on Journalism* (1893).

Stuart, C. (ed.), *The Reith Diaries* (1975).

Sykes, Sir F., *From Many Angles* (1942).

Talbot, P., *An American Witness to India's Partition* (Delhi, 2007).

Templewood, Viscount, *Nine Troubled Years* (1954).
The Times, *India and the Durbar* (1911).
——, *The Times Book of India* (1930).
——, *The History of the Times, 1884–1912* (1947), Vol. III.
——, *The History of the Times. Pt.1, 1912–20* & *Pt.2, 1921–48* (1952), Vol. IV.
Turner, J., *Filming History* (2001).
Twain, M., *Following the Equator* (New York, 1897) 2 vols.
Wheeler, S., *History of Delhi Coronation Durbar* (1904).
Young, D., *Try Anything Twice* (1963).

Secondary Sources

(Place of publication is London unless otherwise stated)

Books and Articles

Adas, M., *Machines as the Measure of Men* (New York, 1989).
Ahuja, B. N., *History of Indian press* (Delhi, 1996).
Amin, S., *Event, Metaphor, Memory* (Berkeley, 1995).
Ananda, P., *A History of the Tribune* (New Delhi, 1986).
Anderson, B., *Imagined Communities* (1983).
Appadurai, A., *Modernity at Large* (Delhi, 1997).
—— (ed.), *Globalization* (North Carolina, 2001).
Arnold, D., *Science, Technology and Medicine in Colonial India* (Cambridge, 2000).
Aspinall, A., *Politics and the Press* (1949).
Ashton, S. R., *British Policy towards the Indian States* (1982).
Ayalon, A., *The Press in the Arab Middle East* (New York, 1995).
Ayerst, D., *Guardian – Biography of a Newspaper* (1971).
——, *Garvin of the Observer* (Kent, 1985).
Ayyar, K. P. V., *et al.* (eds.), *The Indian Press Year Book* 1948 (Madras, 1948).
Barns, M., *India Today and Tomorrow* (1937).
——, *The Indian Press* (1940).
Baron, S. A., Lindquist, E. and Shevlin, E. (eds.), *Agent of Change* (Washington, DC, 2007).
Barrier, N. G., *Banned* (Missouri, 1974).
Bartlett, F. C., *Political Propaganda* (Cambridge, 1942).
Bayly, C., *Information and Empire* (Cambridge, 1996).
——, *The Birth of the Modern World* (Oxford, 2004).
Bean, J. M. W. (ed.), *The Political Culture of Modern Britain* (1987).
Benians, E. A., Butler, J. & Carrington, C. E. (eds.) *Cambridge History of British Empire*, Vol. III (Cambridge 1959).
Beniger, J. R., *The Control Revolution* (Cambridge, Mass, 1986).
Bennett, A., *The History Boys* (2004).
Black, W. R., *Dispatches from the World* (Bloomington, IN, 2012).
Bose, S. & Jalal, A., *Modern South Asia* (1998 edn.).
Bottomore, S., 'Have you seen the Gaekwar Bob?': filming the 1911 Delhi Durbar', *Historical Journal of Film, Radio and Television*, Vol. 17, No. 3, 1997, pp. 309–345.
Boyce, G., Curran, J. & Wingate, P. (eds.), *Newspaper History* (1978).

Boyd-Barrett, O., *The International News Agencies* (1980).

Bridge, C., *Holding India to the Empire* (1986).

Briggs, A., *The BBC The First Fifty Years* (Oxford, 1985).

——, *The Golden Age of Wireless*, Vol. II (1995 edn.).

—— & Burke, P., *A Social History of the Media* (Oxford, 2002).

Bromley, M. & O'Malley, T. (eds.) *A Journalism Reader* (1997).

Brown, F. J., *Cable and Wireless Communications of the World* (1927).

Brown, J. M., *Gandhi's Rise to Power* (Cambridge, 1972).

——, *Gandhi and Civil Disobedience* (Cambridge, 1976).

——, *Prisoner of Hope* (1989).

——, *Modern India* (Oxford, 1985).

Brown, W. N., *The United States and India, Pakistan, Bangladesh* (Cambridge, Mass., 1972 edn.).

Burke, P., *A Social History of Knowledge* (Cambridge, 2000).

Campbell Johnson, A., *Mountbatten in Retrospect* (South Godstone,1997).

Camrose, Viscount, *British Newspapers and their Controllers* (Hampshire, 1947).

Cannadine, D., *Ornamentalism* (2001).

—— (ed.), *History and the Media* (Basingstoke, 2004).

Chakrabarty, D., *Habitations of Modernity* (Chicago, 2002).

Carey, J., *Communication as Culture* (Boston, 1989).

Chatterjee, R. B., *Empires of the Mind* (Oxford, 2006).

Chatterjee, P. C., *The Adventures of Indian Broadcasting* (Delhi, 1998).

Chaudhuri, N. C., *Thy Hand, Great Anarch!* (1990 edn.).

Chester, L. P., *Borders and Conflict in South Asia* (Manchester, 2009).

Chignell, H., *Public Issue Radio* (Basingstoke, 2011).

Chisholm, A. & Davie, M., *Beaverbrook: A Life* (New York, 1993 edn.).

Clymer, K. J., *Quest for Freedom* (New York, 1995).

Codell, J. (ed.), *Imperial Co-Histories* (Madison, NJ, 2003).

Cohn, B. S., *Colonialism and Its Forms of Knowledge* (Princeton, 1996).

Collins, L. & Lapierre, D., *Freedom at Midnight* (1975 and later edns.).

Connelly, M. & Welch, D. (eds.), *War and the Media* (2005).

Cooper, K., *Kent Cooper and the Associated Press* (New York, 1959).

Cotes, E., 'The Newspaper Press of India', *Asiatic Review*, Vol. 19 (1923), pp. 417–441.

Cotton, H. E. A., *The Century in India* (Calcutta, 1901).

Cotton, H. J. S., *New India or India in Transition* (1st edn., 1885; rev. edn., 1907).

Coulton, B., *Louis MacNeice in the BBC* (1980).

Coupland, R., *The Indian Problem 1833–1935* (Oxford, 1942–43), 3 vols.

——, *The Constitutional Problem in India* (1944).

Cousins, N. (ed.), *Profiles of Gandhi* (Delhi, 1969).

Cranfield, L., *The Press & Society* (1978).

Crawley, W. (ed.) 'A Broadcasting Partnership', *Indo-British Review*, Vol. XX, No. 2 (Madras, 1994).

Cross, J. A., *Sir Samuel Hoare* (1977).

Crowley, D. & Heyer, P. (eds.), *Communication in History, Technology, Culture and Society* (New York, 1991).

Cryle, D. & Kaul, C., 'The Empire Press Union and the Expansion of Imperial Air Services 1909–1939 with Special Reference to Australia, New Zealand & India', *Media History*, Vol. 15, No. 1, February 2009, pp. 17–30.

Cudlipp, H., *Publish and Be Damned!* (1953).
——, *The Prerogative of the Harlot* (1980).
Curran, J. (ed.), *The British Press* (1978).
——, *Media and Power* (2002).
——, 'Media and the Making of British Society, c.1700–2000', *Media History*, 2002, Vol. 8, No. 2, pp. 135–154.
—— (ed.), *Media and Society* (2010, 5th edn.).
——, Gurevitch, M. & Woollacott, J. (eds.), *Mass Communication & Society* (1977).
———— & Seaton, J., *Power without Responsibility* (1995 edn.).
Czitrom, D. J., *Media and the American Mind* (North Carolina, 1982).
Dahl, H. F., 'The Pursuit of Media History', *Media Culture & Society*, Vol. 16, No. 2, (1994), pp. 551–563.
Dalton, D., *Mahatma Gandhi* (New York, 1993).
Darwin, J., *After Tamarlane* (2008).
——, *The Empire Project* (Cambridge, 2009).
Das, M. N., *India Under Morley and Minto* (1964).
Dayan, D. & Katz, E., *Media Events* (Cambridge, Mass, 1992).
Deibert, R. J., *Parchment, Printing and Hypermedia* (1997).
Dell'Orto, G., *American Journalism and International Relations* (New York, 2013).
Desai, A. R., *Social Background of Indian Nationalism* (Bombay, 1948).
Desmond, R. W., *Windows on the World 1900–20* (Iowa City, 1980).
——, *Crisis and Conflict* (Iowa City, 1982).
——, *The Press and World Affairs* (New York, 1987).
Devine, K. & Peacock, A. J. (eds.), *Louis MacNeice and His Influence* (1998).
Dewey, C., *Anglo-Indian Attitudes* (1993).
Dilks, D. (ed.), *Retreat from Power* (1981).
Dirks, N., *The Hollow Crown* (Michigan, 1998).
Dodwell, H. H. & Sethi, R. R. (eds.), *Cambridge History of India*, Vol. VI (Delhi, 1964).
Du Boulay, F. R. H., *Servants of Empire* (2011).
Dulffer, J. & Frey, M. (eds.), *Elites and Decolonisation in the Twentieth Century* (Basingstoke, 2011).
Drucquer, S., *Broadcasting* (Bombay, 1945).
Edwards, J., *The Foreign Policy of Col. McCormick's Tribune* (Reno, 1971).
Emery, E., *The Press and America* (New Jersey, 1962, 2nd edn.).
Emery, M., (late) Emery, E. & Roberts N. L. (eds.), *The Press and America* (Needham Heights, MA, 2000, 9th edn.).
Eisenstein, E., *Printing Press as an Agent of Change* (Cambridge, 1979).
——, *Divine Art, Infernal Machine* (Pennsylvania, 2011).
Eldridge, C. C. (ed.), *Empire, Politics and Popular Culture* (Lampeter, 1990).
——, *Imperial Experience* (Basingstoke, 1996).
Finkelstein, D. & Peers, D. M. (eds.), *Negotiating India in the Nineteenth-Century Media* (Basingstoke, 2000).
Fischer, L., *The Great Challenge* (New York, 1946).
Fritzinger, L. B., *Diplomat without Portfolio* (2006).
Frykenberg, R. E. (ed.), *Delhi Through the Ages* (Delhi, 1986).
Furneaux, R., *The First War Correspondent* (1945).
Garnham, N., *Emancipation, the Media, and Modernity* (Oxford, 2000).
George, T. J. S., *Pothan Joseph's India: A Biography* (Delhi, 1992).

Ghosh, A., *Power in Print* (Delhi, 2006).

Ghosh, S., *Modern History of Indian Press* (Delhi, 1998).

Gilmour, D., *Curzon* (1995).

Glendevon, J., *Viceroy at Bay* (1971).

Glynn, I., ' "An Untouchable in the Presence of Brahmins" Lord Wavell's Disastrous Relationship with Whitehall during His Time as Viceroy of India', *Modern Asian Studies*, Vol. 41, No. 3 (Cambridge, 2007), pp. 639–663.

Gopal, S., *The Viceroyalty of Lord Irwin* (Oxford, 1957).

——, *British Policy in India* (Cambridge, 1965).

Gould, H., *Sikhs, Swamis, Students, and Spies* (2006).

Gramling, O., *AP-The story of news* (New York, reissue 1969, 1st edn. 1940).

Grant, M., *Propaganda and the Role of the State in Interwar Britain* (Oxford, 1994).

Greenberger, A. J., *The British Image of India* (1969).

Griffiths, P., *The British Impact on India* (1952).

Guha, R., *Dominance without Hegemony* (Connecticut, Mass., 1997).

—— (ed.), *Subaltern Studies III* (New Delhi, 1989).

Gupta, P. S., *Imperialism and the British Labour Movement, 1914–64* (1974).

——, *Radio and the Raj 1921–47* lectures (Calcutta, 1995).

—— & Bhattacharya, S. (ed.), *Power, Politics and the People* (2002).

Gurevitch, M. (ed.), *Culture, Society & the Media* (1982).

Habermas, J., *The Structural Transformation of the Public Sphere* (Cambridge Mass., 1989 English translation (Thomas Burger), (German 1st edn. 1962).

Hajkowski, T., *The BBC and National Identity in Britain 1922–53* (Manchester, 2010).

Hall, C. & Rose, S. (eds.), *At Home with the Empire* (Cambridge, 2006).

Hamilton, J. M., *Journalism's Roving Eye* (Baton Rouge Louisiana, 2009).

Hampton, M., *Visions of the Press in Britain, 1850–1950* (Urbana & Chicago, 2004).

Hardinge, H. R., 'Broadcasting in India', *Empire Review*, October 1938, pp. 235–236.

Harris, M. & Lee, A. (eds.), *The Press in English Society* (1986).

Headrick, D. R., *The Tools of Empire* (1981).

——, *The Tentacles of Progress* (1988).

——, *Power Over Peoples* (Princeton, 2010).

Hendy, D., 'Biography and the Emotions as a Missing "Narrative" in Media History', *Media History*, Vol. 18, Nos. 3–4, 2012, pp. 361–378.

Herzstein, R. E., *Henry R. Luce* (New York, 1994).

Heyer, P., *Communications and History* (Connecticut, Mass., 1988).

Hiley, N., 'Problems of Media History', *Modern History Review*, Vol. 7, No. 4 (1996).

Hirschmann, E., *Robert Knight* (Delhi, 2008).

Hoare, Sir S., *India by Air* (1927).

Hobsbawm, E. & Ranger, T. (eds.), *The Invention of Tradition* (Cambridge, 2005 edn.).

Hodson, H. V., *The Great Divide* (Karachi, 1997 edn., 1st edn., 1969).

Hoey, B., *Mountbatten the Private Story* (1994).

Holland. R., Williams, S. & Barringer, T. (eds.), *The Iconography of Independence* (Abingdon, 2010).

Hudson, M. & Stanier, J., *War and the Media* (1997).

Hunt, J. D., *Gandhi in London* (Delhi rev. edn., 1993).

Hussey, C., *The Life of Sir Edwin Lutyens* (Woodbridge, 1984 edn.).

Hutchins, F., *The Illusion of Permanence* (Princeton, 1967).

Hyams, E., *The New Statesman* (1963).

Hyde, H. M., *Lord Reading* (1967).

Inden, R., *Imagining India* (Oxford, 1990).

Innis, H. A., *Empire and Communications* (Toronto, 1986, 1st edn., 1950).

——, *The Bias of Communication* (Toronto, 1995, 1st edn., 1951).

Isaacs, H. R., *Scratches on our Minds* (New York, 1958).

Israel, M., *Communications and Power* (Cambridge, 1994).

Jack, H. A. (ed.), *The Gandhi Reader* (New York, 1956).

Jha, M., *Civil Disobedience and After* (Delhi, 1973).

Jones, A., *Powers of the Press* (Aldershot, 1996).

Jones, R., *A Life in Reuters* (1951).

Judd, D., *The Life and Times of George V* (1973).

Kamath, M. V., *The United States and India 1776–1976* (Washington, DC, 1976).

Kaminsky, A. P., *The India Office 1880–1910* (1986).

Kamra, S., *Bearing Witness* (Calgary, 2002).

Kapur, S., *Raising up a Prophet* (Boston, 1992).

Katz, D. *et al.* (eds.), *Public Opinion and Propaganda* (New York, 1954).

Kaul, C., *Reporting the Raj, the British Press and India 1880–1922* (Manchester, 2003, New York, 2004).

—— (ed.), *Media and the British Empire* (Basingstoke, 2006, 2013).

—— (ed.), *Explorations in Modern Indian History and the Media*, 'Media History' special issue, Vol. 15, No. 4, November 2009.

—— (co-ed.), *International Communications and Global News Networks: Historical Perspectives* (New York, 2011).

——, 'Popular Press and Empire: Northcliffe, India and the Daily Mail, 1896–1922', in P. Catterall, C. Seymoure-Ure and A. Smith (eds.), *Northcliffe's Legacy* (Basingstoke, 2000), pp. 45–69.

——, 'Monarchical Display and the Politics of Empire: Princes of Wales and India 1870–1920s', *Twentieth Century British History*, Vol. 17, No. 4, 2006, pp. 464–488.

——, 'Media, India and the Raj', in Thompson (ed.), *Writing Imperial Histories*, pp. 188–215.

——, ' "You Cannot Govern by Force Alone": W. H. Russell, *The Times* and the Great Rebellion', in M. Carter and C. Bates (eds.), *Mutiny at the Margins Global Perspectives*, Vol. 3, (Delhi, 2013), pp. 18–35.

——, 'India, the Imperial Press Conferences and the Empire Press Union', in Kaul (ed.), *Media and the British Empire*, pp. 125–44.

——, 'Washing Dirty Linen in Public: Imperial Spin Doctoring, the British Press and the Downfall of Lord Curzon, 1905', in Kaul (ed.), *Explorations in Modern Indian History and the Media* (2009), pp. 385–406.

Katz, E. & Lazarsfeld, P. F., *Personal Influence* (New Jersey, 2006 edn.).

Kaushik, H. P., *The Indian National Congress in England 1885–1920* (Delhi, 1972).

——, *Indian National Movement: The Role of British Liberals* (Delhi, 1986).

Keay, J., *India A History* (2000).

Kellner, D., *Media Spectacle* (2003).

——, *Media Spectacle and Insurrection, 2011* (2012).

Kendle, J., *The British Empire Commonwealth* (1972).

Kerr, I. J., *Building the Railways of the Raj* (Delhi, 1997).

Kirke-Greene, A., *Britain's Imperial Administrators 1858–1966* (Basingstoke & New York, 2000).

Knightley, P., *The First Casualty* (1975).

Koss, S., *The Rise and Fall of the Political Press in Britain*, Vols I & II (1980, 1984), comb. vol. (1990).

Krishna, B., *Sardar Vallabhbhai Patel* (Delhi, 1995).

Kundu, K., *Rabindranath and the British Press 1912–41* (1990).

Lal, V., *The Other Indians* (New Delhi, 2008).

——, 'Gandhi's West, the West's Gandhi', *New Literary History* (Charlottesville 2009), Vol. 40, No. 2, pp. 281–313.

Lee, A. J., *The Origins of the Popular Press* (1976).

LeMahieu, D. L., *A Culture for Democracy* (Oxford, 2002 edn.).

Lippman, W., *Public Opinion* (New York, 1929).

Lipsette, H. Caldwell, *Lord Curzon in India* (1903).

Lipton, M. & Firn, J., *The Erosion of a Relationship* (1975).

Louis, Wm. Roger (General Editor) *The Oxford History of the British Empire* (Oxford, 1998–99), 5 vols.

——, *Imperialism at Bay* (Oxford, 1977).

Lovett, P., *Journalism in India* (Calcutta, 1926).

Low, D. A., *Eclipse of Empire* (Cambridge, 1991).

—— (ed.), *The Indian National Congress Centenary Hindsights* (Delhi, 1988).

Low, Sir F., 'Present Day Journalism in India and Pakistan', *Asiatic Review*, December 1948, pp. 517–524.

Luthra, H. R., *Indian Broadcasting* (Delhi, 1986).

Lyons, E. (ed.), *We Cover the World* (New York, 1937).

MacDonald, R., *The Awakening of India* (1909).

MacDonald, R. H., *The Language of Empire* (Manchester, 1994).

MacKenzie, J. M., *Propaganda & Empire* (Manchester, 1984).

—— (ed.), *Imperialism & Popular Culture* (Manchester, 1986).

—— (ed.), *Popular Imperialism and the Military* (Manchester, 1992).

Makin., W. J., (& News Chronicle), *The Life of King George the Fifth* (1936/37?).

Mansell, G., *Let Truth Be Told* (1982).

Margach, J., *The Abuse of Power* (1978).

——, *The Anatomy of Power* (1979).

Markovits, C., *The UnGandhian Gandhi* (2004).

Marvin, C., *When Old Technologies Were New* (New York, 1988).

Mathur, A., *The Indian Media* (New Delhi, 2006).

Mathur, L. P., *Indian Revolutionary Movements in the USA* (Delhi, 1970).

Matthew, H. C. G., *The Liberal Imperialists* (Oxford, 1973).

MacNiece L., *The Strings are False* (2007 edn.).

McIntyre, I., *The Expense of Glory* (1993).

McLuhan, M., *The Gutenberg Galaxy* (Toronto, 1962).

——, *Understanding Media* (1967 edn.).

——, *The Medium is the Message* (1967 edn.).

Mehrotra, S. R., *India and the Commonwealth 1885–1929* (1965).

Metcalf, T. R., *Ideologies of the Raj* (Cambridge, 1997).

Misra, M., *Vishnu's Crowded Temple* (2007).

Mody, H. P., 'The King-Emperor's visit: A new epoch', *East and West*, Vol. XI, No. 124, Bombay, February 1912.

Moore, R. J., *Liberalism and Indian Politics* (1966).
——, *The Crisis of Indian Unity 1917–1940* (Oxford, 1974).
——, *Churchill, Cripps and India* (Oxford, 1979).
Mountbatten, Earl, *First Mountbatten Lecture, National Electronics Council* (1978).
Muggeridge, M., *The Thirties* (1967 edn.).
Nanda, B. R., *Gokhale* (Delhi, 1977).
Narain, P., *Press and Politics in India, 1885–1905* (Delhi, 1970).
Nasta, S. (ed.), *India in Britain* (Basingstoke, 2013).
Natarajan, S., *A History of the Press in India* (1962).
Natarajan, J., *History of Indian Journalism* (Delhi, 1997 edn.).
Negrine, R., *Politics and the Mass Media in Britain* (1994 edn.).
Nicholas, S. H., *The Echo of War* (Manchester, 1996).
Nicolson, H., *King George the Fifth* (1952).
Ninan, S., *Headlines from the Heartland* (New Delhi, 2007).
Nye, Jr. J. S., *Power in the Global Information Age* (2004).
——, *Soft Power* (New York, 2004).
——, *The Powers to Lead* (Oxford, 2008).
O'Malley, L. S. S. (ed.), *Modern India & the West* (1941).
O'Malley, T., 'Media History and Media Studies', *Media History*, Vol. 8, No. 2, 2002, pp. 155–173.
Ogilvy-Webb, M., *The Government Explains* (1965).
Osterhammel, J., *Colonialism* (Princeton, 1997).
Owen, N.,'The Conservative Party and Indian Independence 1945–47', *Historical Journal*, Vol. 46, No. 2, 2003, pp. 403–436.
——, *The British Left and India* (Oxford, 2007).
Percy, C. & Ridley, J. (eds.), *Letters of Edwin Lutyens to His Wife Lady Emily* (1985).
Philips, C. H. (ed.), *Politics and Society in India* (1965).
Pinkerton, A., 'Radio and the Raj: Broadcasting in British India 1920–1940', *Journal of the Royal Asiatic Society*, Vol. 3, Nos. 18, 2, 2008, pp. 167–191.
Pope-Hennessy, J., *Lord Crewe 1858–1945* (1955).
Porter, B., *Critics of Empire* (1969).
——, *The Absent Minded Imperialists* (2006).
——, *The Lion's Share* (2012, 5th edn.).
Pradhan, G. P., *Lokamanya Tilak* (New Delhi, 2008 reprint).
Potter, S. J., *Broadcasting Empire* (Oxford, 2012).
Raghavan, G. N. S., *The Press in India* (Delhi, 1994).
Ramsden, J., *The Age of Balfour and Baldwin 1902–1940* (1978).
Ramusack, B., *The Indian Princes and their States, The New Cambridge History of India*, Vol. 111. 6 (Cambridge, 2004).
Ratcliffe, S. K., 'India and the United States', *Asiatic Review*, 26 January 1930.
Read, D., *The Power of News, The History of Reuters* (Oxford, 1992, 1999).
Reed, S. & Cadell, P. R., *India: The New Phase* (1928).
Reddy, E. S. (ed.), *Mahatma Gandhi Letters to Americans* (New Delhi, 1998).
Richards, H., *The Bloody Circus: The Daily Herald and the Left* (1997).
Rizvi, G., *Linlithgow and India* (1978).
Rolph, C. H., *Kingsley* (1973).
Ronaldshay, Lord, *The Life of Curzon*, 3 vols (1928).
Rose, K., *George V* (1983).

Roth, M. P., *Historical Dictionary of War Journalism* (Westport, CT, 1997).

Rothermund, D., *Mahatma Gandhi: An Essay in Political Biography* (New Delhi, 1991).

——, *The Routledge Companion to Decolonization* (2006).

Sahni, J. N., *Truth about the Indian Press* (Delhi, 1974).

Said, E., *Orientalism* (1978).

——, *Culture and Imperialism* (1993).

Sarkar, R. S., *The Press in India* (Delhi, 1984).

Sarkar, S., 'Orientalism Re-visited', *Oxford Literary Review*, Vol. 16, Nos. 1–2, 1994, pp. 204–227.

Scannell, P. & Cardiff, D., *A Social History of British Broadcasting*, Vol. I (Oxford, 1991).

——, Schlesinger, P. & Sparks, C. (eds.), *Culture and Power* (1992).

Seaton, J., 'The BBC and the "Hidden Wiring" of the British Constitution', *Twentieth Century British History*, Vol. 24, No. 3, 2013, pp. 448–471.

Sen, S.P., *The Indian Press* (Calcutta, 1967).

Sengupta, S. & Chatterjee, G. (eds.), *Secret Congress Broadcasts and Storming Railway Tracks during Quit India Movement* (New Delhi, 1988).

Seshachari, C., *Gandhi and the American Scene* (Bombay, 1969).

Seymour-Ure, C., *The Political Impact of the Mass Media* (1974).

Shrivastava, K. M., *Radio and TV Journalism* (New Delhi, 1989).

Singh, A. K., *Indian Students in Britain* (1963).

——, (trans. S. Das), *India Post* (New Delhi, 2009).

Sinha, M. (ed.) K. Mayo, *Mother India* (Michigan, 2003 edn.).

Smith, A., *Politics of Information* (1978).

——, *New Statesman* (1996).

Smith, R. N., *The Colonel* (New York, 1997).

Somervell, D. C., *The Reign of King George the Fifth* (1935).

Stark, U., *An Empire of Books* (Ranikhet, 2007).

Startt, J. D., *Journalists for Empire* (Connecticut, 1991).

Stein, B. rev. Arnold, D., *A History of India* (Oxford, 2010, 2nd edn.).

Stephens, I. M., *Pakistan* (Middlesex, 1964).

——, *Monsoon Morning* (1966).

Stokes, E., *English Utilitarians and India* (Oxford, 1959).

Storey, G., *Reuters' Century 1851–1951* (1951).

Tarlo, E., *Clothing Matters* (1996).

Taylor, P. M., *Projection of Britain* (Cambridge, 1981).

Templewood, Viscount (Sir S. Hoare), *Empire of the Air* (1957).

Terraine, J., *The Life and Times of Lord Mountbatten* (1980).

Tewari, J., *Sabarmati to Dandi* (Delhi, 1995).

Thomas-Symonds, N., *Attlee* (2010).

Thompson, E., *The Reconstruction of India* (1931, 2nd edn.).

——, *Enlist India for Freedom* (1940).

Thompson, A. S., *Imperial Britain* (Essex, 2000).

—— (ed.), *Writing Imperial Histories* (Manchester, 2013).

Thompson, J. B., *The Media and Modernity* (Cambridge, 1995).

Thornton, A. P., *The Imperial Idea and its Enemies* (1959).

Tracey, M., *The Decline and Fall of Public Service Broadcasting* (Oxford, 1998).

Vadgama, K., *India in Britain* (1984).

Ward, K., *Mass Communications in the Modern World* (1985).

Ward, S. (ed.), *British Culture and the End of Empire* (Manchester, 2001).

Watson, Sir A. H., 'The Growth of the Press in English in India', *Journal of the Royal Society of Arts*, January 1948, pp. 121–130.

Weigold, A., *Churchill, Roosevelt and India* (New York, 2008).

Weber, T., *On the Salt March* (New Delhi, 2009).

Weiner, J. H. (ed.), *Papers for the Millions* (Connecticut, 1988).

—— *The Americanization of the British Press, 1830s–1914* (Basingstoke, 2011).

—— & Hampton, M. (eds.), *Anglo-American Media Interactions* (Basingstoke, 2007).

Wenzlhuemer, R., *Connecting the Nineteenth-Century World* (Cambridge, 2013).

Williams, K., *Read All About It!* (2010).

Williams, F., *Dangerous Estate* (1957).

——, *The Right to Know* (1969).

Williams, L. F. R., *Inside Both Indias1914–1938* (Gloucestershire, n.d.).

——, 'Indian Unrest and American Opinion', *Asiatic Review*, July 1930.

Williams, R., *Culture and Society, 1780–1950* (1959 reprint).

——, *The Long Revolution* (1961).

——, *Communications* (1976).

Winseck, D. & Pike, R., *Communication and Empire* (Durham, 2007).

Wrench, J. E., *Geoffrey Dawson and Our Times* (1955).

Ziegler, P., *Mountbatten* (1985 edn.).

Index

Printed in Great Britain
by Amazon